THE BOOK OF
MUSICAL ANECDOTES

Also by Norman Lebrecht

Discord: Conflict and the Making of Music
Hush! Handel's in a Passion

THE BOOK OF
MUSICAL ANECDOTES

NORMAN LEBRECHT

THE FREE PRESS
A Division of Macmillan, Inc.
NEW YORK

The Free Press
A Division of Macmillan, Inc.
866 Third Avenue, New York, N.Y. 10022

First American Edition 1985
Printed in the United States of America

printing number
    3 4 5 6 7 8 9 10

Library of Congress Cataloging-in-Publication Data
Main entry under title:

The Book of musical anecdotes.

   1. Music—Anecdotes, facetiae, satire, etc.
I. Lebrecht, Norman. 1948
ML65.B673   1985   780   85–16809
ISBN 0–02–918710–9

CONTENTS

INTRODUCTION

When Joseph Haydn came to London in 1791 he was so excited by its sheer size and social effervescence that, ever a methodical man, he filled four notebooks[1] with his impressions. 'ANECTOD' he inscribed painstakingly beside episodes worth taking home as souvenirs to the dinner tables of fusty Vienna. For the amazement of his admirers, he recorded the case of the parson who collapsed and died upon hearing the Andante of his 75th Symphony, having had the music revealed to him in a dream the night before. He planned to entertain fellow-musicians with an account of the pompous conductor who, too impatient to wait for the percussion to be fully tuned, ordered his drummer to transpose in the meantime. And for aristocratic patrons, he preserved detailed accounts of the Lord Mayor's dinner, a day at the races at Royal Ascot and, intriguingly, a cryptic note of the stranger's foot spotted beneath the Duchess of Devonshire's petticoat.

As an amateur collector, Haydn hunted the anecdote in its widest contemporary meaning: Samuel Johnson's corollary in the 1773 fourth edition of his Dictionary noting that 'It is now used, after the French, for a biographical incident; a minute passage of private life.'[2]

Following in Haydn's anecdotal footsteps, this volume dips into the lives of great musicians by way of incidents reported by themselves, their friends and loved ones, and more dispassionate contemporaries. The stories are not intended as gossip or a peep-show, but as a means of shedding light, however obliquely, on the circumstances in which outstanding music was created. The anecdotes may be humorous or tragic, superficial or profound, mundane or sublime, domestic or public; they represent an attempt to put a human face on a millennium of music.

In many fields of study – notably in the social and political sciences and certain of the arts – a smattering of anecdotes is indispensable to any acceptable work. English literature abounds in anecdotal collections, among which James Sutherland's *Oxford Book of Literary Anecdotes* is a model to every aspiring anthologist.

In music, however, during the past half-century, the anecdote has

xiii

fallen into disuse and disrepute. 'Today the tendency is to look askance at "anecdotal biography", distrusting every story that cannot be supported by documentary evidence,' observed Frank Walker in his introduction to *The Man Verdi* (1962). Even where good documents exist, modern musical scholars have opted to discard biographical matter in favour of intense notational and structural analysis.[3]

Nowhere is this trend more pronounced than in the great musical reference works. Where Sir George Grove's *Dictionary of Music and Musicians* (1879–89) compressed an abundance of personal insights within its four volumes, the twenty tomes of *The New Grove Dictionary* (1980) provide a multitude of dates, lists and classifications but scarcely a single solid yarn. Percy Scholes' *Oxford Companion to Music* (1938) and its fat successor, *The New Oxford Companion to Music* (1983), betray a similar bleak comparison. Eminent academies and conservatories are producing graduates who are expert in the minutiae of Mahlerian orchestration, yet know nothing of this most self-descriptive composer other than the dates of his birth and death and the fact of his marriage to a celebrated *femme fatale*. The personality of a musical creator has been deemed to be largely immaterial to his or her works.

In an age when the constituency for serious music is visibly shrinking and audiences search in vain for stimulating information, the role of musical literature has been surrendered to factionalizers. The millions who have been turned on temporarily to Mozart by Peter Shaffer's distorted stage and screen image of the composer[4] bear witness to an urgent need to restore genuine portraits of the great musicians to a wide readership.

Obviously it is not essential to know anything about a composer in order to enjoy his or her music. But the personal insight afforded by a relevant anecdote can occasionally provide a deeper understanding and incentive to explore the music further. If the story is sufficiently quirky or inspirational, it adds a certain zest to the music.

The earliest anecdotes of music are found in the Bible; Samuel's account of the Psalmist's immodest entry to Jerusalem (Samuel II, Chapter VI, 14–23) is a prime example. Anecdotes are scattered fairly thinly in histories of music until the late eighteenth century when Charles Burney and Sir John Hawkins, both friends of Samuel Johnson, weaved many older accounts into their rival histories. The first anthology of musical anecdotes appeared in 1828, entitled *Concert Room and Orchestra Anecdotes of Music and Musicians*, and drew heavily on the writings of Burney and Hawkins and the personal observations of its author, Thomas Busby.

Anecdotes abound in thousands of volumes of musical biography, memoirs and correspondence that have long fallen out of print and find no mention in modern studies. This abandoned literature contains much that is irreplaceable: for example, the only eye-witness account of the meeting and parting of Brahms and Liszt, polar opposites of late Romantic music, is contained in the autobiography of an American pianist, published in New York in 1901. Nineteenth-century biographies of past masters are also richly anecdotal. William Rockstro's 1883 *Life of Handel* contains a thirty-page chapter of anecdotes, each story meticulously traced to its source.

Not until the present volume, however, has there been a systematic attempt to survey music through anecdotes of its principal creators. The object of this book is to redress in a small way the prevailing imbalance in the presentation of musical history by reviving long-forgotten narratives from the musical past and, in a few instances, revealing unknown episodes.

In what must, of necessity, be an arbitrary, personal selection, I have undoubtedly overlooked some fine tales and fruitful sources. Some well-known after-dinner stories have failed to get in because they do not reproduce in cold print; others because they hinge upon vernacular witticisms that do not work in English. A number of familiar stories have been rejected as unreliable.

It seemed most sensible to organize the book chronologically; and according to person rather than subject. A few peripheral personalities have crept in on the strength of a stunning anecdote; while, in the early centuries in particular, a handful of significant composers have been omitted due to lack of pungent stories. I especially regret the absence in the book of, among others, Dufay, Palestrina, Alessandro Scarlatti, Alkan, Smetana and Kurt Weill. If readers have suitable anecdotes in their possession, I should be delighted to receive them care of the publisher. I will also welcome corrections to the errors which, inevitably in a work of this size, slipped through the editorial net.

In general, I have sought to include composers or performers who altered the state of music ineradicably. Some twenty or so of the most important have received extended coverage, but no individual should be judged by the size of his or her entry. Extroverts and eccentrics tend to attract the best stories; Paganini, Rossini and Liszt could each fill a complete anecdotography.

Authenticity is forever a problem when dealing with anecdotes. One can never know when a story has been embellished for improved effect, as many of the best ones doubtless are, nor can one always tell when a tale has been made up altogether. Even competent historians have been known to stumble over gems of pure invention:

> At my first visit to Vienna, in 1845, I was once sipping a *demi-tasse* in a coffee-house with the late eminent harpist, Parish-Alvars, and *Kapell-meister* Reuling, when the latter informed me that, on the spot we were sitting, Schubert had sketched many of his songs whilst smoking his cigar in company with Beethoven. Schubert being rather corpulent, the ashes of his cigar accumulated on his waistcoat; and Beethoven, in one of his fitful humours, would blow them on the music-paper and exclaim in a mock-heroic strain, 'Behold Phoenix rising out of the ashes!'[5]

John Ella, the Victorian concert organizer and writer, should have known better. Beethoven never met Schubert in a coffee-house; indeed, he may never have met him at all. What is more, Reuling was not acquainted with Schubert, and Schubert did not smoke cigars. But for these minor inconsistencies you might have read this story in the entry for Schubert.

I have generally traced anecdotes to their earliest published source. Wherever a tale aroused my suspicions, it was included only if I was able to marshal supportive evidence. In a handful of instances a disputed or wholly spurious anecdote of an extraordinary nature has been retained. In each case, the appropriate reservations are stated in the notes at the rear of the book.

With minor exceptions for clarity and fluidity, I have for the most part preserved original texts, spelling and punctuation. Editorial excisions are denoted by three ellipses ... and additions confined within square brackets. Technical terms have been avoided where possible and explained where not; foreign words have been translated.

Occasional passages have been rewritten for reasons of comprehension, brevity or to combine two or more separate accounts. Where this has occurred, the revision is indicated by the preposition 'from' at the head of the source note. Every anecdote is numbered and each numeral refers to its source in the Notes at the end of the book.

In the seven absorbing years of researching and writing this book I have accumulated debts of gratitude so enormous that I could not possibly hope to thank all who have helped me with ideas, hospitality, documents and arrangements, but cannot forgo mentioning the following:

In Austria: Helga Hazelrig, Ferdinand Hennerbichler, Austrian National Tourist Office, Elise and John Holmes, Dr H. Wessely.
In Canada: Professor K. Pringsheim.

In France: René and Gusti Klein, Astrid Schirmer, Nancy Hartmann.

In the Federal Republic of Germany: Ursula and Hermann Kleinstück, Tatiana Hoffman.

In the Netherlands: Sjoerd van den Berg.

In the United States: Gilbert E. Kaplan, Lawrence Schoenberg.

In the United Kingdom: Patrick Carnegy, Carol Felton, Judy Grahame, Howard Hartog, Victor Hochhauser, Camilla Jessel, Ruth Jordan, Dvora Lewis, Calum MacDonald, Robert Maycock, John McMurray, Donald Mitchell, Jasper Parrott, Daniel Snowman, Janis Susskind, Peter Watson, Robin Young.

At my publishers, Dieter Pevsner believed in the book, André Deutsch persevered with it, and Sara Menguç bravely scaled an editorial Everest.

At the *Sunday Times*, many colleagues have encouraged me to pursue ideas that subsequently materialized both in the newspaper and in this book. They include: Don Berry, Tony Bainbridge, Stephen Boyd, Harry Coen, George Darby, David Gwyn Jones, Brian MacArthur, Liam McAuley, Tony Rennell and Stephen Wood.

Finally I must thank all of those who contributed their time and memories and others who permitted me to quote from copyrighted works (see Notes).

Above all, my love and gratitude to Elbie and the girls, whose prolonged patience with my preoccupations has been a source of wonderment and strength.

Notes to the introduction

1. Published in H. E. Krehbiel: *Music and Manners in the Classical Period*. New York 1898.
2. This book follows the Oxford English Dictionary's definition: 'the narrative of a detached incident . . . told as being in itself interesting or striking.'
3. Notable exceptions are David Brown's *Tchaikovsky* (1978), Henry Louis De La Grange's *Mahler* (1973), Maynard Solomon's *Beethoven* (New York, 1977), H. C. Robbins Landon's *Haydn* (1976) and Christopher Hogwood's *Handel* (1985).
4. Peter Shaffer: *Amadeus*. 1980.
5. Programme note by John Ella, 24 June 1856, quoted and refuted in Otto Erich Deutsch: *Schubert, Memoirs by his Friends*. 1958.

GUIDO of Arezzo (b.after 991–d. before 1050)

Guido, a Benedictine monk, motivated by a desire to improve church singing, devised a system of identifying notes by syllables (e.g. 'ut', 're', 'mi'), along with a six-note scale that was easily sight-read and was used to teach singing until 1600.

1

Guido, letter to Michael of Pomposa
Pope John (XIX), who governs the Roman church, heard of our school's reputation. He heard in particular how, by means of our antiphoner [book of liturgical chants], boys could learn songs they had never heard. He was greatly astonished, and sent three messengers to bring me to him. I went to Rome, therefore, together with Dom Grunwald, the venerable abbot, and Dom Peter, the provost of the canons of the church of Arezzo, a most learned man by the standards of our time. The Pope was most glad to see us, talked much with us, and asked a great many questions. He turned the pages of our antiphoner as if it were some great prodigy, pondering in particular the rules prefixed to it. He did not stop, in fact, or move from the place in which he sat, until, fulfilling a vow he made, he had learned to sing one versicle that he had never heard. What he had hardly believed to be true of others he could not but acknowledge in himself. What more is there to say? I had to leave Rome soon – the summer fevers in those wet and swampy places were death to me. We agreed, however, that when the winter returned I would return to explain our work to the Pope, who had already tasted it, and to his clergy.

❧

Chastelain de COUCY (c.1160–1203)

Early *trouvère* (aristocratic poet-minstrel) who went on two Crusades and died in the East.

2

In the time of Philip Augustus and Richard I, Coucy, a valorous and accomplished knight . . . in Picardy, was extremely enamoured with the wife of the lord of Fayel, his neighbour. After many difficulties and sufferings incident to such an attachment, the lover determined to take the cross, and accompany the kings of France and England to the Holy Land. The lady of Fayel, when she discovered his intention, wrought for him a beautiful net, with a mixture of silk and her own hair, which he fastened to his helmet, and ornamented the tassels with large pearls. The parting of these lovers was of course extremely tender. On the arrival of Coucy in Palestine, he performed many gallant and heroic actions, in hopes that their fame would reach the ears of the beloved object whom he had left in Europe; but unfortunately, at a siege, in which the Christians were repulsed by the Saracens, he received a wound, which was soon pronounced to be mortal; upon which he entreated his esquire, the instant he should be dead, to have his heart embalmed, and carry it to the lady of Fayel, together with the ornament which she had worked for him, in a little casket, and other tokens of her affection, and a letter full of tenderness, written with his own hand, on his death-bed.

In this request he was punctually obeyed by his friend and esquire; but unfortunately, on his arrival in France, when he was hovering about the castle of the lady's residence, in order to seize the first opportunity that offered of delivering the casket into her own hands, he was discovered by the lord of Fayel, her husband, who knowing him, and suspecting that he was charged with dispatches to his wife, from the Chastelain, whom he hated more than any other human creature, fell upon the esquire, and would have instantly put him to death, had he not begged for mercy, and informed him of the business with which he was entrusted by his late master. The enraged husband therefore, seizing the casket, dismissed the affrighted esquire, and went instantly to his cook, whom he ordered to dress the embalmed heart, with such sauce as would make it palatable, and serve it up for dinner. In this he was obeyed by the cook, who at the same time prepared a similar dish, in appearance, for his lord's use, of which he ate, while his lady dined upon the heart of her lover. After dinner, the Seigneur de Fayel asked how she liked the dish of which she had been eating. On her answering, 'very well'; 'I thought,' said he, 'you would be pleased with it; supposing it to be a viand of which you were always very fond, and for that reason I had it dressed.' The lady suspecting nothing, made no reply; but her lord continuing the subject, asked her if she knew what she had been eating. She replied in the negative. 'Why then,' said he, 'for your greater satisfaction, I must inform you, that you have eaten the heart of the Chastelain de Coucy.' To be thus reminded of her friend, made her very uneasy, although she could not believe that her husband was serious, till he shewed her the casket and letter; which, when she had examined and perused, her countenance changed; and after a short pause, she said to Fayel, 'It is true, indeed, that you have helped me to a viand which I very much loved; but it is the last I shall ever

2

eat; as, after that, every food would be insipid.' She then retired to her chamber; and as she never more could be prevailed upon to take any kind of sustenance, fasting and affliction soon ended her existence.

❧

Guillaume de MACHAUT (c.1300–1377)

Composer, diplomat and poet of Rheims, leader of the *ars nova* school in fourteenth-century France and Italy. Although a priest, most of his settings are secular.

3

Half-blind, crippled by gout and almost sixty years of age, Machaut received a letter from a teenaged girl of noble ancestry, Peronelle d'Armantières, 'She who has never seen you loves you faithfully and gives you all her heart.' She conspired to join him on a pilgrimage but Machaut dreaded the meeting with her, fearing she would be repelled by his physical decrepitude.

They sat together beneath a cherry tree. She fell asleep, her head upon his lap. Machaut's secretary approached, placed a leaf upon her lips and beckoned him to bend down and kiss it; then he removed the leaf . . . . At Mass they kissed again, secretly behind a pillar.

On a subsequent pilgrimage, Machaut took Peronelle to an inn in the heat of the day. Her sister-in-law, who went along as chaperone, occupied one bed in the room. Machaut shared the other with his beloved and her maid. Peronelle urgently demanded more kisses. Machaut was bashful, protective of her honour, but finally succumbed to her desires. Soon afterwards Peronelle was given in marriage to a young man. In his lonely old age, Machaut celebrated their love in a poem 'Voir Dit'.

❧

Josquin des PRES (c.1440–1521)

Composer of the High Renaissance, his works were published by the first music printer, Ottaviano Petrucci of Venice. 'Josquin,' said Martin Luther, 'is a unique master of the notes: they must do as he wills, while other masters are forced to do as the notes will.'

4

Louis XII [of France] is said to have had a very inadequate voice. He had formerly been pleased by some song and asked Josquin if there was anyone who would compose a song in several voices in which he could also sing some part. The singer, wondering at the demand of the King, whom he knew to be entirely ignorant of music, hesitated awhile and finally decided what he would answer. 'My King,' he said, 'I shall compose a song in which your Majesty will also be given a place in the singing.' The following day, after the King had had breakfast and was to be refreshed with songs according to royal custom, the singer produced his song composed in four parts. In it I* do not approve the skill of his art so much as I praise industry joined with art. For he had composed the song so that two boys would sing the upper part very lightly and delicately in canon, evidently so that the exceedingly thin voice of the King would not be drowned out. He had given the King the next part, consisting of one continuous tone in the alto range, a range suitable to the royal voice. Not content with this device, and so that the King would not waver in pitch, the composer, who was to sing the bass, arranged this part so that at regular intervals he would be supporting the King at the octave. The King laughed merrily at the trick and gladly dismissed the composer with a present and with the desired favour.

5

When Josquin was first admitted into the service of Lewis [Louis] he had been promised a benefice. But this prince, contrary to his usual custom, for he was in general both just and liberal, forgot. Josquin, after suffering great inconvenience from the shortness of his Majesty's memory, ventured to remind him publicly of his promise. Being commanded to compose a motet for the Chapel Royal, he chose part of the 119th Psalm: 'Memor esto verbi tui servo tuo' (Oh think of thy servant, as concerning thy word). The King was not only charmed with the music, but felt the force of the words so effectually, that he soon after granted him the promised preferment. For which act of justice and munificence, Josquin, with equal felicity, composed as a hymn of gratitude another part of the same psalm, 'Bonitatem fecisti cum servo tuo Domine' (Oh Lord, thou has dealt graciously with thy servant).

~∞~

---

* The narrator is Heinrich Glareanus (1488–1563); Swiss philosopher, humanist and musical scholar, a friend of Erasmus.

Martin LUTHER (1483–1546)

Religious reformer, and author of many hymns and chorales that remain the foundation of Protestant church music. Without Luther, it has been said, there could have been no Bach.

6

Often when Luther was at work in his study, Satan perturbed him in many ways. Once he had been locked inside for some time, not even demanding food, when Lucas Edenberger, preceptor of Duke Ernst of Saxony, arrived with some musicians to visit him. When he did not answer their knocking on the door, Edenberger peered through the keyhole and saw Luther lying on the floor unconscious, his arms outstretched. He broke open the door, lifted Luther up in his arms and, together with his companions, began to sing. Dr Luther regained consciousness slowly, his melancholy departed and before long he began to sing with them. He then implored Lucas and his companions to visit him often and never to let themselves be turned away no matter what he was doing; for he believed that the Satanic visitations and sadness left him as soon as he heard music.

ᴄᴊᴀᴀᴄᴐ

Rolande de LASSUS (c.1532–1594)
[Orlando di Lasso]

Franco-Flemish composer, foremost sixteenth-century polyphonist. Widely travelled, his output includes 200 Italian madrigals, 146 French chansons, 93 German lieder and some 500 Latin motets.

7

A violent storm occurred at Munich on the Thursday of the Fête-Dieu [in 1565] and the Duke [Albrecht V] gave orders that the customary procession round the town from the church of St Peter should be confined to the interior of the building. But no sooner had the head of the procession reached the porch of the church, and the choir was heard singing the first notes of Lassus' motet 'Gustate, videte', than a sudden lull occurred in the storm, and the ceremony was performed as usual. This was looked upon as a miracle and the people of Munich 'in their pious enthusiasm looked upon Lassus as a divine being'. Afterwards, whenever fine weather was an object, this motet was chosen.

On his monument is the following humorous epitaph, supposed to have been written by himself.

> Etant enfant, j'ai chanté le dessus,
> Adolescent, j'ai fait le contre-taille,
> Homme parfait, j'ai raisonné la taille;
> Mais maintenant je suis mis au bassus,
> Prie, Passant, que l'esprit sort là sus.

> A *child*, I sang the *treble part*,
> A *youth*, the *counter* claim'd my art;
> A *man*, the *tenor* was my place,
> But *now* I'm station'd in the *bass*,
> Kind passenger, if Christ you love,
> Pray that my soul may chant above.

❧

Don Carlo GESUALDO, Prince of Venosa (c.1561–1613)

Italian madrigalist and murderer, both occupations emotionally interlinked: 'It was not until Gesualdo gave up murder that he seriously took to composing.' His idiosyncratic music was championed in modern times by Stravinsky.

9

Gesualdo took for a wife the most noble D. Maria d'Avalos, who got married only to enjoy a husband. Being unappreciated, she provided herself with a cavaliere, the Duke of Andria. When Gesualdo realized what was going on, he had a false lock made for the door of his wife's room. Then he pretended to go to the country, and the Lady ordered her lover to come on the following night. They retired and eventually tired of the act of love. In the meantime, Prince Gesualdo came incognito to the castle. He took armed men with him to the room of his wife, knocked down the door and, having two guns, upon entering shot at them both, killing the Duke. Gesualdo then went to the bed with a 'stilo' [sharp weapon] and began to molest his wife, who asked pardon for the sins she had committed, and asked for time to confess. But all was in vain, and, pulling the sheets over her head, she expired reciting the 'Salve Regina'.

10

After the double murder Gesualdo was assailed and afflicted by a vast horde of demons which gave him no peace for many days on end unless ten or twelve young men, whom he kept specially for the purpose, were to beat him violently three times a day, during which operation he was wont to smile joyfully.

⌘

Claudio MONTEVERDI (1567–1643)

Italian composer who strove to create music that would 'move the whole man'. In *Orfeo* (1607) he wrote the first mature opera. Born in Cremona – where he returned throughout his life whenever beset by personal crisis – Monteverdi spent twenty years at the ducal court in Mantua and thirty as *maestro di capella* at St Mark's, Venice.

11

Monteverdi, letter to Alessandro Striggio (1573–1630); aristocrat and librettist of Orfeo

I beg to inform Your Honour that while I was in the company of the Mantuan courier on my way back to Venice we were set upon unawares by three ruffians and robbed in Sanguanato – or rather, not in the place itself but a good two miles away. It happened on this wise: from a field by the side of the road, one of the rascals, dark-hued, with sparse beard and of medium height, carrying a long musket with the trigger cocked, suddenly emerged, and another came forward and threatened me with his musket, while the third grasped the bridle of my horse – which continued on its way quite unconcerned and without showing resistance – and led it into the field. I was quickly dismounted and made to go down on my knees, while one of the two armed men demanded my purse and the other took charge of the courier and demanded his portmanteaux which, when the courier himself had lifted them out of the carriage, they opened in turn and one robber packed up everything he could find or that the courier gave him voluntarily. As for me, I remained the whole time on my knees, held fast by the other fellow with the fire-arm. Then both of them seized everything they could lay hands on while the third of the rascals, who held a dagger in his hand, turned watchman and kept a sharp look-out lest anyone might come along the road. When they had thoroughly ransacked all our belongings, the man who had searched the courier came over to me and ordered me to undress so that he could see if I had any more money. As I declared I had none, he went over to my maid-servant and would have submitted her to the same treatment, but she resisted with many prayers, entreaties and tears and succeeded in making him

7

leave her in peace. He then went back to the plunder and to the portmanteaux, made up all the best and most valuable things into a bundle, and as he looked round to see if he could find an article of clothing he lighted upon my cloak. When, however, the rascal saw it was too long for him he said, 'Give me another', and grabbed my little son's cloak, but when he found this was too short, the courier took it upon himself to say, 'Sir, it belongs to the poor innocent; give it up' and he acquiesced. Next, he came across a suit of the boy's and went through the whole procedure again. He also got some more things given to him by the maid-servant after much pleading. Finally the fellows crammed all the remainder into a huge bundle, hoisted it on to their backs and made off with it. Then we packed up what was left and went into the inn. The following morning we lodged a complaint in Sanguanato, and continued on our journey, myself very dispirited.

❦

Heinrich SCHÜTZ (1585–1672)

The first German composer to achieve fame outside his country, Schütz wrote much music for the reformed church – and the first German opera (*Dafne*, 1627).

12

Schütz, letter to Christian Reichsbrod, secretary to the Elector of Saxony, 28 May 1652

I can no longer conceal from you that the bass singer, George Kaiser, who in poverty had to pawn his clothes some time ago and now lives at home like a beast in the woods, has told me through his wife that he must and will leave this place.

It would be a terrible shame to lose such an exquisite voice from the chapel. What does it matter if in other respects he becomes bad-humoured if he cannot wash his tongue every day in keg of wine? After all, a throat as wide as his needs more moistening than a narrow one.

❦

Jean-Baptiste LULLY (1632–1687)
[b. Giovanni Battista Lulli]

Italian musician who, taken to France as an adolescent, became a favourite of Louis XIV. He developed a distinctly French style of opera, wrote comedy-ballets with Molière, and danced in the most famous of these – *Le Bourgeois gentilhomme*.

13

[His opera *Armide*] was at first coldly received, the music not having pleased so much as usual. Lully, who was so passionately fond of his own compositions, that (as he himself confessed) he would have killed any one who said they were bad, had it performed for his own gratification, he himself forming the whole audience. This odd circumstance having been reported to the King, he thought that the opera could not be bad if Lully himself had so good an opinion of it. Having, therefore, ordered it to be performed before him, he was charmed with it; and then both the court and the public changed their opinion.

14

People often begged him to play a little air on the violin, but he refused great lords and his fellow-debauchers alike. The only person who succeeded in making him play was the Marshal de Grammont. He had a footman called La Lande who later became one of the best violinists in Europe. After a meal, the Marshal implored Lully to hear his footman and give him a few words of advice. La Lande came and played, probably as best he could. Lully, however, was so irritated by his mistakes that he seized the instrument from his hand and, having begun, played on for three hours and relinquished the violin only with reluctance.

15

The King was seized with an indisposition that threatened his life, but, on his recovery, Lully was required to compose a Te Deum . . . . He had neglected nothing in the composition of the music, and the preparations for the executing of it; and, the better to demonstrate his zeal, he himself beat the time. With the cane he used for this purpose he struck himself in the heat of action, a blow upon the end of his foot; this caused a small blister to arise thereon, which increasing, Mons. Alliot, his physician, advised him immediately to have his little toe cut off, and after a delay of some days, the foot, and at length the whole limb . . . .

His confessor refused to give Lully absolution unless he would burn the opera of *Achille et Polixene*, which he was composing for the stage. Lully consented, and this music was committed to the flames. A few days after, being a little better, he was visited by one of the young princes of Vendôme: 'Why Baptiste,' said the prince, 'have you been such a fool as to burn your new opera, to humour a gloomy priest?' 'Hush, hush!' said Lully, 'I have another copy of it.'

❧

Alessandro STRADELLA (1638(9)–1682)

Italian vocal and operatic composer.

17

A Venetian nobleman whose mistress was well educated in the art of singing, desired to have her perfected by the fashionable musician, Stradella, and asked that he should teach her at her own house; a thing much against the habits of the Venetians, who are known to be extremely jealous. After a few months' lessons such a reciprocal affection had grown between teacher and pupil that they resolved to elope. The Venetian, driven almost to despair, determined to revenge himself by having them both murdered. He immediately sent for two of the most notorious assassins then in Venice.

They arrived in Rome to find that Stradella, on the next day at five in the afternoon, was to have an oratorio performed at St John Lateran, where the murderers went in the hope of fulfilling their assignment as Stradella went home afterwards with his mistress. But the enthusiasm of the audience for the music, and its effect on the murderers themselves, transformed their anger into piety; they agreed it would be a pity to kill a man whose musical genius held the admiration of all Italy.

On his leaving the church, they complimented him on the oratorio, told him of their mission to kill him and advised him to leave for a place of safety on the very next day.*

❧

---

* After further Venetian attempts on his life in Turin, Stradella was eventually stabbed to death by a soldier in Genoa.

Arcangelo CORELLI (1653–1713)

Corelli's *concerti grossi* laid the foundations of the solo concerto.

18

He was requested one evening to play, to a large and polite company [at Cardinal Ottoboni's], a fine Solo which he had lately composed. Just as he was in the midst of his performance, some of the number began to discourse together a little unreasonably; Corelli gently lay down his instrument. He was asked whether any thing was the matter with him. Nothing, he replied, he was only afraid that he interrupted conversation.

19

Corelli, enjoying 'the Highest Reputation' in Rome, was prevailed upon to play at the court of Naples and brought with him as accompanists two members of his own orchestra. He took some convincing from Alessandro Scarlatti and other maestri to perform his concertos before the King: he did not have his own orchestra, he protested, or enough rehearsal time. But soon he found that the Neapolitan musicians could perform at sight what his Romans required several rehearsals to perfect.

The first piece he played was a sonata, which the king found so long and dry that, being tired, he quitted the room to the great mortification of Corelli. Then Corelli was asked to play a masque by Scarlatti. He failed but was 'astonished beyond measure' to hear the Neapolitan violinists play it to perfection. Finally, he was given a song in C minor; Corelli played C major. '*Riccominciamo*' ('Let's begin again'), said Scarlatti good naturedly. Again Corelli picked the wrong key, until Scarlatti shouted out a correction. Corelli retreated from Naples in disgrace and soon afterwards gave up playing the violin.

Marin MARAIS (1656–1728)

Parisian composer of major works for the viola da gamba, of which he was the foremost player. Among his pieces is a suite depicting a surgical gall bladder removal.

20

After Hotman's* death Sainte-Colombe took over his master's pupil [Marais], but at the end of six months he found that his pupil was likely to surpass him. He told him therefore that he had nothing more to teach him. Marais, who was passionately fond of his viol, was nevertheless anxious to profit by his master's knowledge, and to perfect himself on his instrument. As he had access at any time to his house, he waited till the summer came, when Sainte-Colombe studied in a little wooden summer-house which he had constructed between the branches of a mulberry tree, so as to enjoy absolute quietness and the pleasant position. As soon as Sainte-Colombe had locked himself in this quaint studio, Marais slipped underneath, and benefited by watching how he played certain passages and by studying certain particular bowings which the old masters liked to keep as their secrets. This ruse did, however, not succeed very long, and once discovered, Sainte-Colombe took care that his pupil should no longer overhear his studies.

֍

Henry PURCELL (1659–1695)

England's last significant composer for the next two hundred years, Purcell wrote for theatre, church and Chapel Royal. *Dido and Aeneas* was the first British opera.

21

In the beginning of the year 1689 he became engaged in a dispute with Dr Sprat, the then Dean, and the Chapter of Westminster, the occasion whereof was this. It seems that at the coronation of King William and Queen Mary, he had received and claimed as his right, the money taken for admission into the organ loft of persons desirous of being near spectators of that ceremony, which for the following

---

* Nicholas Hotman (d.1663); Franco-German bass violist and composer.

reasons must be supposed to have amounted to a considerable sum; the profit arising to the owner of one of the houses at the west end of the Abbey, where only the procession could be viewed, amounted at the last coronation to five hundred pounds. The organ in Purcell's time was on the north side of the choir, and was much nearer the altar than now, so that spectators from thence might behold the whole of that august ceremony. . . .

If Purcell had the authority of precedent for his support, he was right in retaining it as a perquisite arising from his office; but his masters thought otherwise, and insisted on it as their due, for in an old chapter book I find the following entry: '18 April, 1689, Mr Purcell, the organ blower, to pay to Mr Needham such money as was received by him for places in the organ loft, and in default thereof his place to be declared null and void, and that his stipend or sallary be detained in the Treasurer's hands until further orders.'

22

Purcell died on the twenty-first day of November, 1695. There is a tradition that his death was occasioned by a cold which he caught in the night, waiting for admittance into his own house. It is said that he used to keep late hours, and that his wife had given orders to his servants not to let him in after midnight: unfortunately he came home heated with wine from the tavern at an hour later than that prescribed him, and through the inclemency of the air contracted a disorder of which he died.

⚬⚬⚬

François COUPERIN (1668–1733)

Known as Couperin Le Grand to distinguish him from other musicians in his family, he published four volumes of harpsichord music that influenced Bach.

23

The first sonata in this collection [the four suites, *Les Nations*] is the first that I composed, and the first to be composed in France. Its story is curious. Charmed by those sonatas of Signor Corelli whose works I shall love as much as I live, much as I love the French works of M. de Lully, I attempted to compose one.

Knowing the greed of the French for foreign novelties, and lacking in self confidence, I pretended that a relative of mine in the service of the King of Sardinia had sent me a sonata by a recent Italian

13

composer. I rearranged the letters of my own name into an Italian one [Coperuni or Pernucio], which I used instead. The sonata was devoured eagerly. I wrote others, and my Italianized name brought me much applause under the disguise.

⌒∽∿∿⌒

Antonio VIVALDI (1678–1741)

Known by his vocation and the colour of his hair as 'The Red Priest', Vivaldi spent most of his career as music master at a girl's orphanage in Venice, creating for his pupils some five hundred concertos (including *The Four Seasons*). He also wrote more than forty operas. In 1741 he moved to Vienna, dying there soon afterwards in great poverty.

24

It is related of him, that one day, while he was saying Mass, a theme for a fugue having suddenly struck him, he quitted the altar to the surprise of the congregation, hastened into the sacristy to write it down, and, having done so, returned to finish his office. For this misdemeanour he was brought before the Inquisition; but the fault having been considered as an aberration of genius, he received no further punishment than a prohibition from saying Mass for the future.

⌒∽∿∿⌒

Georg Philipp TELEMANN (1681–1767)

German composer of around 1,000 suites, 120 concertos and numerous operas. Chosen ahead of Bach as Cantor at Leipzig, he went instead at a higher salary to Hamburg.

25

Though he played on almost every kind of instrument, and had attempted to compose an opera at twelve years old, yet, in obedience to his mother's positive commands, on whom, as his father was dead, he was solely dependent, at about the age of twenty he solemnly renounced his musical pursuits, though with the greatest reluctance, and set out for Leipzig in order to study the law in that university. In the way thither, however, he stopt at Halle, where, says Telemann, 'from my acquaintance with Handel, who was already famous, I again sucked in so much of the poison of music as nearly overset all my resolutions.'

14

'However,' continues Telemann, 'after quitting Handel, I persevered in the plan prescribed by my mother, and went to Leipzig to pursue my studies; but, unfortunately, was lodged in a house where I perpetually heard Music of all kinds, which, though much worse than my own, again led me into temptation. And a fellow-student finding among my papers a psalm which I had set to music, and which, in sacrificing all my other illicit attempts at composition, had chanced to escape oblivion, he begged it of me, and had it performed at St Thomas' church, where it was so much approved, that the burgomaster desired I would compose something of this kind every fortnight.'

26

Telemann's beloved first wife died in childbirth only fifteen months after they married. His second bore him eight children (of whom two survived), but betrayed him with a Swedish officer. Her affair became the talk of Hamburg and was the subject of a satirical play which had to be banned by the authorities. She eventually departed with her lover, leaving Telemann with a massive debt of three thousand thaler. He wrote to friends for help, enclosing a satirical verse of his own:

> My lot is now much easier to bear,
> Extravagance departed with my spouse,
> If I my debts can from time to time repair
> Then Paradise will once more envelop my house.
> Hamburg has rallied round, true and loyal,
> With open hand and magnanimity,
> Perhaps more patrons will be found outside her walls?
> Cheerfully, I am

> > > Your servant Telemann

Jean-Philippe RAMEAU (1683–1764)

At the age of fifty, Rameau – until then a keyboard composer and distinguished theorist – turned to the stage. In the next thirty years he rejuvenated French opera with twenty-five major works.

27

At rehearsal, he had to talk a lot; he did this with so much fire that his mouth would become dry and he had to eat some fruit to enable him to go on; the same thing would happen in conversation and then, at the very instant that he was most excited, he would be seen to fall into silence, open his mouth and indicate in dumb show that he could not speak.

28

At one of the rehearsals of *Les Paladins* Rameau repeatedly told one of the actresses to take a certain air much faster.

'But if I sing it so fast,' said the artiste, 'the public will not be able to hear the words.'

'That doesn't matter,' replied the composer, 'I only want them to hear my music.'

29

As a young organist in Clermont, Rameau longed to get away to Paris to have his *Traité de l'harmonie* published but could not persuade the cathedral authorities to release him from his contract. One Saturday at morning service, however, he played only two chords before leaving the organ loft, banging the door. No one was surprised: they thought he was angry because the organ-blower had not turned up. But at the evening service there was no mistaking Rameau's intentions as he played all the most painful discords. Connoisseurs at the service said only Rameau could play so horribly.

The organist was reprimanded; he replied that he would continue to play that way until his contract was cancelled. The elders of the community gave in. Over the next few days he played magnificently, surpassing himself at his last service with such delicacy, elegance, force and harmony that all in the congregation appreciated the loss they were about to sustain.

30

In spite of the reputation of Rameau, *Les Paladins* did not meet with any success, and was soon withdrawn – before the public had time to learn to appreciate the music, the composer declared; 'The pear was not ripe,' he said.

'That did not prevent it from falling all the same,' retorted Sophie Arnould.*

---

* (1740–1802); French soprano who created roles for Rameau and Gluck.

Near the end of his life he told a friend, 'I have more taste than previously, but no longer any genius.'

❦

Johann Sebastian BACH (1685–1750)

Born at Eisenach to a family which in seven generations produced some sixty professional musicians he was appointed Cantor at St Thomas', Leipzig, in 1723. His music apart, Bach's life was unexciting, his personality unremarkable; few intimate recollections have survived.

32

[In his youth] he counted no hardships or privations too great for the treat of going to Hamburg from time to time, and listening in concealment (for those old masters of the organ were jealous of letting others into the secret of their proficiency) to Reinken's wonderful playing. . . . Once when he had lingered at Hamburg longer than his means allowed, he had only two shillings in his pocket on his way back to Luneburg. Before he reached home he felt very hungry, and stopped outside an inn, from the kitchen of which proceeded such tempting odours as made him painfully aware of the disproportion of his appetite to his purse. His hungry appearance seems to have struck with compassion some casual lookers on, for he heard a window open, and saw two herrings' heads thrown out into the road. The sight of these remains of what are such a popular article of food in Thüringen, his old home, made his mouth water; he picked them up eagerly, but great was his surprise on pulling them to pieces to find a Danish ducat concealed in each of them. This discovery enabled him not only to satisfy his wants at the moment, but to make his next journey to Hamburg in a more comfortable manner. The unknown benefactor, who no doubt peeped out of the window to watch the result of his good nature, made no attempt to know more of the boy.

33

As a young teacher he got into trouble with the Arnstadt authorities over a public brawl with one of his students. Bach, while walking across the market-place in the company of his cousin, Barbara Catharina, was confronted by J. H. Geyersbach and five fellow-students returning from a christening feast. Geyersbach demanded to know why Bach had impugned his abilities as a bassoonist. As tempers rose, he called Bach 'a dirty dog' and lashed his face with a stick. Bach drew his sword and only the intervention of another student averted bloodshed.

When Bach complained, the Consistory determined that he had been principally at fault for having called Geyersbach 'a nanny-goat bassoonist'. He was admonished to try and live in peace with his students. Bach's reaction was to take a prolonged and unauthorized journey to Lübeck, to listen to the organ playing of Buxtehude.

34

He had a very great esteem for Handel, and often wished to be personally acquainted with him. As Handel was also a great performer on the clavier and the organ, many lovers of music at Leipzig and in its neighbourhood wished to hear these two great men confronted. But Handel never could find time for such a meeting. He came three times from London to Halle, his native town. On his first visit, about the year 1719, Bach was still at Cöthen, only four German miles from Halle. He was immediately informed of Handel's arrival, and lost not a moment in paying him a visit; but Handel left Halle the very day of his arrival. At the time of Handel's second visit to Halle, between 1730 and 1740, Bach was at Leipzig, but ill. As soon, however, as he was informed of Handel's arrival at Halle, he immediately sent his eldest son, William Friedemann, thither, with a very polite invitation to visit him at Leipzig. But Handel regretted that he could not come. On Handel's third visit, approximately in 1752 or 1753, Bach was dead.

35

With all Bach's amiable qualities, he had a warm and hasty temper. On one occasion Görner,* the organist at St Thomas', who generally played very well, struck a false chord, and Bach flew into such a passion that tore his wig off, and threw it at the unfortunate man's head, with the thundered exclamation, 'You ought to have become a cobbler rather than an organist!'

36

An amateur who was improvising at the keyboard when Bach entered a crowded room jumped up from his seat [thus creating] a

---

* Johann Gottlieb Görner (1697–1778); Leipzig organist, later guardian to Bach's younger children.

dissonant chord. Walking straight past his host, Bach rushed to the harpsichord, resolved the dissonance and proceeded with a suitable cadence. Only then did he greet his host.

37

He was so fond of full harmony that, besides a constant and active use of the pedals, he is said to have put down such keys by a stick in his mouth, as neither hands nor feet could reach.

38

When he was asked by someone, as frequently happened, for a very easy clavier piece, he used to say, 'I will see what I can do.' In such cases, he usually chose an easy theme, but, in thoroughly working it out, always found so much of importance to say upon it that the piece could not turn out easy after all. If complaints were made that it was still too difficult, he smiled, and said, 'Only practise it diligently, it will go very well; you have five just as healthy fingers on each hand as I.'

39

It occasionally happened that he would turn a recalcitrant scholar out of the choir with no small commotion in the middle of service, and then in the evening dismiss him from the supper table with an equally high hand; and as by these arbitrary proceedings he often sacrificed his dignity as a teacher, he very naturally sometimes found a difficulty in keeping the rout of boys in order.

40

A group of beggars used to whine in a series of dissonances which Bach thought contained an interesting set of intervals. He first made as if to give them something but pretended he could not find any money. As their complaint rose to a high pitch, he gave them several times a very small donation which slightly lowered their cry. Finally, he gave an exceptionally large sum which, to his delight, produced a full resolution of the chord and a satisfying cadence.

41

When he was at Berlin, in 1747, he was shown the new opera house. Whatever in the construction of it was good or faulty in regard to the effect of music, and what others had only discovered by experience, he perceived at the first sight. He was taken into the great saloon within the building; he went up to the gallery that runs round it, looked at the ceiling, and said, without first investigating any further, that ... if a person up there at one corner of the saloon, which was in the form of an oblong parallelogram, whispered a few words against the wall, another, who stood with his face turned to the wall, at the corner diagonally opposite, could hear them distinctly, but nobody else in the whole room, either in the centre or in any other part. This effect arose from the direction of the arches in the ceiling, the particular nature of which he discovered at the first look. Such observations could and naturally did lead him to attempt to produce, by the unusual combination of different stops of the organ, effects unknown before and after him.

42

Charles Philip Emanuel [Bach] entered the service of Frederick the Great in 1740. The reputation of the all-surpassing skill of John Sebastian was at this time so extended that the King often heard it mentioned and praised. This made him curious to hear and meet so great an artist. At first he distantly hinted to the son his wish that his father would one day come to Potsdam. But by degrees he began to ask him directly why his father did not come. The son could not avoid acquainting his father with these expressions of the King's. . . .

[Bach] at length, in 1747, prepared to take this journey, in company of his eldest son, William Friedemann. At this time the King used to have every evening a private concert, in which he himself generally performed some concertos on the flute. One evening, just as he was getting his flute ready and his musicians were assembled, an officer brought him the written list of the strangers who had arrived. With his flute in his hand, he ran over the list, but immediately turned to the assembled musicians and said, with a kind of agitation: 'Gentlemen, old Bach is come.' The flute was now laid aside; and old Bach, who had alighted at his son's lodgings, was immediately summoned to the Palace. William Friedemann, who accompanied his father, told me this story, and I* must say that I still think with pleasure on the manner in which he related it. At that time it was the fashion to make rather prolix compliments. The first appearance of J. S. Bach before so great a King, who did not even give him time to change his travelling dress for a black cantor's gown, must necessarily be attended with many apologies. I will not

---

* Johann Nicolaus Forkel (1749–1818); German musician and author of the first biography of J. S. Bach.

here dwell on these apologies, but merely observe that in William Friedemann's mouth they made a formal dialogue between the King and the apologist.

But what is more important than this is that the King gave up his concert for this evening and invited Bach, then already called the Old Bach, to try his fortepianos, made by Silbermann, which stood in several rooms of the Palace. The musicians went with him from room to room, and Bach was invited everywhere to try them and to play unpremeditated compositions. After he had gone on for some time, he asked the King to give him a subject for a fugue in order to execute it immediately without any preparation. The King admired the learned manner in which his subject was thus executed extempore; and, probably to see how far such art could be carried, expressed a wish to hear also a fugue with six obbligato parts. But as not every subject is fit for such full harmony, Bach chose one himself and immediately executed it to the astonishment of all present in the same magnificent and learned manner as he had done that of the King. His Majesty desired also to hear his performance on the organ. The next day, therefore, Bach was taken to all the organs in Potsdam as he had before been to Silbermann's fortepianos. After his return to Leipzig, he composed the subject which he had received from the King in three and six parts, added several intricate pieces in strict canon on the subject, had it engraved, under the title of Musikalisches Opfer (Musical Offering), and dedicated it to the inventor.

This was Bach's last journey.

43

Count Kaiserling, formerly Russian Ambassador at the Court of the Elector of Saxony, who frequently resided in Leipzig, brought with him Goldberg* to have him instructed by Bach in music. The Count was often sickly, and then had sleepless nights. At these times Goldberg, who lived in the house with him, had to pass the night in an adjoining room to play something to him when he could not sleep. The Count once said to Bach that he should like to have some clavier pieces for his Goldberg, which should be of such a soft and somewhat lively character that he might be a little cheered up by them in his sleepless nights. Bach thought he could best fulfill this wish by variations, which, on account of the constant sameness of the fundamental harmony, he had hitherto considered as an ungrate-

---

* Johann Gottlieb Goldberg (1727–56); organist and composer.

ful task. But as at this time all his works were models of art, these variations also became such under his hand. This is, indeed, the only model of the kind that he has left us. The Count thereafter called them nothing but *his* variations. He was never weary of hearing them; and for a long time, when the sleepless nights came, he used to say, 'Dear Goldberg, do play me one of my variations.' Bach was, perhaps, never so well rewarded for any work as for this: the Count made him a present of a golden goblet, filled with a hundred Louis d'ors.

44

Bach, letter to his cousin Johann Elias, Cantor and Inspector at the Schweinfurt Gymnasium, 1748
Highly honoured Cousin,

Your pleasant letter received yesterday, together with the precious cask of new wine, for which I owe you many thanks, assures me that you and your dear wife are in good health. It is a great pity that the cask was damaged, either by the shaking of the vehicle or some other way, for when it was opened for the ordinary inspection on entering this town, it was found three parts empty, and did not, according to the official's report, contain more than six jugs full; it is a pity that the least drop of this noble gift should have been lost. I congratulate my honoured cousin on the richly blessed vintage, and regret my inability to do anything in return. But '*quod differtur non aufertur*,' I hope yet to have occasion to pay my debt in some way.

It is certainly to be regretted that the distance between our two towns does not permit us personally to visit each other; otherwise I should take the liberty to invite you to the wedding of my daughter Lieschen, who is to be married next January, 1749, to Altnikol, the new organist at Naumburg. But as the distance already mentioned, and the inclement season, would probably make it impossible for us to see you with us, I will only beg you, though absent, to assist us with your Christian good wishes. I salute you from us all, and remain your obedient, faithful cousin and willing servant,

J. S. Bach.

P.S. – M. Birnbaum was buried six weeks ago.

P.M. – Though my honoured cousin has expressed himself willing to continue to assist me with such gifts of liquors, I must decline on account of the immoderate payments to be made for the same, the carriage having cost 16 groschen, the porter having charged 2 groschen, the customs officer 2 gr., the country tax 5 gr. 3 pfennige, and general tax 3 gr., so that you may calculate that for each measure I had to pay almost 5 groschen, which is too much for a gift.

On the evening of 28 July, about a quarter past eight, he passed away quietly in his sleep.

He was buried in St John's Churchyard at Leipzig, but no cross or stone marks the spot where he was laid. The only record of his funeral is an extract from the register of deaths, preserved in the Leipzig town library, in these words: 'A man, age sixty-seven, M. Johann Sebastian Bach, Musical Director and Singing Master of the St Thomas School, was carried to his grave in the hearse, 30 July 1750.'

The *Allgemeine Leipziger Musikzeitung*, May 1800, contains a petition, signed by Bach's warm admirer, Fr. Rochlitz,* in the following words: The Bach family is now extinct except one single daughter of the great Sebastian Bach; and this daughter, now advanced in years, is in want. Very few know this fact, for she cannot – no, she must not, shall not beg!' ...

On 19 May 1801, Rochlitz wrote once more: 'Our appeal for the support of the only survivor of the Bach family, Sebastian Bach's youngest daughter, has not been overlooked by the public. . . . With deep emotion we received on the 10 May, through the Viennese musician, Herr Andreas Streicher, the considerable sum of 307 Viennese florins. . . . At the same time the celebrated Viennese composer and pianist, Herr von Beethoven volunteered to publish one of his newest works through Messrs. Breitkopf and Härtel for the sole benefit of Bach's daughter, that the good old woman might from time to time derive benefit from it, at the same time using all his efforts for the most speedy publication possible, that she may not perchance die before this object is attained.'†

Kirnberger‡ had . . . a portrait of his master, Sebastian Bach; it was my§ constant admiration, and it hung in his room, between two

---

* Johann Friedrich Rochlitz (1769–1842); music critic and editor.
† She died on 14 December 1809.
‡ Johann Philipp Kirnberger (1721–83); composer, theorist and pupil of Bach.
§ Carl Friedrich Zelter (1758–1832), Berlin composer, educationalist and friend of Goethe, letter to Goethe, 24 January 1829. On 11 March 1829, Zelter's twenty-year-old protégé, Felix Mendelssohn, conducted the *St Matthew Passion* in Berlin, in a performance that inaugurated the Bach revival.

windows, on the wall above the piano. A well-to-do Leipzig linen-draper, who had formerly seen Kirnberger, when he was a chorister at the Thomas-Schule, singing in a procession before his father's door, comes to Berlin, and it occurs to him, to honour the now celebrated Kirnberger with a visit. Hardly were they seated, when the Leipziger bawls out, 'Why, good Lord! you've actually got our Cantor, Bach, hanging there; we have him too in Leipzig, at the Thomas-Schule. They say he was a rough fellow; why, the conceited fool did not even have himself painted in a smart velvet coat.' Kirnberger gets up quietly, goes behind his chair, and lifting it up with both hands in the guest's face, exclaims, first gently, then crescendo, 'Out, you dog! Out, you dog!' My Leipziger, mortally frightened, seizes his hat and stick, makes with all haste for the door, and bolts out into the street. Upon this, Kirnberger has the picture taken down and rubbed, the Philistine's chair washed, and the portait, covered with a cloth, restored to its old place.

48

Felix [Mendelssohn] and I* had frequent meetings to consider how the [St Matthew Passion] could be shortened for performance. Giving it in its entirety was out of the question. It necessarily contained much that belonged to a former age, and what we had at heart was to convince people of its intrinsic greatness. Most of the songs would have to be omitted; of others only the symphonies could be given. The part of the Evangelist would have to be shorn of all that was not essential to the recital of the Passion. We often differed, for to us it was a matter of conscience; but what we finally determined upon seems to have been the right thing, for it has been adopted at most of the performances of the work.

It was now time to invite the solo-singers, and we settled to make the round together. Felix was child enough to insist on our being dressed exactly alike on the occasion. We wore blue coats, white waistcoats, black neckties, black trousers, and yellow chamois leather gloves that were then fashionable. [His pocket money being run out, I lent him a thaler for the purchase of the gloves. His mother was displeased with me for this, saying, 'One ought not to assist young people in their extravagances.']

In this 'Bach' uniform we started off gaily, after partaking of some of Felix's favourite chocolate. . . . We were speaking of the strange chance that, just a hundred years after the work could have been last

---

* Writes Eduard Devrient, early friend and biographer of Mendelssohn.

heard, it should now again see the light. 'And to think.' said Felix triumphantly, standing still in the middle of the Opern Platz, 'that it should be an actor and a Jew that gives back to the people the greatest of Christian works.'

49

Pablo Casals, the twentieth-century cellist
One day I told my father I needed especially to find some new solo music for the Café Pajarera. Together we set off on the search. For two reasons I shall never forget that afternoon. First, my father bought me my first full-sized 'cello. . . . Then we stopped at an old music shop near the harbour. I began browsing through a bundle of musical scores. Suddenly I came upon a sheaf of pages, crumbled and discoloured with age. They were unaccompanied suites by Johann Sebastian Bach – for the 'cello only. I looked at them with wonder: Six Suites for Violoncello Solo. What magic and mystery, I thought, were hidden in those words. I had never heard of the existence of the suites; nobody – not even my teachers – had ever mentioned them to me. . . . I hurried home, clutching the suites as if they were the crown jewels, and once in my room I pored over them. I read and reread them. I was thirteen at the time, but for the following eighty years the wonder of my discovery has continued to grow on me. Those suites opened up a whole new world. . . . I studied and worked at them every day for the next twelve years. Yes, twelve years would elapse and I would be twenty-five before I had the courage to play one of the suites in public at a concert. Up until then, no violinist or 'cellist had ever played one of the Bach suites in its entirety. . . . They had been considered academic works, mechanical, without warmth. Imagine that! They are the very essence of Bach, and Bach is the essence of music.

෴

John GAY (1685–1732)

English poet and playwright, Gay wrote *The Beggar's Opera* as a satire on Italian opera and on contemporary society. Gay also wrote the libretto for Handel's *Acis and Galatea* and built the first Covent Garden theatre in 1732.

50

The opera was first offered to Cibber, then manager of Drury Lane, and rejected by him. It was then offered to Rich, the rival potentate of Covent Garden, who had the good sense and good fortune to accept it. Its profits were so very great, both to the author and the manager, that it was said that the *'Beggar's Opera* had made Rich gay and Gay rich'.

∽✺∾

George Frideric HANDEL (1685–1759)

Son of a Halle barber-surgeon, Handel won fame in Italy before becoming *Kapellmeister* to the Elector of Hanover, later George I of England. He emigrated to London ahead of his master and over the next half century produced almost fifty operas. When opera declined in popularity, Handel recaptured his audiences with a series of oratorios on Biblical themes.

51

From his very childhood Handel had discovered such a strong propensity to Music, that his father, who always intended him for the study of the Civil Law, had reason to be alarmed. Perceiving that this inclination still increased, he took every method to oppose it. He strictly forbad him to meddle with any musical instrument; nothing of that kind was suffered to remain in the house, nor was he ever permitted to go to any other, where such kind of furniture was in use. All this caution and art, instead of restraining, did but augment his passion. He had found means to get a little clavichord privately convey'd to a room at the top of the house. To this room he constantly stole when the family was asleep.

52

He had stayed near a year at Florence, and it was his resolution to visit every part of Italy, which was any way famous for its musical performances. Venice was his next resort. He was first discovered there at a Masquerade, while he was playing on a harpsichord in his visor. Scarlatti happened to be there, and affirmed that it could be no one but the famous Saxon, or the devil. Being thus detected, he was strongly importuned to compose an Opera. But there was so little prospect of either honour or advantage from such an undertaking, that he was very unwilling to engage in it. At last, however, he consented, and in three weeks he finished his *Agrippina*, which was performed twenty-seven nights successively. . . .

The theatre, at almost every pause, resounded with shouts and acclamations of *viva il caro Sassone*! [long live the beloved Saxon] and other expressions of approbation too extravagant to be mentioned.

53

He used to say, 'When I came hither first, I found, among the English, many good players and no composers; but now, they are all composers and no players.'

54

Dr Maurice Greene,* whose compositions, whether for the church or the chamber, were never remarkably mellifluous, having solicited Handel's perusal and opinion of a solo anthem, which he had just finished, was invited by the great German to take his coffee with him the next morning, when he would say what he thought of it. The Doctor was punctual in his attendance, the coffee was served, and a variety of topics discussed; but not a word said by Handel concerning the composition. At length Greene, whose patience was exhausted, said, with eagerness, and an anxiety which he could no longer conceal, 'Well, Sir, but my anthem – what do you think of it?' 'Oh, your antum – ah – why I did tink it vanted *air*, Dr Greene?' '*Air*, Sir?' 'Yes, air; and so I did hang it out of de vindow.'

55

Having one day some words with Cuzzoni† on her refusing to sing 'Falsa imagine' in *Ottone*; '*Oh! Madame*' (said he), '*je sçais bien que Vous êtes une veritable Diablesse: mais je Vous ferai sçavoir, moi, que je suis Beelzebub le Chef des Diables* [I know well that you are truly a She-Devil: but I will have you know that I am Beelzebub, chief of the Devils.]. With this he took her up by the waist, and, if she made any more words, swore that he would fling her out of the window.

---

* (1695–1755); composer, organist, Master of the King's Musick from 1735.
† Francesca Cuzzoni (1700–70); volatile Italian soprano.

It is to be noted, that this was formerly one of the methods of executing criminals in some parts of Germany.

56

An English singer, named Gordon, once found fault with his method of accompanying. High words ensued; and Gordon finished by saying, that if Handel persisted in accompanying him in that manner, he would jump upon his harpsichord and smash it to pieces. 'Oh!' replied Handel, 'let me know when you will do that, and I will advertise it; for I am sure more people will come to see you jump, than to hear you sing.'

57

Handel, as is well known, had such a remarkable irritability of nerves, that he could not bear to hear the tuning of instruments, and, therefore, this was always done before he arrived at the theatre. A musical wag, determined to extract some mirth from his irascibility of temper, stole into the orchestra, one night when the Prince of Wales was to be present, and untuned all the instruments. As soon as the Prince arrived, Handel gave the signal to begin, *con spirito*; but such was the horrible discord, that the enraged musician started up from his seat, and, having overturned a double-bass which stood in his way, he seized a kettle-drum, which he threw with such violence at the leader of the band, that he lost his full-bottomed wig in the effort. Without waiting to replace it, he advanced bare-headed to the front of the orchestra, breathing vengeance, but so much choked with passion that utterance was denied him. In this ridiculous attitude he stood staring and stamping for some moments, amidst the general convulsion of laughter; nor could he be prevailed upon to resume his seat, until the Prince went in person, and with much difficulty appeased his wrath.

58

At the close of an air, the voice with which he used to cry out, Chorus! was extremely formidable indeed; and, at the rehearsals of his Oratorios, at Carleton-House, if the Prince [later King George III] and Princess of Wales were not exact in coming into the Music-Room, he used to be very violent; yet, such was the reverence with which his Royal Highness treated him, that, admitting Handel to have had cause of complaint, he has been heard to say, 'Indeed, it is cruel to have kept these poor people, meaning the performers, so long from their scholars, and other concerns.' But if the maids of honour, or any other female attendants, talked, during the performance, I fear that our modern Timotheus, not only swore, but called names; yet, at such times, the Princess of Wales, with her accustomed mildness and benignity, used to say, 'Hush! Hush! Handel's in a passion.'

59

He placed no small happiness in good eating and drinking. Having received a present of a dozen of superior champaigne,* he thought the quantity too small to present to his friends; and therefore reserved the delicious nectar for a *private use*. Some time after, when a party was dining with him, he longed for a glass of his choice champaigne, but could not easily think of a device for leaving the company. On a sudden he assumed a musing attitude, and, striking his forehead with his forefinger, exclaimed, 'I have got one tought! I have got one tought!' (meaning thought). The company, imagining that he had gone to commit to paper some divine idea, saw him depart with silent admiration. He returned to his friends, and very soon had a second, third, and fourth 'tought'. A wag suspecting the frequency of St Cecilia's visits, followed Handel to an adjoining room, saw him enter a closet, embrace his beloved champaigne, and swallow repeated doses. The discovery communicated infinite mirth to the company, and Handel's tought became proverbial.

60

Finding it convenient to dine at a tavern, he ordered dinner for three. The repast was so long in preparation that he grew impatient and sent for the host. 'Why do you keep me so long waiting?' he asked, with the impetuosity of a hungry man. 'We are waiting till the company arrives,' said the innkeeper. 'Then bring up the dinner, *prestissimo*,' said Handel, 'I am the company.'

61

Charles Burney, letter to Lord Mornington, 30 March 1776
[A Lady] being very musical, was invited by him to a private Rehearsal of the *Messiah*, and being struck with the Exceeding dignity of expression in the Chorusses, and other parts of ye oratorio so inimitably sett to the sacred words, after the musick was over she asked him how it was possible for him *who understood the English Language but imperfectly*, to enter so fully into the sublime spirit of

---

* Charles Burney (1726–1814) – English music historian and initiator of the Handel Commemorations – says it was Burgundy.

the Words. His answer is I think a lesson to all Composers, at least of Sacred Musick, *Madam, I thank God I have a little religion.*

62

When [*Messiah*] was first performed [in London] the audience were exceedingly struck and affected by the music in general; but when the chorus struck up, 'For the Lord God omnipotent reigneth', they were so transported, that they all, with the King who happened to be present, started up and remained standing till the chorus was ended: and hence it became the fashion in England for the audience to stand while that part of the music is performing. Some days after the first exhibition of this divine oratorio, Mr Handel went to pay his respects to Lord Kinnoul, with whom he was particularly acquainted. His lordship, as was natural, paid him some compliments on the noble entertainment which he had lately given to the town. 'My lord,' said Handel, 'I should be sorry if I only entertained them; I wish to make them better.'

63

When Handel's servant used to bring him his chocolate in the morning, 'he often stood silent with astonishment to see his master's tears mixing with the ink as he penned his divine compositions.' And Burgh relates that 'a friend,calling upon the great musician when in the act of setting those pathetic words, "He was despised and rejected of men," found him absolutely sobbing.'

64

When Handel went through Chester, on his way to Ireland, this year, 1741 (to give the first performance of *Messiah*), I* was at the Public School in that city and very well remember seeing him smoke a pipe, over a dish of coffee, at the Exchange Coffee House: for being extremely curious to see so extraordinary a man, I watched him narrowly as long as he remained in Chester, which, on account of the wind being unfavourable for his embarking at Parkgate, was several days. During this time, he applied to Mr Baker, the Organist, my first music master, to know whether there were any choirmen in the cathedral who could sing at sight, as he wished to prove some books that had been hastily transcribed, by trying the choruses which he intended to perform in Ireland. Mr Baker mentioned some of the most likely singers then in Chester, and, among the rest, a printer of

---

* Charles Burney.

the name of Janson, who had a good bass voice and was one of the best musicians in the choir . . .

A time was fixed for this private rehearsal at the Golden Falcon, where Handel was quartered; but, alas! on trial of the chorus in the *Messiah*, 'And with his stripes we are healed', poor Janson, after repeated attempts, failed so egregiously, that Handel let loose his great bear upon him; and after swearing in four or five languages, cried out in broken English,' 'You shcauntrel! tit not you dell me dat you could sing at soite?' – 'Yes, sir,' says the printer, 'and so I can, but not at first sight.'

65

One night, when Handel was in Dublin, Dubourg* having a solo part in a song, and a close to make *ad libitum*, wandered about, in different keys, a good while, and seemed indeed a little bewildered, and uncertain of his original key; but, at length, coming to the shake which was to terminate this long close, Handel, to the great delight of the audience, cried out, loud enough to be heard in the most remote parts of the theatre, 'You are welcome home, Mr Dubourg.'

66

'You have taken too much trouble over your opera,' he told Gluck, who wanted an opinion of *La Caduta dei giganti*. 'Here in England, that is mere waste of time. What the English like is something they can beat time to, something that hits them straight on the drum of the ear.'

67

Approached while being shaved, for his subscription to a set of organ concertos by the Rev. Mr Felton,† Handel, putting the barber's hand aside, got up in a fury and, with his face still in a lather, cried out with great vehemence, 'Tamn your seluf and go to der teiffel! A barson make concerto! Why he no make sarmon?' Brown, seeing him in such a rage with razors in his reach, got out of the room as fast he could.

68

In gratitude for the favour shown him by the public, and actuated by motives of benevolence, he performed the *Messiah* for the benefit of an institution, which then stood in need of every assistance, the

---

* Matthew Dubourg (1703–67); eminent violinist.
† William Felton (1715–69); Anglican clergyman, organist and composer.

Foundling-hospital; and this he not only continued to do for several years, but, by presenting the charity with a copy of the score and parts of this composition, gave them such a title to it as seemed to import an exclusive right to the performance of it. This act of bounty was so ill understood by some of the governors of that foundation, that they formed a resolution for an application to Parliament to establish their supposed right; in short, to prohibit, under penalties, the performance of the *Messiah* by any others than Mr Handel and themselves. To facilitate the passing of a law for the purpose, Mr Handel's concurrence was asked, but he was so little sensible of the propriety of it, that upon the bare mention of it he broke out into a furious passion, which he vented in the following terms, 'For vat sal de Foundlings put mein oratorio in de Parlement? Te Teuffel! mein musik sal not go to de Parlement.'

69

One Sunday, having attended divine worship at a country church, Handel asked the organist to permit him to play the people out; to which he readily consented. Handel, accordingly, sat down to the organ, and began to play in such a masterly manner, as instantly to attract the attention of the whole congregation, who, instead of vacating their seats as usual, remained for a considerable space of time, fixed in silent admiration. The organist began to be impatient (perhaps his wife was waiting dinner) and, at length, addressed the great performer, telling him, he was convinced that *he* could not play the people out, and advised him to relinquish the attempt; for while *he* played, they would never quit the church.

70

When Smith* played the organ at the theatre, during the first year of Handel's blindness, *Samson* was performed, and Beard sang, with great feeling,

> *Total eclipse – no sun, no moon*
> *All dark, amid the blaze of noon*

The recollection that Handel had set this air to music, with the view of the blind composer then sitting by the organ, affected the audience so forcibly that many persons present were moved even to tears.

---

* John Christopher Smith (1712–95); Handel's pupil and amanuensis.

When the 'Hallelujah Chorus' was sung, [Haydn] wept like a child and exclaimed, 'He is the master of us all!'

I* sat close by (Beethoven) and heard him assert very distinctly, in German, 'Handel is the greatest composer that ever lived.'. . . Every one of us was moved when he said, 'I would uncover my head and kneel down on his tomb!' – H. and I repeatedly tried to turn the conversation to Mozart, but without effect; I only heard him say, 'In a monarchy we know who is the first' – which might, or might not, apply to the subject.

❧

Nicola PORPORA (1686–1768)

Italian vocal composer and teacher whose pupils included Caffarelli, Farinelli, Haydn and Metastasio.

73

Visiting a monastery in Germany, the monks requested him to be present at the service, in order that he might hear the organist. 'Well,' said the prior afterwards, 'what do you think of our organist?' 'Why,' answered Porpora, 'he is a clever man.' 'And a good chari- table man, too,' interrupted the prior; 'his simplicity is really evangelical.' 'Oh,' said Porpora, 'as to his simplicity, I observed that; for his left hand knoweth not what his right hand doeth.'

❧

Giuseppe TARTINI (1692–1770)

Prodigious violinist and theorist, he lived mostly in Padua, but fled to Assisi after illicitly marrying a pupil. While in hiding in a monastery, he composed the fiendishly difficult 'Devil's Trill' Sonata.

74

Nardini† frequently heard Tartini relate the circumstance, which was neither more nor less than this: He said that one night he

---

* Edward Schulz, English musician who visited Beethoven in 1816 and 1823.
† (1722–93), violinist and composer.

dreamed that he had entered into a contract with the devil, in fulfilment of which his satanic majesty was bound to perform all his behests. He placed his violin in his hands, and asked him to play; and the devil played a sonata so exquisite, that in the delirium of applause which he was bestowing, he awoke, and flew to the instrument to endeavour to retain some of the passages, but in vain! they had fled! yet the sonata haunted his imagination day and night, and he endeavoured to compose one in imitation, which he called the 'Devil's Sonata': but it was so inferior to the sonata of his dream, that he has been heard to say, that if he had had any other mode of gaining a living, he would have left the musical profession.

✺

Johann Joachim QUANTZ (1697–1773)

Flute teacher to Frederick the Great of Prussia, Quantz was author of the first comprehensive flute method (Berlin, 1752).

75

As a young man, Quantz was engaged as assistant to the town musician at Radeberg near Dresden. But he did not keep the position for long. On the great day of penance after the feast of St John in 1714, the town was struck by a violent thunderstorm and burned to the ground 'within the space of four hours'. Quantz, huddled among the refugees in the marketplace, watched the church where he worked go up in flames, ignited by 'a burning side of bacon that lodged in flight on the top of the spire'.

On that very morning the rector had preached a fiery sermon, comparing Radeberg to Sodom and Gomorrah and concluding with the words, 'Ye shall know it. God will strike with thunder! Amen.' The rector's house, Quantz said, was the only one left standing after the fire.

✺

Giovanni Battista SAMMARTINI (c.1700–1775)
[San Martini]

Milanese composer; a key figure in the development of the symphony, in a style similar to Haydn's.

76

Stendhal

I well remember, at Milan, thirty years ago, a musical entertainment was given to the celebrated Mislivicek.* When some old symphonies of San Martini were performed, the Bohemian professor suddenly exclaimed, 'I have discovered the father of Haydn's style.'. . .

This San Martini, a man all fire and originality, was also, though residing at a distance, in the service of Prince Nicholas Esterházy.† A banker of Milan, named Castelli, was ordered by the prince to pay San Martini eight sequins (£4) for every piece of music which he should send him. The composer was bound to supply at least two per month, and had the liberty of sending to the banker as many as he chose. But, in the decline of life, old age rendered him indolent and I well remember hearing the banker complain to him of the remonstrances he received from Vienna on account of the unfrequency of his remittances. San Martini replied, grumbling, 'I'll write some, I'll write some, but the harpsichord kills me.'

⤶⋙⋘⤷

FARINELLI (1705–1782)
[b. Carlo Broschi]

Pre-eminent castrato, born of noble family and raised in Naples, whose surgically preserved voice was one of the wonders of eighteenth-century music.

77

Philip V King of Spain, being seized with a total dejection of spirits, which made him refuse to be shaved, and rendered him incapable of attending council or transacting affairs of state, the Queen, who had in vain tried every common expedient that was likely to contribute to his recovery, determined that an experiment should be made of the effects of music upon the King her husband, who was extremely

---

* Josef Mysliveček (1737–81); Bohemian composer admired by Mozart.
† Haydn's employer.

sensible to its charms. Upon the arrival of Farinelli, of whose extraordinary performance an account had been transmitted to Madrid from several parts of Europe, but particularly from Paris, her Majesty contrived that there should be a concert in a room adjoining to the King's apartment, in which this singer performed one of his most captivating songs. Philip appeared at first surprised, then moved; and at the end of the second air, made the virtuoso enter the royal apartment, loading him with compliments and caresses; asked him how he could sufficiently reward such talents; assuring him that he could refuse him nothing. Farinelli, previously instructed, only begged that his Majesty would permit his attendants to shave and dress him, and that he would endeavour to appear in council as usual. From this time the King's disease gave way to medicine: and the singer had all the honour of the cure.*

78

Having ordered a superb suit of clothes for a gala at court, when the taylor brought it home, he asked him for his bill. 'I have made no bill, Sir,' says the taylor, 'nor ever shall make one. Instead of money,' continues he, 'I have a favour to beg. I know that what I want is inestimable, and only fit for monarchs; but since I have had the honour to work for a person of whom every one speaks with rapture, all the payment I shall ever require will be a song.' Farinelli tried in vain to prevail on the taylor to take his money. At length, after a long debate . . . he took him into his music-room, and sung to him some of his most brilliant airs, taking pleasure in the astonishment of his ravished hearer; and the more he seemed surprised and affected, the more Farinelli exerted himself in every species of excellence. When he had done, the taylor overcome with extacy thanked him in the most rapturous and grateful manner, and prepared to retire. 'No,' says Farinelli, 'I am a little proud; and it is perhaps from that circumstance that I have acquired some small degree of superiority over other singers; I have given way to your weakness, it is but fair, that, in your turn, you should indulge me in mine.' And taking out his purse, he insisted on his receiving a sum amounting to nearly double the worth of the suit of clothes.

სოდოდ

---

* For the next twenty-five years he was obliged to sing for the King the same four songs every night.

Thomas Augustine ARNE (1710–1778)

The composer of 'Rule Britannia!', Arne wrote extensively for the London theatre.

79

Charles Burney, Arne's pupil

He never c^d pass by a woman in the street, to the end of his Life without Concupiscence or, in plain Engl. *picking her up*, if her look was not forbidding, & impracticable. It has frequently happened in walking home with my Wife of a Night, if we have by some accident been separated for a few minutes, that she has been accosted by the D^r with that design, ere I c^d overtake her or he knew to whom she belonged.'

80

Doctor Arne once went to Cannons, the seat of the late Duke of Chandos, to assist at the performance of an oratorio in the Chapel of Whitchurch; but such was the throng of company, that no provisions were to be procured at the Duke's house. On going to the Chandos Arms, in the town of Edgeware, the Doctor made his way into the kitchen, where he found only a leg of mutton on the spit. This, the waiter informed him, was bespoken by a party of gentlemen. 'The Doctor determined to have the mutton, took a fiddle-string, cut it in pieces, and, secretly sprinkling it over the mutton, walked out of the kitchen. Then, waiting very patiently till the waiter had served it up, he heard one of the gentlemen exclaim – 'Waiter! this meat is full of *maggots*: take it away!' This was what the Doctor expected. – 'Here, give it *me*,' he said. 'O, sir,' says the waiter, 'you can't eat it – 'tis full of maggots.' – 'Nay, never mind,' cries the Doctor, 'fiddlers have strong stomachs.' So, bearing it away, and scraping off the catgut, he got a hearty dinner.

81

The father of Dr Arne was an upholsterer in Covent Garden; and, finding that his son was bent on music, engaged a foreigner of some abilities to give him lessons on the violin. The master coming one evening, as usual, discovered, to his astonishment, young Arne practising with his desk on a coffin in the wareroom. Upon this, he expressed some surprise, and added, that he should not be able to study for thinking it contained a corpse. 'So it does,' replied the juvenile musician; and, pushing the lid off, exposed the body; which so affected the master, that he never could be prevailed upon to visit his pupil again.

ᏣᎳᏍᎤᎤ

CAFFARELLI (1710–1783)
[b. Gaetano Majorano]

Italian castrato for whom Handel wrote his famous 'Largo'. His celebrity was second only to Farinelli's.

82

Like many of his neutered kind, Caffarelli was attractive to women, offering virility without risk of conception. He was not safe, however, from the other dangers of illicit carnality. Apprehended in *flagrante delicto* by a returning husband in Rome in 1728, the castrato narrowly escaped vengeance in authentic *opera buffa* style, by hiding all night in a disused water tank where he caught a cold that incapacitated him for weeks. Moreover, the husband was sworn to revenge and Caffarelli had to spend the rest of his time in Rome under the protection of four bodyguards hired by his anxious beloved.

ᏣᎳᏍᎤᎤ

FREDERICK the Great (1712–1786)
Friedrich II of Prussia

Flautist, composer and conqueror, who established Berlin as a musical centre by providing a court orchestra and building an opera house. C. P. E. Bach was his harpsichordist; his father's Musical Offering was composed on a theme of the king's invention.

83

Frederick to his Swiss companion, Henri de Catt
After dinner I play on the flute to aid digestion; I sign my letters and I again read until four o'clock. At that hour you will come to me; we will talk until six when my little concert begins. If passable music can amuse you, it only depends on you to hear it; everything is over at half-past seven. After the concert, which I have only in country quarters, I pitilessly scribble paper with prose and verse until nine o'clock, when I put myself into the arms of Morpheus.

Frederick II, personally fond of music and literature, had a special liking for the philosopher Mendelssohn grandfather of the composer, and would often seat him at his own side at dinner. An ambassador, jealous of the privilege accorded to a commoner and a Jew, insinuated to the King that Mendelssohn was 'a man who would consider nobody, and would offend your Majesty if it so happened that for some imaginary reason he thought himself hurt.'

'I should like to see that,' said the King, 'but I shall give him no reason for feeling hurt, and, any way, he would not offend *me*.'

'Is it a wager?' asked the Ambassador.

'Certainly,' replied the King.

'Will your Majesty at the next supper-party write on a piece of paper, "Mendelssohn is an ass," and put that paper, signed by your own hand on his table?'

'I will not; that would be a gratuitous rudeness.'

'It is only to see what he would do, . . . the paper must be signed "Frederick the Second" so that he cannot afterwards say he did not know that they were written by the King.'

Reluctantly, but with a feeling of curiosity as to how it would all end, the King wrote and signed the paper as required.

The evening came; the table was laid for twelve, the fatal paper was on Mendelssohn's plate, and the guests, several of whom had been informed of what was going on, assembled, eager for the fray.

Mendelssohn sat down, being rather shortsighted and observing the paper, he held it very near his eye, and having read it, gave a start.

'What is the matter?' said the King. 'No unpleasant news, I hope, Mendelssohn.'

'Oh no,' said Mendelssohn, 'it is nothing.'

'Nothing? Nothing would not have made you start. I demand to know what it is.'

'Oh, it is not worth while – '

'But I tell you that it is; I command you to tell me.'

'Oh, if your Majesty commands me, I will say that some one has taken the liberty to make a joke of rather bad taste with your Majesty; I'd rather not –'

'With me? Pray do not keep me waiting any longer. What is it?'

'Why, somebody wrote here, "Mendelssohn is *one* ass, Frederick *the second*." '

꙰

39

Jean-Jacques ROUSSEAU (1712–1778)

The Swiss philosopher was a competent composer (his opera Le Devin du village was widely performed) and historian of music (Dictionnaire de musique, 1768).

85

One morning when I* was at his house I saw various domestics either coming for rolls of music, or bringing them to him to copy. He received them standing and uncovered. He said to some, 'The price is so much,' and received the money; to others, 'How soon must I return my copy?' 'My mistress would like to have it back in a fortnight.' 'Oh, that's out of the question: I have work, I can't do it in less than three weeks.' I inquired why he did not take his talents to better market. 'Ah,' he answered, 'there are two Rousseaus in the world: one rich, or who might have been if he had chosen; a man capricious, singular, fantastic; this is the Rousseau of the public; the other is obliged to work for his living, the Rousseau whom you see.'

86

Rousseau was especially hated by the French orchestral players, of whom, in his writings, he always speaks with unmeasured contempt. Grétry, in his *Mémoires*, says, that while Rousseau was superintending the rehearsals of his *Devin du village*, he treated the band so cavalierly, that they, in revenge, hanged him in effigy. 'Well,' said Rousseau, 'I don't wonder that they should hang me now, after having so long put me to the torture.'

87

Rousseau, at the age of twenty, sets out to win fame and fortune from music
From the name Rousseau I made the anagram Vaussore, and called myself Vaussore de Villeneuve. I knew nothing about composition and boasted of my skill to everybody; and although I could not score the simplest drinking song, I claimed to be a composer. That is not all. Having been introduced to M. de Treytorens, professor of law, who was a music-lover and held concerts at his house, I decided to give him a sample of my talents, and began to compose a piece for his concert with as much boldness as if I had known how to set about it. I had the persistence to work for a fortnight on this fine composition,

---

* J. H. Bernadin de Saint-Pierre (1737–1814), French writer.

to make a fair copy of it, write out the parts, and distribute them with as much assurance as if they had been a musical masterpiece. Finally – a fact that will be hard to believe, though it is really true – to crown this sublime production in a fitting manner, I tacked on a pretty minuet, which was sung in all the streets. . .

Venture had taught me this air with its bass accompaniment, I tacked [it] on to the end of my composition, and claimed it as my own with as much confidence as if I were addressing the inhabitants of the moon.

The players assembled to perform my piece. I explained to each the method of timing, the manner of interpretation and the cues for repeats. The five or six minutes spent in tuning up were five or six centuries to me. At last all was ready. I gave five or six premonitory taps on my conductor's desk with a handsome roll of paper. Attention! All was quiet. Gravely I began to beat time. They began. Throughout all the history of French opera never was there heard such a discordant row. Whatever they might have thought of my pretended talents, the effect was worse than anything they seem to have expected. The musicians were choking with laughter; the audience goggled their eyes, and would gladly have stopped their ears; but they had not the means. My wretched orchestra, who were out to amuse themselves, scraped loudly enough to pierce a deaf man's ear-drums. I had the audacity to go right on, sweating big drops, it is true, but kept there by shame, I had not the courage to bolt and make my escape. For my consolation, I heard the audience around me whisper into one another's ears, or rather into mine: 'It's absolutely unbearable'; or 'What crazy music!'; or 'What a devil of a din!' Poor Jean-Jacques, at that cruel moment you could hardly expect that one day your music would excite murmurs of surprise and applause, when played before the King of France and all his Court, and that in all the boxes around the most charming ladies would say half aloud: 'What delightful sounds! What enchanting music! Every one of those airs goes straight to the heart!'

❧

41

Christoph Willibald von GLUCK (1714–1787)

Bohemian composer active in Vienna and Paris, who altered the course of opera by establishing the supremacy of drama over Italianate ornamental singing. *Orpheus and Eurydice* remains his best-known work.

88

The *Journal de Paris* of 21 January 1777, tells the following story. During the performance of *Alceste* 'tragédie de Mons. W. A. Gluck,' Mdlle. Levasseur sang the verse, *'Il me déchire et m'arrache le coeur'* with such deep expression that a gentleman in the stalls felt perfectly enchanted with her and applauded with frenzy. A neighbour of his, however, of quite different opinion, shouted to the singer. 'It is not the heart, it is my ears you tear off'; whereupon the first gentleman got up and said, 'That's lucky for you; now go quickly and get another pair.'

89

During the height of the musical feud between the partisans of Gluck and Piccini,* an attempt was made by Berton, at that time director of the opera, to appease the parties by reconciling the chiefs. Accordingly (says Ginguené) he gave a great supper, where Gluck and Piccini, after embracing each other, were placed side by side. They conversed during the evening with great cordiality. After supper, Gluck, like a true German, a little warmed by wine, began to talk very frankly, and so loud as to be heard by all the company. 'The French,' he said, 'are a good sort of people, but they really amuse me; they want to have songs composed for them, and yet they know nothing about singing. My dear friend, you are a man celebrated throughout Europe. You think only of supporting your reputation: you compose beautiful music for them, – but what are you the better for it? Believe me, you must think here of making money, and nothing else.' Piccini politely replied, that the example of M. Gluck proved that it was possible to attend to one's fame and fortune at the same time. 'They parted,' adds Ginguené, 'as they met, and there is no doubt that their mutual expressions of friendship were sincere. Yet the war, of which they were the cause, did not cease; and it may truly be said of them, as has been said of political leaders, that they themselves were the men who seemed least to belong to their parties.'

---

* [1728–1800]; Italian opera composer.

One morning, after I* had been singing with him, he said, 'Follow me up stairs, Sir, and I will introduce you to one, whom, all my life, I have made my study, and endeavoured to imitate.' I followed him into his bedroom, and, opposite to the head of the bed, saw a full-length picture of Handel, in a rich frame. 'There, Sir,' said he, 'is the portrait of the inspired master of our art; when I open my eyes in the morning, I look upon him with reverential awe, and acknowledge him as such, and the highest praise is due to your country for having distinguished and cherished his gigantic genius.'

91

In the early days of January 1775, *Iphigenia in Aulis* was revived. Gluck had made several additions and alterations in the score, and, very much against his will, had lengthened the ballets. Indeed he seemed so willing to oblige anybody and everybody, that old Vestris asked him to insert a chaconne for the younger Vestris to dance.

'Do you think the Greeks danced the chaconne?' growled the composer.

'Didn't they?' asked the old dancer in honest amazement, 'then they were greatly to be pitied.'

'Well, well?' said the composer, 'you shall have your chaconne, though *the opera stinks of music already*.'

92

[After a serious seizure, Gluck] was put to bed. His friends tried to deceive him about the danger his life was threatened with, and began a discussion about a sacred trio he had written, and very much disputed the tone in which the part of the Saviour should be sung. 'Well, my friends,' he said, 'as you cannot decide how we can make the Saviour sing, I'll go to Him and ascertain from His holy countenance what to do.' He died placidly on 15 November in the year 1787.

---

* Michael Kelly (1762–1826); Irish singer.

Charles BURNEY (1726–1814)

English musical historian; friend of Haydn, biographer of Metastasio, and father of the novelist, Fanny Burney.

93

Among the peculiarities of Dr Burney, were two of a very innocent kind: the first was the constant possession of wine of the best vintage; the next, the dread of a current of air. 'Shut the door,' was the first salutation uttered by him to any one who entered his apartment; and but few of his associates ever neglected the rule. This custom did not abandon him on the most trying occasions; for having been robbed . . . while returning home one evening in his carriage . . . he called the [thieves] back, as they were making off, exclaiming to them, in his usual peremptory tone, 'Shut the door!' A voice so commanding had the desired effect – he was instantly obeyed.

⚬⚬⚬

François André PHILIDOR (1726–1795)
[b. Danican]

Innovative composer of *opéras comiques* – *Tom Jones* is the best remembered – and the earliest modern chess master. He is reputedly the first composer to receive a curtain call.

94

The only *bon mot* recorded of him appears to have been uttered very seriously, without the least thought of being witty. 'One day, he entered the house at the moment when two of his sons, of about fourteen and sixteen, were trying their strength at Chess. He looked at their game, and after following it for two or three moves, said to his wife, *Ma chère amie*, our children have fairly succeeded in making Chess a game of chance.'

95

The only picture we have of him in the theatre . . . represents him in company with his handsome [son] André, at the moment of meeting, behind the scenes, a certain pretty Opera-singer (Mademoiselle Colombe), who had condescended to become the boy's 'first love'. 'I hope you will be pleased,' said the father bowing to the ground before her, and politely thanking her for having taken the raw youth into training, with the most innocent unconsciousness of the strange confusion, with which he was overwhelming both lad and lady, by taking such parental cognizance of their little private arrangements.

⌒◡⌒

Franz Joseph HAYDN (1732–1809)

Haydn – affectionately known as 'Papa' to his contemporaries – encouraged Mozart, taught Beethoven, and in his own compositions fathered the moden symphony and the string quartet.

96

The Austrian composer Dittersdorf and Haydn were friends as young men. One night while roaming the streets they stopped outside a common beer hall in which the musicians, half drunk and half asleep, were fiddling away miserably at a Haydn minuet. . . .

'Let's go in,' proposed Haydn.

'In we go!' agreed Dittersdorf.

Entering the taproom, Haydn sat down beside the leader and asked casually, 'Whose minuet?' The man snapped, 'Haydn's.' Haydn moved in front of him and, feigning anger, declared: 'That's a stinking minuet!'

'Says who?' demanded the fiddler, jumping out of his seat with rage. The other musicians rallied round him and were poised to smash their instruments over Haydn's head but Dittersdorf, a big fellow, shielded Haydn with his arm and pushed him out of the door.

97

In 1759 Haydn gained his first appointment as music director to Count Morzin in Vienna. He liked to tell in later years how, while he was sitting one day at the harpsichord, the beautiful Countess Morzin leaned over him to see the notes and her neckerchief came undone. 'It was the first time I had seen such a sight; I became confused, my playing faltered, my fingers stuck to the keys. "What is it, Haydn? What are you doing?" cried the Countess. Very respectfully, I answered, "But your Grace, who would not be undone at such a sight?"'

98

In Prince Esterházy's orchestra there were a number of vigorous young men who in summer, when the Prince stayed at Esterháza, had to leave their wives behind in Eisenstadt. The Prince once

45

prolonged his stay in Esterháza uncustomarily by some weeks: thoroughly dismayed, the loving husbands turned to Haydn for help.

Haydn had the inspiration of writing a symphony . . . in which one instrument after the other falls silent. Each of the musicians was directed, as soon as his part was finished, to blow out his candle, put his instrument under his arm and walk out. The Prince and his audience immediately took the point . . . next day came the order to leave Esterháza.

Thus Haydn told me* the origin of the 'Farewell' Symphony.

99

Many years afterwards when Haydn was in England, he perceived that the English, who were very fond of his instrumental compositions when the movement was lively and allegro, generally fell asleep during the andantes or adagios, in spite of all the beauties he could accumulate. He therefore wrote an andante, full of sweetness, and of the most tranquil movements; all the instruments seemed gradually to die away; but, in the middle of the softest pianissimo, striking up all at once, and reinforced by a stroke on the kettledrum, they made the slumbering audience start.†

100

In his bedroom, he hung a set of twenty-four canons that he had composed. 'I am not rich enough,' said Haydn, 'to buy good paintings, so I have found myself hangings that few others possess.' When his wife complained one day that there was not enough money in the house to bury him if he died suddenly, Haydn replied, 'If such a calamity occurs, take these canons to the publisher. I am sure they will cover a decent funeral.'

101

'Where Mozart is, Haydn cannot appear,' he wrote, when invited at the same time as Mozart to Prague for the coronation of Emperor Leopold II.

102

On the eve of Haydn's departure [for London], Mozart said: 'Papa,' (as he usually called him), 'you have no education for the great world and you speak too few languages.' 'Oh!' replied Haydn, 'my language

---

* Georg August von Griesinger (1769–1845), official at Saxonian embassy in Vienna; biographer of Haydn.
†This work became known as the 'Surprise' Symphony.

is understood all over the world.' . . . Mozart, that day, never left his friend Haydn. He dined with him and, when they parted, said, 'We are probably saying our last adieu in this life.' Tears welled in both men's eyes. Haydn applied Mozart's words to himself: it never occurred to him that Mozart's life would be cut short the very next year.

103

One morning a neat little gentleman came into [Howell's] shop and asked to look at some pianoforte music, and he laid before him some sonatas by Haydn which had just been published. The stranger turned them over and said, 'No, I don't like these.' Howell replied, 'Do you see they are by Haydn, Sir?' 'Well, Sir, I do, but I wish for something better.' 'Better,' cried Howell indignantly, 'I am not anxious to serve a gentleman of your taste,' and was turning away when the customer made it known that he was Haydn himself. Howell, in astonishment, embraced him and the composer was so flattered by the interview that a long and intimate friendship followed.

104

Haydn, in his London notebooks
On 14 December I dined for the first time at the house of Mr Shaw. He received me below stairs at the door, and conducted me thence to his wife, who was surrounded by her two daughters and other ladies. While I was bowing all around I suddenly perceived that the lady of the house, besides her daughters and the other ladies, wore on their headdresses a pearl-coloured band, of three-fingers' breadth, embroidered in gold with the name of Haydn, and Mr Shaw wore the name on the two ends of his collar in the finest steel beads. The coat was of the finest cloth, smooth, and bore beautiful steel buttons. The mistress is the most beautiful woman I ever saw. N.B. Her husband wanted me to give him a souvenir, and I gave him a tobacco-box which I had just bought for a guinea. He gave me his in exchange. A few days afterward I visited him and found that he had had a case of silver put over the box I had given him, on the cover of which was engraved Apollo's harp, and round it the words *Ex dono celeberrimi Josephi Haydn*. N.B. The mistress gave me a stickpin as a souvenir.

105

He related an anecdote of his dining in company with Mrs Billington,* at some house where there was a picture of her [by Sir Joshua Reynolds] hanging in the room, representing her listening to

---

* Elizabeth Billington (1765–1818); English soprano.

an angel singing; Haydn said it ought to be reversed – she ought to have been drawn singing and the angel listening to her; he got a kiss for this elegant compliment.

106

At the end of the first part of the concert Haydn had the distinguished honour of being formally introduced to His Majesty George III, by His Royal Highness the Prince of Wales. My* station at the time was so near to the King, that I could not avoid hearing the whole of their conversation. Amongst other observations, His Majesty said (in English), 'Doctor Haydn, you have written a great deal.' To which Haydn modestly replied, 'Yes, Sire, a great deal more than is good.' To which the King neatly rejoined, 'Oh no, the world contradicts that.'

107

He showed me† his Aria in D from the *Creation*, which depicts the movements of the sea and the rising of the cliffs out of the sea. 'Can you see,' he said jokingly, 'how the notes behave like waves? Up and down they go! Look, you can also see the mountains. You have to amuse yourself sometimes after being serious for so long.'

108

In 1805 he became so debilitated and disabled, as to give birth to the report of his death. The Paris papers echoed the mortal announcement: and the National Institute (of which he was a member) acknowledged his claims to its honourable notice, by the celebration of a Mass to his memory. The intelligence of this amused him exceedingly: 'O, why did not the learned and liberal body apprize me of their munificent intention, that I might be present to beat time to the performance of my own mortal rites.'

109

On 10 May [1809] in the morning a French army corps advanced to the Mariahülf line, not far from Haydn's home. They were just getting him out of bed and dressed when four canister shots exploded, violently rattling the windows and doors of his house. He called out aloud to his frightened servants, 'Don't be afraid, children; where Haydn is, no harm can reach you!'

---

* William Thomas Parke (1762–1847); English oboist.
† Frederik Samuel Silverstolpe, diplomat at Swedish embassy in Vienna.

On removing the body of the deceased composer from Gumpendorf to its present abiding place in Vienna, it was found *minus* the skull! Medical men, it seems, had noticed some ailment of the great master. Without entering into particulars, I* will merely state that, during my last visit to Vienna, in November 1873, I had the honour of dining with the Baron Rokitanzky, the chief director of the great hospitals. After dinner, the Baron took me into his studio, and carefully placed in my hands a well-preserved relic – the missing skull of Papa Haydn.

❧

Johann Christian BACH (1735–1782)

'The English Bach', eleventh and youngest son of J. S. Bach, settled in 1762 in London. He composed some forty piano concertos and was greatly esteemed by Mozart, who mourned his passing in the adagio of his 12th piano concerto (K414).

111

Christian Bach was a very lighthearted and merry man. When a serious friend reproached him for his easy ways – he would toss off the light and ephemeral pieces demanded of him and throw away and money they earned on frivolities and sensual delights – he would point to the example of his elder brother in Berlin [C. P. E. Bach], who wrote big works and held onto what he earned, and say, 'My brother lives to compose while I compose to live; he works for others, I work for myself.'

112

The Mozarts were summoned to court on 19 May [1764]. Wolfgang accompanied the Queen in a song, a flute-player in a solo and, finally, took the bass of an air by Handel and improvised a charming melody to it. None took more interest in the young musician than the Queen's music-master, Joh. Christian Bach. He liked to play with the boy; took him upon his knee and went through a sonata with him, each in turn playing a bar with so much precision that no one would have suspected two performers.

---

* John Ella (1802–88), English concert organizer and writer on music.

His Majesty George III patronized the oratorios at the King's Theatre in the Haymarket on the Friday evenings during Lent, conducted by Mr Bach. These performances notwithstanding were thinly attended. On Friday morning, General Fitzpatrick meeting Mr Hare, the witty member of Parliament, said to him, 'Do you go to the oratorio in the Haymarket this evening?' 'Oh no,' replied Mr Hare, 'I have no wish to intrude on His Majesty's privacy.'

114

The conversation in every circle was of 'poor Dr Dodd', a preacher condemned to death for fraud.

The kind-hearted Abel,* who was a libertine in his sentiments, insisted that a mere act of fraud ought not to be visited with the same dreadful penalty as that of the rascal assassin.

Bach, though no less good hearted, asserted, rather too coldly and pertinaciously for the warm temper of Abel, that fraud was the act of a dirty mind. 'What the debbel do you talk of Tocdor Todd being in tebdt, are not you somedimes in tebdt? am nod I always in tebdt? and is it prober and right, pecause of dat, I am to commit forgery? I do insist upon it, mine teare friend, Misder Abel, dat he vot gommits forgery of notes, ought to be hanged. Such a man is a rogue, and not fit to live in society.'

Abel, who was ever addicted to drolling, instantly replied, 'O! O! Master Bach! Vell den, Sir, you and mineself should be hanged; for have we not both of us forged notes enough in our dimes?'

'Dat is not chendeel of you, mine tear Abel,' said Bach. 'To be sure, as you say, friend Abel, us gombosers are birates, and blagiarists, and forgers of nodes; pote,' adding, with a sly look, 'some gombosers forge false nodes, and I only forge true.'

❧

---

* Carl Friedrich Abel (1723–87); German musician, co-founder of the Bach-Abel concerts.

Sir William HERSCHEL (1738–1822)

German-born composer, organist and English concert organizer, Herschel became preoccupied by astronomy, discovered the planet Uranus and in 1781 abandoned music.

115

Such was his ardour for discovery, that in some benefit concert which he gave, he had his telescope fixed in the window, and was making his observations between the acts.

116

Haydn, in his London notebooks
On 15 June I went from Windsor to Slough to Dr Herschel, where I saw the great telescope. It is forty feet long and five feet in diameter. The machinery is vast, but so ingenious that a single man can put it in motion with ease. . . .

[Herschel's] landlady was a widow. She fell in love with him, married him, and gave him a dowry of £100,000. Besides this he has £500 for life, and his wife, who is forty-five years old, presented him with a son this year, 1792. Ten years ago he had his sister come; she is of the greatest service to him in his observations. Frequently he sits from five to six hours under the open sky in the severest cold.

117

The most privileged visitors were allowed to walk through the giant tube of Herschel's telescope before it was raised to the sky. King George III, calling on Herschel one day in 1787, took great pleasure in showing 'the way to Heaven' to the Archbishop of Canterbury.

~

Giovanni PAISIELLO (1740–1816)

Prolific composer who established Italian opera at the Russian Court and achieved such popularity with his *The Barber of Seville* that a Roman audience rioted when Rossini dared to re-set it.

118

Arriving in Paris, [Paisiello], the cunning Italian, like an experienced courtier, was no sooner introduced to Napoleon than he addressed him as 'sire!'

'"Sire," what do you mean?' replied the first consul, 'I am a general, and nothing more.'

'Well, General,' continued the composer, 'I have come to place myself at your Majesty's orders.'

'I must really beg you,' continued Napoleon, 'not to address me in this manner.'

'Forgive me, General,' answered Paisiello, 'but I cannot give up the habit I have contracted in addressing sovereigns who, compared with you, seem but pygmies. However, I will not forget your commands, sire; and if I have been unfortunate enough to offend, I must throw myself upon your Majesty's indulgence.'

119

One day, during the stay of Paisiello, I* heard him relate an anecdote illustrative of the kindness of the Empress Catherine of Russia towards him. She was his scholar; and while he was accompanying her one bitter cold morning, he shuddered with the cold. Her Majesty perceiving it, took off a beautiful cloak which she had on, ornamented with clasps of brilliants of great value, and threw it over his shoulders. Another mark of esteem for him, she evinced by her reply to Marshal Beloselsky. The Marshal agitated, it is believed, by the 'green-eyed monster', forgot himself so far as to give Paisiello a blow; Paisiello, who was a powerful athletic man, gave him a sound drubbing. In return, the Marshal laid his complaint before the Empress, and demanded from her Majesty the immediate dismissal of Paisiello from the court, for having had the audacity to return a blow upon a marshal of the Russian Empire. Catherine's reply was, 'I neither can nor will attend to your request; you forgot your dignity when you gave an unoffending man and a great artist a blow; are you surprised that he should have forgotten it too? and as to rank, it is in my power, Sir, to make fifty marshals, but not one Paisiello.'

I give the above anecdote as I heard it, although I confess it is rather a strange coincidence, that a similar circumstance should have occurred to Holbein, when a complaint was made against him to Henry VIII by a peer of Great Britain.

❧

---

* Michael Kelly (1762–1826); Irish singer.

52

André GRETRY (1741–1813)

Franco-Flemish composer of about fifty operas, of which *Richard Cœur de Lion* was the most successful.

120

Related by Hector Berlioz at his wedding reception in 1852
On New Year's day, it was the custom of the Emperor to receive the congratulations of the most distinguished men of science, literature, and art of France. On the first visit of Grétry, Napoleon (who had no partiality for French music) affected not to know him, and thus abruptly accosted him, 'Who are *you*?' 'Grétry, sire.' On the next visit of Grétry, the Emperor again interrogated him, 'Who are *you*?' Feeling rather humiliated, Grétry replied, after a short silence, 'Grétry, sire.' The third year that the composer of *Richard Cœur de Lion* presented himself at the Tuileries, the Emperor again asked 'Who are *you*?' '*Hélas! – toujours Grétry, sire!*'

Luigi BOCCHERINI (1743–1805)

Italian 'cellist and composer who spent most of his working life in Spain. A contemporary once said of him, 'If God chose to speak to man he would employ the music of Haydn; but if he desired to hear an earthly musician, he would select Boccherini.'

121

The King of Spain was fond of playing with Boccherini, and the Emperor of Austria occasionally joined them in a trio. The Emperor one day asked Boccherini whether he played better than Charles IV; upon which the diplomatic musician replied, 'Sire, Charles IV plays like a King, but Your Imperial Highness plays like an Emperor!'

Domenico CIMAROSA (1749–1801)

Italian composer of *opera buffa* whose *Il Matrimonio Segreto* (*Secret Marriage*) so enthralled Leopold II at its première in Vienna in 1792 that he ordered supper for the cast and made them perform it again. Cimarosa was condemned to death in Naples in 1799 for Napoleonic sympathies, but was reprieved and banished.

122

The Emperor Napoleon once inquired of the celebrated Grétry what was the difference between Mozart and Cimarosa. 'Sire,' replied Grétry, 'Cimarosa places the statue on the stage, and the pedestal in the orchestra; while Mozart puts the statue in the orchestra and the pedestal on the stage.'

123

Cimarosa and Paisiello, were not only contemporaries and rivals, but sworn enemies. They were never seen in the same company. It was impossible for any person to be on friendly terms with the one, if he had ever been guilty of applauding the other. These two men, so great in their art, were even known to visit the theatres in disguise, in order to hiss, in security, each other's compositions.

೦⋙೦

Antonio SALIERI (1750–1825)

Rumours that he killed Mozart provided the subject for Pushkin's poem, Rimsky-Korsakov's opera (*Mozart and Salieri*, 1898) and Peter Shaffer's play, *Amadeus*. Born near Verona, Salieri lived from 1776 in Vienna, where he taught Beethoven, Schubert and Liszt.

124

Rossini: After Mozart's death it was suggested – even seriously – that [Salieri] had killed him out of professional jealousy, using a slow poison.
Wagner: That rumour was still about in Vienna in my time.
Rossini: One day, I said to Salieri as a joke, 'It's lucky for Beethoven that his instinct for self-preservation leads him to avoid dining with you. Otherwise you might pack him off to the next world, as you did Mozart.' 'Do I look like a poisoner?' Salieri replied.

Moscheles* wished also to visit poor Salieri, who, weak, old, and nigh to death, was lying in the common hospital. 'Our meeting,' writes Moscheles, 'was a sorrowful one; for already his appearance shocked me, and he spoke to me in broken sentences of his nearly impending death. At last he said, "I can assure you as a man of honour that there is no truth in the absurd report; of course you know – Mozart – I am said to have poisoned him; but no – malice, sheer malice; tell the world, dear Moscheles, old Salieri, who is on his death-bed, has told this to you." I was deeply moved, and when the old man in tears repeated his thanks for my visit (having already overwhelmed me with gratitude on my arrival), it was time for me to rush out of the room before I was entirely overcome with emotion. . . .

'[But] morally speaking, he had no doubt by his intrigues poisoned many an hour of Mozart's existence.'

❧

Muzio CLEMENTI (1752–1832)

Italian-born composer of more than one hundred sonatas; keyboard artist, piano manufacturer and Beethoven's British publisher.

Clementi, owing to intense study, had become an extremely absent [-minded] man; so much so, that he had gone out in the morning with a black and a white stocking on; but because he had never gone out without any at all, some of his friends considered his absence mere affectation. But I† am inclined to think the following fact will prove they were in error. Clementi and Crosdill‡ were together on a visit in the summer to the Earl of Pembroke, at his fine seat at Wilton. A prominent ornament in this park is a beautiful and extensive sheet of water, in which, one sultry evening, they agreed to go bathing. After remaining in the water a certain time, Crosdill retired to the dressing rooms, and secretly took Clementi's shirt into the house.

Clementi returned, perfectly dressed as he believed, and while he was expatiating largely on the pleasure he had received by his

---

* Ignaz Moscheles (1794–1870); pianist and composer, a pupil of Salieri's.
† William Thomas Parke (1762–1847); English oboist.
‡ John Crosdill (1751–1825); cellist.

immersion, a gentleman and his lady arrived on an evening visit. After the usual introductions had taken place, the lady expressed a desire to hear Clementi play one of his own sonatas on the piano-forte, to which he readily assented. Having taken his seat, and fidgeted a little in his peculiar way, he played he first movement of one of his most difficult pieces, and was about to begin the adagio, when, being oppressed with heat, he unconsciously unbuttoned nearly the whole of his waistcoat, and was proceeding, when the lady, greatly surprised, hastily retired to the farthest part of the room, while Lord Pembroke, almost convulsed with laughter, apprised Clementi of his situation.

∾❦∾

Giovanni Battista VIOTTI (1755–1824)

Italian violinist and composer, Viotti was the founder of modern violin technique. His political sentiments resulted in expulsion from Britain in 1798.

127

On the fifth story, in a little street in Paris, not far from the *Place de la Révolution*, in the year 1790, lodged a deputy of the Constituent Assembly, an intimate and trusty friend of Viotti's. The conformity of their opinions, the same love of the arts and of liberty, an equal admiration of the genius and works of Rousseau had formed this connection between two men who thenceforward became insepar-able. It was during the exciting times of enthusiasm and of hope, that the ardent heart of Viotti could not remain indifferent to sentiments which affected all great and generous minds. He shared them with his friend. This person solicited him strongly to comply with the desire which some of the first personages in the kingdom expressed to hear him – if only for once. Viotti at last consented, but upon one condition – namely, that the concert should be given in the modest and humble retreat of *the fifth floor! La fortune passe par tout* – 'We have,' said he, 'long enough descended to *them*: but the times are changed; they must now mount, in order to raise themselves to *us*.'

128

[Ferdinand] Langlé, a professor of harmony in the French Con-servatoire, was an intimate friend of Viotti, and one charming summer evening the two were strolling on the Champs Elysées. They sat down on a retired bench to enjoy the calmness of the night, and became buried in reverie. But they were brought back to prosaic matters harshly by a babel of discordant noises that grated on the sensitive ears of the two musicians. They started from their seats, and Viotti said:

'It can't be a violin, and yet there is some resemblance to one.'

'Nor a clarinet,' suggested Langlé, 'though it is something like it.'

They approached the spot whence the extraordinary tones issued, and saw a poor blind man standing near a miserable-looking candle and playing upon a violin made of tin-plate.

'Fancy!' exclaimed Viotti, 'it *is* a violin, but a violin of tin-plate! Did you ever dream of such a curiosity!' and, after listening a while, he added, 'I say, Langlé, I must possess that instrument. Go and ask the old blind man what he will sell it for.'

Langlé approached and asked the question, but the old man was disinclined to part with it.

'But we will give you enough for it to enable you to purchase a better,' he added; 'and why is not your violin like others?'

The aged fiddler explained that ... his good, kind nephew Eustache, who was apprenticed to a tinker, had made it.

'Well,' said Viotti, 'I will give you twenty francs for your violin. You can buy a much better one for that price; but let me try it a little.'

He took the violin in his hands, and produced some extraordinary effects from it. A considerable crowd gathered around, and listened with curiosity and astonishment to the performance. Langlé seized on the opportunity, and passed round the hat, gathering a goodly amount of chink from the bystanders, which, with the twenty francs, was handed to the astonished old beggar.

'Stay a moment,' said the blind man, recovering a little from his surprise; 'just now I said I would sell the violin for twenty francs, but I did not know it was so good. I ought to have at least double for it.'

Viotti had never received a more genuine compliment, and he did not hesitate to give the old man two pieces of gold instead of one, and then immediately retired from the spot. He had scarcely gone forty yards when he felt some one pulling at his sleeve; it was a workman, who politely took off his cap, and said:

'Sir, you have paid too dear for that violin; as it was I who made it, I can supply you with as many as you like at six francs each.'

❦

Wolfgang Amadeus MOZART (1756–1791)

Son of the Kapellmeister to the Prince-Archbishop of Salzburg, Mozart spent his adult life in Vienna as a freelance musician. 'I must tell you before God and as an honest man,' declared Haydn to Leopold Mozart in 1785, 'that your son is the greatest composer I ever heard of.'

129

Letter to Mozart's sister, Maria Anna, from Johann André Schachtner, court trumpeter at Salzburg, 24 April 1792

Once I went with your father after the Thursday service to your house, where we found Wolfgängerl, then four years old, busy with his pen.

Father: What are you doing?

Wolfg.: Writing a concerto for the clavier; it will soon be done.

Father: Let me see it.

Wolfg.: It's not finished yet.

Father: Never mind; let me see it. It must be something very fine.

Your father took it from him and showed me a daub of notes, for the most part written over ink-blots. (The little fellow dipped his pen every time down to the very bottom of the ink-bottle, so that as soon as it reached the paper, down fell a blot; but that did not disturb him in the least, he rubbed the palm of his hand over it, wiped it off, and went on with his writing.) We laughed at first at this apparent nonsense, but then your father began to note the theme, the notes, the composition; his contemplation of the page became more earnest, and at last tears of wonder and delight fell from his eyes.

'Look, Herr Schachtner,' said he, 'how correct and how orderly it is; only it could never be of any use, for it is so extraordinarily difficult that no one in the world could play it.' Then Wolfgängerl struck in, 'That is why it is a concerto; it must be practised till it is perfect; look! this is how it goes.'

He began to play, but could only bring out enough to show us what he meant by it. He had at that time a firm conviction that playing concertos and working miracles were the same thing.

130

'I saw him,' said Goethe, 'at seven years old, when he gave a concert while travelling our way. I myself was about fourteen years old, and remember perfectly the little man, with his frisure and sword.'

As the two archduchesses were one day leading the boy between them to the empress, being unused to the highly polished floor his foot slipped and he fell. One of them took no notice of the accident but the other, Marie Antoinette, afterwards the unfortunate Queen of France, lifted him up and consoled him. He said to her, 'You are very kind, I will marry you.' She related this to her mother, who asked Wolfgang how he came to form such a resolution. 'From gratitude,' he replied, 'she was so good, but her sister gave herself no concern about me.'

132

Maria Anna Mozart recalls
On 5 August [1764] we had to rent a country house outside London, in Chelsea, so that Father could recover from a throat ailment which brought him near to death. . . . While our father lay dangerously ill, we were forbidden to touch the piano. And so, to occupy himself, Mozart composed his first symphony [K16] for all the instruments of the orchestra.

133

Until he was almost ten years old, he had an insurmountable horror of the horn, when it was sounded alone, without other instruments; merely holding a horn towards him terrified him as much as if it had been a loaded pistol. His father wished to overcome this childish alarm, and ordered me* once, in spite of his entreaties, to blow towards him; but, O! that I had not been induced to do it. Wolfgang no sooner heard the clanging sound than he turned pale, and would have fallen into convulsions, had I not instantly desisted.

134

I† well remember a long illness, during which I attended (Constanze) for full eight months. I was at her bedside and Mozart likewise, composing – both of us as silent as the grave; for after much suffering she had just sank into a sweet and refreshing slumber. On a sudden a noisy messenger entered the apartment. Mozart, alarmed lest his wife should be disturbed, pushed his chair back and rose hastily, when the penknife, which was open in his hand, slipped and buried

---

* Johann André Schachtner.
† Sophie Haibl, Constanze Mozart's sister.

itself in his foot. Although very sensitive to pain on ordinary occasions, he was now silent; but beckoned me to follow him into another room, where I found that the wound was really a very serious one. Johannisöl, the surgeon, attended him, and he was cured without his wife's knowing that an accident had happened; although the pain made him for some time lame in walking.

135

Seeing the impossibility of altogether weaning Mozart from the habit of writing far into the night, and very often as he lay in bed in the morning, [his doctor] endeavoured to avert the hurtful consequences in another way. He recommended him not to sit so long at the clavier, but at all events to compose standing, and to take as much bodily exercise as he could. His love of billiard-playing gave the doctor a welcome pretext for turning this motive into a regular one; Mozart was equally fond of bowls, and he was the more ready to follow the doctor's directions with regard to both games ... since they did not interfere with his intellectual activity. It happened one day in Prague that Mozart, while he was playing billiards, hummed an air, and looked from time to time into a book which he had with him; it appeared afterwards that he had been occupied with the first quintet of *The Magic Flute*.

136

His barber used to relate in after-years how difficult it was to dress his hair, since he would never sit still; every moment an idea would occur to him, and he would run to the clavier, the barber after him, hair-ribbon in hand.

137

After hearing the rehearsal of *The Abduction from the Seraglio* which he had himself demanded of Mozart the Emperor Joseph II said to the composer, 'My dear Mozart that is too fine for my ears; there are too many notes.' 'I ask your Majesty's pardon,' replied Mozart, 'there are just as many notes as there should be.'

138

He was once required, in consequence of one of the general government orders frequent at Vienna, to deliver in a statement of the amount of his salary. He wrote, in a sealed note, as follows, 'Too much for what I have done: too little for what I could have done.'

Mozart was one day accosted in the streets of Vienna by a beggar, who not only solicited alms of him, but by strong circumstances endeavoured to make it appear that he was distantly related to him. Mozart's feelings were excited; but being unprovided with money he desired the beggar to follow him to the next coffee-house, where, taking writing-paper, and drawing lines on it with his pen, he in a few minutes composed a minuet and trio. This, and a letter, Mozart directed him to take to his publisher, of whom the mendicant received a sum equal to five guineas.

140

The finest virtuosi and composers in Vienna would assemble at von Keess' concerts where Haydn's symphonies were performed; Mozart would play the piano, Jarnovick* would give a concerto and the mistress of the house sang. One evening Mozart, who had promised her a song, was late in arriving. One servant after another was sent to find him, and he was eventually located in a tavern. Mozart suddenly remembered that he had promised a song but had not written a note of it. He sent the servant for a sheet of paper and sat down to compose. When the song was finished he went to the concert.

141

Mozart found an old Salzburg acquaintance at Vienna in the person of the horn-player Joseph Leutgeb. . . . He was a capital solo-player on the French horn, but was wanting in higher cultivation. Mozart was always ready to help him, but frequently made him the butt of his exuberant spirits. Whenever he composed a solo for him, Leutgeb was obliged to submit to some mock penance. Once, for instance, Mozart threw all the parts of his concertos and symphonies about the room, and Leutgeb had to collect them on all fours and put them in order; as long as this lasted Mozart sat at his writing-table composing.

142

One day when I† was sitting at the pianoforte playing the 'Non più andrai' from *Figaro*, Mozart, who was paying a visit to us, came up behind me; I must have been playing it to his satisfaction, for he

---

* Giovanni Marie Giornovichi ['Jarnovick'] (*c.*1740–1804); virtuoso violinist.
† Karoline Pichler (1769–1843); Viennese novelist.

hummed the melody as I played and beat the time on my shoulders; but then he suddenly moved a chair up, sat down, told me to carry on playing the bass, and began to improvise such wonderfully beautiful variations that everyone listened to the tones of the German Orpheus with bated breath. But then he suddenly tired of it, jumped up, and, in the mad mood which so often came over him, he began to leap over tables and chairs, miaow like a cat, and turn somersaults like an unruly boy.

143

Mozart fortified himself with a glass of wine or punch when he was in the throes of composition. In one of his apartments his immediate neighbour was Joh. Mart. Loibl, who was musical and a Freemason, [and] consequently intimate with Mozart; he had a well-filled wine-cellar, of the contents of which he was never sparing in entertaining his friends. The partition wall between the houses was so thin, that Mozart had only to knock when he wished to attract Loibl's attention; whenever Loibl heard the clavier going and taps at his wall between the pauses, he used to send his servant into the cellar, and say to his family, 'Mozart is composing again; I must send him some wine.'

144

Michael Haydn* had been ordered by the Archbishop to compose some duets for violin and tenor, perhaps for his special use, but owing to a violent illness, which incapacitated him for work during a lengthened period, he was unable to finish them; the Archbishop thereupon threatened to deprive him of salary. When Mozart heard of the difficulty he at once undertook the work, and, visiting Haydn daily, wrote by his bedside to such good purpose that the duets (K423, 424) were soon completed and handed over to the Archbishop in Haydn's name.

145

At the final rehearsal [in Prague of Don Giovanni] Mozart was not at all satisfied with the efforts of a young and very pretty girl, the possessor of a voice of greater purity than power, to whom the part of Zerlina had been allotted. Zerlina, frightened at Don Giovanni's too pronounced love-making, cries for assistance behind the scenes (but) in spite of continued repetitions, Mozart was unable to infuse sufficient force into the poor girl's screams, until at last, losing all

* (1737–1806); Salzburg composer, brother of the more eminent Joseph.

patience, he clambered from the conductor's desk on to the boards. At that period neither gas nor electric light lent facility to stage mechanism. A few tallow candles dimly glimmered among the desks of the musicians, but over the stage and the rest of the house almost utter darkness reigned. Mozart's sudden appearance on the stage was therefore not noticed, much less suspected, by poor Zerlina, who at the moment when she ought to have uttered the cry received from the composer a sharp pinch on the arm, emitting, in consequence, a shriek which caused him to exclaim: 'Admirable! Mind you scream like that tonight!'*

146

The evening before the production of *Don Giovanni* at Prague, the dress rehearsal having already taken place, he said to his wife that he would write the overture during the night if she would sit with him and make him some punch to keep his spirits up. This she did, and told him tales about Aladdin's lamp, Cinderella, etc., which made him laugh till the tears came. But the punch made him sleepy, so that he dozed when she left off, and only worked as long as she told tales. At last the excitement, the sleepiness, and his frequent efforts not to doze off were too much for him, and his wife persuaded him to go to sleep on the sofa promising to wake him in an hour. But he slept so soundly that she could not find it in her heart to wake him until two hours had passed. It was then five o'clock. At seven o'clock the overture was finished and in the hands of the copyist.

147

The ink, Swoboda recalled, was hardly dry on some of the pages when they were placed on the desks of the orchestra. A rehearsal was impossible. Nevertheless, the overture was played with a spirit which not only roused the enthusiasm of the audience to the highest pitch, but so greatly delighted the illustrious composer that, turning to the orchestra, he exclaimed, '*Bravo, bravo, Meine Herren, das war ausgezeichnet!*' (Bravo, bravo, gentlemen, that was admirable!)

148

Lorenzo da Ponte (1749–1838); Mozart's librettist, recalls
The Emperor sent for me [in Vienna] and ... told me that he was longing to see *Don Giovanni.* . . .

---

* Both this and anecdote 147 are recounted by Wenzel Swoboda, double-bass player in the Prague Opera House Orchestra.

Need I recall it? . . . *Don Giovanni* did not please! Everyone, except Mozart, thought that there was something missing. Additions were made; some of the arias were changed; it was offered for a second performance. *Don Giovanni* did not please! And what did the Emperor say? He said, 'That opera is divine; I should even venture that it is more beautiful than *Figaro*. But such music is not meat for the teeth of my Viennese!'

I reported the remark to Mozart, who replied quietly, 'Give them time to chew on it!'

149

The success [of *The Magic Flute*] was not at first so great as had been expected, and after the first act Mozart rushed, pale and excited, behind the scenes to Schikaneder,* who endeavoured to console him. In the course of the second act the audience recovered from the first shock of surprise, and at the close of the opera Mozart was recalled. He had hidden himself, and when he was found could [only] with difficulty be persuaded to appear before the audience, not certainly from bashfulness, for he was used by this time to brilliant successes, but because he was not satisfied with the way in which his music had been received. . . .

Schenck† relates . . . that after the overture, unable to contain his delight, he crept along to the conductor's stool, seized Mozart's hand and kissed it; Mozart, still beating time with his right hand, looked at him with a smile, and stroked his cheek.

150

Italian ears were slow to approve the piquant chromatic harmony of the Germans, or to perceive in it the source of unnumbered beautiful effects in instrumental music. When [the music publisher] Artaria sent [Mozart's six] quartets to Italy they were speedily returned with the excuse, *'the engraving is full of mistakes.'* Nissen relates that the Hungarian Prince Grassalkowitsch was one day hearing them performed by the musicians of his chapel, when he called out repeatedly, 'You are playing wrong;' and on the parts being handed to convince him of the contrary, he tore them up on the spot.

---

*Emanuel Schikaneder (1751–1812); German theatre manager and playwright, librettist of *The Magic Flute*.
† Johann Schenck (1753–1836); Austrian composer, teacher of Beethoven.

Beethoven arrived in Vienna in the spring of 1787 as a youth of great promise and was taken to play before Mozart. Assuming that his music was a showpiece specially prepared for the occasion, Mozart responded coolly. Beethoven begged him to state a theme on which he could improvise and began playing as if inspired by the Master's presence. Mozart became engrossed. Finally he rejoined his friends in the next room and pronounced emphatically, 'Keep your eyes on that young man. Some day he will give the world something to talk about.'

152

Once, when a new quartet of Haydn's was being performed in a large company, Kozeluch,* standing by Mozart, found fault, first with one thing and then with another, exclaiming at length, with impudent assurance, 'I should never have done it in that way!' 'Nor should I,' answered Mozart; 'but do you know why? Because neither you nor I would have had so good an idea.'

153

When he was travelling with his wife through beautiful scenery, [Mozart] used to gaze earnestly and in silence on the scene before him; his usually absent and thoughtful expression would brighten by degrees, and he would begin to sing, or rather to hum, finally breaking out with: 'If I could only put the subject down on paper!' And, when [Constanze] sometimes said that he could do so if he pleased, he went on: 'Yes, of course, all in proper form! What a pity it is that one's work must all be hatched in one's own room!'

154

One fine day in the autumn [of 1791] his wife drove with him to the Prater. As soon as they had reached a solitary spot, and were seated together, Mozart began to speak of death, and said that he was writing this *Requiem* for himself. She tried to talk him out of these gloomy fancies, but in vain, and his eyes filled with tears as he answered her, 'No, no, I am but too well convinced that I cannot last long. I have certainly been poisoned. I cannot rid myself of this idea.'

---

* Leopold Kozeluch (or Kozeluh, 1747–1818); Czech composer who refused to occupy Mozart's post in Salzburg but later accepted his court position in Prague.

Stendhal's account of the Requiem *has acquired legendary status: it is substantially untrue*

One day, when he was plunged in a profound reverie, he heard a carriage stop at his door. A stranger was announced, who requested to speak to him. A person was introduced, handsomely dressed, of dignified and impressive manners. 'I have been commissioned, Sir, by a man of considerable importance, to call upon you.' – 'Who is he?' interrupted Mozart. 'He does not wish to be known.' – 'Well, what does he want?' – 'He has just lost a person whom he tenderly loved, and whose memory will be eternally dear to him. He is desirous of annually commemorating this mournful event by a solemn service, for which he requests you to compose a requiem.' Mozart was forcibly struck by this discourse, by the grave manner in which it was uttered, and by the air of mystery in which the whole was involved. He engaged to write the *Requiem*. The stranger continued, 'Employ all your genius on this work; it is destined for a connoisseur.' – 'So much the better.' – 'What time do you require?' – 'A month.' – 'Very well: in a month's time I shall return. What price do you set on your work?' 'A hundred ducats.' The stranger counted them on the table, and disappeared.

Mozart remained lost in thought for some time; he then suddenly called for pen, ink, and paper, and, in spite of his wife's entreaties, began to write. This rage for composition continued several days. He wrote day and night, with an ardour which seemed continually to increase; but his constitution, already in a state of great debility, was unable to support this enthusiasm: one morning, he fell senseless, and was obliged to suspend his work. Two or three days after, when his wife sought to divert his mind from the gloomy presages which occupied it, he said to her abruptly, 'It is certain that I am writing this *Requiem* for myself; it will serve for my funeral service.' Nothing could remove this impression from his mind.

As he went on, he felt his strength diminish from day to day, and the score advanced slowly. The month which he had fixed being expired, the stranger again made his appearance. 'I have found it impossible,' said Mozart, 'to keep my word' – 'Do not give yourself any uneasiness,' replied the stranger; 'what further time do you require?' – 'Another month. The work has interested me more than I expected, and I have extended it much beyond what I at first designed.' – 'In that case, it is but just to increase the premium; here are fifty ducats more.' – 'Sir,' said Mozart, with increasing astonishment, 'who, then, are you?' – 'That is nothing to the purpose; in a month's time I shall return.'

Mozart immediately called one of his servants, and ordered him to follow this extraordinary personage, and find out who he was; but the man failed for want of skill, and returned without being able to trace him.

Poor Mozart was then persuaded that he was no ordinary being: that he had a connexion with the other world, and was sent to announce to him his approaching end. He applied himself with the more ardour to his *Requiem*, which he regarded as the most durable monument of his genius. While thus employed, he was seized with the most alarming fainting fits, but the work was at length completed before the expiration of the month. At the time appointed, the stranger returned, but Mozart was no more!

His career was as brilliant as it was short. He died before he had completed his thirty-sixth year; but in this short space of time he has acquired a name which will never perish, so long as feeling hearts are to be found.

156

It was late in the evening of 5 December 1791, that his sister-in-law [Sophie Haibl] returned, but only to witness his dissolution. Her own account may now be given.

'How shocked was I, when my sister, usually so calm and self-possessed, met me at the door, and in a half-distracted manner said, "God be thanked that you are here. Since you left he has been so ill that I never expected him to outlive this day. Should he be so again he will die to-night. Go to him, and see how he is." As I approached his bed he called to me – "It is well that you are here: you must stay to-night and see me die." I tried as far as I was able to banish this impression, but he replied, "The taste of death is already on my tongue – *I taste death*: and who will be near to support my Constance if you go away?" I returned to my mother for a few moments to give her intelligence, for she was anxiously waiting, as she might else have supposed the fatal event already over; and then hurried back to my disconsolate sister. Süssmayr* was standing by the bedside, and on the counterpane lay the *Requiem*, concerning which Mozart was still speaking and giving directions. He now called his wife, and made her promise to keep his death secret for a time from every one but Albrechtsberger, that he might thus have an advantage over other candidates for the vacant office of kapellmeister to St Stephen's. His desire in this respect was gratified, for Albrechts-

---

* Franz Xaver Süssmayr (1766–1803); composer, pupil of Mozart whose *Requiem* he eventually completed.

berger received the appointment. As he looked over the pages of the *Requiem* for the last time, he said, with tears in his eyes. "Did I not tell you that I was writing this for myself?"

'On the arrival of the physician, Dr Closset, cold applications were ordered to his burning head, a process endured by the patient with extreme shuddering, and which brought on the delirium from which he never recovered. He remained in this state for two hours, and at midnight expired.'

157

A contemporary musician (Salieri must be meant) did not scruple to say to his acquaintances: 'It is a pity to lose so great a genius, but a good thing for us that he is dead. For if he had lived much longer, we should not have earned a crust of bread by our compositions.'

158

At three o'clock in the afternoon of 6 December the corpse of Mozart received the benediction in the transept chapel on the north side of St Stephen's Church. A violent storm of snow and rain was raging, and the few friends who were assembled – among them Van Swieten, Salieri, Süssmayr, Kapellm. Roser, and the violoncellist Orsler – stood under umbrellas round the bier, which was then carried through the Schulerstrasse to the churchyard of St Mark's. The storm continued to rage so fiercely that the mourners decided upon turning back before they reached their destination, and not a friend stood by when the body of Mozart was lowered into the grave. For reasons of economy no grave had been bought, and the corpse was consigned to a common vault, made to contain from fifteen to twenty coffins, which was dug up about every ten years and filled anew: no stone marked the resting-place of Mozart.

159

'I was beside myself,' wrote Haydn from London. 'I only regret that before his death he could not convince the English, who walk in darkness in this respect, of his greatness ... I shall make every possible effort to promote his works for the widow's benefit; I wrote to the poor woman and told her that when her favourite son reaches the necessary age I shall give him composition lessons to the very best of my ability and at no cost.'

160

When Mendelssohn visited Italy in 1831, he had an introduction to the wife of the military commandant at Milan, Dorothea von Ertmann, the intimate friend of Beethoven. Her name is immortalized on the title-page of the Sonata, Op. 101. Mendelssohn was invited to her house, and had played her own special sonata and a great deal of Beethoven besides, when a little modest Austrian official* who had been sitting in the corner came up and said timidly, '*Ach! Wollen sie nicht etwas vom lieben Vater spielen?*' (Won't you play something of my dear father's?)

Mendelssohn: 'Who was your father?'
Austrian official: 'Ach! Mozart.'

'And,' said Mendelssohn, 'I *did* play Mozart for him, and for the rest of the evening.'

161

At an Augarten concert [in 1799, Beethoven and J. B. Cramer]† were walking together and hearing a performance of Mozart's Pianoforte Concerto in C minor (K491); Beethoven suddenly stood still and, directing his companion's attention to the exceedingly simple but equally beautiful motive which is first introduced towards the end of the piece, exclaimed, 'Cramer, Cramer! We shall never be able to do anything like that!'

━━━

Luigi CHERUBINI (1760–1842)

Italian composer of some thirty operas, who spent twenty years as Director of the Paris Conservatoire. Famously acerbic, he offended Napoleon and was forced to flee to Vienna, where he impressed Beethoven.

162

Before Napoleon became First Consul, he had been on familiar terms with Cherubini. One evening, when an opera of Cherubini was being performed, and he and Napoleon were present in the same box, Napoleon turned to Cherubini and said, 'My dear Cherubini, you are certainly an excellent musician; but really your music is so noisy

---

* Carl Thomas Mozart (1786–1859), elder surviving son of the composer, became an Austrian government official and landowner in Italy; his younger brother, Franz Xaver Wolfgang (1791–1844), was a pianist and composer of minor repute.
†Johann Baptist Cramer (1771–1858); pianist and composer, Beethoven's London publisher.

and complicated, that I can make nothing of it;' to which Cherubini replied, 'My dear general, you are certainly an excellent soldier; but, in regard to music, you must excuse me if I don't think it necessary to adapt my compositions to your comprehension.'

163

One day Cherubini was walking along the boulevard when it began to rain. A gentleman, driving by, recognized the maestro, and, alighting, placed his vehicle at Cherubini's disposal, who got in. The gentleman, who was going a different way, said, 'M. Cherubini, will you lend me your umbrella?' 'No; I never lend my umbrella,' was Cherubini's reply; and he drove off!

164

Berlioz, Memoirs
No sooner was Cherubini appointed director [of the Conservatoire], after the death of Perne, than he at once set to work to signalize his accession to power by the introduction of all sorts of restrictions in the internal economy of the school, which had not, up to that time, been organized on exactly puritan principles. In order to prevent the intermingling of the two sexes, except in the presence of the professors, he issued an order that the men were to enter by the door in the Faubourg Poissonnière, and the women by that in the Rue Bergère; the two being at opposite ends of the building.

Wholly ignorant of this moral decree, I betook myself one morning to the library, entering as usual by the Rue Bergère, the female door, and was making my way to the library, when I found myself suddenly confronted by a servant, who stopped me in the middle of the courtyard, and ordered me to go back and return to the very same spot by the other entrance. I thought this so absurd that I sent the liveried Argus about his business, and went on my way. The rascal, hoping to find favour in the eyes of his new master by emulating his severity, ran off to report the circumstance. I had forgotten all about it, and was absorbed in [studying Gluck's] *Alceste*, when Cherubini entered the reading-room, his face more cadaverous, his hair more dishevelled, his eyes more wicked, and his step firmer than ever. He and my accuser made their way round the table, examining several unconscious students, until the servant stopped in front of me and cried, 'Here he is!' Cherubini was in such a passion that he could not utter a word. 'Ah! ah, ah, ah!' he cried at last, his Italian accent comically intensified in his anger, 'and so you are the man who, who, who dares to come in by the door by which I forbid you to enter?' 'I was not aware, sir, of your order, and another time I will obey it.'

'Another time! another time! What – What – what are you doing here?' 'As you see, sir, I am studying Gluck's scores.' 'And what – what – what – are Gluck's scores to you? and who allows you to – to – to enter the library?' 'Sir!' (I was getting angry) 'Gluck's music is the grandest I know, and I need no one's permission to come here to study. The Conservatoire library is open to the public from 10 till 3, and I have a right to use it.' 'The – the – the right?' 'Yes, sir.' 'I – I forbid you to come here!' 'Nevertheless, I shall return.' 'What – what – what is your name?' he cried, trembling with passion. I was, by this time, white with anger too. 'Sir, perhaps you may hear my name some day . . . but you will not hear it now!' 'Sei – sei – seize him, Hottin' (that was the servant's name), 'seize him, and – and – take him away to prison!' Then, to the astonishment of everyone, master and servant pursued me round the table, knocking over stools and reading-desks in the vain effort to catch me, until at last I escaped, calling out as I vanished, 'You shall neither have me nor my name, and I shall soon come back and study Gluck's scores again!'

This was my first interview with Cherubini.

❧

Ludwig van BEETHOVEN (1770–1827)

Born in Bonn of Flemish ancestry, he moved in 1792 to Vienna. Beethoven's music, personality and the events of his life assumed almost mythological proportions during the nineteenth century: he was considered the apotheosis of genius and creator.

165

In Bonn [when Beethoven was a boy] there was a middle-aged man by the name of Stommb who had formerly been a musician and learned to compose. Thereby, it was said, he had become insane; he used to wander through the town with a conductor's wand in his right hand and a music roll in his left; not a word would he say. When he came into the ground floor at Rheinstrasse 934, where no one had thought to see him, he would strike with his wand on the table . . . and point up towards the Beethovens' home as if to indicate that musicians were there, too, and then beat time with the conductor's wand on the music roll, not saying one word.

Ludwig van Beethoven often laughed about it and once said, 'We can see by that how it goes with musicians; music has already made this one mad – what may happen to us?'

166

When Johann van Beethoven had visitors, Ludwig would sidle over to the piano and play chords with his right hand. His father would say, 'what are you splashing around for? Go away, or I'll box your ears.' One day Ludwig was playing as usual, without notes, when his father came in, 'Won't you ever stop after all I've told you?' He played again and said to his father, 'Now isn't that beautiful?' His father said, 'That is something else, you made it up yourself. You are not to do that yet.'

167

He told me* once that as a boy he was neglected, and his musical education had been very bad. 'But' he added, 'I had talent for music.'

168

When [Griesinger]† was still only an attaché, and Beethoven was little known except as a celebrated pianoforte player, both being still young, they happened to meet at the house of Prince Lobkowitz. In conversation with a gentleman present, Beethoven said in substance, that he wished to be relieved from all bargain and sale of his works, and would gladly find some one willing to pay him a certain income for life, for which he should possess the exclusive right of publishing all he wrote; adding, 'and I would not be idle in composition. I believe Goethe does this with Cotta, and, if I mistake not, Handel's London publisher held similar terms with him.'

'My dear young man,' returned the other, 'You must not complain; for you are neither a Goethe nor a Handel, and it is not to be expected that you ever will be; for such masters will not be born again.' Beethoven bit his lips, gave a most contemptuous glance at the speaker, and said no more.

169

He seemed to think strangeness and originality the chief objects to be aimed at in composition, as appears from his answer to a lady who asked whether he frequently attended Mozart's operas, that 'he was not acquainted with them, and did not care to hear other than his own music, lest he should impair his originality.'

---

* Karl Czerny (1791–1857); Austrian pianist, composer and teacher.
† Georg August von Griesinger (1769–1845); later to become Saxon Minister in Vienna, biographer of Haydn.

At the performance of the [C minor Piano] Concerto he asked me* to turn the pages for him, but – heaven help me! – that was easier said than done. I saw almost nothing but empty leaves; at the most on one page or the other a few Egyptian hieroglyphs wholly unintelligible to me scribbled down to serve as clues for him; for he played nearly all of the solo part from memory, since, as was so often the case, he had not had time to put it all on paper. He gave me a secret glance whenever he was at the end of one of the invisible passages and my scarcely concealable anxiety not to miss the decisive moment amused him greatly and he laughed heartily at the jovial supper which we ate afterwards.

171

Beethoven once found Streicher's daughter practising the Variations [in C minor of 1806]. After he had listened for a while he asked her, 'By whom is that!' 'By you.' 'Such nonsense by me! O Beethoven, what an ass you were!'

172

In whatever company he might chance to be, he knew how to produce such an effect upon every hearer that frequently not an eye remained dry, while many would break out into loud sobs; for there was something wonderful in his expression in addition to the beauty and originality of his ideas and his spirited style of rendering them. After ending an improvisation of this kind he would burst into loud laughter and banter his hearers on the emotion he had caused in them. 'You are fools!' he would say. . . . 'Who can live among such spoiled children!' he would cry.

173

In writing his compositions Beethoven often had some special object in mind. . . . In his [Third] Symphony he had thought of Bonaparte, but Bonaparte when he was still First Consul. At that time Beethoven held him in the highest esteem and compared him to the great consuls of ancient Rome. I,† as well as several other intimate friends, have seen this Symphony, already scored, lying on

---

* Ignaz Ritter von Seyfried (1776–1841); Austrian composer and conductor.
† Ferdinand Ries (1784–1858); German musician and Beethoven biographer; this incident is contested by modern scholars.

his table, with the name Bonaparte at the very top of the title page and at the very bottom 'Luigi van Beethoven', but not another word. How and with what the gap between was to be filled in I do not know. I was the first announce to him that Napoleon had declared himself Emperor, whereupon he flew into a rage and cried out: 'Then he, too, is nothing but an ordinary mortal! Now he, too, will trample on the rights of man and indulge only his own ambition. He will raise himself above all others and become a tyrant!' Beethoven went to the table, took hold of the title page by the top, tore it apart and flung it on the ground. The first page was rewritten and not until then was the Symphony entitled Sinfonia 'Eroica'.

174

In 1802, facing the gradual onset of deafness, Beethoven gave expression to his appalling predicament in a document found among papers after his death, the so-called Heiligenstadt Testament

FOR MY BROTHERS CARL AND [JOHANN] BEETHOVEN
Oh, you men who think or say that I am malevolent, stubborn, or misanthropic, how greatly do you wrong me. You do not know the secret cause which makes me seem that way to you. From childhood on, my heart and soul have been full of the tender feeling of goodwill, and I was ever inclined to accomplish great things. But, think that for six years now I have been hopelessly afflicted, made worse by senseless physicians, from year to year deceived with hopes of improvement, finally compelled to face the prospect of *a lasting malady* (whose cure will take years or, perhaps, be impossible). Though born with a fiery, active temperament, even susceptible to the diversions of society, I was soon compelled to withdraw myself, to live life alone. If at times I tried to forget all this, oh how harshly was I flung back by the doubly sad experience of my bad hearing. Yet it was impossible for me to say to people, 'Speak louder, shout, for I am deaf.' Ah, how could I possibly admit an infirmity in the *one sense* which ought to be more perfect in me than in others, a sense which I once possessed in the highest perfection, a perfection such as few in my profession enjoy or ever have enjoyed. Oh I cannot do it; therefore forgive me when you see me draw back when I would have gladly mingled with you. My misfortune is doubly painful to me because I am bound to be misunderstood; for me there can be no relaxation with my fellow men, no refined conversations, no mutual exchange of ideas. I must live almost alone, like one who has been banished; I can mix with society only as much as true necessity demands. If I approach near to people a hot terror seizes upon me, and I fear being

exposed to the danger that my condition might be noticed. Thus it has been during the last six months which I have spent in the country. By ordering me to spare my hearing as much as possible, my intelligent doctor almost fell in with my own present frame of mind, though sometimes I ran counter to it by yielding to my desire for companionship. But what a humiliation for me when someone standing next to me heard a flute in the distance and *I heard nothing*, or someone heard a *shepherd singing* and again I heard nothing. Such incidents drove me almost to despair; a little more of that and I would have ended my life – it was only *my art* that held me back. Ah, it seemed to me impossible to leave the world until I had brought forth all that I felt was within me. So I endured this wretched existence – truly wretched for so susceptible a body, which can be thrown by a sudden change from the best condition to the very worst. *Patience*, they say, is what I must now choose for my guide, and I have done so – I hope my determination will remain firm to endure until it pleases the inexorable Parcae to break the thread. Pehaps I shall get better, perhaps not; I am ready. Forced to become a philosopher already in my twenty-eighth year, – oh it is not easy, and for the artist much more difficult than for anyone else. Divine One, thou seest my inmost soul; thou knowest that therein dwells the love of mankind and the desire to do good. Oh fellow men, when at some point you read this, consider then that you have done me an injustice; someone who has had misfortune may console himself to find a similar case to his who despite all the limitations of Nature nevertheless did everything within his powers to become accepted among worthy artists and men. You, my brothers Carl and [Johann], as soon as I am dead, if Dr Schmidt is still alive, ask him in my name to describe my malady, and attach this written document to his account of my illness so that so far as is possible at least the world may become reconciled to me after my death. At the same time, I declare you two to be the heirs to my small fortune (if so it can be called); divide it fairly; bear with and help each other. What injury you have done me you know was long ago forgiven. To you, brother Carl, I give special thanks for the attachment you have shown me of late. It is my wish that you may have a better and freer life than I have had. Recommend *virtue* to your children; it alone, not money, can make them happy. I speak from experience; this was what upheld me in time of misery. Thanks to it and to my art, I did not end my life by suicide – Farewell and love each other – I thank all my friends, particularly *Prince Lichnowsky* and *Professor Schmidt* – I would like the instruments from Prince L. to be preserved by one of you, but not to be the cause of strife between you, and as soon as they can serve

75

you a better purpose, then sell them. How happy I shall be if I can still be helpful to you in my grave – so be it. With joy I hasten to meet death. If it comes before I have had the chance to develop all my artistic capacities, it will still be coming too soon despite my harsh fate, and I should probably wish it later – yet even so I should be happy, for would it not free me from a state of endless suffering? – Come *when* thou wilt, I shall meet thee bravely. Farewell and do not wholly forget me when I am dead; I deserve this from you, for during my lifetime I was thinking of you often and of ways to make you happy – please be so –

LUDWIG VAN BEETHOVEN
(seal)

Heiglnstadt [Heiligenstadt]
6 October, 1802

For my brothers Carl and [Johann] to be read and executed after my death.

Heiglnstadt, 10 October, 1802, thus I bid thee farewell – and indeed sadly – Yes, that fond hope – which I brought here with me, to be cured to a degree at least – this I must now wholly abandon. As the leaves of autumn fall and are withered – so likewise has my hope been blighted – I leave here – almost as I came – even the high courage – which often inspired me in the beautiful days of summer – has disappeared – Oh Providence – grant me at last but one day of *pure joy* – it is so long since real joy echoed in my heart – Oh when – Oh when, Oh Divine One – shall I feel it again in the temple of nature and of mankind – Never? – No – Oh that would be too hard.

175

One day Neate* was with Beethoven and while urging him to visit England mentioned the excellence of the English aurists, and was sure B. would find there some remedy for his deafness.

'No,' said Beethoven, in substance, 'I have already had all sorts of medical advice. I shall never be cured. I will tell you how it happened. I was once busy writing an opera.'

---

* Charles Neate (1784–1877); English pianist, founder-member of the Royal Philharmonic Society, visited Beethoven in 1815.

Neate – *Fidelio?*

B. – No, it was not *Fidelio*. I had a very ill-tempered *primo tenore* to deal with. I had already written two grand airs to the same text, with which he was dissatisfied, and now a third, which, upon trial, he seemed to approve and took away with him. I thanked the stars that I was at length rid of him and sat down immediately to a work which I had laid aside for those airs and which I was anxious to finish. I had not been half an hour at my work when I heard a knock at my door which I immediately recognized as that of my *primo tenore*. I sprang up from my table under such an excitement of rage that as the man entered the room I thew myself upon the floor as they do on the stage [here B. spread out his arms and made an illustrative gesture], coming down upon my hands. When I arose I found myself deaf and have been so ever since. The physicians say the nerve is injured.'

176

After ordering his dinner with his funny old cook and telling his nephew to see to the wine, we all five took a walk. Beethoven was generally in advance humming some passage. He usually sketches his subjects in the open air; it was on one of these occasions, Schuppanzigh* told me,† that he caught his deafness. He was writing in a garden and was so absorbed that he was not sensible of a pouring rain, till his music paper was so wet that he could no longer write. From that day his deafness commenced, which neither art nor time has cured.

177

Beethoven was playing a new Pianoforte Concerto of his, but forgot at the first tutti, that he was a Soloplayer and springing up, began to direct in his usual way. At the first sforzando he threw out his arms so wide asunder, that he knocked both the lights off the piano upon the ground. The audience laughed, and Beethoven was so incensed at this disturbance, that he made the orchestra cease playing, and begin anew. Seyfried, fearing, that a repetition of the accident would occur at the same passage, bade two boys of the chorus place themselves on either side of Beethoven, and hold the lights in their

---

* Ignaz Schuppanzigh (1776–1830); leader of string quartet at Rasoumovsky's, introduced several new Beethoven works.
† Sir George Smart (1776–1867); English composer and conductor who visited Beethoven in 1825.

hands. One of the boys innocently approached nearer, and was reading also in the notes of the piano-part. When therefore the fatal sforzando came, he received from Beethoven's out thrown right hand so smart a blow on the mouth, that the poor boy let fall the light from terror. The other boy, more cautious, had followed with anxious eyes every motion of Beethoven, and by stooping suddenly at the eventful moment he avoided the slap on the mouth. If the public were unable to restrain their laughter before, they could now much less, and broke out into a regular bacchanalian roar. Beethoven got into such a rage, that at the first chords of the solo, half a dozen strings broke. Every endeavour of the real lovers of music to restore calm and attention were for the moment fruitless. The first allegro of the Concerto was therefore lost to the public. From that fatal evening Beethoven would not give another concert.

178

We* went one afternoon to the Alservorstadt, and mounted to the second storey of the so-called Schwarzspanier house. We rang, no one answered; we lifted the latch, the door was open, the ante-room empty. We knocked at the door of Beethoven's room, and receiving no reply, repeated our knock more loudly. But we got no answer, although we could hear there was someone inside. We entered, and what a scene presented itself! The wall facing us was hung with huge sheets of paper covered with charcoal marks; Beethoven was standing before it, with his back turned towards us, but in what a condition! Oppressed by the excessive heat, he had divested himself of everything but his shirt, and was busily employed writing notes on the wall with a lead pencil, beating time and striking a few chords on his stringless pianoforte. He did not once turn towards the door. We looked at each other in amused perplexity. It was no use trying to attract the deaf master's attention by making a noise; and he would have felt embarrassed had we gone up to him. I said to Atterbom, 'Would you, as a poet, like to take away with you to the north the consciousness of having, perhaps, arrested the loftiest flights of genius? You can at least say, "I have seen Beethoven create." Let us leave, unseen and unheard!' We departed. We had certainly caught him *in flagrante*.

---

* Alois Jeitteles, Austrian poet, author of *An die Ferne Geliebte* cycle, set by Beethoven; Per Daniel Amadeus Atterbom (1790–1855); Swedish poet and philosopher.

When I* came early in the morning to Beethoven, he was still lying in bed; he happened to be in remarkably good spirits, jumped up immediately, and placed himself, just as he was, at the window looking out on the Schottenbastei, with the view of examining the *Fidelio* numbers which I had arranged. Naturally, a crowd of street boys collected under the window, when he roared out, 'Now what do these confounded boys want?' I laughed, and pointed to his own figure. 'Yes, yes; you are quite right,' he said, and hastily put on a dressing-gown.

Goethe, letter to Zelter

Karlsbad, 2 September 1812

I made the acquaintance of Beethoven in Teplitz. His talent amazed me. However, unfortunately he is an utterly untamed personality, not entirely in the wrong if he finds the world detestable, but does not thereby make it more enjoyable for himself or for others.

Beethoven, letter to Bettina von Arnim†

When two such come together as I and Goethe great lords must note what it is that passes for greatness with such as we. Yesterday, as we were returning homewards, we met the whole Imperial family; we saw them coming at some distance, whereupon Goethe disengaged himself from my arm, in order that he might stand aside; in spite of all I could say, I could not bring him a step forwards. I crushed my hat more furiously on my head, buttoned up my top coat, and walked with my arms folded behind me, right through the thickest of the crowd. Princes and officials made a lane for me: Archduke Rudolph took off his hat. The Empress saluted me the first: – *these great people know me!* It was the greatest fun in the world to me, to see the procession file past Goethe. He stood aside, with his hat off, bending his head down as low as possible. For this I afterwards called him over the coals properly and without mercy.

---

* Ignaz Moscheles (1794–1870); pianist and composer.
† (1785–1859); recipient of Goethe's *Correspondence with a Child* and, briefly, a love-object of Beethoven's. The autograph of this letter has never been traced and its dates conflict with known events, but the story appears to have some basis in fact.

Everywhere in public, said Simrock,* Beethoven railed at Emperor Franz because of the reduction of the paper money. 'Such a rascal ought to be hanged to the first tree,' said he. But he was known and the police officials let him do what he pleased.

183

He was requested to improvise on the pianoforte, which he did not wish to do. A table had been spread with food in an adjoining room and finally the company gathered about it. I† was a young lad and Beethoven interested me so greatly that I remained always near him. Search was made for him in vain and finally the company sat down without him. He was in the next room and now began to improvise; all grew quiet and listened to him. I remained standing beside him at the pianoforte. He played for about an hour and one by one all gathered around him. Then it occurred to him that he had been called to the table long before – he hurried from his chair to the dining-room. At the door stood a table holding porcelain dishes. He stumbled against it and the dishes fell to the floor. Count Dönhoff, a wealthy cavalier, laughed at the mishap and the company again sat down to the table with Beethoven. There was no more thought of playing music, for after Beethoven's fantasia half of the pianoforte strings were broken.

184

Beethoven asked me‡ if I had not observed how village musicians often played in their sleep, occasionally letting their instruments fall and remaining entirely quiet, then awaking with a start, throwing in a few vigorous blows or strokes at a venture, but generally in the right key, and then falling asleep again; he had tried to copy these poor people in [the merrymaking of the country folk] in his 'Pastoral' Symphony.

185

Beethoven was at times exceedingly passionate. One day when I§ dined with him at the 'Swan', the waiter brought him a wrong dish.

---

* Peter Joseph Simrock (1796–1870); son and successor of Beethoven's publisher in Bonn.
† Franz Glöggl, Austrian music publisher.
‡ Anton Schindler (1796–1864); Beethoven's amanuensis and early biographer.
§ Ferdinand Ries.

Beethoven had no sooner uttered a few words of reproof (to which the other retorted in no very polite manner), than he took the dish, amply filled with the gravy of the stewed beef it contained, and threw it at the waiter's head. Those who know the dexterity of Viennese waiters in carrying at one and the same time numberless plates full of different viands, will conceive the distress of the poor man, who could not move his arms, while the gravy trickled down his face. Both he and Beethoven swore and shouted, whilst all the parties assembled roared with laughter. At last Beethoven himself joined the chorus, on looking at the waiter, who was licking in with his tongue the stream of gravy which, much as he fought against it, hindered him from uttering any more invectives; the evolutions of his tongue causing the most absurd grimaces. The picture was worthy of Hogarth.

186

His housekeeper told me I* would probably be unable to speak to him, since he had returned home in a rage. He at once gave free rein to his feelings and said he was the most wretched man in the world; he had just returned from the tavern, where he had asked for some veal which he felt like eating – and none was available! All this he said in a very serious, gloomy way. I consoled him, we talked and thus he kept me for nearly two hours.

I hurried back to Vienna and at once asked my innkeeper's son whether he had some roast veal ready. I made him put it in a dish, carefully cover it and, without a word of explanation, sent it back to Baden. I was still lying in bed the next morning when Beethoven came to me, kissed and embraced me and told me I was the most kind-hearted person he had ever met; never had anything given him such pleasure as the roast veal, coming at the very moment when he so greatly longed for it.

187

Among his favourite dishes was bread soup, made in the manner of pap, in which he indulged every Thursday. To compose this, ten eggs were set before him, which he tried before mixing them with the other ingredients; and if it unfortunately happened that any of them were musty, a grand scene ensued; the offending cook was summoned to the presence by a tremendous ejaculation. She, however, well knowing what might occur, took care cautiously to stand on

---

* Ferdinand Ries.

the threshold of the door, prepared to make a precipitate retreat; but the moment she made her appearance the attack commenced, and the broken eggs, like bombs from well directed batteries, flew about her ears, their yellow and white contents covering her with viscous streams.

188

He once dismissed a housekeeper, who was in other respects an excellent servant, because she had told an untruth with a view to benefitting him. A lady friend who had procured him this house-keeper, was questioning him about his severity, when he replied, 'Anyone who tells a lie has not a pure heart, and cannot make pure soup!'

189

The use of the bath was as much a necessity to Beethoven as to a Turk; and he was in the habit of submitting himself to frequent ablutions. When it happened that he did not walk out of doors to collect his ideas, he would not unfrequently, in a fit of the most complete abstraction, go to his wash-hand basin, and pour several jugs of water upon his hands, all the while humming and roaring, for sing he could not. After dabbling in the water till his clothes were wet through, he would pace up and down the room, with a vacant expression of countenance, and his eyes frightfully distended; the singularity of his aspect being often increased by an unshaven beard. Then he would seat himself at his table and write; and afterwards get up again to the wash-hand basin, and dabble and hum as before. Ludicrous as were these scenes, no one dared venture to notice them, or to disturb him while engaged in his inspiring ablutions, for these were his moments, or I should rather say his hours, of profoundest meditation. It will be readily believed, that the people in whose houses he lodged were not very well pleased when they found the water trickling through the floor to the ceiling below.

190

He again removed with bag and baggage to Döbling. On arranging his musical matters there, he missed the score of the first movement ('Kyrie') of his grand Mass. All search for it proved to be in vain, and Beethoven was irritated to the highest degree at the loss, which was irreparable; when lo! several days afterwards the whole 'Kyrie' was found, but in what condition! The large sheets, which looked just like waste paper, seemed to the old housekeeper the very thing for wrapping up boots, shoes, and kitchen utensils, for which purpose she had torn most of them in half. When Beethoven saw the treatment to which this production of his genius had been subjected, he could not refrain from laughing.

191

One summer . . . I* frequently visited my grandmother, who had a country-house in . . . Döbling; Beethoven was at Döbling at the same time. Opposite to my grandmother's windows was the tumbledown house of a peasant, named Flohberger, notorious for his profligate life. Besides his unsightly dwelling, Flohberger had a daughter with a very pretty face, but not a very good reputation. Beethoven seemed to take great interest in this girl; I can still see him walking along the Hirschengasse, with his white handkerchief in his right hand trailing along the ground, stopping at Flohberger's yard gate, behind which the giddy girl was working vigorously with a fork on the top of a waggon of hay or manure, laughing incessantly. I never saw Beethoven speak to her; he used to stand silently gazing, till the girl, who preferred the company of peasant lads, would vex him with a jeer, or persistently take no notice. Then he would suddenly dash off, but he never failed to stop there the next time he passed. His interest was so intense that when the girl's father was thrown into the village jail (called the *Kotter*) on account of a drunken brawl, he interceded personally for his release. But, in his fashion, he treated the parish authorities so brusquely that he very nearly became the involuntary companion of his imprisoned protégé.

192

One evening, on coming to Baden to continue my lessons, I† found Beethoven sitting on the sofa, a young and handsome lady beside him. Afraid of intruding my presence, which I judged might be unwelcome, I was going to withdraw, but Beethoven prevented me, saying, 'You can play in the mean time.' He and the lady remained seated behind me. I had been playing for some time, when Beethoven suddenly exclaimed, 'Ries, play us an Amoroso,' shortly after, 'a Malinconico,' then an 'Appassionato,' &c. From what I heard I could guess that he had in some way given offence to the lady, and was now trying to make up for it by such whimsical conduct. At last he started up, crying, 'Why that is my own, every bit!' I had all along been playing extracts from his own works, linked together by short

---

* Franz Grillparzer (1791–1872); Austrian dramatist and poet.
† Ferdinand Ries.

transitions, and thus seemed to have pleased him. The lady soon left, and I found to my utter astonishment that Beethoven did not know who she was.

193

Professor Höfel, . . . was one evening with Eisner (still living in Vienna) and others of his colleagues; also the Police Commissary of W[iener] Neustadt, in the garden of the Wirthshaus 'Zum Schleifen,' a little way out of town. It was autumn and already dark when a constable came out and said to the commissary, '*Herr Commissär, wir haben Jemand arretirt welcher uns kein' Ruh gibt. Er schreit immer dass er der Beethoven sei. Er ist aber ein Lump, hat kein Hut, alter Rock, etc., kein Aufweis wer er ist, etc.*' (Mr Commissary, we have arrested one who will give us no peace. He keeps on yelling that he is Beethoven. But he's a ragamuffin; has no hat, an old coat, etc.; nothing by which he can be identified.)

The Commissär ordered that the man be kept in arrest until morning, '*dann werden wir verhören wer er ist*' (then we will examine him and learn who he is). Next morning the company was very anxious to know how the affair turned out, and the Commissary said that about 11 o'cock he was woken up by a policeman with the information that the prisoner gave them no peace, and demanded that Herzog, Musikdirektor in Wiener Neustadt, be called to identify him. So the Commissary got up, dressed, went out and waked up Herzog, and, in the middle of the night, went with him to the watchhouse. Herzog, as soon as he cast eyes upon the man exclaimed, '*Das ist der Beethoven!*' (That is Beethoven.) He took him home with him, gave him his best room, etc. Next day came the Bürgermeister, making all sorts of apologies. As it turned out Beethoven had got up early in the morning, and slipping on a miserable old coat, and without a hat, had gone out to walk a little. . . He had been seen looking in at the windows of the houses, and as he looked so like a beggar the people had called a constable and arrested him. Upon his arrest the composer said, '*Ich bin Beethoven*' (I am Beethoven). '*Warum nich gar?*' (Of course, why not?) said the policeman, '*ein Lump sind sie; so sieht der Beethoven nicht aus*' (You're a tramp; Beethoven doesn't look like that.)

194

On 6 April 1822, Beethoven had inquired of his old pupil [Ries], '**What would the [Royal] Philharmonic Society be likely to offer me for a symphony?**' Ries, evidently, laid the matter before the directors of the society who, at a meeting on 10 November 'resolved to offer Beethoven fifty pounds for a MS symphony'. . . . Beethoven, although he protested that the remuneration was not to be compared with what other nations might give, accepted the offer, adding, 'I would write gratis for the first artists of Europe if I were not still poor Beethoven. If I were in London, what would I not write for the Philharmonic Society! For Beethoven can write, God be thanked, though he can do nothing else in this world.'

195

In the midst of the noisy whirl of discussion about Weber's *Euryanthe* and the skirmishing of defence and attack, the giant Beethoven entered [Steiner's and Haslinger's* music] shop 'How did the new opera go?' he cried, as he bustled in. 'A great success!' replied Haslinger. 'I am delighted,' cried the great man, 'delighted! Yes, the German can still hold his own above all their Italian sing-song! And little Sontag,† how did she sing?' he asked again, eagerly. 'Exquisitely.' Beethoven positively smirked with pleasure. Then, turning to young Benedict,‡ who was present, he said, 'Tell Herr von Weber I would have come, but – for many long years, you know –'. He pointed to his ears and rushed from the shop.

196

The [singers] pleaded with the composer for changes [in the finale of the Ninth Symphony] which would lighten their labors, but he was adamant. Unger§ called him a 'tyrant over all the vocal organs' to his face, but when he still refused to grant her petitions she turned to Sontag and said: 'Well, then we must go on torturing ourselves in the name of God!'

197

Never in my life did I¶ hear such frenetic and yet cordial applause. Once the second movement of the Symphony was completely interrupted by applause – and there was a demand for a repetition. The reception was more than imperial – for the people burst out in a

---

* Tobias Haslinger (1787–1842), partner of Sigmund Anton Steiner (1773–1838); Viennese music publishers and booksellers.
† Henrietta Sontag (1806–54); celebrated German soprano.
‡ (Sir) Julius Benedict (1804–85); German-born composer, pupil of Weber.
§ Caroline Unger-Sabatier (1803–77); Hungarian contralto and songwriter.
¶ Anton Schindler, reporting to Beethoven in his Conversation books.

storm four times. At the last there were cries of *Vivat!* – The wind-instruments did very bravely – not the slightest disturbance could be heard. – When the parterre broke out in applauding cries the fifth time the Police Commissioner yelled 'Silence!'

198

Questions have frequently been addressed to me* respecting the motivo of the last movement of the Quartet in F, op. 135; to which Beethoven affixed as a superscription the words – *Der schwer-gefasste Entschluss. Un effort d'inspiration. 'Muss es sein?' 'Es muss sein!'*† [The difficult resolution. An effort of inspiration. 'Must it be?' 'It must be!'] Between Beethoven and the people in whose houses he at different times lodged, the most ludicrous scenes arose whenever the period arrived for demanding payment of the rent. The keeper of the house was obliged to go to him, almanack in hand, to prove that the week was expired, and that the money must be paid. Even in his last illness he sang with the most comical seriousness to his landlady the interrogatory motivo of the quartet above mentioned. The woman understood his meaning, and, entering into his jocose humour, she stamped her foot, and emphatically answered, *'Es muss sein!'*†

199

To the question, 'How do you do,' he would often answer, 'As well as a poor musician can do.'

200

A weekly musical meeting was generally held at Streicher's house . . . and Beethoven, who seldom failed to be present, often took his nephew, Karl, with him on these occasions. One day, in the year [1825] while someone else was playing, the boy was asleep on Beethoven's knee in front of the piano. Then something by Beethoven was played, and at the first chord Karl suddenly awoke, and looked up with pleasure. He was asked how he could go to sleep, and what made him awake so suddenly; and whether he knew who the piece was by. He replied quickly, 'It is my uncle's music.' This incident increased not a little Beethoven's strong affection for the child.

---

* Anton Schindler.
† Thayer attributes the *Muss es sein?* motif to an anecdote related to Beethoven about the reluctance of a patron to pay his musicians. 'He laughed and instantly wrote down a canon on the words, "it must be! . . . out with the purse!"'

When his nephew Karl was about to take his examination in tech-
nics and, in addition, loaded with debts, felt himself as unprepared
in purse as he was in knowledge; besides, furthermore, dreading his
uncle's reproaches, of which 'he had already long since tired and
which he found silly' – he resolved to kill himself. He bought two
pistols, drove out to Baden, climbed the tower of the ruinous Castle
Rauenstein, and high up in the air, putting both pistols to his
temples, pressed the triggers – and merely superficially injured the
periosteum, yet so that he had to be taken to the General Hospital in
Vienna.

The news was a terrible blow to Beethoven. The sorrow which the
occurrence caused him was indescribable; he was as downcast as a
father who has lost his well-beloved son. My mother met him,
seemingly quite deranged, on the Escarpment. 'Do you know what
has happened to me? My Karl has shot himself!' 'And – is he dead?'
'No, he only grazed himself; he is still alive and they hope to be able to
save him. But how he has disgraced me, and I love him so very
dearly!'

Schindler tells us that Beethoven copied out three ancient Egyptian
inscriptions 'and kept them framed and mounted under glass, on his
work table.' The first two of these read:

I AM THAT WHICH IS.

I AM EVERYTHING THAT IS, THAT WAS, AND THAT WILL BE.
NO MORTAL MAN HAS LIFTED MY VEIL.

And the third:

HE IS OF HIMSELF ALONE, AND IT IS TO THIS ALONENESS
THAT ALL THINGS OWE THEIR BEING.

When Beethoven heard, in the last days of his life, that Hummel* was
expected at Vienna, he was overjoyed, and said, 'Oh! if he would but
call to see me!' Hummel did call, the very day after his arrival, . . .
and the meeting of the old friends, after they had not seen each other

---

* Johann Nepomuk Hummel (1778–1837); composer and pianist.

for so many years, was extremely affecting. Hummel, struck by Beethoven's suffering looks, wept bitterly. Beethoven strove to appease him, by holding out to him a drawing of the house at Rohrau in which Haydn was born, sent to him that morning by Diabelli,* with the words, 'Look, my dear Hummel, here is Haydn's birth-place; it is a present that I received this morning, and it gives me very great pleasure. So great a man born in so mean a cottage!' Hummel afterwards paid him several visits; . . . ten or twelve days afterwards Beethoven expired, and Hummel attended him to the grave.

204

Early in the afternoon of 26 March Hüttenbrenner† went into the dying man's room. . . . Beethoven had then long been senseless. Telscher began to draw the dying face of Beethoven. This grated on Breuning's feelings, and he remonstrated with him. . . . Then Breuning‡ and Schindler left to go out to Währing to select a grave. . . . The storm passed over, covering the Glacis with snow and sleet. As it passed away a flash of lightning lighted up everything. This was followed by an awful clap of thunder. Hüttenbrenner had been sitting on the side of the bed sustaining Beethoven's head – holding it up with his right arm. His breathing was already very much impeded, and he had been for hours dying. At this startling, awful peal of thunder, the dying man suddenly raised his head from Hüttenbrenner's arm stretched out his own right arm majestically – 'like a General giving orders to an army'. This was but for an instant; the arm sunk back; he fell back. Beethoven was dead.

205

Beethoven's funeral was, as in justice it should be, that of a great man. Some 30,000 persons crowded on the glacis, and surged through the streets where the processions were to pass. I§ cannot describe the scene. If you remember the fête in the Prater, on the occasion of the Congress [of Vienna] in the year 1814, you will have some idea of it. Eight Kapellmeisters were pall-bearers. . . . There were six-and-thirty torchbearers, amongst them Grillparzer, Castelli,¶ Haslinger, Steiner, Schubert, &c.

---

* Antonio Diabelli (1781–1858); Austrian composer and publisher; he supplied the theme for Beethoven's 33 variations, Op. 120.
† Anselm Hüttenbrenner (1794–1868); composer, friend of Beethoven and Schubert;
‡ Stephan von Breuning (1774–1827); dedicatee of Beethoven's violin concerto.
§ Anton Schindler, letter to Ignaz Moscheles, 4 April 1827.
¶ Ignaz Franz Castelli (1781–1862); poet.

A passing stranger asked of a woman caretaker, 'Whose funeral is this?' – 'Well, don't you know,' answered the old crone, 'the general of the musicians has died . . .'

'Turn up the wick,' I* say to Goubaux, 'we can't see a bit.' Instead of which he turns it down, and we are absolutely in the dark. I might say, in a dense gloom, and this sudden change from light to darkness emphasized by the first notes of the piano has the effect of moving all of us very deeply. . . . Liszt, whether by sheer accident or from the unconscious influence, begins the mournful and heartrending andante of [Beethoven's] Sonata in C sharp. Everyone remains as if rooted to the spot where he happens to be at that self-same moment, and does not attempt to stir. Now and then the expiring embers pierce through their ashes and throw strange, lurid and fitful gleams into the room and invest us with wierd, uncouth shapes. I had dropped into an armchair, while above my head I heard stifled cries and sobs. It was Berlioz trying to master his emotion. At the termination of the piece we remained absolutely mute for a moment or so; then Goubaux lights a candle and while we are passing from the drawing-room into the study, Liszt lays his hand on my arm and stops and points to Berlioz with the tears streaming down his cheeks.

'Look at him,' says Liszt in a low voice, 'he has been listening to this as the "heir presumptive" to Beethoven.'

A Soviet Congress was just being held in Moscow; as a musical introduction to the first session, the 'Internationale' had been played, and the last movement of Beethoven's Ninth with choir and soloists. After this, Stalin is said to have exclaimed, 'This is the right music for the masses. It can't be performed often enough, and it ought to be heard in the smallest of our villages.'. . .

The result was a Beethoven epidemic far surpassing anything of the sort which we had experienced in Germany during the Great War. Orchestras and choirs toured the country, including the far-eastern provinces, performing nothing but Beethoven's Ninth. . . . The official art periodical . . . kept exclaiming, 'Poor Beethoven. For a hundred years he has been homeless. Now at last he has found his

---

* Ernest Legouvé (1807–1903); French playwright and long-standing friend of Berlioz.

true dwelling place – the only country where he is really understood and loved: the Soviet Union.'

❧

Gaspare SPONTINI (1774–1851)

Italian whose bombastic operas left indelible impressions on Wagner and Berlioz.

209

A wealthy [Berlin] amateur had become deaf and suffered much from his deprivation of the enjoyment of his favourite art. After trying many physicians, he was treated in novel fashion by his latest doctor. 'Come with me to the opera this evening,' wrote down the doctor. 'What's the use? I can't hear a note,' was the impatient rejoinder. 'Never mind,' said the other, 'come and you will see something at all events.'

So the twain repaired to the theatre to hear Spontini's *Olympie*. All went well until one of the overwhelming finales which happened to be played that evening more fortissimo than usual. The patient turned around exclaiming, 'Doctor, I can hear.' As there was no reply, the happy patient said again, 'Doctor, you have cured me.' A blank stare alone met him. The doctor was as deaf as a post.

210

Wagner recalls
From Berlioz, who was at Spontini's deathbed until the end, I heard that the master had struggled most determinedly against death and had cried repeatedly, *'Je ne veux pas mourir, je ne veux pas mourir.'* [I don't want to die!] When Berlioz tried to comfort him by saying, *'Comment pouvez-vous penser mourir vous, mon maître, qui êtes immortel?'* [How can you think of dying, you my master, who are immortal!] Spontini retorted angrily, *'Ne faites pas de mauvaises plaisanteries!'* [Don't make bad jokes!]*

❧

---

* Since Berlioz was in Paris when Spontini died in his native village of Majolati, this tale is apocryphal.

Daniel AUBER (1782–1871)

French composer of forty-two operas. His *Dumb Girl of Portici* (or *Masaniello*) depicted the Naples uprising of 1647 so vividly that its first Brussels performance in 1830 triggered the Belgian rebellion.

211

... My dear old friend Auber came to see me this afternoon. ...* He had been in Paris all through the war and had suffered intensely, both physically and mentally; he looked wretched, and for the first time since I had known him seemed depressed and unhappy. He is eighty-six years old and now he looks his age. He is a true Parisian, adores his Paris, and never leaves it, even during the summer, when Paris is insufferable. One can easily imagine his grief at seeing his beloved city as it is now. He was full of uneasy forebodings and distress. He gave me the most harrowing description of the killing of General Lecomte! It seems that the mob had seized him in his home and carried him to the garden of some house, where they told him he was to be judged by a *conseil de guerre*, and left him to wait an hour in the most pitiable frame of mind.

The murder of General Clément Thomas was even more dreadful. Auber knew him well; described him as kind and gentle, and 'honest to the tips of his fingers'. They hustled him into the same garden where poor General Lecomte already was, pushed him against the wall, and shot him, killing him instantly. Then they rushed upon their other victim, saying, 'Now is your turn.' In vain did Lecomte beg to be judged by his equals, and spoke of his wife and children. But his tormentors would have none of that, and shot him then and there. Lecomte fell on his knees; they dragged him to his feet, and continued firing into his still warm body. When the populace was allowed to come in they danced a saturnalia over his corpse. Auber said, 'My heart bleeds when I gaze on all that is going on about me. Alas! I have lived too long.'

212

Auber would never attend a performance of any of his [own] operas. 'If I did,' he said, 'I could never write another note.' The delight he took in Rossini's music made him one evening go to hear *William Tell*,

---

* Entry for 24 March 1871 in the Paris diary of Lillie de Hegermann-Lindencrone, 'formerly Miss Lillie Greenhough of Cambridge, Massachusetts', an amateur singer whose marriages to an American banker and a Danish diplomat brought her into high society in Paris and Rome and into the confidence of prominent musicians.

and he sat quietly waiting for the charming violoncello trio, which begins the overture. The conductor arrived and gave the sign. Oh, horror! Instead of the low E on the 'cello, a smashing diminished seventh. . . . Through a prima donna's indisposition *William Tell* could not be given, and . . . *Masaniello* was put in [its] place. [Auber] jumped up as quickly as his green eighty-seven years would allow, and ran away from his own work.

John FIELD (1782–1837)

Irish composer, virtuoso and pedagogue, Field invented the piano nocturne. He settled in St Petersburg. His pupils included Glinka – and the fictional pianist at Count Rostov's in *War and Peace*.

213

Nothing can afford a more glaring contrast than a Field's Nocturne and a Field's manners, which are often of the cynical order. There was such a commotion yesterday amongst the ladies, when at a party he drew from his pocket a miniature portrait of his wife, and loudly proclaimed the fact that she had been his pupil, and that he had only married her because she never paid for her lessons, and he knew she never would. He also bragged of going to sleep whilst giving lessons to the ladies of St Petersburg, adding that they would often rouse him with the question, 'What does one pay twenty roubles an hour for, if you go to sleep?'

214

As he lay dying in Moscow, friends asked if he wanted a priest. Field declined, but an English clergyman was none the less summoned to his bedside.

'Are you a Protestant?' asked the pastor.
'No,' said Field.
'Perhaps a Catholic?'
'No.'
'Then you must be a Calvinist?' he persisted.
'Not quite,' retorted the dying pianist. 'I am a Clavecinist.'

Niccolò PAGANINI (1782–1840)

Born in Genoa, Paganini transformed the nature of violin playing and the public persona of the player. His second Caprice (in A minor) has inspired variations by, among others, Brahms, Rachmaninov, Lutoslawski and Lloyd Webber.

215

As it was the first time we* had seen the great player, except in the criticisms of our musical friends, which had rendered us doubly curious, we looked up with interest at him from our abysm in the pit. A lucky interval between a gentleman's head and a lady's bonnet favoured our endeavour, and there we beheld the long, pale face of the musical marvel, hung, as it were, in the light, and looking as strange as need be. He made divers uncouth obeisances, and then put himself in a masterly attitude for his work, his manner being as firm and full of conscious power when he puts the bow to the instrument as it is otherwise when he is not playing. We thought he did not look so old as he is said to be; but he is long-faced and haggard, with strongly-marked prominent features, wears his black hair flowing on his neck like an enthusiast, has a coat of ancient cut which astonishes Fop's Alley; in short, is very like the picture of him in the shops. He is like a great old boy, who has done nothing but play the violin all his life, and knows as much about that as he does little of conventional manners. His face at the same time has much less expression than might be looked for. At first it seemed little better than a mask; with a fastidious, dreary expression, as if inclined to despise his music and go to sleep. And such was his countenance for a great part of the evening. His fervour was in his hands and bow. Towards the close of the performances, he waxed more enthusiastic in appearance, gave way to some uncouth bodily movement from side to side, and seemed to be getting into his violin. Occasionally also he put back his hair. When he makes his acknowledgments, he bows like a camel, and grins like a goblin or a mountain-goat.

His playing is indeed marvellous. What other players can do well, he does a hundred times better. We never heard such playing before; nor had we imagined it. His bow perfectly talks. It remonstrates, supplicates, answers, holds a dialogue. In a word, we never heard anything like *any* part of his performance, much less the least marvel we have been speaking of. The people sit astonished, venting themselves in whispers of 'Wonderful!' – 'Good God!' – and other

---

* The narrator is Leigh Hunt (1784–1859); English writer.

unusual symptoms of English amazement; and when the applause comes, some of them take an opportunity of laughing, out of pure inability to express their feelings otherwise.

But even after what we have heard, how are we to endure hereafter our old violins and their players? How can we consent to hear them? How crude they will sound, how uninformed, how like a cheat! When the Italian goes away, violin-playing goes with him, unless some disciple of his should arise among us and detain a semblance of his instrument. As it is, the most masterly performers, hitherto so accounted, must consent to begin again, and be little boys in his school.

216

When playing at Lord Holland's someone asked him to improvise on the violin the story of a son who kills his father, runs away, becomes a highwayman, falls in love with a girl who will not listen to him, leads her to a wild country spot and suddenly jumps with her from a rock into an abyss where they disappear forever. He listened quietly and, when the story was at an end, asked that all the lights should be extinguished. He then began playing, and so terrible was the musical interpretation of the idea that had been given to him that several ladies fainted and the salon, when relighted, looked like a battlefield.

217

[In Dublin] such was the eagerness to hear Paganini that a man pawned his coat and I* saw him go into the gallery without one. . . .

A carriage, with four horses and outriders, was sent to bring us from Dublin to Black Rock [Seat of the Lord Lieutenant of Ireland].

I had to hand one of the handsome daughters into dinner. I was seated next to her and she asked me if it were true that Paganini had cut off his wife's head, for so it had been reported amongst other remarkable things that were said about him. I could not answer either yes or no, therefore I said, 'Your Ladyship may rest assured that he will not meddle with yours or mine.'

Paganini, letter to F.–J. Fétis†, 1831
I will relate what occurred to me at Padua, nearly fifteen years since. I had played at a concert with great success. The next day, seated at

---

* Sir George Smart (1776–1867); English composer and conductor.
† (1784–1871); Belgian critic, composer and musical biographer.

the *table d'hôte* (I was the sixtieth) my entrance in the room passed unobserved. One of the guests spoke of the great effect I had produced the previous evening. His neighbour concurred in all that was said, and added, 'There is nothing surprising in Paganini's performance – he acquired his talent while confined in a dungeon during eight years, having only his violin to soften the rigours of his confinement. He was condemned for having, coward-like, stabbed one of my friends, who was his rival.' As you may imagine, every one was shocked by the enormity of my crime. I then addressed myself to the person who was so well acquainted with my history, and requested to know when and where this had taken place. Every eye was directed towards me. Judge the surprise when they recognized the principal actor in this tragical history. The narrator was embarrassed. It was no longer his friend who had been assassinated. He heard – it had been affirmed – he believed; but it was not improbable he had been deceived. This is how an artist's reputation is trifled with, because indolent people will never comprehend that one may study at liberty as well as under lock and key.

A still more ridiculous report, at Vienna, tested the credulity of some enthusiasts. I had played the the variations entitled 'Le Streghe' (the Witches), and they produced some effect. One individual, who was represented to me as of a sallow complexion, melancholy air, and bright eye, affirmed that he saw nothing surprising in my performance, for he had distinctly seen, while I was playing my variations, the devil at my elbow directing my arm and guiding my bow. My resemblance to him was a proof of my origin. He was clothed in red – had horns on his head – and carried his tail between his legs.

219

One fine day Paganini walked into Vuillaume's workshop with his violin case in his hand. The instrument was examined by the expert and an operation deemed necessary. The violin would have to be opened, and Paganini stood aghast. After long hesitation he agreed to allow Vuillaume to repair it on condition that he worked under its owner's eye. Paganini sat at the end of the room . . . watching the operation with deep anxiety. The chisel was introduced between the table and the rib; a slight cracking noise – Paganini bounded from his chair. Every moment of the tool brought fresh beads of perspiration to the brow of the tortured man who loved this fiddle more than he cared for any other inanimate thing in the world. He said, 'It was as if the chisel were entering his own flesh.'

Paganini was to be seen nearly every afternoon in the music shop of Bernard Latte, Passage de l'Opéra, where he sat for an hour, enveloped in a long cloak, taking notice of nobody, and hardly ever raising his piercing black eyes. He was one of the sights of Paris, and I* had often gone to stare at him with wonder until a friend introduced me to him, and he invited me to visit him, an invitation I accepted most eagerly. . . .

He sat there, taciturn, rigid, hardly ever moving a muscle of his face, and I sat spellbound, a shudder running through me whenever his uncanny eyes fell upon me. He made me play to him often, mostly by pointing with his bony hand to the piano without speaking, and I could only guess from his repeating the ceremony that he did not dislike it, for never a word of encouragement fell from his lips. How I longed to hear him play it is impossible to describe, perhaps even to imagine. From my earliest childhood I had heard of Paganini and his art as of something supernatural, and there I actually sat opposite to the man himself, but only looking at the hands that had created such wonders. On one never-to-be-forgotten occasion, after I had played and we had enjoyed a long silence, Paganini rose and approached his violin-case. What then passed in me can hardly be imagined; I was all in a tremble, and my heart thumped as if it would burst my chest; in fact, no young swain going to the first rendezvous with his beloved could possibly feel more violent emotions. Paganini opened the case, took the violin out, and began to tune it carefully with his fingers without using the bow; my agitation became almost intolerable. When he was satisfied, and I said to myself, with a lump in my throat, 'Now, now, he'll take the bow!' he carefully put the violin back and shut the case. And that is how I heard Paganini.

Hector Berlioz recalls
I composed *Harold in Italy* at the instigation of Paganini. Though performed several times during his absence, it had not figured at any of my concerts since his return; he therefore was not acquainted with it, and heard it that day for the first time.

The concert was just over; I was in a profuse perspiration, and trembling with exhaustion, when Paganini, followed by his son Achilles, came up to me at the orchestra door, gesticulating violently. Owing to the throat affection of which he ultimately died, he

---

* Sir Charles Hallé (1819–95); conductor.

had already completely lost his voice, and unless everything was perfectly quiet, no one but his son could hear or even guess what he was saying. He made a sign to the child, who got up on a chair, put his ear close to his father's mouth, and listened attentively.

Achilles then got down, and turning to me, said, 'My father desires me to assure you, sir, that he has never in his life been so powerfully impressed at a concert; that your music has quite upset him, and that if he did not restrain himself he should go down on his knees to thank you for it.' I made a movement of incredulous embarrassment at these strange words, but Paganini, seizing my arm, and rattling out, 'Yes, yes!' with the little voice he had left, dragged me up on the stage, where there were still a good many of the performers, knelt down, and kissed my hand. I need not describe my stupefaction; I relate the facts, that is all.

[Next day Achilles delivered a letter to Berlioz with instructions not to open it until he had left.] I must evidently have grown quite pale, for my wife coming in at that moment, and finding me with a letter in my hand and a discomposed face, exclaimed, 'What's the matter now? Some new misfortune? Courage! we have endured as much before.'

'No, no; quite the contrary.'

'What, then?'

'Paganini.'

'Well, what of him?'

'He has sent me – twenty thousand francs.'

'Louis! Louis!' cried Henrietta, rushing distractedly in search of my son, who was playing in the next room. 'Come here! come with your mother; come and thank God for what He has done for your father.' And my wife and child ran back together, and fell on their knees beside my bed, the mother praying, the child in astonishment joining his little hands beside her. O Paganini! what a sight! . . . Would that he could have seen it! . . .

222

On the last night of his existence, he appeared unusually tranquil. He had slept a little; when he awoke, he requested that the curtains of his bed should be drawn aside to contemplate the moon, which, at its fullest, was advancing calmly in the immensity of the pure heavens. While steadily gazing at this luminous orb, he again became drowsy, but the murmuring of the neighbouring trees awakened in his breast that sweet agitation which is the reality of the beautiful. At this solemn hour, he seemed desirous to return to Nature all the soft sensations which he was then possessed of;

stretching forth his hands towards his enchanted Violin – to the faithful companion of his travels – to the magician which had robbed care of its stings – he sent to heaven, with its last sounds, the last sigh of a life which had been all melody.

❧

Ludwig (Louis) SPOHR (1784–1859)

German composer, virtuoso violinist and conductor who claimed to have introduced the baton to England.

223

Eager to catch sight of Napoleon, Spohr went to Erfurt where a congress of princes was gathered in 1808. He persuaded the second horn in the orchestra to give up his place for an evening and, never having played the instrument before, practised all day until his lips were black and swollen. On entering the theatre he discovered that the musicians had to sit with their backs to the noble audience and had strict orders not to turn round. Undaunted, Spohr produced a mirror from his pocket and observed Napoleon throughout the performance.

224

Spohr recalls
My turn had come to direct one of the Philharmonic concerts [in London], and I created no less sensation than with my solo play. It was at that time still the custom there that when symphonies and overtures were performed, the pianist had the score before him, not exactly to conduct from it, but only to read after and to play in with the orchestra at pleasure, which when it was heard, had a very bad effect. The real conductor was the first violin, who gave the *tempi*, and now and then when the orchestra began to falter gave the beat with the bow of his violin. So numerous an orchestra, standing so far apart from each other as that of the Philharmonic, could not possibly go exactly together, and in spite of the excellence of the individual members, the *ensemble* was much worse than we are accustomed to in Germany. I had therefore resolved when my turn came to direct, to make an attempt to remedy this defective system. Fortunately at the morning rehearsal on the day when I was to conduct the concert, Mr [Ferdinand] Ries took the place at the piano, and he readily assented to give up the score to me and to remain wholly excluded from all participation in the performance. I

then took my stand with the score at a separate music desk in front of the orchestra, drew my directing baton from my coat pocket and gave the signal to begin. Quite alarmed at such a novel procedure, some of the directors would have protested against it; but when I besought them to grant me at least one trial, they became pacified. The symphonies and overtures that were to be rehearsed were well known to me, and in Germany I had already directed at their performance. I therefore could not only give the *tempi* in a very decisive manner, but indicated also to the wind instruments and horns all their entries, which ensured to them a confidence such as hitherto they had not known there. I also took the liberty, when the execution did not satisfy me, to stop, and in a very polite but earnest manner to remark upon the manner of execution, which remarks Mr Ries at my request interpreted to the orchestra. Incited thereby to more than usual attention, and conducted with certainty by the visible manner of giving the time, they played with a spirit and correctness such as till then they had never been heard to play with. Surprised and inspired by this result the orchestra immediately after the first part of the symphony expressed aloud its collective assent to the new mode of conducting . . .

The result in the evening was still more brilliant than I could have hoped for. It is true, the audience were at first startled by the novelty, and were seen whispering together; but when the music began and the orchestra executed the well-known symphony with unusual power and precision, the general approbation was shown immediately on the conclusion of the first part by a long-sustained clapping of hands. The triumph of the baton as time-giver was decisive, and no one was seen any more seated at the piano during the performance of symphonies and overtures.

~~~

Carl Maria von WEBER (1786–1826)

The son of a *Kapellmeister* and pupil of Michael Haydn, he triumphed in 1821 with his opera *Der Freischütz*.

225

Weber hated the King [Frederick of Württemberg], of whose wild caprice and vices he witnessed daily scenes, before whose palace-gates he was obliged to slink bareheaded, and who treated him with unmerited ignominy.

. . . Smarting under some foul indignity, he had just left the private apartment of the King, when an old woman met him in the passage, and asked where she could find the room of the court washerwoman. 'There!' said the reckless youth, pointing to the door of the royal cabinet. The old woman entered, was violently assailed by the King, who had a horror of old women, and, in her terror, stammered out that a young gentleman who had just come out had informed her that there she would find the 'royal washerwoman'. The infuriated monarch guessed who was the culprit, and dispatched an officer on the spot to arrest [him] . . . and throw him into prison.

226

It was unfortunate for Weber that Rossini was in London this season [1826], for he was invited to many musical parties but Weber to only a few. At one of these parties, given by Mrs Coutts, the banker's wife, who paid him twenty-six pounds, five shillings, a lady asked him to play the overture to *Der Freischütz*. He declined, saying it was not composed for the pianoforte. The lady immediately brought him a printed copy, on which was written, 'Arranged for the Pianoforte by the composer'. Weber instantly went to the instrument and played it. When it was over, he came to me* asking, 'Who is that lady?' I answered, 'Lady Guildford.' 'She has taught me a lesson,' he said. 'I never will again arrange overtures for the pianoforte.'

227

The general rehearsal, conducted by Mori, with Weber sitting in an arm-chair, went off with great *éclat* and to the complete satisfaction of the master, who only on one occasion raised his voice from the customary whisper. The chorus in a prayer, an appeal to the Deity in the cantata, began to sing at the top of their voices; Weber stopped them at once, exclaiming, 'Hush, hush, would you scream like that in the presence of God?'

228

5 June – Early this morning I† was summoned in all haste to Sir G. Smart's. At eleven o'clock last night Fürstenau had conducted Weber to his bedroom; his friends went to his door at an early hour, but found it locked inside, contrary to Weber's promise. To do this he must have got up during the night. It was in vain to knock or call for admission; no answer came. So Sir George sent to me and other friends, and the door was broken open in our presence. The noise did not disturb the sleeper; it was his sleep of death. His head, resting on

---

* Sir George Smart (1776–1867); English composer and conductor.
† Ignaz Moscheles (1794–1870); pianist and composer.

his left arm, was lying quietly on the pillow.' . . . Any attempt to describe the depth of my sorrow would be profanation. I thought Weber a composer quite *sui generis*; one who had the imperishable glory of leading back to our German music a public vacillating between Mozart, Beethoven, and Rossini. On his dressing-table lay a small washing-bill written by him. This I put in my pocket-book, where I carried it ever after.

❧

Giacomo MEYERBEER (1791–1864)
[b. Jakob Liebmann Beer]

Berlin-born composer who lived principally in Paris and used inherited wealth to indulge a taste for lavish stage spectacle and infinite rehearsal.

229

Once in Berlin the chorus sang rather tamely in *Les Huguénots*. Meyerbeer, afraid that the great scene – the 'Bénédiction des Poignards' – would lose its effect through want of energy on the part of the chorus, sent for the leader, and asked him what he could do to infuse some spirit into the performance of the chorus.

'Why,' said the learned man, *'similia similibus curantur* – infuse some spirits into the singers.'

'What sum,' said Meyerbeer, 'would it require to make these gentlemen do their best?'

The *Chef des Chœurs* named a sum, and was instantly authorized to give it. Off they went round the corner to spend it. And tell it did! When the grand chorus came on they were full of spirit, and screamed so, that the performance was utterly spoiled.

230

Hector Berlioz
Meyerbeer has not merely the luck to have talent, but in a very high degree the talent to have luck.

231

[Pauline Viardot]* had a disfiguring front tooth which somewhat protruded. She had been cast for the part of Fidès in the *Prophète*, and several of her *intimes* begged her to have it out, without success. At

---

* (1821–1910); mezzo-soprano, sister of Maria Malibran, and intimate friend of Turgenev.

one of the final rehearsals Meyerbeer came to her and said that with infinite regret he must take the part away from her unless she had the offending incisor removed. This was too much for her; out it came, and she sent it to the composer. After the first performance, Meyerbeer came round to her room and presented her with a bracelet in the centre of which was a white enamel set in precious stones; the white enamel was the front tooth.

232

Rossini was going along the Boulevards with a friend, when they met Meyerbeer, and exchanged cordial greetings.

'And how is your health, my dear Maestro?' asks Meyerbeer.

'Shaky, *cher maître*, very shaky. My digestion, you know, my poor head. Alas! I'm afraid I am going down hill.'

They pass on. 'How could you tell such stories?' asks the friend; 'you were never in better health, and you talk of going down hill.'

'Ah, well,' answered Rossini, 'to be sure – but why shouldn't I put it that way? It gives him so much pleasure.'

233

Meyerbeer, who had a mania for hearing his music rehearsed *sans fin*, would not authorize the first performance to be given. He came towards Rossini complaining, sighing as usual. 'Well,' said Rossini, 'what are you suffering from to-day?' 'O maestro,' he said, 'I am so sick – all over pains; I do not know what to do.' Rossini, who knew that he had just come from a rehearsal, said: '*Je vais vous dire ce que c'est, vous vous écoutez trop.*' [I'll tell you what it is: you listen to yourself too much.]

234

Soon after Meyerbeer's death, his young nephew composed a funeral march and took it to Rossini. 'Very good, very good,' said Rossini when the young man had finished at the piano. 'But, truthfully, wouldn't it have been better if *you* had died and your poor uncle had composed the march?'

Karl CZERNY (1791–1857)

Viennese composer who from the age of fifteen made his living, and his reputation, as a piano teacher, instructing both Liszt and Thalberg and producing exercises that torment pupils to the present day.

235

Before my* departure from Vienna, in 1845, Czerny desired me to pay him a visit. Up three flights of stone stairs lived this venerable musician in a suite of ample-sized rooms. . . .

As I passed through his library, he begged me to observe his collection of English literature. 'You see, I have your Byron, Scott, all complete in that case; and your immortal Shakespeare – your Beethoven, eh? – *Gottes lieber Mann*, eh?' Our interview lasted some time, in the course of which I inquired, 'how it was possible he had ever found time to publish so many works?' He replied, 'I will surprise you the more when I tell you that I was twenty-eight years of age before I published my first work, and that I have written more music in my lifetime than any living copyist. You may imagine this when I state that I have written more than one thousand pieces that have never been printed, and have never employed a copyist to prepare any of my publications.'

I was curious to know the truth of what had been described, as to his mode of working at four different publications at a time. Czerny smiled at my feeling astonished at his *modus operandi*.

In each corner of his study was a desk with an unfinished score in hand.

'You see, my dear Mr Ella, that I am working for the English,' showing me at the same time a long list of national tunes to be arranged for D'Almaine and Co. At a second desk I found Beethoven's Symphonies *à quatre mains*, half finished, for Cocks and Co. At a third desk he was editing a new edition of Bach's fugues; and at a fourth he was composing a Grand Symphony. After finishing a page of one score, he passed on to another desk; and by the time he had written a page at the fourth desk, he resumed his labours at desk No. 1. Such, then, was the mechanical labour of this musician's life. No wonder that his own compositions smelt of the lamp.

ᴄᴀᴡꞓ

---

* John Ella (1802–88); English concert organizer and writer on music.

Gioacchino ROSSINI (1792–1868)

By the age of thirty, Rossini had attained world fame with a string of *opera buffa* successes. After 1829 he wrote nothing more for the stage and passed the second half of his life in Parisian indolence.

236

The rigorists of Bologna . . . reproached him, and not without reason, with having transgressed against the rules of composition. Rossini did not deny the charge. 'I should not have so many faults to reproach myself with,' was his reply, 'if I had leisure to read my manuscript twice over; but you know very well, that scarcely six weeks are allowed me to compose an opera. I take my pleasure during the first month; and, pray, when would you have me take my pleasure if not at my present age, and with my present success? Would you have me wait till I am grown old and full of spleen? At length the two last weeks arrive; I compose every morning a duo or air, which is to be rehearsed that very evening. How then would you have me detect little faults of grammar in the accompaniments?'

237

I mounted the stairs leading to the poor lodgings of the great man [said Rossini, recalling his visit with the poet Carpani to Beethoven in 1822.] . . . I found myself in a sort of attic, terribly disordered and dirty. I particularly remember the ceiling. It was under the roof and showed crevices through which the rain must have poured down in streams. . . .

When we entered, he paid no attention to us but remained bent over proofs which he was finishing. Then, raising his head, he said, in reasonably comprehensible Italian: 'Ah, Rossini, you the composer of the *Barber of Seville*? My congratulations; that is an excellent *opera buffa*. I have read it with pleasure and I enjoyed myself. It will be played so long as Italian opera will exist. Never try your hand at anything but *opera buffa*!' . . .

The visit was short. One side of the conversation had to be conducted in writing. I expressed to him all my admiration for his genius. He answered with a deep sigh and the single phrase, 'Oh, *un infelice!*' Then, wishing me success with *Zelmira*, he rose and showed us out with the remark, 'Above all do a lot of the *Barber*'. . .

When I descended those dilapidated stairs I could not repress my tears. . . .

Liszt came to see him in his little room, and improvised rather madly on the small Pleyel piano. When he had done, Rossini said, *'J'aime mieux l'autre'* [I prefer the other]. *'L'autre?'* asked Liszt, stupefied. 'Yes, Haydn's Chaos,* said Rossini.

Baron James Rothschild sent Rossini some splendid grapes from his hothouse. Rossini, in thanking him, wrote, *'Bien que vos raisins soient superbes, je n'aime pas mon vin en pillules.'* [Splendid though your grapes certainly are, I don't take my wine in pills.] This Baron Rothschild read as an invitation to send him some of his celebrated Château-Lafitte.

(He) once said quite frankly, 'I know of no more admirable occupation than eating, that is, really eating. Appetite is for the stomach what love is for the heart. The stomach is the conductor, who rules the grand orchestra of our passions, and rouses it to action. The bassoon or the piccolo, grumbling its discontent or shrilling its longing, personify the empty stomach for me. The stomach replete, on the other hand, is the triangle of enjoyment or the kettledrum of joy. As for love, I regard her as the *prima donna par excellence*, the goddess who sings cavatinas to the brain, intoxicates the ear, and delights the heart. Eating (note that Rossini puts eating first!), loving, singing, and digesting are, in truth, the four acts of the comic opera known as life, and they pass like the bubbles of a bottle of champagne. Whoever lets them break without having enjoyed them is a complete fool.'

That the musician who could make such a frank gastronomic confession of faith, who once declared that 'The truffle is the Mozart among the mushrooms,' was an accomplished gourmand cannot be denied. Yet on the morning when I† saw him [first] he seemed quite content with his bread and milk.

'Every one comes to him, you know; and he was sitting yawning in his *robe de chambre*, when a fellow was shown in, wretchedly shabby

---

* In the *Creation*
† Leopold Auer (1845–1930); Hungarian violinist and teacher.

and poor, – eager of course to have his fortune made, and certain Rossini would make it: he is very generous to all those *misérables*!'

' "Well," said he, "what am I to do for you? An artist? What sort of a voice have you got?"

"No voice, Monsieur Rossini; I am an instrumentalist; but if you will only – "

"Ah! What instrument then?"

"The drum, *Monsieur*! and if you will let me play to you –"

"*O, par exemple!*" exclaimed Rossini, bursting into a fit of laughter. "No, thank you: and besides we have no drum here."

"But I have brought mine with me."

"*Diable*! but I cannot think of your taking so much trouble!"

But the Professor was not to be got rid of. In the drum came, and Rossini screwed himself up for an infliction. "I shall have the honour." said the suitor, "of playing for you the overture to *La Gazza Ladra*."

"Ah!" . . . and Rossini laughed again. Well, the fellow began without more waiting; and after the tremendous roll which opens the march in the overture, looked up, delighted with the noise he made.

"*Monsieur*," said he, "here are now sixty bars' rest – we will pass them over, and –."

"I beg you will do no such thing," replied Rossini, gravely. "*Pray count them!*" '

242

At noon, he put on his wig, which until then lay quietly on the table, his big bald head being covered with a towel for the time being; then he dressed, and by one o'clock every day he was out. He hailed the first cabman he met and asked him, '*Est-ce que vos chevaux sont fatigués?*' (Are your horses tired?) When the unfortunate driver said, 'Non, monsieur,' Rossini never [hired] him: he would never trust himself to other but tired horses; and during all his life he had never entered a railway carriage.

243

One morning, when in Paris, a wandering organ grinder accidentally played the tune of a romance from Halévy's *Guido and Ginevra*, under his windows. Rossini summoned the luckless boy into his chamber, and catching hold of and shaking him, exclaimed:

'What do you mean by this, you little rascal?'

'Signor!' exclaims the unfortunately small malefactor, 'don't beat me!'

'Have you not been paid, to play that infernal *charivari* under my windows? Answer, little whelp! and at once.'

The boy swore, by all his Italian gods, that this was not the case.

'You lie! Confess, who sent you here to dose me with all this horrid music.'

'No one, Signor!'

But the frantic Rossini was not to be persuaded that the infliction was not an intended foretaste of the pleasures of Purgatory. At length, he gave two napoleons to the street-musician, who opened his eyes when his fingers touched the gold.

'Here! take these,' he said. 'Order for your organ a new barrel, with an aria from *Tancredi*. Then, go and play it sixty times under the windows of M. Halévy. Do you understand me? Sixty times!'

'Yes, Signor!' stammered the boy.

'It may be, that, afterwards, he will learn how to write music!'

244

Auber asked him how he had liked the performance of *Tannhäuser*? Rossini answered, with a satirical smile, 'It is a music one must hear several times. I am not going again.'

245

Rossini said: '*M. Wagner a de beaux moments, mais de mauvais quarts d'heure*' (Mr Wagner has beautiful moments, but bad quarters of an hour).

246

'My immortality?' said Rossini, 'do you know what will survive me? . . . The third act of *Tell*, the second act of *Otello*, and the *Barber of Seville* from one end to the other. . . . Of the 'Prayer of Moses' [from *Mosè in Egitto*, 1810], that piece magnificent in its simplicity . . . I* asked him was he in love, or very hungry and miserable, when he wrote that inspired page; for hunger as well as love has the power of making people write with lofty inspiration. 'I will tell you,' he said, and from his ironical smile I saw some fun was coming: 'I had a little misfortune; I had known a Princess B – g – e, and she, one of the most passionate women living, and with a magnificent voice, kept me up all night with duos and talking, etc. A short time after this exhausting performance, I had to take a *tisane* [herb potion] which stood before

---

* Louis Engel; English critic.

me, while I wrote that prayer. When I was writing the chorus in G minor I suddenly dipped my pen into the medicine bottle instead of the ink; I made a blot, and when I dried it with sand (blotting-paper was not invented then) it took the form of a natural, which instantly gave me the idea of the effect which the change from G minor to G major would make and to this blot is all the effect – if any – due.'

247

This sublime prayer* was an after-thought, and introduced to cover an absurdity in the scenic representation of Crossing the Red Sea. Rossini was lounging in bed, with his friends about him, when Tottola, the author of the drama, burst into the room, exclaiming. 'Maestro! I've saved the third act! I've made a prayer for the Hebrews before the passage of the Red Sea,' giving the words to Rossini. While the Maestro was deciphering the scrawl, the poet whispered to the company that he had done it in an hour. 'What! in an hour?' exclaimed Rossini, 'give me a pen, and I will make you the music in a quarter.'

248

Sir Arthur Sullivan
'One morning when I called in to see [Rossini], he was trying over a small piece of music as I entered. "Why, what is that?" I exclaimed. He answered me very seriously, "It's my dog's birthday and I write a little piece for him every year." '

249

It was late on the day of Rossini's death, and he had breathed his last. His faithful spouse† was not present. More serious duties had called her away: she was giving a sulphur bath to her dog. But when apprised of the sad event she came in and laid her hand on the dead man's head, and assuming a melodramatic pose, she said, '*Je jure sur la tête de Rossini, de garder son nom pur à l'avenir*' (I take my oath upon Rossini's head to keep his name pure for all time to come). Considering that she was then near seventy, the self-denial did really seem enormous!

∽⚮∾

---

* Of Moses.
† His second wife, Olympe; the first was the soprano Isabella Colbran (1785–1845).

Franz SCHUBERT (1797–1828)

Viennese composer of more than six hundred songs, as well as much orchestral and chamber music: 'the product of my genius and my misery, and that which I have written in my greatest distress, is that which the world seems to like best.'

250

[While] still a mere boy, and after the performance of some of his Lieder set to Klopstock's poems, he enquired of a friend who had heard them, whether he really thought that he should ever do anything. The friend replied that he, Schubert, was already something first-rate; and the latter answered, 'Sometimes quietly to myself I think so too. But who can ever do anything after Beethoven?'

251

Coming home one evening with several friends after hearing *Tancredi*, there was a general chorus of praise of Rossini's music, and especially the overtures to his operas, whereupon Schubert, who thought the praise overdone, declared it would be the easiest thing for him to write down, at the shortest notice, overtures of the style alluded to. His companions promised, on their part, to reward Schubert's effort with a glass of good wine. Schubert there and then set to work and wrote an orchestral overture, which was subsequently followed by another, under the names of 'Overtures in the Italian Style'.

252

There were Schubert evenings when wine flowed generously, when the good Vogl sang all those lovely Lieder and poor Franz Schubert had to accompany him endlessly so that his short and fat fingers would hardly obey him any longer. It was even worse for him at our* social entertainments, only *Würstelbälle* (hot-dog parties) in those frugal times, but with no lack of charming ladies and girls. Here our 'Bertl', as Schubert was familiarly called by his friends, was made to play, and play again and again, his latest waltz until the endless cotillon was finished and the small, corpulent and freely perspiring little man could finally take a rest and eat his modest dinner. Small wonder that he sometimes fled and some 'Schubertiads' had to take place without Schubert.

---

* The narrator is Eduard von Bauernfeld; Austrian playwright, translator of Dickens.

A place of rendezvous [for Schubert and his friends] was the still-existing extra room on the ground floor of the 'Hungarian Crown' [restaurant] on the Himmelpfortgasse. Amongst the evening guests were . . . painters . . . poets . . . government officials. Schubert is said to have been nicknamed by these people 'The Kanevas', because when a stranger was introduced to his society, the first question Schubert invariably asked of his neighbour was '*Kann er was?*' [Can he do anything? or Is he capable?].'

He was surely as fond of wine as any young worshipper of the loveliest art. But when the blood of the grape glowed within his veins, he was not violent, but liked to retire to a secluded corner, and there nurse himself comfortably into a passion; he became a laughing tyrant, who would destroy everything he could without making a noise – glasses, plates, cups, &c. – and sit simpering and screwing up his eyes into the smallest possible compass. At a wine-shop, when he had drunk more than he ought, he used, when the time of reckoning came, to put his hand quietly under the table, and the *Kellner* had to guess, by the number of fingers held up by their owner, the quantity of pints consumed. A friend of Schubert's mentions the so-called 'Vertrunkenen Quartet', a quartet for men's voices, before writing which Schubert had steeped himself in liquor.

On a summer afternoon, with Franz Lachner* and others, we strolled over to Grinzing for the *Heurige* [new wine], which Schubert particularly liked, though I was unable to acquire a taste for its dryness. We talked over our wine until evening and when we walked back I wanted to go straight home but Schubert dragged me along to a tavern and afterwards to the coffee house where he tended to round off his evenings. At one o'clock we were having a spirited musical discussion over hot punch when by some mischance two professional artists, well-known members of the Opera orchestra, came in. Schubert stopped in the middle of his argument. The musicians rushed up to him, clasped his hands, showered him with compliments and it soon became clear that they wanted a new composition

---

* (1803-90); German conductor and composer. The narrator is Eduard von Bauernfeld.

for their concert, with solos for thir individual instruments, and were sure that *Meister* Schubert would kindly oblige. . . .

After repeated petitions, he said suddenly: 'No, for you I will write nothing.'

'Nothing for us?' asked the men, surprised.

'No, under no circumstances.'

'And why not, Herr Schubert? We are artists just as you are. No better ones can be found in all Vienna.'

'Artists!' exclaimed Schubert, tossing back his glass of punch and rising from the table. 'Musical hacks, you are! Nothing more! One of you bites the brass stem of a wooden stick, the other blows his cheeks out on the horn. Call that art? It's a trade, a knack. I am an artist, I! I am Schubert, Franz Schubert, whom everybody knows and recognizes, who has written great and beautiful things that you cannot begin to understand and who will write more beautiful things cantatas and quartets, operas and symphonies! I am not just a composer of Ländler, as the idiot newspapers say and the idiot people repeat, I am Schubert, Franz Schubert!' . . .

Next morning, I hurried round to my friends and found Schubert still in bed, fast asleep, his spectacles on his face as usual. 'So it's you?' he said on recognizing me, adjusted his spectacles and sheepishly offered me his hand. I could not avoid mentioning the [previous night's] scene. 'The rogues,' replied Schubert in quiet good humour. 'I will write them the solos they want and they will still come wheedling to me. I know these people!'

256

Lachner called on Schubert one day when he was not in the mood for work. 'Let's have some coffee,' said Schubert, and fetching out an old coffee mill – 'my most precious possession', he called it – measured out the beans, took off his glasses and began to grind. Suddenly he exclaimed, 'I've got it! I've got it! You rusty little machine!' He threw the coffee mill into the corner, sending the beans flying. 'What have you got, Franzl?' asked Lachner. 'This coffee mill is a wonderful thing,' explained Schubert excitedly. 'Melodies and themes come flying in. You see, it's the ra-ra-ra, that's what. . . . You search for days for an idea, and the little machine finds it in a second.' And he began singing the themes of the String Quartet in D minor, 'Death and the Maiden', which Lachner faithfully wrote down.

Schubert, one morning, brought [Michael Vogl] several songs for perusal. The singer was busy at the moment, and put off the musician to another time; the songs were laid aside. Vogl afterwards examined all the songs at his leisure. . . . One that pleased him particularly . . . was too high for him, so he transposed it, and had a fresh copy made. About a fortnight elapsed, and the two artists and friends were enjoying music together. Something new was proposed, and Vogl, without saying a word further, placed [the song] in the handwriting of the transposer upon the piano. When Schubert heard the composition in its transposed state, he called out with exultation, in the Viennese dialect, 'H'm! pretty good song. Whose is it then?'

258

In the winter of 1827, on a visit to Vienna with his teacher Hummel, Ferdinand Hiller* heard Michael Vogl sing Schubert songs with the composer as accompanist. The sixteen-year-old Hiller watched in astonishment as Hummel, 'with half a century of music behind him', wept openly throughout the recital. Determined to meet the unknown composer, Hiller next morning searched him out in his sparsely-furnished rooms. When he entered, Schubert was working, standing up beside a broad, high desk. 'You compose a great deal,' exclaimed Hiller, seeing mounds of fresh manuscript scattered around. 'I compose every morning,' replied Schubert seriously. 'When one piece is finished, I begin another.'

259

He once called on [Bendedikt] Randhartinger and asked him for the loan of fifteen florins to pay the rent of his lodgings, in order to avoid being turned out. Randhartinger at once gave him the necessary sum, and they both went to the proprietor and paid the fifteen florins. As they passed the 'Graben', the street where the music publisher Diabelli had his shop, Schubert said: 'Dear Benedictus, I would repay you at once if these people here could pay me for my songs; they have a great many of my compositions, but every time I ask for money they always say they had too much outlay and too little income from my songs. I called twelve times at Diabelli's, but I have not yet received one penny; but I shall never give them a song again.' He sold Diabelli the copyright of twelve volumes of his songs for 800

---

* (1811–85); German composer and conductor.

florins; while on one single song, the 'Wanderer', Diabelli is said to have made a profit of no less than 36,000 florins.

260

Among the 20,000 mourners who followed Beethoven's coffin on 29 March 1827, was Franz Schubert. After the ceremony at the Währing cemetery Schubert and his friends went to an inn to have a drink. Schubert lifted his glass and his first toast was 'to him whom we have buried!' At the second glass he said: 'to him who will go next!' Twenty months later, on 19 November 1828, Schubert was dead, aged only thirty-one.

261

Schubert's mood became more gloomy. When I asked him what the matter was, he merely said, 'Well, you will soon hear it and understand.' One day he said, 'Come to Schober's* today, I will sing you a cycle of awe-inspiring songs.' So, in a voice wrought with emotion, he sang the whole of the *Winterreise*. We were quite dumbfounded by the gloomy mood of these songs and Schober said he had liked only one, 'Der Lindenbaum'. To which Schubert replied, 'I like these songs more than all the others, and you will come to like them too.' They were his swansong. From then on he was a sick man.

262

Schubert's last letter

11 November 1828

Dear Schober,
I am ill. I have eaten and drunk nothing for eleven days, and am so tired and shaky that I can only get from the bed to the chair, and back. Rinna is attending me. If I taste anything, I bring it up again directly.

   In this distressing condition, be so kind as to help me to some reading. Of Cooper's I have read the *Last of the Mohicans*, the *Spy*, the *Pilot*, and the *Pioneers*. If you have anything else of his, I entreat you to leave it with Frau von Bogner at the Coffee house. My brother, who is conscientiousness itself, will bring it to me in the most conscientious way. Or anything else. Your friend,

Schubert

---

* Franz von Schober (1796–1882); poet.

Gaetano DONIZETTI (1797–1848)

Italian composer of some seventy operas, providing in *Lucia di Lammermoor* and *Anna Bolena* outstanding vehicles for dramatic sopranos.

263

Donizetti, when asked which of his own operas he thought the best, spontaneously replied, 'How can I say which? A father always has a preference for a crippled child, and I have so many.'

264

A remarkable man I* met now and then in 1840 and 1841 was Donizetti, a most distinguished, amiable, and fashionable gentleman, as elegant as most of his music. He was young still, but such a prolific composer that at that time he had already written upwards of forty operas. I remember talking with him about Rossini, and asking if Rossini had really composed the *Barbiere* in a fortnight. 'Oh, I quite believe it,' said he, 'he has always been such a lazy fellow!' I confess that I looked with wonder and admiration at a man who considered that to spend a whole fortnight over the composition of an opera was a waste of time.

265

A Milanese theatre manager had been let down by another composer and desperately needed a new opera in two weeks. He begged Donizetti to revamp an existing work. 'Are you making fun of me?' retorted the composer. 'I am not accustomed to patching up my own old operas, let alone another composer's. I'll give you a new opera in fourteen days. Now send me Felice Romani.'

'I give you one week to prepare the text,' he told the librettist. 'It must be set to music within fourteen days. Let's see which of us has guts!' The fruit of this challenge was *L'Elisir d'amore*.

❦

---

* Sir Charles Hallé (1819–95); German-born conductor, founder of eponymous orchestra in Manchester.

Jacques Fromental HALÉVY (1799–1862)

Parisian-Jewish composer of *La Juive*, teacher of Gounod, Saint-Saëns and Bizet (who became his son-in-law) and uncle of Offenbach's librettist, Ludovic Halévy.

266

[Watching] the first performance of one of Halévy's operas from the composer's box Cherubini kept silence until after the second act. Halévy, his pupil, asked, 'Maestro, have you nothing to say to me?' when Cherubini snarled back, 'I have been listening to you for two hours and *you* have said nothing to *me.*'

267

Auber sat down at the piano, played a magnificent [new] march with which everybody was delighted, and the talk turned to other topics. Shortly afterwards one of the guests sidled up to Halévy, who was known to be at work on his opera of *Charles VI*, and begged him to favour them in his turn with a specimen of his forthcoming production. In the most affable manner the maestro acceded to the request and placed himself before the instrument. Instead, however, of playing anything of his own, to the astonishment of all present, and by a wonderful effort of memory, Halévy repeated as it appeared, note for note, Auber's magnificent march which they had all just heard for the first time. A clamour of ejaculations and compliment arose at the end of this feat. 'He has remembered every note, without change or omission,' cried one. 'Not quite,' remarked Auber, 'he has made several changes, and very happy ones, which I shall certainly adopt.'

Vincenzo BELLINI (1801–1835)

Creator of great soprano roles in *La Sonnambula* and *Norma*.

268

Bellini, when a student at the Conservatory of Music in Naples, was introduced to the house of Signor Francesco Fumaroli, President of the Supreme Court, to whose beautiful and talented daughter, Maddalena, he gave lessons in singing. [He] naturally fell madly in love with his charming scholar, who fully reciprocated his passion.

As usual in such cases, everybody knew the state of affairs except the father and mother of the love-sick girl.

After Bellini's first opera, *Adelson e Salvini*, had been produced, with fair success, he, through a mutual friend, Sig. Marsigli by name, asked for the hand of Maddalena, and of course the request was refused by the parents, who were surprised at his audacity, the refusal being accompanied by a decided prohibition of any further visits to the house. The lovers were in despair at first, and then exchanged mutual resolutions and vows never to belong to any one else.

'Before I shall have written ten operas, your parents will be only too glad to offer me your hand,' said Bellini to Maddalena.

'It takes a long time to write ten operas,' sighed poor Maddalena.

'Only a few years, and we are young and can wait,' returned Bellini.

'Well, then, let us swear to be true to each other till then, and that we shall be united after your tenth opera, dead or alive,' exclaimed the romantic and poetical Maddalena.

Bellini did swear.

His second opera, *Bianca e Fernando*, had a great success and Bellini was called to Milan to write for the theatre of La Scala the opera *Il Pirata*, which made a sensation and established Bellini's reputation through Europe.

The operas of *Straniera*, *Zaira*, *I Capuletti e Montecchi* followed in rapid succession, and *La Sonnambula* sealed Bellini's fame throughout the civilized world.

As Bellini had predicted, the parents of Maddalena Fumaroli did not wait till his tenth opera was finished, and after the enormous success of *La Sonnambula*, he received a letter from his beloved Maddalena informing him that her father, yielding to her urgent entreaties, had given his consent to their union. This letter reached him when he was writing *Norma* for Mme. Pasta and Giula Grisi,* but he who had formerly sent every day to Maddalena letters vowing everlasting fidelity, had lately become less enthusiastic in his visions of their mutual future bliss.

His great triumphs, which filled poor Maddalena's heart with hopes of the realization of her only desire in life, were the very causes that undermined Bellini's early love for her.

Whether it was ambition of passion for glory, or Giulia Grisi that produced a change in his feeling, has never been decided, but Bellini

---

* Giuditta Pasta (1797–1865); Giulia Grisi (1811–1869); sopranos.

answered in a lukewarm letter that he was then occupied in finishing the score of *Norma*, and after its production he would go to Naples and decide about their union.

He never went! . . . Poor Maddalena soon after died of a broken heart, but in her last letter to Bellini conjured him not to forget that 'after his tenth opera they must be united live or dead!'

Her death and last letter, however, made an everlasting impression on him, and a continual sadness took hold upon him. According to the general belief in Italy, he was haunted by the ghost of Maddalena, in the shape of a white dove, who fluttered nightly in his bedroom. When he composed his tenth opera, *I Puritani*, the dove [would] alight on the score of that opera, give ten sighs and disappear.

Bellini died shortly after the first performance of *I Puritani*.

269

Heinrich Heine writes
Though he had lived several years in France, he spoke its language so badly that its like was not to be heard even in England. I will not say that he spoke it badly, for the word bad would here be entirely too good. One must say outrageously, incestuously, world-destroyingly – as a cataclysm. Yes, when one was in society with him, and he like a public executioner broke the poor French words on the wheel, and without sign or trembling dealt out a tremendous *coq à l'âne*, one felt as if the very world must split as with a thunder-crack. A deathly stillness then spread over the entire hall, for death himself seemed to be painting terror on every face with chalk and cinnabar; ladies knew not whether they should faint or fly; men looked in sudden amazement at their breeches to realize that they really wore such things; and, what was worst of all, this horror awoke at the same time a convulsive, maddening desire to laugh which could hardly be repressed.

270

Heine, again
The last time I was destined to see him in his life was one evening after supper in the house of a great lady, who had the smallest foot in Paris, and when he had become merry, and the sweetest melodies rang from the pianoforte. I can see him now, the good Bellini, when, exhausted by the many mad Bellinisms which he had chattered, he sat on a seat – it was very low, almost like a footstool, so that he found himself at the feet of a fair lady who had reclined opposite him on a sofa, and with sweet mischievousness looked down on him, while he toiled away to entertain her with a few French phrases, getting ever

deeper into difficulties, commenting in his Sicilian jargon in order to prove that what he said was not foolish, but, on the contrary, the most refined flattery. I do not think that the beautiful lady paid much attention to Bellini's phrases. She had taken his little cane, wherewith he often helped himself out of weak places in rhetoric, and calmly used it to disarrange the elaborate arrangements of the hair on both temples of the young maestro.

త◆⌇

Joseph LANNER (1801–1843)

Austrian dance composer. He founded a quartet in 1819 with Johann Strauss I, but the two soon became rival waltzmasters.

271

After a gruelling evening's music, the Archduchess Sophie approached Lanner and favoured him with a few compliments. 'You have certainly worked hard,' she said graciously. Lanner, wiping his brow with a handkerchief, replied in coarse Viennese dialect, 'Yes, Your Imperial Highness, I sure did.' And, throwing off his coat, added, 'look how I am sweating!' He was promptly suspended from duty.

త◆⌇

Hector BERLIOZ (1803–1869)

Son of a Grenoble doctor, he was sent to medical school in Paris but turned to music. He outraged a conservative establishment with Romantic compositions and pungent essays.

272

Someone sitting next to him in the theatre who, noticing his sobbing during the performance of one of Beethoven's symphonies, said kindly, 'You seem to be greatly affected, monsieur. Had not you better retire for a while?'

'Are you under the impression that I am here to enjoy myself?' replied Berlioz brusquely.

273

Berlioz writes
It was the first performance of [Cherubini's] *Ali Baba*, about the emptiest, feeblest thing he ever wrote. Near the end of the first act,

tired of hearing nothing interesting, I called out, '20 francs for an idea!'

In the middle of the second I raised my bid. '40 francs for an idea!'

The finale commenced. '80 francs for an idea!'

The finale ended, and I took myself off, remarking, 'By Jove, I give up. I'm not rich enough!'

Berlioz

I was sorely tried when [my fellow-student] Robert announced one morning that he had bought a *subject* (a corpse), and asked me to accompany him to the dissecting-room at the Hospital de la Pitié. When I entered that fearful human charnel-house, littered with fragments of limbs, and saw the ghastly faces and cloven heads, the bloody cesspool in which we stood, with its reeking atmosphere, the swarms of sparrows fighting for scraps, and the rats in the corners gnawing bleeding vertebrae, such a feeling of horror possessed me that I leapt out of the window, and fled home as though Death and all his hideous crew were at my heels. It was twenty-four hours before I recovered from the shock of this first impression, utterly refusing to hear the words anatomy, dissection, or medicine, and firmly resolved to die rather than enter the career which had been forced upon me.

Robert wasted much eloquence and finally induced me to make another effort, and I consented to return to the hospital, and face the dread scene once more. How strange! I now merely felt cold disgust at the sight of the same things which had before filled me with such horror; I had become as callous to the revolting scene as a veteran soldier. It was all over. I even found some pleasure in rummaging in the gaping breast of an unfortunate corpse for the lungs, with which to feed the winged inhabitants of that charming place.

'Well done!' cried Robert, laughing; 'you are growing quite humane.' . . .

I went on with my course of anatomy, stoically, if not enthusiastically.

. . . I was thus in a fair way to swell the ranks of the medical students, and might have added another name to the long list of bad doctors but for a visit I paid to the Opéra. There I saw *Les Danaïdes*, by Salieri. The gorgeous splendour of the spectacle, the rich fullness of the orchestra and the chorus, the wonderful voice and pathetic charm of Madame Branchu . . . the crashing bacchanal and the voluptuously dreamy dance-music added by Spontini to the score of his countryman, [all] filled me with excitement and enthusiasm. I was like a lad with the inborn instincts of a sailor, who, never having seen anything but fishing-boats on a lake, suddenly finds himself transported to a three-decker in mid-ocean. Not a wink did I sleep the night after that performance, and my anatomy lesson the next morning suffered in proportion. I sang the air of Danäus . . . while sawing away at the skull of my 'subject'; and when Robert, irritated by my constantly humming . . . when I should have been reading a chapter of Bichat, cried, 'Do attend to your work; we are not getting on at all, our subject will be spoiled in three days; eighteen francs wasted. You must really be sensible!' I retorted by singing the hymn of Nemesis 'Divinité de sang avide!' [Bloodthirsty Divinity!] and the scalpel fell from his hands.

275

On one of the examination days [at the Conservatoire], Cherubini, reading a composition of [Berlioz] asked, 'What does this pause of two bars mean?' 'I thought,' answered Berlioz, 'that the prolonged silence would produce a certain effect upon the public.' 'Oh, you thought so, did you?' replied Cherubini, with his habitual bad temper. 'Well, I think the effect would be still greater if you length-ened the pause. . .'

276

I* had, out of sheer enthusiasm, translated *Romeo and Juliet*, he was madly in love with the celebrated artist, Miss Smithson,† who played Juliet. His love passion virtually set our friendship ablaze. First of all he scarcely knew a sentence of English, and Miss Smithson was even more ignorant of our language than he was of hers; a fact which made their conversation rather awkward, not to say comical. Secondly, she was more or less afraid of her savage admirer. Lastly, Berlioz' father strenuously opposed all idea of marriage. All this was enough and more than enough to create the demand for a confidant, and he raised me to the dignity of counsellor in ordinary. . . .

Our consultations partook of a strange character indeed, and an accident which had happened to Miss Smithson, (she had sprained her ankle while getting out of a cab) gave rise one day to a very characteristic conversation. On that morning Berlioz had sent me a note in a short cramped handwriting. It ran as follows:

---

* Ernest Legouvé (1807–1903); French playwright and long-standing friend of Berlioz.
† Harriet Constance Smithson (1800–54); Anglo-Irish actress whom Berlioz married in 1833.

'I wish to see you most urgently. Send word to [Eugène] Sue. Oh, my friends, the agony of it.'

Thereupon I send a note to Sue.

'A wild hurricane is blowing. Berlioz has summoned us to appear. Tonight, at supper, at my place at midnight.'

At the time appointed, Berlioz makes his appearance, his eyes beclouded with tears, his hair drooping over his forehead like a weeping willow and uttering sighs which he seemed to draw from his boots.

'Well, what is the matter?' we asked.

'Oh my friends, life has become impossible to me.'

'Is your father as relentless as ever?'

'My father,' shouts Berlioz at the top of his voice and trembling with rage, 'My father says, "Yes." He wrote to me to that effect this morning.'

'Well, then it seems to us. . .'

'Wait, wait, do not interrupt me. The receipt of this letter drives me frantic with joy. I rush to her place, I enter her room, almost out of my senses and dissolved in tears. I exclaim, "My father consents, my father consents." And would you know her answer? "Well," she said very calmly, "Not yet, Hector; not yet. My foot hurts me too much." What do you say to that?'

'What we say is this, that the poor girl was no doubt in great pain.'

'In great pain?' he replied. 'Is there such a thing as great pain with people who are in ecstasies?'

277

Heinrich Heine

A young gentleman who sat by me in the box, talkative and lively, pointed out to me the composer, who sat at the extreme end of the hall, in a corner of the orchestra, and played on the kettledrum, for this is his instrument. 'Do you see in the front scene,' asked my neighbour, 'that plump young English lady? That is Miss Smithson, with whom Berlioz has been for three years dead in love, and we may thank this passion for the wild symphony which you now hear.' And, truly enough, there in the front scene or proscenium-box sat the celebrated actress of Covent Garden Theatre, while Berlioz stared steadily at her alone, and when her glance met his, then he pounded away on his drum like mad. . . .

Since then Miss Smithson has become Madame Berlioz, and her husband has had his hair cut. When I this winter again heard his symphony, he again sat drumming in the background of the orchestra; the plump English lady was, as before, in the proscenium-box.

Their glances met as before, but this time he did not at once attack so furiously the drum, nor bang thereon as he had done of yore.

'My dear Legouvé,' he says, 'there are people in hell who have deserved their fate less than I have.'

Accustomed as I was to these kind of outbursts, I was, nevertheless, startled.

'Great heavens, what is the matter?'

'You know that my poor wife is living in humble lodgings at Montmartre.'

'Whither you often go to see her, I also know that, and where your anxious care and respect for her have made her as comfortable as possible under the circumstances.'

'There is not much credit due to me for that,' he replies quickly. 'A man would indeed be a monster if he did not love and respect such a woman as that.' Then with indescribable bitterness, he adds, 'Well, I am a monster.'

'Another case of your conscience pricking you?'

'Judge for yourself. I am not living by myself.'

'I know it.'

'Someone else* has taken her place. It's of no use, I am as weak as a child. Well, a few days ago, there was a ring at my wife's door. She opens it herself and finds herself face to face with a young and elegant woman, who with a smile on her lips, says to her: "Madame Berlioz, if you please, madame." – "I am Madame Berlioz," replies my wife. – "You are mistaken," says the other one, "I am asking for Madame Berlioz" – "I am Madame Berlioz."

'"No you are not Madame Berlioz; you mean old Madame Berlioz, the deserted Madame Berlioz, and I am talking of the young and pretty and tenderly beloved one. That Madame Berlioz stands before you." Saying which she makes her exit, slamming the door on the poor creature who sinks to the ground, almost swooning with grief.'

Thereupon he stopped, then after a short pause went on, 'Isn't it simply atrocious and wasn't I right in saying that. . . .'

'Who told you of that abominable act?' I exclaimed excitely. 'No doubt she who performed it. I feel certain she boasted of it. And do you mean to tell me that you did not turn her out after that?'

'I could not have done it,' he said in a broken voice, 'I love her.'

---

* Marie-Geneviève Reccio (1814–62); Berlioz's domineering mistress from 1841 and second wife from 1854.

Berlioz

There are, perhaps, one thousand bars in my *Requiem*. Precisely in *the* one bar where the conductor's motion is absolutely indispensable, Habeneck* puts down his baton, quietly takes out his snuffbox, and proceeds to take a pinch of snuff. I always had my eye in his direction, and instantly turned rapidly on one heel, and, springing forward before him, I stretched out my arm and marked the four great beats of the new movement. The orchestras followed me, each in order. I conducted the piece to the end, and the effect which I had longed for was produced. When, at the last words of the chorus, Habeneck saw that the 'Tuba mirum' was saved, he said, 'What a cold perspiration I have been in! Without you we should have been lost.' 'Yes, I know,' I answered, looking fixedly at him. I did not add another word. . . . Had he done it on purpose? . . . Could it be possible that this man had dared to join my enemy, the Director, and Cherubini's friends, in plotting and attempting such rascality? I don't wish to believe it . . . but I cannot doubt it. God forgive me if I am doing the man injustice!

I† asked [George] Osborne if he remembered anything about this episode [recounted above], and he said that he had reason to, for he was sitting in the nave with Berlioz, that he never stood up, that Habeneck never put down his bâton, did not take a pinch of snuff, and that there was no necessity or opportunity for fixed significant flashes of the composer's eye. Moreover that when the *Memoirs* were published, he asked Berlioz why upon earth he had put upon record such a wholesale piece of pure invention; that Berlioz burst out laughing and said that the story seemed to him far too good a one to be lost!

Berlioz

At one of the nocturnal festivals [in Vienna] I was once in a mournful reverie – for Strauss' waltzes, with their fervid airs resembling love voices, have the gift of putting me into a profound melancholy –

* François Antoine Habeneck (1781–1849); influential Parisian conductor.
† Sir Charles Villiers Stanford (1852–1924); Irish composer. Adding further confusion to the incident, Charles Hallé, who claims to have sat beside Berlioz, endorses anecdote 279 in every detail.

when a small man, with a clever, intelligent face, made his way to me through the crowd. It was the day after one of my concerts.

'Sir,' he said briskly, 'you are French, and I am Irish; so there is no national *amour-propre* in my opinion, and' (seizing my left hand) 'I beg your permission to grasp the hand that wrote the symphony of 'Romeo'. You understand Shakespeare!'

'Certainly,' I answered, 'but you are mistaken in the hand, as I always write with this one.'

The Irishman smiled, took the right hand I offered him, pressed it very cordially, and went off, saying:

'Oh, these Frenchmen! these Frenchmen! They must laugh at everything and everybody; even at their own admirers.'

282

Related by Edmond and Jules Goncourt*, 15 November 1862
Every now and then at Compiègne a writer or artist is included at the end of a batch of guests: tradition has to be respected! Here is an instance of the sort of gracious welcome which is accorded to them. . . . The Emperor [Napoleon III] was complaining that his sight was failing, 'The queer thing is that I can't tell the difference between black and blue any more. Who is that over there?'

'Sire, it is Monsieur Berlioz.'

He raised his voice. 'M. Berlioz, is your tail-coat blue or black?'

'Sire,' Berlioz hastened to reply, 'I should never take the liberty of appearing before Your Majesty in a blue tail-coat; it is black.'

'Good,' said the Emperor.

And that is all the Emperor said to him in four days.

❦

Mikhail (Ivanovich) GLINKA (1804–1857)

'Father of Russian Music'; Glinka's *A Life for the Tsar* is the first genuine Russian opera.

283

My wife was one of those women for whom finery, balls, carriages, horses, livery, and so on were everything. She had a poor understanding of music, or, to put it better, with the exception of light romances she really understood nothing at all – then, too, anything of an

---

* Edmond (1822–96) and Jules (1830–70) Goncourt; French historians, novelists and critics.

elevated or poetic nature was wasted on her. Here is an example of Maria Petrovna's indifference to music: when I began to write *A Life for the Tsar* in 1835, she complained to my aunt (my father's sister), Maria Nikolaevna Zelepugina, that I was spending money on manuscript paper!

284

When Liszt visited Russia in 1843, he played *Ruslan and Lyudmila* through on the piano and declared it a masterpiece. 'You and Weber,' he told its composer, 'are like two rivals courting the same woman.' In the following year, Glinka went to Paris. 'How come, M. Glinka,' asked Meyerbeer, 'that we know only your reputation, not your works?' 'That's perfectly natural,' retorted the Russian, 'I am not in the habit of *peddling* my compositions.'

⚜

Wilhelmine SCHRÖDER-DEVRIENT (1804–1860)

German soprano. Seeing her in *Fidelio* convinced Wagner to compose opera. She created roles in *Rienzi*, *Flying Dutchman* and *Tannhäuser*.

285

[Schröder] was fulfilling an engagement in Budapest, under the frenzied enthusiasm of the hot-blooded Magyars. She always appeared with a brilliant suite of admirers.

'. . . I* remember the end of an act in which [Schröder-Devrient] as Fidelio uttered that famous heart-rendering cry, and then, still trembling all over her body, rushed into the wings. A circle of enthusiasts who awaited her there were applauding even more madly than the audience in the pit. The great artiste was panting, and threw herself upon a chair in the dressing-room, whilst all those admirers were standing around her singing her praises. Suddenly she jumped up, seized one of the most loquacious by the collar and cried violently, " Has my representation really pleased you as much as you are at pains to assure me? Very well; but I have been told that beside this art-criticism, you, Doctor, are very much concerned also about criticizing my private life! Ah, my most respected sir, do place one of your so very moral citizen-wives, for whom I have the greatest respect, out there upon the stage, and let one of these calm, sedate

---

* Karoline Bauer; German actress.

125

dames sing and play Fidelio as I did. When I am to represent a passion I must have one too, for only that can carry you away which you feel yourself. . . ." '

❦

Johann STRAUSS [I] (1804–1849)

Viennese founder of the dynasty that made an art and a fortune of the waltz. He wrote some 250 pieces, of which the Radetzky March is best known, but was eclipsed by his sons.

286

Mother turned the conversation to a less dangerous subject. We spoke about the respective merits of Strauss and Lanner.

I* had often heard both of them in the Prater. It was quite a pleasure to see Strauss conduct his dance-music – the nimble little man with the small magic violin in his hand; he hopped, nodded fiddled, and moved to and fro in gladsome excitement to the time of the intoxicating tones. The performance of the orchestra was exquisite. Oberon's horn could not invite to dance with greater magic force.

'To whom do you give the preference – Strauss or Lanner?' one beau asked me.

'I am equally fond of both artistes; but I would dance to Strauss' music with the best dancer, and to Lanner's with the dearest. The waltzes of Strauss are gayer, those of Lanner more poetical.'

❦

Michael William BALFE (1808–1870)

Irish composer and singer (London's first Papageno), Balfe wrote *The Bohemian Girl*, and the ballad 'Come into the Garden, Maud'.

287

Balfe's method of finding melodies when inspiration failed may be new to some. He would put the letters of the musical alphabet on separate bits of paper, duplicating each letter several times, then draw them out from a hat, one by one, and note them down, having

---

* Karoline Bauer; German actress.

previously decided upon his key and time. The reiterated notes of some of his melodies certainly warrant the truth of this.

ℰ∾ℳℯ

María MALIBRAN (1808–1836)

Revered Spanish mezzo-soprano.

288

The opera was *Sonnambula*, and the new theatre [in Venice] was filled to the remotest corners. At the conclusion of the rondo finale, 'Ah! non giunge', Malibran's foot slipped . . . one of her slippers was suddenly disengaged and found its way into the pit. A scramble ensued, which amidst so large an assembly must have offered a scene of fearful tumult, in which even those sitting in the boxes became involved in the anxiety to seize a morsel of the object that had touched the foot of the divine artiste, as a prized relic. Never was the game of 'hunt the slipper' played before on so gigantic a scale. Malibran, partly delighted at this amusing display of the public adulation, and partly to prevent a probable catastrophe by effecting a diversion, cast her remaining slipper in another direction, and the uproar was thus prolonged with renewed violence. Not till her slippers, more worshipped than even the Pope's, were reduced to shreds and patches – each a treasured memento – was the tempest appeased. The manager then . . . announced that henceforth the new theatre should bear the title of Teatro Malibran, which it does to this day.

289

Malibran, who entered heart and soul into every character she undertook, was reduced almost to despair at first by the stupidity and *gaucherie* of Mr Templeton* who had not the slightest idea of acting. . . . At the first rehearsal she bore this imperturbability of manner with some degree of patience, thinking that she could rouse 'the man', as she called him, into something like enthusiasm by her own manner. But when, at the next and the succeeding *répétition*, she found him 'no better than a stick', she suddenly seized him by the arm, and hissed into his ear, 'Good heavens, sir, don't you know you are my lover? You must make love to me with some show of passion

---

* John Templeton (1802–86), sang Elvino in *La Sonnambula* opposite Malibran in 1833; he was subsequently known as 'Malibran's tenor'.

in the first act, and in the second you must pull me about the stage as if you would tear me into little bits.' 'But,' replied Mr Templeton, as meekly as a lamb, 'but, madame, I shall hurt you.' 'And what if you do?' screamed out the impetuous woman. 'Never you mind. That's my affair; and if you don't do it' – suiting the action to the words by stamping her pretty little foot – 'by heaven, I'll kill you!'

290

On one occasion, certain visitors thought to gratify Malibran by speaking lightly of English music. She gravely and cunningly pretended to agree with the detractors, and proceeded to sing, to Italian words, a slow, 'melodious' theme, adorned with many wonderful flourishes. Her auditors were enraptured, and were more fully confirmed than ever in their prejudices.

The great vocalist appeared solemnly to assent. She then became more vigorous in her efforts, and gradually hastened the time into something like a *presto*. The applause was unbounded. Amid all this flattering excitement, Malibran suddenly changed the words, and her crest-fallen victims had the pleasure of hearing part of the classical poem:

'Polly, put the kettle on; we'll all have tea!'

291

Malibran's death [at the age of twenty-eight] may have been accelerated by her extraordinary exertions whilst singing in a duet with Madame Caradori-Allan;* they settled the manner at rehearsal as to how it was to be sung, but when the time came Madame Caradori-Allan made some deviation; this prompted Malibran to do the same, in which she displayed most wonderful execution. During the well-deserved encore she turned to me and said, 'If I sing it again it will kill me.' 'Then do not,' I replied, 'let me address the audience.' 'No,' said she, 'I will sing it again and annihilate her.' She was taken ill with a fainting fit after the duet and carried into her room.

❧

---

* Maria Caradori-Allan (1800–65); Italian-born soprano. The narrator here is Sir George Smart (1776–1867); English composer and conductor.

Felix MENDELSSOHN-BARTHOLDY (1809–1847)

Grandson of the Jewish philosopher Moses Mendelssohn, he was raised a Protestant. By the age of seventeen he had composed twelve string symphonies, an opera and overture to the *Midsummer Night's Dream*; at twenty he conducted the first performance of the *St Matthew Passion* since Bach's death.

292

In the evening, we assembled in Goethe's rooms to tea; for he had invited a large party of his Weimar musical acquaintances to make them acquainted with the boy's extraordinary talents. Presently Goethe made his appearance: he came from his study, and had a habit – at least I* generally noticed it – of waiting till all the guests were assembled, ere he showed himself. . . . His 'good evening' was addressed to all; but he walked up to Zelter† first, and shook his hand cordially. Felix Mendelssohn looked up, with sparkling eyes, at the snow-white head of the poet. The latter, however, placed his hands kindly on the boy's head, and said, 'Now you shall play us something.' Zelter nodded his assent.

The piano was opened, and light arranged on the desk. Mendelssohn asked Zelter, to whom he displayed a thoroughly childish devotion and confidence, 'What shall I play?'

'Well, what you can,' the latter replied, in his peculiarly sharp voice; 'whatever is not too difficult for you.' . . .

It was at length arranged that he should play a fantasia; which he did to the wonder of all. But the young artist knew when to leave off; and thus the effect he produced was all the greater. A silence of surprise ensued when he raised his hands from the keys after a loud finale. . . .

Goethe was a great admirer of Bach's fugues, which a musician of Berka, a little town about ten miles from Weimar, came to play to him repeatedly. Felix was therefore requested to play a fugue of the grand old master. Zelter selected it from the music-book; and the boy played it without any preparation, but with perfect certainty.

Goethe's delight grew with the boy's extraordinary powers. Among other things, he requested him to play a minuet.

'Shall I play you the loveliest in the whole world?' he asked, with sparkling eyes.

'Well, and which is that?'

---

* Ludwig Rellstab (1799–1860); German author and critic.
† Carl Zelter (1758–1832); Mendelssohn's mentor.

He played the minuet from *Don Giovanni*.

Goethe stood by the instrument, listening; joy glistening in his features. . . .

'Well, come,' he said, 'you have only played me pieces you know; but now we will see whether you can play something you do not know. I will put you on trial.'

Goethe went out, re-entered the room in a few moments, and had a roll of music in his hand. 'I have fetched something from my manuscript collection. Now we will try you. Do you think you can play this?'

He laid a page, with clear but small notes, on the desk. It was Mozart's handwriting. Whether Goethe told us so, or it was written on the paper, I forget, and only remember that Felix glowed with delight at the name; and an indescribable feeling came over us all, partly enthusiasm and joy, partly admiration and expectation. Goethe, the aged man, laying a manuscript of Mozart, who had been buried thirty years, before a lad so full of promise for the future, to play at sight, – in truth such a constellation may be termed a rarity.

The young artist played with the most perfect certainty, not making the slightest mistake, though the manuscript was far from easy reading.

Goethe adhered to his good-humoured tone; while all the rest applauded. 'That is nothing,' he said: 'others could read that too. But I will now give you something over which you will stick; so take care.'

With these words, he produced another paper, which he laid on the desk. This certainly looked very strange. It was difficult to say if they were notes or only a paper, ruled, and splashed with ink and blots. Felix Mendelssohn, in his surprise, laughed loudly. 'How is that written? who can read it?' he said.

But suddenly he became serious; for while Goethe was saying, 'Now, guess who wrote it?' Zelter, who had walked up to the piano, and looked over the boy's shoulder, exclaimed, 'Why, Beethoven wrote that! any one could see it a mile off. He always writes with a broomstick, and passes his sleeve over the notes before they are dry. I have plenty of his manuscripts. They are easy to know.'

At the mention of the name, as I remarked, Mendelssohn had suddenly grown serious, – even more than serious. . . .

He played it through once . . . generally correctly, but stopping at times, and correcting several mistakes with a quick 'No, so;' then he exclaimed, 'Now I will play it to you.' And, this second time, not a note was missing. 'This is Beethoven, this passage,' he said once turning to me, as if he had come across something which sharply displayed the master's peculiar style. 'That is true Beethoven. I recognize him in it at once.'

293

How he composed I* enjoyed only one opportunity of witnessing. I went one morning into his room, where I found him writing music. I wanted to go away again directly, so as not to disturb him. He asked me to stop, however, remarking, 'I am merely copying out.' I remained in consequence, and we talked of all kinds of subjects, he continuing to write the whole time. But he was not copying, for there was no paper but that on which he was writing. The work whereon he was busy was the Grand Overture in C major, there was no looking forwards or backwards, no comparing, no humming over, or anything of the sort; the pen kept going steadily on, slowly and carefully, it is true, but without pausing, and we never ceased talking. The copying out, therefore, as he called it, meant that the whole composition, to the last note, had been so thought over, and worked out in his mind, that he beheld it there as though it had been actually lying before him.

294

When he revived Bach's Passion Music, and conducted the first performance of that immortal work after it had been dormant for about a century, he found, stepping to the conductor's desk, that a score similar in binding and thickness, but of another work, had been brought by mistake. He conducted this amazingly complicated work by heart, turning leaf after leaf of the book he had before him, in order not to create any feeling of uneasiness on the part of the executants.

295

One of Mendelssohn's favourite stories was an ancient Roman tradition of a motionless assembly of senators, seated in death-like silence, whom a guileless Gaul mistook for stone statues, and was therefore bold enough to pluck the beard of one of the circle, when the supposed statue started into life and cut down the audacious Gaul with his sword. In remembrance of this anecdote, Mendelssohn and Hildebrandt agreed, that whenever they met, no matter where, even in the most aristocratic society, never to say good day to each other without a certain form. Hildebrandt was suddenly to stand

---

* Julius Schubring (b. 1806); German composer.

still and assume a stony face, when Mendelssohn was to go up to him slowly and solemnly and pull his beard, while he was in turn to submit to a sharp Roman blow on the shoulder, which dissolved the magic spell, and they were then to greet each other with their usual cordiality.

296

Mendelssohn, letter to his mother

Prince Albert had asked me to go to him on Saturday at two o'clock, so that I might try his organ before I left England. I found him alone; and as we were talking away Queen Victoria came in, also alone, in a simple morning dress. She said she was obliged to leave for Claremont in an hour, and then, suddenly interrupting herself, exclaimed, 'But goodness! what a confusion!' for the wind had littered the whole room, and even the pedals of the organ (which, by the way, made a very pretty feature in the room), with leaves of music from a large portfolio that lay open. As she spoke, she knelt down and began picking up the music; Prince Albert helped, and I, too, was not idle. Then Prince Albert proceeded to explain the stops to me, and she said that she would meanwhile put things straight. I begged that the Prince would play me something, so that, as I said, I might boast about it in Germany; and he played a chorale by heart, with the pedals, so charmingly and clearly and correctly, that it would have done credit to any professional; and the Queen, having finished her work, came and sat by him and listened, and looked pleased. . . .

The Queen asked if I had written any new songs, and she said she was very fond of singing my published ones. 'You should sing one to him,' said Prince Albert, and after a little begging she said she would try the 'Frühlingslied' in B flat, 'if it is still here', she added, 'for all my music is packed up for Claremont.' Prince Albert went to look for it, but came back saying it was already packed.

[But I] rummaged about amongst the music, and soon discovered my first set of songs. So of course I begged her to sing one of these, to which she very kindly consented; and which did she choose? 'Schöner und schöner schmückt sich' – sang it quite charmingly, in strict time and tune, and with very good execution. Only in the line 'Der Prosa Last und Müh', where it goes down to D and up again by semitones, she sang D sharp each time; and as I gave her the note the first two times, the last time she sang D where it ought to have been D sharp. But with the exception of this little mistake it was really charming, and the last long G, I have never heard better or purer or more natural from any amateur. Then I was obliged to confess that

Fanny* had written the song (which I found very hard, but pride must have a fall), and to beg her to sing one of my own also. If I would give her plenty of help she would gladly try, she said, and then she sang the Pilgerspruch, 'Lass dich nur', really quite faultlessly, and with charming feeling and expression.

297

He had been once more making music with the Queen, and had been genuinely delighted with her rendering of his songs. As he was about to leave, she said:

'Now, Dr Mendelssohn, you have given me so much pleasure; is there nothing I can do to give you pleasure?'. . .

'Well, to speak the truth, I have a wish, and one that only Your Majesty can grant.'

'It is granted,' she interposed.

And then he told her that nothing could give him greater pleasure than to see the nurseries and all the domestic arrangements connected with the royal children. The most consummate courtier could not have expressed a wish better calculated to please the Queen. She most cordially responded, and herself conducted him through the nurseries. Nor was the matter treated lightly; she had to show him the contents of the wardrobes and give him particulars of the service, and for the time being the two were not in the relative position of gracious sovereign and obedient servant, but rather of an experienced materfamilias and an enlightened paterfamilias, comparing notes, and giving one another points on the management of their respective children.

298

Anonymous letter received by Sir Thomas Beecham in Leipzig, November 1936
Sir Thomas Beecham
c/o Gewandhaus, Leipzig

When you conduct tomorrow evening in the Gewandhaus you will see in the first row, exactly as in Berlin, the Leaders (*Führer-Persönlichkeiten*) assiduously applauding. You will be in a better position to judge the real musical culture of these gentlemen when

---

* Fanny Cäcilie Mendelssohn-Bartholdy (1805–47), amateur pianist and composer; Mendelssohn's sister.

you have been informed of the following facts which, perhaps, nobody else will tell you:

Some days ago, late at night, the monument of Felix Mendelssohn-Bartholdy, the immortal composer and conductor of the Gewandhaus, was pulled down and removed.

May you, dear Sir, be comforted by the fact that this act of racial hatred brings the blush of shame to the cheeks of millions of music-loving Germans.

◦◦◦◦◦

Ole BULL (1810–1880)

Eccentric, untutored Norwegian violin virtuoso who devoted his fortune to founding a musical conservatory in Norway and a Norwegian colony in the USA; both ventures collapsed.

299

Going down the Mississippi, he met on the steamboat a party of half-savage men, colonists from the far West. While reading his newspaper he was accosted by one of the men, who had been sent as spokesman by his companions, with the request that the fiddler would take a drink with them, offering him a whisky flask at the same time. 'I thank you,' said Ole Bull politely, 'but I never drink whisky.' With a curse, the fellow asked if he was a teetotaler. 'No, but whisky is like poison to me.' 'If you can't drink, come and fight then!' The man's comrades had gathered round him meantime, and they all cried, 'If you won't drink, you must fight. You look d–n strong; show us what you are good for.' 'A Norseman can fight as well as anybody when his blood is up, but I can't fight when my blood is cold, and why should I?' 'You look like a strong fellow, and d–n it, you shall fight.' Seeing no way of escape, Ole Bull quietly said, 'Since you insist on testing my strength and there is no reason for fighting, I will tell you what I will do. Let any one of you take hold of me in any way he likes, and I'll wager that in half a minute he shall lie on his back at my feet.' A big fellow was chosen, who stepped forward and grasped the violinist round the waist, but was instantly thrown over his head by a sudden wrench and lay senseless on the deck. Ole Bull now felt himself in a very uncomfortable position, for he saw one of the man's comrades draw his bowie knife, but was relieved when it was used only to open a flask. A good dose of its contents poured down his throat soon revived the fainting man. . . . The same fellow later went to an editor to call him to account for an adverse criticism on Ole

134

Bull's playing. [The former adversary was] ready to fight for 'the strongest fiddler he had ever seen, anyhow!'

300

He loves to tell the story of King Frederick VII of Denmark, who said to him, 'Where did you learn to play the violin? Who was your teacher?'

Ole Bull answered, 'Your Majesty, the pine forests of Norway and the beautiful *fjords* taught me!'

The King, who had no feeling for such high-flown sentiments, turned to one of his *aides-de-camp* and said, '*Sikken vrovl!*' – the Danish for 'What rubbish!'

301

He had been engaged by the Princess Damerond to arrange and take part in some quartet music at one of her soirées, and had secured the aid of Ernst* and the brothers Boucher.† As the musicians descended the stairs some white Polish dogs followed them, snarling and barking to the salon. Ernst, who had on silk stockings and low shoes, began to retreat, thus encouraging one of the little brutes to bite him. The cur then rushed at Ole Bull, who deliberately lifted it on his toe and sent it up among the lights of the great chandelier. The attendant found on picking it up that the fall had killed it. The princess ... sent a messenger to request the musicians to leave immediately.

❧

Frédéric (Fryderyk) CHOPIN (1810–1849)

Writing mainly for the piano, Chopin avoided public concerts, living from teaching and the sale of his works. For nine years he cohabited with the novelist Georges Sand.

302

During the time of Chopin's greatest brilliancy and popularity, in the year 1835, he once played his musical portraits in a certain Polish salon, where the three daughters of the house were the stars of the evening, in all splendour of beauty and power. After a few portraits

---

* Heinrich Wilhelm Ernst (1814–65); Austrian violinist and composer
† One of whom was Alexander Boucher (1778–1801); French violin virtuoso renowned for his striking resemblance to Napoleon.

had been extemporized, one of these ladies (Mme Delphine Potocka) demanded hers. Chopin, in reply, drew her shawl from her shoulders, threw it on the keyboard, and began to play, implying in this way: firstly, that he knew the character of the brilliant and famous queen of fashion so well, that he was able to depict it; secondly, that the character and soul were hidden under the externals of *mondaine*, as his piano was under the shawl.

303

Chopin gave a recital of his own compositions in Paris, which Dreyschock* attended in company with Thalberg.† They listened with delight throughout the performance, but on reaching the street Thalberg began shouting at the top of his voice.

'What's the matter?' asked Dreyschock, in astonishment.

'Oh,' said Thalberg, 'I've been listening to *piano* all the evening, and now, for the sake of contrast, I want a little *forte*.'

304

When I‡ visited Chopin in Paris, I asked him to introduce me to Kalkbrenner,§ Liszt, and Pixis. 'That is unnecessary,' answered Chopin, 'wait a moment, and I will present them to you, but each separately.' Then he sat down to the piano after the fashion of Liszt, played in his style and imitated all his movements to the life; after which he impersonated Pixis. The next evening I went to the theatre with Chopin. He left his box for a short time, and turning round I saw Pixis beside me. I thought it was Chopin, and I laughingly clapped him on the shoulder, exclaiming, 'Leave off your mimicry!' My neighbour was quite flabbergasted by such familiarity on the part of a total stranger, but fortunately at that moment Chopin returned to the box, and we had a hearty laugh over the comical mistake. Then, with his own peculiar grace of manner, he apologized both for himself and me to the real Pixis.

305

One evening, when they were all assembled in the *salon*, Liszt played one of Chopin's nocturnes, to which he took the liberty of adding

---

* Alexander Dreyschock (1818–69); Czech pianist of whom J. B. Cramer declared: 'The man has no left hand – here are two right hands!'

† Sigismond Thalberg (1812–71); Swiss-born Austrian pianist, rival of Liszt's.

‡ Joseph Nowakowski, compatriot-friend of Chopin's.

§ Friedrich Kalkbrenner (1785–1849), German pianist whose classes Chopin attended; Johann Peter Pixis (1788–1874), German pianist, teacher and composer.

some embellishments. Chopin's delicate intellectual face, which still bore the traces of recent illness, looked disturbed; at last he could not control himself any longer, and in that tone of *sang froid* which he sometimes assumed he said, 'I beg you, my dear friend, when you do me the honour of playing my compositions, to play them as they are written or else not at all.' 'Play it yourself then,' said Liszt, rising from the piano, rather piqued. 'With pleasure,' answered Chopin. At that moment a moth fell into the lamp and extinguished it. They were going to light it again when Chopin cried, 'No, put out all the lamps, the moonlight is quite enough.' Then he began to improvise and played for nearly an hour. And what an improvisation it was! Description would be impossible, for the feelings awakened by Chopin's magic fingers are not transferable into words.

When he left the piano his audience were in tears; Liszt was deeply affected, and said to Chopin, as he embraced him, 'Yes, my friend, you were right; works like yours ought not to be meddled with; other people's alterations only spoil them. You are a true poet.' 'Oh, it is nothing,' returned Chopin, gaily, 'We have each our own style.'

306

Five days afterwards the friends were again assembled in the same place and at the same time. Liszt asked Chopin to play, and had all the lights put out and all the curtains drawn; but when Chopin was going to the piano, Liszt whispered something in his ear and sat down in his stead. He played the same composition which Chopin had played on the previous occasion, and the audience was again enchanted. At the end of the piece Liszt struck a match and lighted the candles which stood on the piano. Of course general stupefaction ensued.

'What do you say to it?' said Liszt to his rival.

'I say what everyone says; I too believed it was Chopin.'

'You see,' said the virtuoso rising, 'that Liszt can be Chopin when he likes; but could Chopin be Liszt?'

307

He had asked me* to give a newspaper report of [a rare public concert] but Liszt claimed the honour. I quickly went to Chopin to tell him the good news. 'I should have preferred you to do it,' he said very sweetly.

'You are jesting, my dear Chopin. An article by Liszt! It is a positive

---

* Ernest Legouvé, (1807–1903); French playwright.

piece of luck both for the publc and for you. You may safely trust to his great admiration for your talent. I feel certain that he will map you out a magnificent kingdom.'

'Yes,' he answered, smiling, 'a magnificent kingdom within his empire.'

308

[Countess Pauline Plater, a Polish noblewoman living in Paris] said one day to Chopin; '*Si j'étais jeune et jolie, mon petit Chopin, je te prendrais pour mari, Hiller pour ami, et Liszt pour amant.*' (If I were young and pretty, my little Chopin, I would take you for a husband, Hiller for a friend and Liszt as a lover.)

309

Chopin's purse was always open to assist his emigrant Polish countrymen; he had put aside the necessary means for [our] journey [to a music festival]; but the journey having been postponed, forty-eight hours had been quite sufficient to empty his cash-box. As I* would not on any condition give up his company, he said, after much consideration, that he thought he could manage it, produced the manuscript of his lovely E flat waltz, ran off to Pleyel's with it, and came back with 500 francs.

310

There was an infallible means of dragging him away from the piano – namely to ask him to play the funeral march he composed after the disasters in Poland. He never refused to play it, but the moment he had finished, he took his hat and went away.

311

Ferdinand Hiller, open letter to Franz Liszt
One evening you had assembled in your apartments the aristocracy of the French literary world – Georges Sand was of course one of the company. On the way home Chopin said to me, 'What a repellent woman the Sand is! But is she really a woman? I am inclined to doubt it.'

312

Georges Sand did not say a word when Chopin introduced me.† That was hardly civil of her and for that reason I immediately sat down

---

* The narrator is Ferdinand Hiller (1811–85); German composer and conductor.
† Wilhelm von Lenz (1809–93); civil servant and writer on music.

close to her. Chopin hovered around like a frightened bird in a cage. . . .

Georges Sand rose, strode across the room like a man, and sat down at the glowing fire. I followed at her heels, and primed ready for the next encounter, sat down beside her. She had to say something, at last. She drew from her apron pocket an enormously thick Trabucco cigar and called back into the drawing-room: 'Frédéric, a light!' I felt insulted for him – my great lord and master. I understood Liszt's remark 'Poor Frédéric!' in all its bearings.

Chopin obediently brought a light.

313

Georges Sand had a little dog which was in the habit of turning round and round in the endeavour to catch its tail. One evening when it was thus engaged, she said to Chopin, 'If I had your talent, I would compose a pianoforte piece of this dog.' Chopin at once sat down at the piano, and improvised the charming Waltz in D flat (Op. 64), which hence has obtained the name of *Valse du petit chien*.

314

'You will play in memory of me,' he said to friends the dearest to him and the greatest comrades in music, 'and I will hear you from beyond.' Franchomme,* his nearest friend and helper in composition, with whom he wrote his sonata for piano and violoncello, answered him, 'Well, we will play your sonata.' 'Oh, no, not mine, play really good music, Mozart, for instance.'

315

From this hour [of receiving Extreme Unction] he was a saint. The death struggle began and lasted four days. Patience, trust in God, even joyful confidence, never left him, in spite of all his sufferings, till the last breath. He was really happy, and called himself happy. In the midst of the sharpest sufferings he expressed only ecstatic joy, touching love of God, thankfulness that It† had led him back to God, contempt of the world and its good, and a wish for a speedy death.

He blessed his friends, and when, after an apparently last crisis, he saw himself surrounded by the crowd that day and night filled his chamber, he asked me, 'Why do they not pray?' At these words all fell on their knees, and even the Protestants joined in the litanies and prayers for the dying.

---

* Auguste-Joseph Franchomme (1808–84); French 'cellist.
† Abbé Jelowicki, boyhood friend of Chopin's who became a priest.

His usual language was always elegant, with well chosen words, but at last to express all this thankfulness and, at the same time, all the misery of those who die unreconciled to God, he cried, 'Without you I should have croaked like a pig.'

While dying he still called on the names of Jesus, Mary, Joseph, kissed the crucifix and pressed it to his heart with the cry, 'Now I am at the source of Blessedness!'

316

A gentleman of undoubted musical abilities . . . played very well and was extremely fond of Chopin's music, playing many of his pieces, even some of the very difficult ones. I* brought him the sad tidings of Chopin's death. 'Capital!' he exclaimed; 'now I can have his complete works bound!'

∾

Robert SCHUMANN (1810–1856)

German Romantic, he composed piano works while courting Clara Wieck, daughter of his piano teacher who violently opposed their union. From 1854 he was confined to an asylum.

317

Schumann once attended a masquerade during the carnival of 1830, in company with his friend Rosen, for the purpose of paying some attention to a pretty but otherwise insignificant girl. He knew that she would be present at the ball, and, as a pretext for approaching her, put a poem in his pocket. Fortune favoured him: he met and recognized her; but, as he was about to take a carnival liberty, and hand her the poem, the girl's mother stepped threateningly between, 'Keep your poems to yourself, Mask: my daughter does not understand poetry.'

318

It was a habit of Schumann to collect Wieck's children in his room at twilight, and to frighten them by the recital of the most horrible ghost stories of his own invention. Then he would sometimes shut the door, and appear suddenly by the light of a spirit-lamp as a spectre in a fur coat turned inside out, exciting universal terror. Another thing

---

* Sir Charles Hallé (1819–95); English conductor.

which afforded him great pleasure was to make one of Wieck's two sons stand on one foot for a long time, while he walked up and down the room with twinkling eyes.

319

Schumann's genius was so little appreciated that when he entered the store of Breitkopf and Härtel with a new manuscript under his arm, the clerks would nudge one another and laugh. One of them told me* that they regarded him as a crank and a failure because his pieces remained on the shelf and were in the way.

320

When Schumann had just finished [the piano quintet] Liszt unexpectedly came to Leipzig and insisted on hearing it performed the same night. 'It was difficult,' Clara Schumann told us, 'to get four other artists to come at such short notice, but I took a cab and drove about Leipzig until I was fortunate enough to succeed in my mission.' It was arranged that the performance should take place at 7 o'clock that evening at the Schumanns' house. At that hour all were assembled with the exception of Liszt, who did not make his appearance until 9 o'clock. The quintet was duly played, but at the end Liszt moved towards Schumann and, patronizingly touching his shoulder, exclaimed: 'No, no, my dear Schumann, this is not the real thing; it is only *Kapellmeister* music.' At supper afterwards Liszt indulged in some deprecatory remarks about Mendelssohn. Schumann immediately rose, seized Liszt by the shoulder, and cried, 'How dare you talk like that of our great Mendelssohn!' He then left the room. Liszt, the polished man of the world, also rose, and, bowing low to Clara Schumann, said: 'I am deeply sorry to have been the cause of such an unpleasant incident. I feel I am in the wrong place here; pray accept my humble excuses and allow me to depart.'

321

Once, when expecting a visit from Joachim, Schumann jokingly proposed our composing a violin sonata all together, and then letting Joachim guess who was the author of each movement. The first movement fell to me,† the intermezzo and finale were composed by Schumann, whilst Brahms wrote the scherzo on a theme from my

---

* William Mason (1829–1908); American pianist.
† Albert Hermann Dietrich (1829–1908); German composer and conductor.

first movement. After having played the sonata with Clara Schumann, Joachim immediately recognized the author of each part.

The manuscript of this joint production was presented to Joachim, Schumann writing the following dedication:

F. A. E.*
'In Erwartung der Ankunft des verehrten und geliebten Freundes JOSEF JOACHIM*; schrieben diese Sonate*

'ROBERT SCHUMANN, JOHANNES BRAHMS, ALBERT DIETRICH.'

In expectation of the arrival of their revered and beloved friend, Joseph Joachim, this sonata was written by R.S., J.B., A.D.

322

Madame Schumann had played at one of the [Düsseldorf] subscription concerts some unaccompanied solo pieces. Her husband sat not far from her, behind the piano. When she had finished there was a general rivalry among the audience and the musicians on the platform to give expression to their delight, which she, however, little heeded, for she saw her husband motionless and cold. 'Have I not played well, Robert?' But there came no response, and she wept whilst the hall was ringing with ecstastic applause.

323

On Shrove Monday, 27 Feb. 1854, he received a noonday visit from his physician, Dr Hasenclever (a member of the board of health), and his musical friend, Albert Dietrich. They sat and chatted together sociably. During the conversation, Schumann, without a word, left the room. They supposed he would return; but when some time passed, and he did not come, his wife went in search of him. He was nowhere to be found. His friends hastened out to look for him – in vain. He had left the house in [his] dressing-gown and, bare headed, gone to the bridge that spans the Rhine, and sought to end his misery by plunging into the stream. Some sailors jumped into a boat, rowed after him, and pulled him out.

324

Before his final collapse, Schumann had some intervals of peace during which he wrote some Variations on a theme brought to him during the first stages of his illness by 'angels as a greeting from Mendelssohn and Schubert.' As though Schumann had had some sort of presentiment he had put all his domestic affairs in order, down to the minutest details; latterly, he had even written the most

---

* *'Frei aber einsam'* [free but lonely] – Joachim's motto.

precise instructions on all his manuscripts. In one of his earlier notebooks, which he filled with all kinds of remarks, there is the sentence: 'The artist should beware of losing touch with society, otherwise he will be wrecked, as I am.'

325

Extracts from Clara Schumann's diary
[10 February 1854]
Throughout the night Robert had such terrible sounds in his ears that he couldn't sleep for a single minute. First there was a continuous drone on one note, then an occasional second note as well. During the day it eased off. The next night was just as bad, and the following day as well – he had a mere two hours respite in the early morning, and at ten it all came back afresh. He is in terrible agony. Every sound he hears turns to music – music played on glorious-sounding instruments, he says, more beautiful than any music ever heard on earth. It utterly exhausts him. The doctor says there is nothing he can do.
[17 February]
In the night, not long after we had gone to bed, Robert got up and wrote down a melody which, he said, the angels had sung to him. Then he lay down again and talked deliriously the whole night, staring at the ceiling all the time. When morning came, the angels transformed themselves into devils and sang horrible music, telling him he was a sinner and that they were going to cast him into hell. He became hysterical, screaming in agony that they were pouncing on him like tigers and hyænas, and seizing him in their claws.

✆✘✆

Franz (Ferencz) LISZT (1811–1886)

Liszt's impact on nineteenth-century music and society was immense, arousing what Heine called 'Lisztomania'. Late in life he took minor religious orders to become the 'Abbé Liszt'.

326

When I* saw Liszt in 1880, I remember his saying to me, '*J'ai reçu le célébre baiser de Beethoven*' ['I received the celebrated kiss of Beethoven'].

---

* The Reverend Hugh Reginald Haweis (1838–1901); Anglican clergyman and writer on music.

143

I find that Beethoven's secretary, Schindler, wrote in 1823 to Beethoven, 'You will be present at little Liszt's concert, will you not? It will encourage the boy. Promise me that you will go.' And Beethoven went. When the 'little Liszt' stepped on to the platform, he saw Beethoven in the front row; it nerved rather than staggered him – he played with an abandon and inspiration which defied criticism. Amidst the storm of applause which followed, Beethoven was observed to step up onto the platform, take the young virtuoso in his arms, and salute him, as Liszt assured me, 'on both cheeks'.*

327

Pixis was an old-fashioned player of considerable reputation in his day. . . . Among his works was a duo for two pianofortes. While this composition was yet in manuscript it was played in concert with the assistance of Liszt. Pixis, knowing Liszt's habit of playing from memory, requested him on this occasion at least to have the music open before him on the piano-desk, as he himself did not like to risk playing his part without notes. . . .

When the time came the pianists walked on the stage, each carrying his roll of music. Pixis carefully unrolled his and placed it on the piano-desk. Liszt, however, sat down at the piano, and, just before beginning to play, tossed his roll over behind the instrument and proceeded to play his part by heart. Liszt was young at that time, and – well – somewhat inconsiderate.

328

At an orchestral concert given by him and conducted by Berlioz, the 'March to the Scaffold' from the latter's Symphonie Fantastique . . . was performed, at the conclusion of which Liszt sat down and played his own arrangement, for the piano alone, of the same movement, with an effect even surpassing that of the full orchestra.

329

To Liszt considerable credit is due for having been the first to draw the attention of the French musical world to Schumann. He played his compositions and wrote enthusiastically of them in the Press. He

---

*Widely related, this is a prime example of Lisztian legend. Beethoven did not attend the boy's concert, let alone embrace him publicly. He may, however, have received him at home. To one of his pupils Liszt said, 'Beethoven caught hold of me with both hands, kissed me on the forehead and said gently: "Go, you are one of the fortunate ones. For you will give joy and happiness to many other people. There is nothing finer or better." '

also published a long and highly appreciative article on Clara Schumann in one of the leading musical papers of Paris, and subsequently asked her whether it satisfied her. She said that it did, but added, 'What made you say I practised with a black cat on each side of the pianoforte desk? You know that isn't true.' 'My dear madam,' replied Liszt, 'in order to make an article like that go down with the French public it must have something piquant about it.'

330

As the closing strains began, I* saw Liszt's countenance assume that agony of expression, mingled with radiant smiles of joy, which I never saw in any other human face, except in the paintings of our Saviour by some of the early masters; his hands rushed over the keys, the floor on which I sat shook like a wire, and the whole audience were wrapped in sound, when the hand and frame of the artist gave way; he fainted in the arms of the friend who was turning over for him, and we bore him out in a strong fit of hysterics. The effect of this scene was really dreadful. The whole room sat breathless with fear, till Hiller came forward and announced that Liszt was already restored to consciousness, and was comparatively well again. As I handed Mme de Circourt to her carriage, we both trembled like poplar leaves, and I tremble scarcely less as I write.

331

It† did not hear Liszt again until his visit to London in 1840, when he puzzled the musical public by announcing 'Pianoforte Recitals'. This now commonly accepted term had never previously been used, and people asked, 'What does he mean? How can any one *recite* upon the pianoforte?' At these recitals Liszt, after performing a piece set down in his programme, would leave the platform, and, descending into the body of the room, where the benches were so arranged as to allow free locomotion, would move about among his auditors and converse with his friends, with the gracious condescension of a prince, until he felt disposed to return to the piano.

332

During a *soirée* at the court of St Petersburg, where he was always very well received, it happened that the Tsar Nicolas, who did not care much for music, began talking with a lady, and, caring little for Liszt's playing, talked very loud. All of a sudden Liszt stopped dead,

---

* Henry Reeve, reporting a Paris concert, April 1835.
† Charles Kensington Salaman (1814–1901); English pianist.

and went away from the piano. The Tsar was puzzled, and approaching the master said to him:

'Why have you stopped playing?'

'When the Emperor speaks, one ought to be silent,' was the Machiavellian answer.

333

'Do you remember the time,' said King Louis Philippe of France, 'when you played at my house as a little boy, when I was yet Duke of Orleans? Things have greatly changed since then!'

'Yes, sire; but not for the better,' replied Liszt, dryly.

334

The infatuated maid of honour at the court of Saxe-Weimar, [had a] peculiar personal flavour of stale tobacco. [It] mystified all her friends and fellow-courtiers until an accident one day revealed the astounding fact that she permanently wore in her bosom, as a sacred relic of her musical idol, an old cigar-stump that Liszt had thrown away in the street under her very eyes – she had reverently picked up the unsavoury morsel, enshrined it in a costly locket enriched with the monogram 'F.L.' in brilliants, and suspended it round her virgin neck, whence it steadfastly gave forth the sickly reek that so long perplexed the Grand Ducal Household.

335

When her turn came [at the concert, the Russian countess] was very graciously received, and she commenced her ballad, of course playing by heart. All went well until the sixth page, when she hesitated and became confused. In desperation she began again, encouraged by indulgent applause. But at the very same passage her overwrought nerves betrayed her again. Pale as a sheet she rose. Then the master [Liszt], thoroughly irritated, stamped his foot and called out from where he was sitting: 'Stop where you are!' She sat down again, and, in the midst of a sickening silence, she began the wretched piece for the third time. Again her obstinate memory deserted her. She made a desperate effort to remember the final passages, and at last finished the fatal piece with a clatter of awful discords.

I was never present at a more painful scene. Going out, the master upbraided her more than angrily, as she clung to his arm. . . .

The countess went home, took a dose of laudanum, and slept for forty-eight hours. They thought she was dead, but she woke up again.

After letters had passed between them, the master insisted on her leaving Budapest immediately. They say she went to Liszt's apartments one morning with a revolver. She deliberately took aim at him. 'Fire!' said Liszt, advancing towards her. The unhappy woman dropped her hand, and threw herself at his feet.

336

He was widely believed to be the natural father of, among many others, the pianist Franz Servais. Liszt's reply to such speculation was characteristically polished, '*Ich kenne seine Mutter nur durch Correspondenz, und so was kann nicht durch Correspondenz abmachen* (I know his mother only by correspondence, and one cannot arrange that sort of thing by correspondence).

337

A young lady pianist had announced a recital [in Berlin] advertising herself (in the hope of attracting a larger audience) as a 'pupil of Liszt'. As she had never laid eyes upon him in her life, she was horrified to read in the papers on the morning of her concert that the Abbé had arrived in the city. The only thing to be done was to make a clean breast of it; she went to his hotel and asked for an interview. When she was shown in she confessed with many tears, and asked for absolution. Liszt asked her the name of the pieces she was going to play, chose one and made her sit down at the piano and play it. Then he gave her some hints about her performance, and dismissed her with a pat on the cheek, and the remark, 'Now, my dear, you can call yourself a pupil of Liszt.'

338

Liszt is not always so amiable. He resents people counting on his playing [for them]. When Baroness K. inveigled him into promising to take tea with her because he knew her father, she, on his accepting, invited a lot of friends, holding out hopes that Liszt would play. She pushed the piano into the middle of the room – no one could have possibly failed to see it. Every one was on the *qui vive* when Liszt arrived, and breathless with anticipation. Liszt, who had had many surprises of this sort, I imagine, saw the situation at a glance. After several people had been presented to him, Liszt, with his most captivating smile, said to the hostess:

'*Où est votre piano, chère madame?*' and looked all about for the piano, though it was within an inch of his nose.

'Oh, Monseigneur! Would you, really . . .?' advancing toward the piano triumphantly. 'You are too kind. I never should have dared to ask you.' And, waving her hand toward it, '*Here* is the piano!'

'Ah,' said Liszt, who loves a joke, '*c'est vrai. Je voulais y poser mon chapeau.*' [I want to put my hat on it.]

Very crestfallen, but undaunted, the Baroness cried, 'But, Monseigneur, you will not refuse, if only to play a scale – merely to *touch* the piano!'

But Liszt, as unkind as she was tactless, answered, coldly, 'Madame, I never play my scales in the afternoon,' and turned his back on her and talked with Madame Helbig.

339

Edvard Grieg

'I had fortunately just received the manuscript of my pianoforte concerto from Leipzig, and . . . [was] very anxious to see if he would really play my concerto at sight. I, for my part, considered it impossible; not so Liszt. "Will you play?" he asked, and I made haste to reply: "No, I cannot" (you know I have never practised it). Then Liszt took the manuscript, went to the piano, and said to the assembled guests, with his characteristic smile, "Very well, then, I will show you that I also cannot." With that he began. I admit that he took the first part of the concerto too fast, and the beginning consequently sounded helter-skelter; but later on, when I had a chance to indicate the tempo, he played as only he can play. It is significant that he played the cadenza, the most difficult part, best of all. His demeanour is worth any price to see. Not content with playing, he at the same time converses and makes comments, addressing a bright remark now to one, now to another of the assembled guests, nodding significantly to the right or left, particularly when something pleases him. In the adagio, and still more in the finale, he reached a climax both as to his playing and the praise he had to bestow.

'A really divine episode I must not forget. Toward the end of the finale the second theme is, as you may remember, repeated in a mighty fortissimo. In the very last measures, when in the first triplets the first tone is changed in the orchestra from G sharp to G, while the piano part, in a mighty scale passage, rushes wildly through the whole reach of the keyboard, he suddenly stopped, rose up to his full height, left the piano, and with big theatric strides and arms uplifted walked across the large cloister hall, at the same time literally roaring the theme. When he got to the G in question he stretched out his arms imperiously and exclaimed: "G, G, not G sharp! Splendid! That is the real Swedish Banko!" He went back to the piano repeated the whole strophe, and finished. In conclusion, he handed me the manuscript, and said, in a peculiarly cordial tone: "*Fahren Sie fort, ich sage Ihnen, Sie haben das Zeug dazu, und – lassen Sie sich nicht abschrecken!*" (Keep steadily on; I tell you, you have the capability, and – do not let them intimidate you!)

'This final admonition was of tremendous importance to me; there was something in it that seemed to give it an air of sanctification.'

340

The orchestra played Wagner's overture to *Tannhäuser*. The applause was not as enthusiastic as Liszt thought it ought to be, so he stood up in the box, and with his great hands clapped so violently that the whole audience turned toward him, and, recognizing him (indeed, it would have been difficult not to recognize him, such a striking figure as he is), began clapping their hands for him. He cried, '*Bis!*' And the audience in chorus shouted, '*Bis!*' And the orchestra repeated the whole overture. Then the audience turned again to Liszt and screamed, '*Vive* Liszt!'

Auber said such a thing had never been seen or heard before in the annals of these severe and classical concerts. People quite lost their heads, and Auber, being afraid that there would be a demonstration at the *sortie*, advised us to leave before the end.

Liszt was very pleased with his afternoon.

341

As soon as the Wagner concert was announced in Budapest, opposition immediately arose. Voices were raised in the Press, claiming that Budapest was not a German city, and that no defence could be put forward for the attempt to spend Hungarian money on the support of a German undertaking. . . .

Tickets for the Wagner concert were selling so badly that we* began to fear a fiasco, which would have been very unpleasant for the Master, and not exactly to the credit of our capital. Liszt was informed of the state of things, and he at once said: 'I will play Beethoven's Concerto in E Flat major at the same concert.' – On that day when this decision of the Master became known, all the tickets for the concert were sold out. . . .

---

* The narrator is Count Albert Apponyi, Hungarian politician.

Lilli Lehmann recalls

I sang several times for Frau Cosima,* especially, Liszt's 'Mignon', even before he, himself, appeared in Bayreuth. One day when I was doing it again 'by request', I saw Wagner enter and listen to the end. Then, with his head thrown back, a bearing that gave him the appearance of great self-consciousness, he strode rather stiffly through the drawing-room with a bundle of music under his arm, and turned, before leaving, to Frau Cosima. 'Really, my dear,' he said, 'I did not know that your father had written such pretty songs; I thought he had rendered service only in fingering for piano playing.'

343

As soon as we were alone, he said to me† in a low voice:
'You have seen Cosima?'
I had none of that sentiment which the high personality of Liszt evoked among his intimates. . . . So I was not in the least intimidated, and, believing him to be hostile to his daughter [who had left her husband to live with Wagner] it was with a decided vehemence that I replied to him:
'I beg of you, do not say anything against your daughter to me. I am her partisan to such an extent that I cannot admit any blame. In the face of a personality so superhuman as Richard Wagner's, the prejudices and even the laws of men cannot prevail. Who would not feel the fascination and submit joyfully to the supremacy of such a genius? In Cosima's place, you would do as she does, and it is your duty as a father not to put any obstacle in the way of the realization of the great event to which she has the right to look forward.'
Liszt grasped me warmly by the arm.
'I am entirely of your opinion, but I may not express it,' said he in a still lower voice. 'The habit which I wear imposes certain opinions which I cannot openly deny. I know the temptations of the heart too well to judge severely: conventions force me to be silent, but within myself, I desire more than anyone else for a legal solution of this painful affair.'

---

* Liszt's second daughter (1837–1930), she married the pianist and conductor Hans von Bülow in 1857, but from 1864 was intimate with Wagner, whom she married in 1870.
† Judith Gauthier (1850–1917); French writer and admirer of Wagner.

One day Pius IX came to see the master in his solitude at Monte Mario, where he was living in an old Dominican monastery. The Holy Father was sad, and directly he arrived he gave Liszt to understand that he had come on purpose to be cheered up by his talent. He begged him to improvise. He also was particularly fond of this kind of music, maintaining that the originality and the individuality of the artist was more clearly marked when nothing fettered the inspiration of the soul. 'I played, therefore,' said the master, 'as the spirit moved me. Perhaps my sympathetic hearer inspired me; but, without wishing to praise my "strumming," I must tell you that the Holy Father was deeply affected, and when I had finished he said rather a curious thing to me:

'"The law, my dear Palestrina,* ought to employ your music, in order to lead hardened criminals to repentance. Not one could resist it, I am sure; and the day is not far distant, in these times of humanitarian ideas, when similar psychological methods will be used to soften the hearts of the vicious."'

The conductor, Felix Weingartner, recalls Liszt's death
The Wagner family gave no outward sign of mourning. The daughters wore black dresses and that was all. We had confidently expected that at least one of the festival performances would be cancelled. . . .

If at least the flag on the roof of the theatre had been removed or hung at half-mast! But nothing, nothing at all was done to show outward reverence to his memory. Not even the receptions in the Villa Wahnfried were interrupted. Everything was made to look – as if on purpose – that Franz Liszt's passing was not of sufficient importance to dim the glory of the Festivals even temporarily by a veil of mourning.

From that time on I never entered the portals of Wahnfried again.

Anton Rubinstein [would] say of him, 'Let us never put anybody on a parallel with Liszt, either as pianist or as musician, and least of all as man, for Liszt is more than all that – *Liszt is an Idea!*'

---

* Favoured Papal composer in the sixteenth century.

'Have you written the history of your life?' I* asked him one day.

'It is enough to have lived such a life as mine,' he replied in a grave voice.

❦

Louis JULLIEN (1812–1860)

French conductor; won great popularity at London promenade concerts and signalled the rise of the conductor as a cult figure.

348

He determined to set the Lord's Prayer to music. Like a good many of his friends, I† pointed out to him, as gently, of course, as I could, that the public would probably consider the idea somewhat incongruous of a composer of dance music attempting so sacred a subject, but with the self-sufficiency that was one of this remarkable man's characteristics, Jullien replied that a composition bearing on its title-page two of the greatest names in history could not fail to be a success. Asked to explain his meaning more fully, he turned to me and said:

'The Lord's Prayer
Words by
Jesus Christ
Music by
Jullien'

349

He had a daïs built in the centre of the orchestra, the floor of which was covered with white cloth having a gold-lace border. On the daïs he had a splendid arm-chair of white and gold. When he directed, he stood up and faced the audience, his string forces being on either hand, part way between him and the audience, but leaving him in full view; and the wood and wind were on each side, with the brass in the rear.

At the end of a piece he would drop down into the splendid arm-chair, mop his face, and appear to be in a state of collapse, which drew out enormous applause.

---

* Janka Wohl, author of a Liszt memoir.
† Jules Rivière (1819–1901); conductor.

Dance music and his own compositions he conducted with a baton of white or black wood, which was changed for a jewelled stick when a symphony by Beethoven, or other classical composer, was performed.

He was sitting at the pianoforte one morning, when he suddenly rose with a knife in his hand, and, addressing a young lady who was on a visit in the house, told her he had an inspiration from Heaven to kill her. With wonderful presence of mind, she declared she was prepared to die, but asked him to grant her one favour before fulfilling his mission. 'What is it?' he replied, 'I have power to agree to what you may demand.' She begged that he would let her hear him play some of his own compositions on the piccolo. He consented, and went into an adjoining room to fetch the instrument. She turned the key upon him and rang for assistance. He was taken to Dr Pinet's Maison de Santé, known as La Folie St James, where he died raving mad, on 14 March, 1860.

〜〜〜

Sigismond THALBERG (1812–1871)

Virtuoso pianist and composer; rival of Liszt.

The agent who had the local management of the concert in Belfast refused to provide a grand piano [for Thalberg], fearing it might be injured. A small upright instrument, called a cottage, very much the worse for wear, was all he would allow upon the platform. Thalberg had his revenge for this meanness of the agent. The programme passed off with éclat; the audience was enthusiastic, notwithstanding the absence of a 'grand'. As Thalberg went on the platform to play the last piece, he quietly observed to my father, 'Now good-bye to the piano', and when he came off, the unlucky instrument had not a note to speak with – he had smashed the strings, already in a very attenuated condition, and the hammers were all more or less disabled.

'I expected as much,' growled the agent, when examining the wreck, 'the same thing would have happened had I given him the best piano in my shop.'

〜〜〜

Giuseppe VERDI (1813–1901)

Verdi's operatic masterpieces form the core of the modern Italian repertoire.

353

He was only seven when, under the following circumstances, he gave the first proof of the influence which music exercised upon his young mind.

It was on a fête day, and he was helping as choir-boy at Mass in the little church of Le Roncole. The Mass was accompanied on the organ, which he heard for the first time. At the sound of this harmony, then so new to him, the child remained positively in ecstasy. Just at the moment when the priest asked him for the water – *'Acqua!'* – Verdi was so completely absorbed that he did not hear him. The priest, therefore, repeated *'Acqua!'* and Verdi remained deaf. At last a third demand remaining without result, this brutal man, to awake him from his torpor, gave the poor child such a push that he sent him rolling down the three steps of the altar. The fall was so violent that the child fainted, and had to be carried into the sacristy. When he came to himself, and was able to be taken home to his parents, what does the reader suppose he did, instead of complaining and crying, as many others would have done in his place? He renewed a request which he had already made to his father, and begged him to allow him to learn music.

354

Verdi's recollections

'But now began for me the greatest misfortunes. My *bambino* fell ill at the beginning of April, the doctors were unable to discover the cause of his ailment, and the poor little thing, fading away, expired in the arms of his mother, who was beside herself with despair. That was not all. A few days after my little daughter fell ill in turn, and her complaint also terminated fatally. But this even was not all. Early in June my young companion herself was attacked by acute brain fever, and on the 19th June, 1840, a third coffin was carried from my house.

'I was alone! – alone! In the space of about two months three loved ones had disappeared for ever. I had no longer a family! And, in the midst of this terrible anguish, to avoid breaking the engagement I had contracted, I was compelled to write and finish a comic opera!

'*Un Giorno di Regno* did not succeed. A share of the want of success certainly belongs to the music, but part must also be attributed to the performance. My soul rent by the misfortunes which had overwhelmed me, my spirit soured by the failure of my opera, I persuaded myself that I should no longer find consolation in art, and formed the resolution to compose no more! I even wrote to the engineer Pasetti (who since the fiasco of *Un Giorno di Regno* had shown no signs of life) to beg him to obtain from Merelli the cancelling of my contract.

'Merelli sent for me, and treated me as a capricious child. He would not allow me to become disgusted with art on account of one failure, etc., etc. But I held to my point so firmly that Merelli finished by returning to me my agreement, saying:

'"Listen, Verdi, I cannot make you write by force. My confidence in you is not lessened. Who knows but that one day you may decide to take up your pen again? In that case, it will be enough for you to give me notice two months before the beginning of a season, and I promise that the opera which you bring me shall be put on the stage."

'I thanked him; but these words did not have the effect of making me reconsider my determination, and I went away.

'I fixed my residence at Milan, near to the Corsia de' Servi. I was out of spirits, and thought no more of music, when one winter evening, coming out of the Cristoforis gallery, I found myself face to face with Merelli, who was going to the theatre. It was snowing great flakes, and Merelli, drawing my arm in his, induced me to accompany him as far as his office at La Scala. We chatted on the way, and he told me that he was in difficulties for a new opera which he had to bring out. He had engaged [Otto] Nicolai to write this opera, but he was not satisfied with the libretto.

'"Fancy," said Merelli, "a libretto by Solera, superb !! . . . magnificent !! . . . extraordinary !! . . . splendid dramatic situations, full of interest, fine poetry ! . . . but this obstinate Nicolai will not hear of it, and declares that it is an impossible libretto ! . . . I would give my head to find another immediately."

'" . . . I will get you out of the difficulty," said I at once. "Did you not have *Il Proscritto* written for me? I have not composed a note of it; I put it at your disposal."

'" . . . Oh! bravo! This is a piece of luck."

'Thus conversing, we had arrived at the theatre. Merelli called Bassi, who was at the same time poet, stage manager, librarian, *régisseur*, etc., etc., and told him to look at once among the archives to try and find a manuscript of *Il Proscritto*. As a matter of fact, he did find it. But at the same moment, Merelli took another manuscript, and showing it to me, cried out:

155

'"... Stop; here is a libretto of Solera's. So fine a subject, and to refuse it! Take it; read it!"

'"... What the deuce do you want me to do with it? I have no wish to read libretti."

'"... Well, I suppose it will not hurt you! Read it, and then bring it me back."

'And he put it into my hands. It was a large paper book, written in big letters, as was the custom then. I rolled it up, and taking leave of Merelli, made my way to my lodging.

'As I walked, I felt myself seized with a kind of undefinable uneasiness; a profound sadness, a genuine anguish, took possession of my heart. I went into my room, and with an impatient gesture I threw the manuscript on the table, and remained standing before it. In falling on the table, it had opened by itself; without knowing how, my eyes fixed on the page which was before me, and on this verse:

'"Va pensiero sull' ali dorate."
(Go, my thought, on gilded wings.)

'I ran through the following verses, and was much impressed by them, the more so that they formed almost a paraphrase of the Bible, the reading of which was always dear to me.

'I read first one fragment, then another, but, firm in my resolution to compose no more, I tried to command myself. I shut the book, and went to bed. But bah! *Nabucco* ran in my head; I could not sleep. I got up and read the libretto, not once, but twice, three times, so that in the morning I was able to say that I knew Solera's poem by heart, from one end to the other.

'In spite of all this, I felt no disposition to change my determination, and during the day I went back to the theatre to return the manuscript to Merelli.

'"Oh!" said he, "it is fine."

'"Very fine."

'"Well, set it to music."

'"Not at all! I will have nothing to do with it."

'"Set it to music, I say; set it to music."

'And with these words he took the libretto, rammed it into the pocket of my overcoat, took me by the shoulders, and not only pushed me roughly out of his office, but shut the door in my face and locked himself in.

'What was I to do?

'I returned home with *Nabucco* in my pocket. One day one verse, one day another, one time a note, another time a phrase, and little by little the opera was written.'

'Ah!' said Verdi, 'the people have always been my best friends, from the very beginning. It was a handful of carpenters who gave me my first real assurance of success.

'It was after I had dragged on in poverty and disappointment for a long time in Busseto, and had been laughed at by all the publishers, and shown to the door by all the impresarios. I had lost all real confidence and courage, but through sheer obstinacy I succeeded in getting *Nabucco* rehearsed at the Scala in Milan. The artistes were singing as badly as they knew how, and the orchestra seemed bent only on drowning the noise of the workmen who were busy making alterations in the building. Presently the chorus began to sing, as carelessly as before, the "Va, pensiero", but before they had got through half a dozen bars the theatre was as still as a church. The men had left off their work one by one, and there they were sitting about on the ladders and scaffolding, listening! When the number was finished, they broke out into the noisiest applause I have ever heard, crying, *"Bravo, bravo, viva il maestro!"* and beating on the woodwork with their tools. Then I knew what the future had in store for me.'

Alzira, given in 1845 at ... San Carlo, obtained but a moderate success, in spite of the renown which Verdi had already acquired by his previous works. The friends whom he had in Naples, with the superstition usual in that country, had maintained that the unhappy fate of that work was due to the influence of the composer Cape- celatro, an amateur musician whose talent was open to question, but who passed in the eyes of his fellow-countrymen for an accom- plished *jettatore*. Now the mischievous influence attributed to the 'evil eye' by the Neapolitans is well known. They therefore wished on this occasion to do everything possible and impossible to avert the unlucky influence of Capecelatro. . .

Scarcely had Verdi set foot in Naples, and become installed at the Hotel de Russie, when his friends, to prevent any meeting between him and the dreaded *jettatore*, began to mount guard at his door, without stirring an inch, relieving each other on duty as best they could in unfailing succession. Did Capecelatro appear at the hotel? Presto! he was sent about his business without pity. Did he protest? Harshness had to be used. . .

As soon as Verdi went out he was surrounded by a little group of friends, who did not leave him alone a moment, but accompanied him everywhere – to the theatre, to the restaurant, for a walk. Their sole efforts were directed to a single end: to prevent Capecelatro speaking to him, touching him, even approaching him. . . .

Be this as it may, these novel body-guards were untiring, and courageously persevered in their campaign to the end. The production of *Luisa Miller* took place at San Carlo on 8 December 1849, without Capecelatro having once succeeded in forcing the guard and approaching Verdi, and, naturally, the work obtained a great success.

357

However:

The first acts of *Luisa Miller* had obtained a complete success. Verdi was on the stage arranging the last groups, when a man, rushing from the wings, ran and fell on his neck; at the same moment a side scene broke loose and fell upon the stage; Verdi, happily perceiving it, made a great step backwards, dragging with him Capecelatro (it was he!), and the scene fell at the foot of the maestro, who had a narrow escape of being crushed while in the embrace of Capecelatro! But that was not all. The last act was begun, and it is not known wherefore, but its success was much less than that of the previous acts. After that go and disbelieve in *la jettatura* if you have the courage!

358

In Rome, towards the end of 1847, the Italians for a time looked on [Pope Pius IX] as the liberator and future saviour of their country. It lasted a very short time, but it is certain that the pontiff was then, especially in the eyes of the Romans, the object of a respect and an affection which bordered on adoration. *Ernani* was being played at the Tordinona Theatre, and every night the public applauded with frenzy certain pieces [which] excited the enthusiasm, and raised the patriotic passions, of the multitude. [In the opera,] instead of singing, 'A Carlo Quinto sia gloria e onor!' they sang 'A Pio Nono', etc., and naturally [Italian] tricoloured banners and cockades replaced the Austro-Spanish cockades and banners [on stage]. At each performance they had this scene repeated. One night a person in the costume of the National Guard, up in the gallery, with one leg over the balustrade, the piece having been already repeated, kept on shouting, 'Bis! Viva Italia! Viva Pio Nono!' Others joined in chorus, and the curtain rose for the third time. Still the fellow was not satisfied; he continued shouting, so that at last the public lost patience and hissed him. At that, redoubling his noise, and reaching the paroxysm of his patriotic fury, he took off his shako, and threw it into the pit; to his shako succeeded his tunic, then his waistcoat; the occupiers of the pit began to be nervous, fearing that he might throw himself over next; but he did worse than that: he drew his sword and hurled it with such violence, that it embedded itself in the stage, two steps from the footlights, in the midst of general alarm. At this moment an officer made his way to this madman, seized him, not without difficulty, and turned him out of the theatre.

359

His chief recognition at the hands of the Monarch had been his nomination as a Senator in the Upper House. He had no taste for practical politics, and mainly amused himself by setting 'Divide! Divide!' (*ai Voti! ai Voti!*) as a choral libretto, using the orders of the day as music paper. He had no taste for titular distinction. The morning after the performance I* went to see him with Boito,† and he was pacing the room, thoroughly out of temper. Boito asked him what was the matter and he tossed a telegram to him from the King. It contained the offer to make him Marchese di Busseto.

Boito: Well, Master, what have you said?

Verdi: I have answered him, 'Musician I was born, musician I remain.'

360

Verdi . . . greatly gratified me‡ by asking me to send him the songs and perhaps some other of my compositions. His answer to my question to what address I should send them was most characteristic. Without the slightest suspicion of conceit or affection he said, '*Oh – adressez simplement "Maestro Verdi, Italia."* '

361

When he came to superintend his *Vêpres Siciliennes* at Paris, and the orchestra did not arrive for an additional rehearsal, and kept him waiting, he complained to the conductor, who said, '*Mon Dieu, ils ont autre chose à faire.*' 'Ah!' said Verdi, 'they have something else to do than their duty?' And there and then he took his hat, left the theatre and Paris.

---

* Sir Charles Villiers Stanford (1852–1924); Irish composer.
† Arrigo Boito (1842–1918); composer and Verdi's librettist.
‡ Sir George Henschel (1850–1934); baritone and founder conductor of the Boston Symphony Orchestra.

When *La Traviata* was a failure at Venice, Varesi, the baritone, and other interpreters of the work, thinking to console Verdi, paid him their condolences; but he only exclaimed, 'Make them to yourself and your companions, who have not grasped my music.'

'My terms,' said Maurel,* 'will be the same as Monsieur Tamagno's.†
If Monsieur Tamagno asks two thousand francs a night, then I will sing for two thousand francs. If Monsieur Tamagno asks ten thousand francs a night, then my terms will be the same.'

Ten thousand francs a night was, as Maurel knew, precisely the price that Tamagno was asking. Maurel's fee at the Scala had been only two thousand francs, for which reason Maurel hated Tamagno much as Iago hated Othello: Iago, the superior in intellect, hating Othello the superior in position.

Maurel then expatiated on the general imbecility of tenors, and by implication on his own superiority to such people.

'When God,' he said, 'has created a perfect idiot, He says to him, "You shall be a tenor!" '

Maurel talked eloquently and wittily, but not reasonably; and nothing, he declared, would induce him to accept less than was paid to Tamagno.

'So like Maurel!' said Verdi. 'The baritone may, of course, be a better artist than the tenor, and Maurel is infinitely more intelligent than Tamagno. But the diamond is more valuable than other stones, not because it is more beautiful, but because it is more rare.'

When they came to study the fourth act [of *Rigoletto*] the tenor Mirate, cast for the part of the Duke of Mantua, perceived that a piece which he had to sing alone was wanting in his part.

'*Mi manca un pezzo*' (There is a piece missing), said he to the composer.

'*Cè tempo; te lo darò*' (There is plenty of time; I will give it you), replied the latter.

Every day the same demand was repeated, and every day the same reply was given. Mirate began to be anxious and out of patience, when at last, the evening before the orchestral rehearsal, Verdi

---

* Victor Maurel (1848–1923); French baritone, created the role of Falstaff for Verdi.
† Francesco Tamagno (1850–1905); Italian tenor, Verdi's first Otello.

brought him a paper on which was the famous *canzone*, 'La donna è mobile'.

'Stop! read this,' said he.

Mirate opened the paper, saw that the music was easy, and appeared enchanted.

'Mirate,' then added Verdi, 'you give me your word of honour that you will not sing this melody at home, that you will not hum it, that you will not even whistle it, – in a word, that you will allow no one whatever to hear it?'

'I promise,' answered Mirate; and Verdi became easy.

This is the reason of the mystery made by Verdi on this occasion. The master counted much, and with reason, on the effect of this *canzone*, of so new a rhythm, and so full of elegant ease. He knew, besides, that it was of a melodic turn easy to retain, and being aware of the powers of the Italians in this respect, he feared not only lest they should carry off his melody, but lest they should spread it abroad in Venice before the performance, and thus when it was heard in the theatre every one should accuse him of plagiary, instead of applauding his invention.

The recommendation made to Mirate was not, therefore, as one has seen, useless; but it would have been insufficient, as the master well knew. Therefore the day of the full rehearsal he addressed not only the orchestra, but the whole of the staff of the theatre, begging each person to keep it the most profound secret. The secret was well kept, and thus the effect of the song was prodigious. Even from the elegant opening passage of the violins the public was aroused by the form and freedom of the subject; and when the tenor had finished the first verse, thunders of applause broke out in the house, followed after the second by a formidable encore. It was a perfect triumph, as spontaneous as possible.

365

Although many families had already left [Vienna] for the summer holidays, Verdi's name was powerful enough to recall them from all parts of the country, and the ticket-office of the opera was besieged by an eager crowd, anxious to secure places. All the seats were occupied, and the public was enthusiastic over the *Requiem*, of which the soli were remarkably well rendered by Mesdames Stolz and Waldmann, Monsieurs Masini and Medini, while the chorus, strengthened by a private choral society and the orchestra from the opera-house, surpassed themselves under the master's magic baton. Verdi has often remarked since that it was a real pleasure to conduct such an excellent orchestra and chorus. On the night of the first

161

performance, as Verdi was leaving the theatre and preparing to enter his carriage, he was suddenly surrounded by a crowd of students, who cheered him enthusiastically. Being of a retiring disposition, and always having a horror of stormy ovations, he jumped quickly into the carriage; but when he observed that the hot-headed youths intended unhitching the horses, he sprang out at the opposite door and ran like lightning to the hotel, never leaving the theatre on the following nights until he was sure that no one was lying in wait for him.

366

A friend who went to see Verdi when he was staying in a villa at Moncalieri found him in a room which, Verdi said, was his drawing-room, dining-room, and bedroom combined, adding, 'I have two other large rooms – but they are full of things that I have hired for the season.' Verdi threw open the doors and showed him a collection of several dozen piano-organs.

'When I arrived here,' he said, 'all these organs were playing airs from *Rigoletto*, *Travatore*, and my other operas from morning till night.

'I was so annoyed that I hired the whole lot for the season. It has cost me about a thousand francs, but at all events I am left in peace.'

367

To Giuseppe Verdi   *Reggio, 7 May 1872*

On the second of this month, attracted by the sensation which your opera, *Aida*, was making I went to Parma. Half an hour before the performance began I was already in my seat, No. 120. I admired the scenery, listened with great pleasure to the excellent singers, and took pains to let nothing escape me. After the performance was over, I asked myself whether I was satisfied. The answer was in the negative. I returned to Reggio and on the way back in the railroad carriage, I listened to the verdicts of my fellow travellers. Nearly all of them agreed that *Aida* was a work of the highest rank.

Thereupon I conceived a desire to hear it again, and so on the fourth I returned to Parma. I made the most desperate efforts to obtain a reserved seat, and there was such a crowd that I had to spend five lire to see the performance in comfort.

I came to the following conclusion: the opera contains absolutely nothing thrilling or electrifying, and if it were not for the magnificent scenery, the audience would not sit through it to the end. It will fill the theatre a few more times and then gather dust in the archives.

Now, my dear Signor Verdi, you can imagine my regret at having spent 32 lire for these two performances. Add to this the aggravating circumstance that I am dependent on my family, and you will understand that this money preys on my mind like a terrible spectre. Therefore I address myself frankly and openly to you, so that you may send me this sum. Here is the account:

Railroad: one way	2.60 lire
Railroad: return trip	3.30 "
Theatre	8.00 "
Disgustingly bad dinner at the station	2.00 "
	15.90 lire
Multiplied by 2	× 2 "
	31.80 lire

In the hope that you will extricate me from this dilemma, I am yours sincerely,

BERTANI

My address: Bertani, Prospero; Via San Domenico, No. 5

Verdi to Ricordi   *May, 1872*

As you may readily imagine, in order to save this scion of his family from the spectres that pursue him, I shall gladly pay the little bill he sends me. Be so kind, therefore, as to have one of your agents send the sum of 27 lire, 80 centesimi to this Signor Prospero Bertani, Via San Domenico, No. 5. True, that isn't the whole sum he demands, but for me to pay for his dinner too would be wearing the joke a bit thin. He could perfectly well have eaten at home. Naturally, he must send you a receipt, as well as a written declaration that he promises never to hear another one of my new operas, so that he won't expose himself again to the danger of being pursued by spectres, and that he may spare me further travel expenses!

368

Tosca was written originally by Luigi Illica not for Puccini, but for another Ricordi composer, the wealthy and spectacular Alberto Franchetti, known as 'the Italian Meyerbeer'. Franchetti, however, was unhappy with the libretto and, when Illica refused to amend it, proposed that they go with Ricordi to Verdi to seek his adjudication. Accordingly, they proceeded to the octogenarian maestro's suite at the Hotel Milan, where Illica read out the three acts of his libretto. When he had finished, Verdi sprang to his feet and pronounced it excellent. Franchetti, somewhat abashed, asked how the great composer would tackle the tenor's role. 'My dear Franchetti,' said Verdi, 'I would simply make some music – a little music, that's all.'

Puccini, on hearing Verdi's verdict, became so covetous of the libretto that he made Ricordi abrogate his contract with Franchetti and surrender Illica's text to his own talents.

369

In 1899, Verdi noticed that his friend Leopoldo Mugnone* was making frequent trips to the town of Pistoia, 'to supervise the casting of the bells for *Tosca*'.

'How many bells, and what are they used for?' demanded Verdi.

'Eleven,' replied the conductor. 'In the third act they represent dawn breaking over Rome with the chimes of the different churches.'

'Eleven bells!' exclaimed Verdi, '*Per Bacco*! And to think that when I composed *Il Trovatore* I hardly dared introduce one bell in the 'Miserere' for fear of the impresarios' curses. . . . There's nothing more to say except that the world has progressed – the operatic world, at least.'

370

Toscanini joined the Scala orchestra as a 'cellist shortly before *Otello* went into rehearsal. He was overwhelmed by the experience of playing for Verdi and, at the première, on 5 February 1887, was ovecome by the music itself. Returning to Parma some days later, he reached home at night and found his mother asleep in bed. He shook her awake. '*Otello* is a masterpiece!' he shouted. 'Get on your knees, mother, and say, "*Viva, Verdi!*" ' The befuddled woman duly obliged.

371

The occasion of the performance [of *Otello*] was a remarkable one. Repeated delays had intensified interest rather than abated it, and 'all the city was moved' because of the opera. The hotels filled with strangers who had secured seats, and others who had come on the chance of obtaining admission; everywhere *Otello* was talked about; the press, annoyed at being shut out from rehearsals, kept up an agitation, and the man who could let out any of the well-guarded secrets of La Scala became for the time a hero. Meanwhile Verdi, superintending the many rehearsals, pursued the even tenor of his

---

* (1858–1941); conductor of the premières of *Tosca* and *Cavalleria Rusticana*.

way, calm and undisturbed. Visiting nobody, and allowing nobody to visit him, the master reserved all his energy for duty. Rising early each morning, he took a little exercise in the quiet streets; spent most of the day at the theatre, and about ten o'clock went to bed. On the memorable Saturday evening, a crowd gathered before the Hotel de Milan to see him pass to his carriage. This was the beginning of an extraordinary series of demonstrations. A far larger crowd around the theatre cheered Verdi in confident anticipation of an artistic triumph; while within the house and during the performance of the opera, the old composer was summoned at every possible opportunity. So long as the curtain remained up the brilliant gathering let him alone, but whenever it was down they kept him exercised at coming forward, bowing, and retiring. Several times after each act two of the principal artists would lead him on, and then, perhaps by way of suggestion that he had had enough of it, Verdi would step forward alone, hat in hand, with his frock coat tightly buttoned around him. For this the audience reserved their loudest and longest cheer. They became frantic with enthusiasm. At the close there was a special scene of wreaths and flowers and whatnot appropriate to such occasions, but the master preserved his calm demeanour. Agitated he must surely have been, though not a muscle of his face moved, and he appeared as the most unconcerned person in all that delirious assembly. Another ovation awaited Verdi outside, where the constant crowd had become larger and denser. No horses should draw him home that night, but rather the willing arms of his enthusiastic countrymen. The design was fulfilled to the letter, and being able to regulate the pace of the carriage, the people gave their hero an embarrassing example of slow travelling. However, even such a journey must have an end. Verdi reached his hotel, the corridors of which were crowded, and, gaining his apartments, went speedily to bed, where, if he slept, it was not because his lingering admirers in the street failed to make a noise. So ended one of the greatest personal triumphs ever awarded to a composer.

❧

Richard WAGNER (1813–1883)

Wagner is the subject of more biographies than any historical figure other than Jesus and Napoleon. He participated in revolutionary activities in 1849; took up with Cosima, Liszt's daughter and von Bülow's wife; propounded a union of all the arts in a single form; composed mammoth operas and built a theatre at Bayreuth in which to stage them.

372

We reached Zürich on 5 June 1852, and, the next morning, armed with the letter, I* made my way to Wagner's chalet, which was situated on a hill in the suburbs. It was then about ten o'clock in the morning.

When I asked the maid who opened the door if Herr Wagner was at home and to be seen, she answered, as I had feared she would, that he was busily at work in his study, and could not be disturbed. . . .

Just as I was turning to leave, I heard a voice at the head of the stairs call out, *'Wer ist da?'* [Who is there?] I told the maid to deliver my letter immediately. As soon as Wagner had glanced through it, he exclaimed, *'Kommen Sie herauf! Kommen Sie herauf!'* [Come up! Come up!]

At that time Wagner was known, and that not widely, only as the composer of *Rienzi, The Flying Dutchman, Tannhäuser*, and *Lohengrin*. I had heard only *The Flying Dutchman*, but considered it a most beautiful work, and was eager to meet the composer.

Wagner's first words, as I met him on the landing at the head of the stairs, were, 'You've come just at the right time. I've been working away at something, and I'm stuck. I'm in a state of nervous irritation, and it is absolutely impossible for me to go on. So I'm glad you've come.'

I remember perfectly my first impression of him. He looked to me much more like an American than a German. . . . In some way Beethoven was mentioned. After that the conversation became a monologue with me as a listener, for Wagner began to talk so fluently and enthusiastically about Beethoven that I was quite content to keep silent and to avoid interrupting his eloquent oration. . . .

'Mendelssohn,' he said, 'was a gentleman of refinement and high degree; a man of culture and polished manner; a courtier who was always at home in evening dress. As was the man, so is his music, full

---

* William Mason, (1829–1908); American pianist and composer.

of elegance, grace, finish, and refinement, but carried without variance to such a degree that at times one longs for brawn and muscle. Yet it is music that is always exquisite, fairylike, and fine in character. In Beethoven we get the man of brawn and muscle. He was too inspired to pay much attention to conventionalities. He went right to the pith of what he had to say, and said it in a robust, decisive, manly, yet tender way, brushing aside the methods and amenities of conventionalism, and striking at once at the substance of what he wished to express. Notwithstanding its robustness, his music is at times inexpressibly tender; but it is a manly tenderness, and carries with it an idea of underlying and sustaining strength. Some years ago, when I was *Kapellmeister* in Dresden, I had a remarkable experience, which illustrates the invigorating and refreshing power of Beethoven's music. It was at one of the series of afternoon concerts of classic music given at the theatre. The day was hot and muggy, and everybody seemed to be in a state of lassitude and incapacity for mental or physical effort. On glancing at the programme, I noticed that by some chance all of the pieces I had selected were in the minor mode – first, Mendelssohn's exquisite A Minor Symphony, music in dress-suit and white kid gloves, spotless and *comme il faut*; then an overture by Cherubini; and finally Beethoven's Symphony No. 5 in C Minor.' At this point Wagner rose from his chair, and began walking about the room. 'Everybody,' he continued, 'was listless and languid, and the atmosphere seemed damp and spiritless. The orchestra laboured wearily through the symphony and overture, while the audience became more and more apathetic. It seemed impossible to arouse either players or listeners, and I thought seriously of dismissing both after the overture. I was very reluctant to subject Beethoven's wonderfully beautiful music to such a crucial test, but after a moment's reflection I appreciated the fact that here was an opportunity for proving the strength and virility of it, and I said to myself, "I will have courage, and stick to my programme."'

Wagner stopped walking a moment, and looked about the room as if searching for something. Then he rushed to a corner, and seizing a walking-stick, raised it as if it were a baton.

'Here is Beethoven,' he exclaimed, 'the working-man in his shirtsleeves, with his great herculean breast bared to the elements.'

His straightened himself up, and, giving the stick a swing, brought it down with an abrupt 'Ta-ta-ta-tum!' – the opening measure of Beethoven's C Minor Symphony.

The whole scene was graphically portrayed. Then throwing himself into a chair, he said, 'The effect was electrical on orchestra and audience. There was no more apathy. The air was cleared as by a passing thunder-shower. There was the test.'

373

Wagner writes

Bakunin* [apart from his ideas] proved a really amiable and tender-hearted man. He was fully alive to my own anxiety and despair with regard to the risk I ran of forever destroying my ideals and hopes for the future of art. It is true, he declined to receive any further instruction concerning these artistic schemes, and would not even look at my work on the Nibelungen saga. I had just then been inspired by a study of the Gospels to conceive the plan of a tragedy for the ideal stage of the future, entitled *Jesus of Nazareth*. Bakunin begged me to spare him any details; and when I sought to win him over to my project by a few verbal hints, he wished me luck, but insisted that I must at all costs make Jesus appear as a weak character. As for the music of the piece, he advised me, amid all the variations, to use only one set of phrases, namely: for the tenor, 'Off with His head!'; for the soprano, 'Hang Him!'; and for the basso continuo, 'Fire! fire!' And yet I felt more symphathetically drawn towards this prodigy of a man when I one day induced him to hear me play and sing the first scenes of my *Fliegender Holländer*. After listening with more attention than most people gave, he exclaimed, during a momentary pause, 'That is stupendously fine!' and wanted to hear more.

374

Like Beethoven, Wagner was slightly under middle height, well built, quick in movement, speech and gesture. . . . He made the impression of being somewhat taller than he actually was. After the political disturbances of 1849 when he was 'wanted' by the Saxon police, the following *Signalement* was issued:

Wagner is thirty-seven to thirty-eight years old, of middle height, has brown hair, wears glasses; open forehead; eyebrows brown; eyes grey-blue; nose and mouth well proportioned; chin round. Particulars: in moving and speaking he is hasty. Clothing: *surtout* [coat] of dark green buckskin, trousers of black cloth, silk neckerchief, [ordinary] felt hat and boots.

---

* Mikhail Alexandrovich Bakunin (1814–76); Russian anarchist ideologue.

Rossini was no more an admirer of Wagner than were other Parisians of his day.

A friend who entered his study found him studying the score of *Tristan and Isolde*, and asked him what he thought of it.

'Ah,' said the master, 'it is a beautiful work! I never expected to find such grace of expression, such power of invention in the music of the reformer of our old dramatic operas, the scores of Mozart, Gluck, Cimarosa, Weber, Mercadante, Meyerbeer – and my own.'

His visitor, coming closer, was dumbfounded when he observed that Rossini was reading Wagner's score wrong side up.

Whereupon, inverting the score, Rossini said after a glance, 'Alas, now I cannot make head or tail of it!'

376

'Do you know what Wagner's music sounds like?' [Rossini] asked me* one day. Opening the piano and seating himself heavily on the keys, he exclaimed, 'There! that's the music of the future.'

377

'Direction for Composing a Wagner Overture'

> 'A sharp where you'd expect a natural;
> A natural where you'd expect a sharp;
> No rule observe but the exceptional;
> And then (first happy thought!) bring in a
> HARP!

> 'No bar a sequence to the bar behind;
> No bar a prelude to the next that comes;
> Which follows which you really need not mind;
> But (second happy thought!) bring in your
> DRUMS!

> 'For harmonies, let wildest discords pass;
> Let key be blent with key, in hideous hash;
> Then (for last happy thought!) bring in your
> BRASS!

> 'And clang, clash, clatter – clatter, clang, and clash!'

---

* Louise Héritte–Viardot (1841–1918); contralto.

Wagner writes

Cosima appeared to have lost the shyness she had evinced towards me . . . and a very friendly manner had taken its place. While I was singing 'Wotan's Farewell' to my friends I noticed the same expression on Cosima's face as I had seen on it, to my astonishment, in Zürich on a similar occasion, only the ecstasy of it was transfigured into something higher. Everything connected with this was shrouded in silence and mystery, but the belief that she belonged to me grew to such certainty in my mind, that when I was under the influence of more than ordinary excitement my conduct betrayed the most reckless gaiety. As I was accompanying Cosima to the hotel across a public square, I suddenly suggested she should sit in an empty wheelbarrow which stood in the street, so that I might wheel her to the hotel. She assented in an instant. My astonishment was so great that I felt all my courage desert me, and was unable to carry out my mad project.

379

Hans von Bülow to Cosima, his wife

Munich, 17 June 1869

You have preferred to devote your life and the treasures of your mind and affection to one who is my superior and, far from blaming you, I *approve* your action from every point of view and admit you are perfectly right. I swear that the only consoling thought has been this: Cosima is happy over there.

380

Behind the house, in that court which formed a part of the garden, and from which the carriage-drive started, there was a high swing, which the children were allowed to use very carefully, and with which the older people sometimes amused themselves. One day Madame Cosima was sitting on the narrow board. Wagner offered to start the swing and give her a good flight through the air.

All went well for a time, but, little by little, the motion became more rapid; higher and still higher went the swing! In vain Madame Cosima begged for mercy. Carried away by a kind of frenzy, the Master paid no attention, and the incident began to have a terrifying aspect.

Cosima grew white; her hold relaxed, and she was about to fall.

'Do you not see that she is fainting?' I* cried, throwing myself toward Wagner.

He grew pale, in his turn, and the danger was quickly averted. But, as the poor woman continued to be dizzy and trembling, the Master concluded it would be wise to create a diversion. He ran rapidly toward the house, and by the aid of the shutters, the mouldings and projections of the stones, he climbed nimbly up the side, and reaching the balcony of the floor above, leaped over it.

He had obtained the desired effect, but in replacing one evil by another. Trembling with anxiety, Cosima turned to me, saying under her breath:

'Above all things, do not notice him; do not look surprised, or you can never tell where he will end.'

381

15 July [1876]

Yesterday morning I† took to Brahms the orchestral score of Wagner's *Götterdämmerung*. In the afternoon he said to me, '*Why* did you bring it to me?' (He had particularly asked me for it!) 'The thing interests, and fascinates one, and yet, properly speaking, is not always pleasant. With the *Tristan* score it is different. If I look at that in the morning, I am cross for the rest of the day.'

. . . To-day I read out, from a Berlin paper, the news of the death, at Bayreuth, of a member of the Wagner orchestra. 'The first corpse,' said Brahms, dryly.

382

Among [Brahms'] admirers it was the fashion to despise Wagner, but to this he demurred, and a remark he often made, 'His imitators are monkeys but the man himself has something to say,' was cited as proof of his noble, generous disposition. People like Joachim and Herzogenberg‡ considered Wagner a colossal joke, and I remember their relating how, as a sort of penance, they sat through a whole act of *Siegfried*, keeping up each other's spirits by exchanging a 'Good morning' whenever a certain chord, let us say a diminished ninth, occured in the score.

---

* Judith Gauthier (1850–1917); French writer.
† Sir George Henschel (1850–1918); conductor and baritone.
‡ Heinrich Freiherr von Herzogenberg (1843–1900), Austrian composer; the narrator is the English composer, Dame Ethel Smyth.

Two windows of the little room that we* were in faced the lake [of Lucerne], a third, a side window, was open and overlooked the court, where a blacksmith was at work. Wagner listened to the ringing stroke of the hammer on the anvil. Suddenly he opened the piano and began to play the *motif* of Siegfried forging the sword. At the measure where the blade is struck he stopped, and it was the blacksmith who, striking the iron with an astonishing precision, unconsciously completed the theme.

'You see,' said the Master, 'how well I have calculated the time, and how exactly the blow falls.'

384

An orchestral violinist recalls Wagner's London rehearsals, May 1877
The immortal Wagner is coming to London when at the zenith of his glory. A large orchestra is engaged for a series of ten concerts.

On a particular day, the first rehearsal is held in the lower room of St James' Hall (now demolished), beginning at 10 o'clock, and expected to last till about 3 in the afternoon, the work selected being *Das Rheingold*, and Herr Wagner to take the baton, although Hans Richter is looked upon as the probable conductor of the festival. The orchestra numbers nearly two hundred members, containing something like fifty first and fifty second violins. The descriptive music of the Rhine, which opens the work, gives a deal for the second violins to do, and is exceedingly difficult to perform.

The members of the orchestra are all in their places, when Herr Wagner appears, descending some steps, followed by Herren Richter and Franke. By some strange accident, in descending Herr Wagner has his hat crushed through coming in contact with some projection, and this gives a most undignified, if not comical appearance, as, strutting into the room, he approaches the orchestra, assuming a very haughty air. Those in his immediate presence seem to look at him with too much awe to propose taking off his hat and restoring it to a proper shape. Amongst the English members of the orchestra the incident provokes unmistakable signs of merriment, as the individual players call each other's attention to the condition of the hat. But this is not shared by the German members of the orchestra, who view the English conduct in the matter as almost sacrilegious and most reprehensible. Herr Wagner, noticing this hilarity, and not divining the cause, glares at the perpetrators with surprise and disgust. However, a tap with the baton, and the

---

* The narrator is Judith Gauthier.

rehearsal begins. The second violins with their long, rolling *arpeggi* like waves, make the atmosphere quite damp with the water of the Rhine, and this is more strongly emphasized, as, after rehearsal, I see two or three members of the orchestra causing a small crowd to collect as they pretend to wring water from the tails of their frock coats. The work has not proceeded far before the conductor taps his desk violently, and shouts, '*Zürück*' (Again). A fresh start is made, but ere long another misunderstanding, this time through the conductor, who, carried away by the music, relinquished his baton, expecting this huge machine to follow a beat, given only with one of his fingers on his shirt-stud. This time, white with ill-concealed rage, the composer turns to Richter, and walking to and fro, repeats the word '*Schlecht*' [Bad] two or three times. This little performance is not lost on the English portion of the orchestra, who, seemingly unable any further to control their mirth, burst into an unmistakable chuckle, to the consternation of the German and other foreign elements.

Here Herr Deichman, leader of the second violins, springs to his feet, and passionately tapping the music stand with his bow, says in bad English. 'It is no tink to laugh.' So violently does he strike his desk, that the little piece of ivory at the top of his bow flies across the room and strikes Herr Wilhelmj in the face. This last occurrence draws perfect howls of laughter, in which a good number of the foreign section freely join. Herr Wagner is by this time in a frenzy of passion. But this is the opportunity for that perfect tactician, Herr Richter, who, taking the great composer by the arm, leads him away, speaking in a soothing, conciliatory tone. The orchestra in the meantime indulge in unrestrained jubilation. In a few moments the conductor returns, without Herr Wagner, and with the baton in his hand, says only two words, 'Now, boys!' Every man in that orchestra looks back to the eye which seems to read into their very souls, as, electrified by the wonderful personality of the great conductor, each one pushes his chair nearer to his music-stand, and a volume of sound, as if from one instrument, conveys to the ear the glorious effects in that wonderful conception of one of the greatest musical and dramatic geniuses of the century.

Now we know we are playing *Das Rheingold*, for we feel it illuminated by the soul of Richard Wagner.

385

The conductor Felix Mottl began his career as a composer and first called on Wagner to ask him to read his opera. Wagner agreed to look at the libretto. 'It's terrible,' he announced when Mottl called again.

'Shall I bring the score?' asked the young man. 'No, I don't understand anything about music,' said Wagner, 'you had better go to Liszt.'

386

In one respect opera at Bayreuth in the lifetime of the composer had a virtue which has gradually tended to disappear since his death. The composer did not permit his conductor to exaggerate slowness of pace. This was especially noticeable, when Hermann Levi directed *Parsifal* in 1883 (the year of the composer's death). Dannreuther,* who stayed at 'Wahnfried' for the rehearsals in 1882, told me that Wagner frequently called out from the stalls, '*Schneller! Schneller! Die Leute werden sich langweilen*' (Quicker, quicker, the people will be bored).

387

During [a performance of *The Ring*] my† friend Mihàlovich wanted to speak to one of the Wagner family, and for this purpose went up into a part of the theatre which was reserved to them. By chance, he entered a room in which he found the Master sitting alone before a writing table and musing. Seeing someone he knew, Wagner rose and said, almost in a tone of discouragement:

'No, that isn't what I imagined. It falls far short of what I intended.' Mihàlovich, thinking that the performance was responsible for his dissatisfaction, began to defend it. Wagner answered, 'It's nothing to do with that. I know the people are doing their best; but what I have written is not what lived in my imagination.'

388

One day, in talking with several persons who abused Wagner's music, Massenet turned to another individual and said calmly, 'Since you are just back from Bayreuth you will understand this: so overwhelming is the power of Wagner that after hearing one of his works one vows never to compose another thing. Afterward,' he added with a sigh, 'one forgets a little and begins again.'

389

He was usually very affable and joked a great deal with his children – his eldest daughter had just returned from boarding school. If one or

---

* Edward Dannreuther (1844–1905); Alsatian-born Wagnerite.
† The narrator is the Hungarian politician, Count Apponyi. Ödön von Mihàlovich (1842–1929); Hungarian composer, pupil of Hans von Bülow.

the other, however, appeared upon the scene, he would ask her, rather sarcastically, what was the word for lamp, cup, book, etc., in French, and tease her because the use of French in his own house was very disasteful to him. His antipathy to it went so far that, in 1876, he issued a formal prohibition of it in his house, and expressed the wish to his guests that only German might be spoken at 'Wahnfried'. During the year of the first rehearsals it was avoided, although, to Frau Cosima, French was her mother tongue, and to Liszt his language for conversation, and both being accustomed to speak it they did not like to use German.

390

Speaking of the eccentricities of Wagner, Liszt explained them to us in a few words, 'In the matter of glory Wagner had fasted almost continuously for thirty years. Now fasting weakens, and when glory at last did come to him, not drop by drop like to other mortals, but in a flood, he was not able to receive it with calmness.'

391

I* was strolling down Broadway with Seidl one day when we met Steinberg of the *New York Herald*. He said to Seidl, 'I think you have forgotten, *Herr Kapellmeister*, the sad occasion on which we met many years ago.'

'When was that?' Seidl asked.

'It was that windy morning when the body of Wagner reached Bayreuth.'

'Ah,' said Seidl, 'that was very sad', and they both shook their heads gravely.

Suddenly Steinberg, in a pert, biting manner, said, 'But on the level, *Herr Kapellmeister*, what did you think of the "Träuermarsch" as played by the town band?'

Seidl burst into shrieks of laughter. They had arranged a version of [Siegfried's Funeral March] to suit the local band. Having no cards to fit in the holders on the instruments they resorted to notepaper. When the cortège was formed and the band moved forth from the station, a gust of wind took the band parts and swirled them up into the heavens. Immediately, each bandsman was chasing his part.

---

* Francis Neilson, American conductor; Anton Seidl (1850–98); Hungarian conductor.

I* never visited Brahms' home in the Karlsgasse 4, without finding one or another of Wagner's scores lying open on the piano, and he once spontaneously told me, that he would have liked to have gone to Bayreuth if he had not feared that capital would be made out of his presence there.

I† recalled a visit to that grave, when Madame Wagner had not yet taken up the noble mission which now causes her to live and to take interest in life. It was in 1883. The sudden death of her beloved husband had almost destroyed her reason. She had cut off her beautiful long tresses (because Wagner had admired them) and placed them in his coffin; Liszt had come to Bayreuth, but she refused to see him; only the boy, Siegfried, because he was the favourite of his father, was suffered to approach her; and every day, in rain or sunshine, she would sit two hours or more beside that lonely grave. She allowed none other near it, and it was only by the connivance of an underling that I was finally able to visit the resting place of the greatest composer of his epoch.

❧

Sir William Sterndale BENNETT (1816–1875)

Precocious English composer, invited to Germany at the age of sixteen by Mendelssohn. On returning to England, however, his creative talent declined.

There was a composer called Bennett,
Whose career – it won't take long to pen it:
In his youth, like a lark,
Up to Mendelssohn's mark,
He rose; since when, silent is Bennett.

❧

---

*Sir Felix Semon (1849–1921); British laryngologist.
† Louis Charles Elson (1848–1920); American music historian.

Charles GOUNOD (1818–1893)

Composer of *Faust*, one of the most successful nineteenth-century operas.

395

I* remember meeting him once in the rue de la Chaussée d'Antin.

It was just after Gounod's *Faust* had been given at the Théâtre Lyrique, and, to my amazement, had met with rather doubtful success. The 'Soldiers' Chorus', the waltz especially, [was] very much applauded, praised, and bought, but what is really grand in the opera people seemed very slow to appreciate; and so I said to him, 'Is is not curious that people should take so to that "Soldiers' Chorus", which, you must really agree with me, is not exactly the most distinguished piece in the opera?' 'Ah, my dear E.,' he said, 'don't you see, operas are not born like men, head foremost; operas are born feet foremost.'

396

Gounod did not arrive in London until nearly seven o'clock on the night of [the British première of *Faust*] and all I† heard from him was that he wanted a good pit box in the centre of the house. With this, for reasons which I will at once explain, I had no difficulty whatever in providing him.

One afternoon, a few days before the day fixed for the production of the opera, I looked in upon Mr Nugent at the box-office and asked how the sale of places was going on.

'Very badly indeed,' he replied.

Only thirty pounds' worth of seats had been taken.

This presaged a dismal failure, and I had set my mind upon a brilliant success. I told Mr Nugent in the first place that I had decided to announce *Faust* for four nights in succession. He thought I must be mad, and assured me that one night's performance would be more than enough, and that to persist in offering to the public a work in which it took no interest was surely a deplorable mistake.

I told him that not only should the opera be played for four nights in succession, but that for the first three out of these four not one place was to be sold beyond those already disposed of. That there

---

* Louis Engel, British critic.
† James Henry Mapleson (1830–1901); English impresario

177

might be no mistake about the matter, I had all the remaining tickets for the three nights in question collected and put away in several carpet bags, which I took home with me that I might distribute them far and wide throughout the Metropolis and the Metropolitan suburbs. At last, after a prodigious outlay in envelopes, and above all postage stamps, nearly the whole mass of tickets for the three nights had been carefully given away.

I at the same time advertised in *The Times* that in consequence of a death in the family, two stalls secured for the first representation of *Faust* – the opera which was exciting so much interest that all places for the first three representations had been bought up – could be had at twenty-five shillings each, being but a small advance on the box-office prices. The stalls thus liberally offered were on sale at the shop of Mr Phillips, the jeweller, in Cockspur Street, and I told Mr Phillips that if he succeeded in selling them I would present him with three for the use of his own family. Mr Phillips sold them three times over, and a like success was achieved by Mr Baxter, the stationer, also in Cockspur Street.

Meanwhile demands had been made at the box-office for places, and when the would-be purchasers were told that 'everything had gone', they went away and repeated it to their friends, who, in their turn, came to see whether it was quite impossible to obtain seats for the first performance of an opera which was now beginning to be seriously talked about. As the day of production approached the inquiries became more and more numerous.

'If not for the first night, there must surely be places somewhere for the second,' was the cry.

Mr Nugent and his assistants had, however, but one answer, 'Everything had been sold, not only for the first night, but also for the two following ones.'

The first representation took place on 11 June 1863 and the work was received with applause, if not with enthusiasm. I had arranged for Gounod to be recalled; and he appeared several times on the stage. . . .

The second night *Faust* was received more warmly than on the first, and at each succeeding representation it gained additional favour, until after the third performance the paying public, burning with desire to see a work from which they had hitherto been debarred, filled the theatre night after night.

397

[Charles] Hallé had visited Paris to give a recital, which took place at the Salle Erard in the afternoon; and he had gone to a party in the evening where he met Gounod. Gounod seized him by both hands and thanked him profusely for the pleasure his recital had given him, instancing one passage in a Beethoven Sonata which he hummed, which proved to him that 'No one – no one, my dear friend, except you could have interpreted that passage in so masterly a way. Even with my eyes shut, I should have known that Hallé was playing.' Immediately after up came Madame Gounod, who began by apologizing for her and her husband's absence from the concert owing to a previous engagement.

398

My husband had no sooner left us than the black fury of Gounod burst out in all its violence [The narrator is Georgina Weldon (1837–1914), Gounod's landlady and mistress in London, where he took refuge from the Franco-Prussian War]. In vain I tried to calm him. I tried to take him in my arms and coax him; he pushed me brutally away, almost with blows. 'Don't touch me,' he shrieked, 'it is *you* who have incited your husband to insult me, to outrage me, to defy me. I will die,' he shrieked, 'and all shall perish with me!' I was terrified. The thought struck me that he meant to set the place on fire, but I followed him with my eyes, hoping that my looks might subdue him. He rushed like a madman to the cupboard where the orchestral score of *Polyeucte* was carefully stowed away. He seized hold of it, crying out, '*Polyeucte* first; *Polyeucte* shall burn!' It was his custom, at the least contrariety, to burn the manuscript he was composing. It was his best way of getting anything he wanted out of me. It made me wretched to see him destroy his work.

With strength lent me by the horror of despair, I threw myself on Gounod with all my weight; I knocked him down; I rolled on him; we tussled violently for possession of the treasure. I tore it from him; I flung it on the sofa; I suddenly picked myself off the floor; I sat upon it and screamed, 'You shall kill me first, but you shall not burn *Polyeucte*!' My strength then gave way, I burst into sobs, I stretched out my arms to him – 'My old man! My old treasure! why are you so wicked to me? Don't you see you are killing me? I suffer too much: I can bear it no longer. I do all that is possible to save you useless trouble – useless work. It is in vain.'

Gounod, to whom the fight had done good, had calmed down, thank God: the score of *Polyeucte* was saved.

⌖

Jacques OFFENBACH (1819–1880)
[b. Jacob Eberst]

Son of the cantor at a Cologne synagogue, he captivated and satirized Second Empire France in about a hundred operettas.

399

Offenbach's *Orphée aux Enfers*, given under the composer's own direction at the Gaiété [was] ... impudent music perhaps but fascinating too. Offenbach always seemed to reflect in his work the spirit of his 'cheeky' reply to a questioner who asked him if he was not born at Bonn. 'No, Beethoven was born at Bonn; I was born at Cologne.' [He sometimes signed himself 'O. de Cologne'.]

400

An ageing comic actor called at Offenbach's Paris apartment, near the Opéra, on the morning of 5 October 1880.

'How is he?' he asked the servant.

'M. Offenbach is dead; he died peacefully, without knowing anything about it,' was the reply.

'Ah,' sighed the actor, 'he will be surprised when he finds out.'

401

On 8 December 1881 fire broke out at the Ring Theatre in Vienna during a performance of *Tales of Hoffmann*; 384 members of the audience burned to death. Richard Wagner commented, 'When miners in a coal pit are buried alive, I am deeply moved and horrified, filled with disgust for a society which obtains its heating fuel by such means. But it leaves me cold and scarcely moved when members of an audience perish while listening to an Offenbach operetta, which contains not one iota of moral worth.'

☙❧

Clara SCHUMANN (1819–1896)

The foremost woman pianist in Europe, devoted wife of Schumann and beloved friend of Brahms.

402

At an evening party at the house of the family Preusser of Leipzig ... among the works performed was Schumann's quintet, in which Madame Schumann took the pianoforte part. In all this is, of course, nothing unusual; but the reader may perhaps think it sufficiently remarkable that the composer, to prevent his wife, a great pianist, from hurrying the *tempi*, beat time on her shoulders.

403

A large number of friends had been invited to hear Mendelssohn, Clara Schumann amongst them. He played Beethoven's great F minor Sonata ('Appassionata'); at the end of the Andante he let the final chord of the diminished seventh ring on for a long time, as if he wanted to impress it very forcibly on all present; then he quietly got up, and turning to Madame Schumann, said 'You must play the Finale.' She strongly protested. Meanwhile all were awaiting the issue with the utmost tension, the chord of the diminished seventh hovering over our* heads all the time like the sword of Damocles. I think it was chiefly the nervous, uncomfortable feeling of this unresolved discord which at last moved Madame Schumann to yield to Mendelssohn's entreaties.

cᴀᴗᴗ੭

Jenny LIND (1820–1887)

Swedish soprano who caused a sensation throughout Europe. In 1849 she retired from opera for religious reasons, singing thereafter only in oratorio and concerts, but touring the United States with the circus master, P. T. Barnum.

404

The old Duke of Wellington† [was] as badly bitten by the Jenny Lind mania as any schoolboy in the audience. In four months after her arrival in London the old warrior had become a captive to the enchantress. He courted the lady so ostentatiously as to rouse the jealousy of the Italian faction; his enthusiasm was rather awkward at times to the object of his homage. I have her own authority for saying that the Duke always arrived early and seated himself in his box on a level with the stage; directly he saw Jenny Lind he opened fire, 'Good evening, Miss Lind, how are you to-night? All right, I hope!' These well-meant utterances were a trifle out of place at the particular time, for the Lucia, Amina, or Daughter of the Regiment

---

* The narrator is Clara Louise Kellogg (1842–1916); American soprano.
† Arthur Wellesley, First Duke of Wellington (1769–1832).

was always so absorbed in her part as to be out of touch with all outside influence.

405

The London hangman went one night to the pit of Her Majesty's Theatre to hear Jenny Lind, and on seeing the Swedish nightingale, exclaimed, breathless with admiration and excitement, 'What a throat to scrag!'

406

Jenny Lind, who was staying with her connections the Brockhaus family, had received a deputation from the Directors of the Gewand-haus Concerts, in grateful acknowledgement of her services, followed by a torchlight serenade, as a tribute to the admired singer, in which so large a portion of the public were interested that the spacious courtyard of the Brockhaus mansion was entirely filled. Weber's Jubel Ouverture was performed, succeeded by various songs. Quite perplexed by this ovation, Jenny Lind asked Mendelssohn what she ought to do with these people? Mendelssohn advised her to go down and thank them herself in a few words, if she wished to cause real pleasure to the musicians. 'Very well,' said she after a pause, 'I will go to them, but you must accompany me, and speak for me.'

Mendelssohn instantly offered her his arm, and escorted her into the circle of performers, who greeted the appearance of their two favourites together with a burst of applause. Mendelssohn then spoke as follows: 'Gentleman! You must not think that I am Mendelssohn, for at this moment I am Jenny Lind, and as such I thank you from my heart for your delightful surprise. Having now, however, fulfilled my honourable commission, I am again transformed into the Leipzig Music-Director, and in that capacity I say, "Long live Jenny Lind!!"'

407

'At one of the concerts I conducted during the progress of Queen Victoria through Germany,' [Meyerbeer] continued, 'Lind and Viardot sang. Out of compliment to the conductor they chose my duet, 'La Mère Grand', to sing together. At the rehearsal nothing was said about a cadenza, and none was tried. I thought the ladies would arrange one among themselves. During the evening, I asked them what they intended doing, and they replied they had not yet determined. The moment arrived for the duet to be performed, and they had evidently settled nothing. We went into the orchestra, and the duet was sung with immense effect, being constantly interrupted by applause. At the pause for the cadenza I raised my *baton*, and waited to hear what the fair vocalists would do. Viardot led off with a series of the most elaborate 'runs' and *fioritura* I ever listened to – her cadenza was a composition of itself. I was in some anxiety as to what Lind would follow with, when to my amazement every note that Viardot had sung was repeated, without a fault or the slightest hesitation. This, to my mind, was a most remarkable instance of the complete perfection of vocal facility which both of these singers have attained. I cannot say who, in my opinion, is the greatest living vocalist.'

408

It was after Mendelssohn's remarkable exhibition of virtuosity [in the Beethoven G major piano concerto] and in my hearing, that the late Mr Bartholomew* congratulated him on his fine performance, to which Mendelssohn replied, 'I am glad that I did well, as there were two ladies present I particularly wished to please; one was the Queen, and the other Jenny Lind.'

༺⌇Ⱥⱥ⌇༻

Henri VIEUXTEMPS (1820–1881)

Belgian violinist and composer, his six concertos are still performed as showpieces.

409

Leopold Auer, the eminent violinist, visited Vieuxtemps when a student
We were received very cordially by Vieuxtemps himself, and very coldly by his wife, who played the accompaniments at his concerts. After a few polite words regarding my studies had been exchanged, I was permitted to take out my violin – a poor enough instrument – and play. Mme Vieuxtemps sat down at the piano looking decidedly bored. I myself, nervous by nature trembling with emotion, began to play the 'Fantaisie Caprice'. I do not recall how I played it, but it seems to me that I put my whole soul into every tone, though poorly

---

* William Bartholomew (1793–1867); English translator of most of Mendelssohn's vocal works.

supported by an insufficiently developed technique. Vieuxtemps encouraged me with an amiable smile. Then, at the very moment when I was in the midst of a cantabile phrase which I was playing all too sentimentally, Mme Vieuxtemps leaped from the piano stool, and began to walk precipitately around the room. She bent down to the ground, looked here, looked there, beneath the furniture, under the bureau and the piano, as though she were hunting for something she had lost and could not find in spite of all the trouble she took. Brusquely interrupted by her strange action, I stood with wide-open mouth, with no suspicion of what all this might mean. I felt as though I had been cast down from illuminated heights by a fiery explosion rising from the abyss. Vieuxtemps, himself astonished, followed his wife's progress about the room with a surprised air, and asked her what she was looking for so nervously under the furniture. 'One or more cats must be hidden in this room,' said she, 'miaowing in every key!' She was alluding to my over-sentimental glissando in the cantabile phrase. I was so overcome by the shock that I lost consciousness, and my father was obliged to hold me in his arms lest I fall. Vieuxtemps turned the whole affair into a joke, patted me on the cheek, and consoled me by saying that later on everything would go better. I was then no more than fourteen.

❦

César FRANCK (1822–1890)

Organist and composer. Born in Liège, the son of a banker, his much-played D minor symphony, violin sonata and string quartet all appeared in the four years before his death.

410

Félicité Franck turned on her husband's pupils one day and blamed them, not without reason, for the hostility he encountered and for the advanced style of his later works. 'You don't have to tell me that Franck has once written some beautiful works,' she cried. 'I am a musician myself. . . . But that quintet! Ugh!'

411

If no one turned up for his class at the Paris Conservatoire, he would open the door of Massenet's classroom and ask gently, 'Isn't there anyone for me?' Alternatively he would say, 'Perhaps one of you gentlemen would come to my room for a minute or two to keep me company?'

After performing the Franck quartet in November 1916 in the rue de Tournon, the musicians were approached by a pale, moustachioed stranger wearing a fur coat, who asked if they would play the piece for him privately. Some days later, at midnight, the stranger arrived by taxi to summon the violist from his bed. They drove together to rouse his colleagues and proceeded to an apartment at 102 boulevard Haussmann. There, the organizer of the concert, Marcel Proust, stretched out on his bed amid the scattered manuscript pages of *À la recherche du temps perdu* and luxuriated in the music. When it was over, he served the players with fried potatoes and champagne, then asked them to do him 'the immense kindness' of playing the work again. He paid them well. On leaving, they found four taxis waiting for them in the blacked-out street.

The quartet, led by Gaston Poulet, subsequently played many times during the War for Proust. For a while he contemplated taking the group with him to Venice to play music as he watched dawn break over the Grand Canal. The Franck quartet with which they had first captured his imagination formed the basis for the Vinteuil septet in his literary masterpiece.

ᴄᴀᴀᴄᴐ

Anton BRUCKNER (1824–1896)

Austrian symphonist whose rural origins, religious certainties and admiration of Wagner were derided by Viennese sophisticates.

413

Gustav Mahler recalls
After an illness, Bruckner was ordered by his doctor to take a daily hip-bath. Loath to waste time, he would take music paper and compose while in the tub. While absorbed in his work one day, the mother of Rudolf Krzyanowski, one of his pupils, knocked at the door. 'Come in!' called Bruckner. Imagine her consternation on entering the apartment to see Bruckner's portly person in the bathtub naked as the good Lord had fashioned him. As she stood there transfixed, Bruckner politely got up and walked over, dripping, to greet her. Only her shriek and hasty exit made the poor man aware of his condition. And this had to happen to Bruckner, who blushed like a schoolboy if he so much as looked at a woman.

The violinist Fritz Kreisler was a pupil of Bruckner's

Bruckner had a chubby, fat pug dog named Mops. He would leave us with Mops munching our sandwiches while he himself hastened off to luncheon. We decided we'd play a joke on our teacher which would flatter him. So while the Meister was away, we'd play a motif by Wagner, and as we did so, would slap Mops and chase him. Next we'd start Bruckner's *Te Deum*, and while this music was in progress, would give Mops something to eat. He soon showed a convincing preference for the *Te Deum*! When we thought we had trained him sufficiently so that he would automatically run away when Wagner was played and joyfully approach us at the sound of a Bruckner strain, we deemed the moment appropriate for our prank.

'Meister Bruckner,' we said one day as he returned from lunch, 'we know that you are devoted to Wagner, but to our way of thinking he cannot compare with you. Why, even a dog would know that you are a greater composer than Wagner.'

Our guileless teacher blushed. He thought we were serious. He reproved us, paid tribute to Wagner as unquestionably the greatest contemporary, but was nevertheless filled with enough curiosity to ask what we meant by claiming even a dog could tell the difference.

This was the moment we had waited for. We played a Wagner motif. A howling, scared Mops stole out of the room. We started in on Bruckner's *Te Deum*. A happy canine returned, wagging his tail and pawing expectantly at our sleeves. Bruckner was touched.

415

Eduard Hanslick spearheaded the critical offensive against Bruckner with such thunderous pejoratives as *traumverwirrten Katzenjammerstil* (nightmarish hangover style). Bruckner acknowledged the critic's enmity and feared him deeply. When the Emperor Franz Joseph, bestowing a decoration on the composer, asked if there were any other favour he might show him, Bruckner replied, 'Perhaps Your Majesty would be so gracious as to ask Mr Hanslick not to write such bad criticisms of my symphonies?'

416

Invited by Hans Richter to conduct the Vienna Philharmonic Orchestra in one of his symphonies, Bruckner stood beaming but motionless on the conductor's platform at rehearsal. When after several minutes he had still failed to lift the baton, the orchestra's leader, Arnold Rosé*, prompted him gently, 'We are quite ready,

Herr Bruckner,' he urged, 'do begin'. 'Oh no,' replied Bruckner, 'after *you*, gentlemen!'

417

Rehearsing a Bruckner symphony in the composer's presence, Richter called down from the podium, 'F, or F sharp?' Leaping to his feet, his face suffused with pleasure, Bruckner shouted, 'Whichever you like, *Herr Kapellmeister*, go on, go on!'

418

His *Te Deum* triumphed in Berlin in 1891. 'Imagine,' he told his pupils, 'one of the honourable critics wrote that I was a second Beethoven. Good Lord, how can anyone say such a thing?' And he crossed himself quickly to expunge the possibility of sin.

419

When Mahler called upon him during his last illness, Bruckner talked about his Ninth, and final, Symphony. 'I must at least finish' [it], he fretted, 'or I'll cut a poor figure when I appear soon before the good Lord and he says, "Well, my boy, why did I give you so much talent if not to sing to my honour and glory? You have not done nearly enough with it!"'

⁂

Eduard HANSLICK (1825–1904)

Powerful and feared music critic of the *Neue Freie Presse* of Vienna, 1864–95, Hanslick was the scourge of Wagner – who caricatured him as Beckmesser in *Die Meistersinger* – and foremost advocate of Brahms.

420

Wagner, in his memoirs
I had to read *Die Meistersinger* aloud to the Standhartner family, as I had done everywhere else. As Dr Hanslick was now supposed to be well disposed towards me, it was considered the right thing to invite him too. We noticed that as the reading proceeded the dangerous critic became more and more pale and depressed, and it was remarked by everyone that it was impossible to persuade him to stay on at the close, but that he took his leave there and then in an

---

* (1863–1946); led the VPO for fifty-seven years; brother-in-law of Gustav Mahler.

unmistakably vexed manner. My friends all agreed in thinking that Hanslick looked on the whole libretto as a lampoon aimed at himself, and had felt an invitation to the reading to be an insult. And undoubtedly the critic's attitude towards me underwent a very remarkable change from that evening. He became uncompromisingly hostile.

421

The Prelude to *Tristan and Isolde* [wrote Hanslick] reminds me of the old Italian painting of a martyr whose intestines are slowly unwound from his body on a reel.

⌘

Johann STRAUSS [II] (1825–1899)

'The Waltz King', formed a rival orchestra to his father's when aged nineteen, then merged both bands when Strauss senior died, enlisting his brothers Josef and Eduard as co-conductors.

422

Brahms never missed one of the afternoon concerts by Johann Strauss. It is said that Mme Strauss once asked Brahms for an autographed photo of himself. In the course of a few days he presented her with a picture on which he had jotted down the first measure of The Beautiful Blue Danube, beneath which he had written his signature, preceded by the exclamation, 'Alas, *not* by Johannes Brahms!'

423

When a mere stripling of nineteen, he contrived to get together a scratch orchestra of young players and started from Vienna upon a concert-tour through Transylvania and Roumania. The slender fund with which this joyous company set out on its wild expedition was soon exhausted, and at Pancsova, a small town in the Lower Banat, Strauss and his merry men found themselves one fine morning without a kreuzer in their collective pockets. What was to be done? The band performed a serenade under the mayor's bedroom windows, and its leader succeeded in borrowing from that functionary a sum sufficient to purchase the immediate necessaries of life, but only on condition that the loan should be repaid out of the proceeds of certain concerts to be given in Pancsova itself. To these concerts, however, the Pancsova public so steadfastly refrained from coming, that the Strauss orchestra fell into grave embarrass-

188

ment, culminating in the seizure of its instruments, at the instance of hard-hearted creditors, by the myrmidons of the law, one evening in the middle of a performance at the Town Hall. Long and animated negotiations ensued between Strauss and the local authorities, resulting in the restitution of the instruments, with permission to their owners to prosecute their professional tour – in the charge, however, of the Pancsova chief constable, who was to accompany them at their costs and charges until their debts in the town should be discharged to the last penny.

Seated on the box of the van in which their instruments, music-stands, etc., were packed, this official stuck to them for several weeks with unappeasable appetite and insatiable thirst. With him they visited and performed at Semlin, Arad, Temesvar, Gross-wardein, Hermannstadt and Kronstadt, *en route* for Bucharest, paying instalments into his hands whenever their receipts exceeded their expenses. At last, on their arrival in the Transylvanian *chef-lieu*, he informed them that, as far as the town of Pancsova was concerned, their liabilities were discharged, and took leave of them with the assurance that he had enjoyed his trip amazingly.

By this time the members of the Strauss orchestra were in an alarmingly dilapidated condition, ragged, dirty, unshaven and way-worn, presenting the outward and visible aspect of incorrigible 'rogues and vagabonds'. No Kronstadt inn-keeper would accord them food and shelter or allow them to perform within his premises, the view taken of them being that they were highwaymen disguised as wandering musicians. Consequently, although it was the depth of winter, they and their instruments were crammed into an open haywaggon and conveyed across the Carpathians to the Wallachian frontier under a strong military escort. At the close of this remark-able episode in their tour, the members of the band mutinied against their leader, and vowed they would go no further. Upon this Strauss harangued them in the following terms: 'Comrades! We must see this thing out together. One man is as good as another, if not better. Let our watchword be "One for all and all for one". We will give a farewell performance in the nearest town, divide the proceeds, and then get back to Vienna the best way we can!' To this proposal they all agreed; but a fresh difficulty arose, the offspring of their fears (in which Strauss himself largely participated) of being attacked by brigands whilst working their way down the Roumanian slopes of the Carpathian pass, at that time infested by more than one predatory band of blood-chilling reputation. It was resolved to purchase weapons at the sacrifice of two violins, in exchange for which they managed to obtain a few old rusty pistols, but no ammunition. Thse were distributed amongst them by Strauss, who, however, kept three for himself, sticking them in his belt, where they imparted to him a highly impressive air of robber-chieftainship. His trombone-player, one Seidl, a man of exceptional thew and sinew, scornfully rejected the pistol tendered to him, remarking 'he would back himself to settle any ten bandits of the whole neighbourhood with his trombone.'

So formidable was the appearance of the Strauss cohort, numbering thirty-four ferocious-looking musicians, that the peasants of the villages on their road fled or hid themselves as they approached, taking them for brigands of the deepest dye; and, between Kympena and Ploesti, a real robber-band which chanced to encounter them took to its heels, panic-stricken, in the full belief that a rival association had come down the mountain-side in overwhelming force for the purpose of putting an end to local enterprise.

Eventually Strauss and his formidable cohort reached Bucharest in safety, where for some time they did extremely well, from a pecuniary point of view. Their conductor's amatory proclivities, however, brought the tour to a premature and somewhat tragical conclusion. A Wallachian lady of rank, who had conceived an irresistible passion for the handsome young Viennese, made a tender appointment with him at the house of her washerwoman, whither, however, she was followed by her husband, an energetic and vindictive Boyar. This much-wronged personage bought half-dozen of his man-servants with him, to whose unmerciful hands he committed the luckless musician, whilst he himself beat his wife almost to death with a heavy dog-whip.

424

Massenet, asked define the difference between Strauss and Brahms, said, '*Brahms est l'âme* [spirit] *de Vienne, Strauss en est le parfum.*'

❧

Stephen Collins FOSTER (1826–1864)

American composer whose ballads ('Oh, Susanna': 'My Old Kentucky Home'; etc.), have attained the status of folk songs.

425

Morrison Foster, the composer's brother
One day in 1851, Stephen came into my office, on the bank of the Monongahela, Pittsburgh, and said to me, 'What is a good name of

two syllables for a Southern river? . . .' I asked him how Yazoo would do. 'Oh,' said he, 'that has been used before.' I then suggested Pedee. 'Oh pshaw,' he replied, 'I won't have that.' I then took down an atlas from the top of my desk and opened the map of the United States. We both looked over it and my finger stopped at the 'Swanee', a little river in Florida emptying into the Gulf of Mexico. 'That's it, that's it exactly,' exclaimed he delighted, as he wrote the name down; and the song was finished, commencing 'Way Down Upon de Swanee Ribber.' He left the office, as was his custom, abruptly, without saying another word, and I resumed my work.

━━━━━

Louis Moreau GOTTSCHALK (1829–1869)

America's first world-famous musician. Born in New Orleans of Anglo-Jewish and French-Creole parentage, Gottschalk became an itinerant pianist and composer, touring Europe and the Americas.

426

Gottschalk writes

California, 1865

I am wanting a pianist. I had executed on fourteen pianos the March of *Tannhäuser* arranged by myself. Its success had been so great that I had to announce another concert on fourteen pianos. On the eve of the concert one of my pianists fell sick. What am I to do? Put off the concert? Never! . . .

Announce only thirteen pianos. Another error, still more dangerous. The public wish to hear fourteen pianos, and if you give it one less it will think itself robbed. . . .

The difficulty was becoming insurmountable. San Francisco, although filled with all the corruption and with all the plagues arising from civilization, did not then possess but thirteen first-class pianoforte players. The proprietor of the hall, seeing my embarrassment, offered to speak to his son, an amateur pianist, he said, of the first class, who played Thalberg, Liszt, and Gottschalk without difficulty, and for whom it would be only play to take the part that was wanted for the March of *Tannhäuser*. . . .

The concert was to take place in the evening. I suggested that a rehearsal would be necessary. The son, who in the interval had been introduced to me, expressed surprise, and said it was useless. The part was very easy; he played the fantasies of Liszt. . . .

He then placed himself at the piano, and like all amateurs, after having executed a noisy flourish, attacked with the boldness of innocence the piece of *Tannhäuser*. At the end of two bars, my mind was made up. . . .

I thought seriously of putting off the concert, under the pretence of indisposition, when my tuner, a man of resources, said to me, 'Sir, if this young man plays, trouble is inevitable with the other pianos; it is absolutely necessary to prevent his being heard, and the only way to do it is this' – and at the same moment he pushed a *crochet* in the piano I designed for the amateur, a vertical piano, took out the whole of the interior mechanism, and, looking triumphantly at me, added: 'The keyboard remains, but I assure you that there will be no more false notes.' The mode was excellent.

The evening came. The hall was full. My amateur, in white cravat and evening dress, was showing himself in the hall. His friends awaited the moment of his entrance with impatience. He requested me to give him a piano near the footlights in full view (for it must be stated that amateurs, who should be less familiarized with the public, have an impassibility and *sang froid* which we never acquire – again innocence).

I placed his dumb piano in the middle of the stage, close to the prompter.

Before going on the stage, I made my thirteen acolytes take notice, that, in order to produce the greatest effect, it was indispensable not to make any preludes, that thus the public might be more surprised on hearing all at once the fourteen pianos attack the flourish of trumpets with which the March in *Tannhäuser* commences.

One, two, three – we begin. It goes on marvellously. In the midst of the piece I looked at my amateur: he was superb; he was sweating great drops; he was throwing his eyes carelessly on the audience, and performed with miraculous ease the passages apparently the most difficult. His friends were in raptures. They applauded to excess. Some enthusiasts even cried out, 'Hurrah for —!' (the amateur's name). 'Encore!' 'Encore!!' We must repeat the piece. But at the moment of commencing the amateur forgot my recommendation not to prelude, and could not resist the temptation to play a little chromatic scale. I see him now! The stupor which was printed on his countenance is inexpressible. He recommenced his scale. Nothing. . . .

'Pst! pst!!' said he with a wild air, but I had seen the danger, and without loss of time, I had given the signal and the March was recommenced. My young man, to save appearances before the audience, made the pantomine of the passages, but his countenance, which I saw from below, was worth painting, it was a mixture of discouragement and of spite. The fury with which he struck the poor instrument, which could do nothing, was very funny.

'That was very well done, gentlemen,' I said, on entering into the artists' room, 'but the effect was less than the first time.'

427

An imaginative Spanish girl, who ... was too ill to attend his concerts, had a passionate desire to hear him play, and pined away in the fretfulness of ungratified desire. Her family ... made the circumstances known to the artist. Gottschalk did not hesitate a moment, but ordered his piano to be conveyed to the humble abode of the patient. Here by her bedside he played for hours to the enraptured girl, and the strain of emotion was so great that her life ebbed away before he had finished the final chords.

428

Gottschalk writes
I wish to speak of my death. This sad event took place at Santiago three months ago. I was carried off in three days by a frightful attack of black vomit; it is the newspaper of *Savana la grande* who tells it; but the *Revue de Villa Clara*, without doubt better informed, makes me succumb to an aneurism of the heart, which I much prefer, the aneurism being much more poetical than the vomit. I have written to these gentlemen, assuring them that I am still alive, and requesting them to publish my letter when it reaches them. The newspaper *Savana la grande* has already been at the expense of a lithograph of the '*deceased and ever to be regretted Gottschalk*'.

✧✦✧

Anton RUBINSTEIN (1829–1894)

Russian pianist and composer. He taught Tchaikovsky and founded St Petersburg Conservatory (1862); his brother, Nikolay, founded the Moscow Conservatory.

429

At the last rehearsal of one of [his operas in Hamburg] Rubinstein was so well pleased with the work of the orchestra that he turned to them and said, 'Gentlemen, if my opera is a success you must all come to my hotel after the performance for a champagne supper.' Unfortunately, the opera was a decided frost and the audience so undemonstrative that Rubinstein, in absolute disgust, laid down the stick after the second act, and, bidding the local conductor finish the opera, returned dejectedly to his hotel and went to bed. At eleven o'clock there was a knock at his door. 'Who is it?' he shouted in great irritation. 'It is I, Herr Rubinstein, the double-bass player from the opera orchestra.' 'What do you want?' 'I have come for the champagne supper.' 'What nonsense!' raged Rubinstein. 'The opera was a ghastly failure.' 'Well, Herr Rubinstein,' answered the thirsty and undaunted double-bass player, '*I* liked it!'

430

Sarasate and Rubinstein were playing whist at a hotel in Leipzig when people began returning from the first performance of a new symphony. 'What was it like?' demanded Rubinstein. 'Oh, very musical,' said a concertgoer. 'Well it's damned then,' swore Rubinstein, banging his fist on the table. 'When Germans say a work is "musical", it is bound to be boring.'

431

Rubinstein entertained us with a recital of his experiences in the United States, whence he had just returned after a tour of two hundred and fifteen concerts in eight months – and there were no Sunday concerts then – and where once, somewhere out in the wild, woolly West, a man, about an hour before the concert, had thrust his head into Rubinstein's room with the words, 'Don't you think, boss, it's about time to have your face blacked?'

432

Anton did not drink. He had another passion, which in the course of years became a vice – the fair sex. . . .

He once told me* in confidence: 'If I had to educate and provide for all my children, the fortune of two Rothschilds would scarcely suffice.'

433

Lilli Lehmann, the soprano, recalls
A few months before his death we met each other by chance, at the Nordwest station at Vienna, and we had been on the same train without knowing it. From fear of annoying him, I meant to pass by without recognition, but I had not the heart to do it. Walking up to him courageously, I greeted him cordially. It took some time for him to recognize me; he had trouble with his eyes, and now could see

---

* Louise Héritte-Viardot (1841–1918); contralto.

only very poorly. Then his face lighted up, he stroked my hair tenderly, and said in his dear, veiled voice almost sadly, slowly, and gently as though he did not want to hurt me, 'Lilli, you have grown quite grey.' 'I have been so for a long time! We have not seen each other for such a while! But you have become so, too, dear friend!' 'Yes, I, of course; but *you*, my Noëmi!'

⌘

Hans von BÜLOW (1830–1894)

Virtuoso conductor and pianist, acolyte to Wagner, then standard-bearer to Brahms. His wife, Cosima, left him for Wagner.

434

Bülow's most famous exploit in Italy had been with a drummer at a rehearsal of the Ninth Symphony of Beethoven. The unfortunate man could not get the rhythm of the solo in the Scherzo.

After various objurgations –

Bülow: 'What is your instrument called?'

Drummer: 'Tympani.'

Bülow: 'There you have it. Tȳmpănī! Tȳmpănī!'

The drummer grasps the rhythm and triumphantly smacks his drums as loud as possible.

Bülow: '*Forte!*'

The drummer puts more force into it.

Bülow: 'FORTE!!'

The drummer nearly bursts the vellum.

Bülow: 'FORTE!!! Not *fortissimo!*'

435

After a brilliant performance of Beethoven's Ninth at Hamburg, Bülow imperiously silenced the applause. 'Like you, I am over-whelmed,' he announced. 'I am also touched by your delight in this work of genius. In accordance with your sincere wishes, I shall perform it again here and now.' When some of the audience made to leave, he requested, with exquisite courtesy, that they resume their seats. He had, he explained, ordered the exits to be locked.

436

It so happened that two ladies were making their way to their seats at the very moment he finished the introduction of the first movement of Beethoven's Sonata Pathétique. This so irritated him that he purposely commenced the *allegro* at such an absurdly slow pace as to make the quavers in the bass correspond exactly to the time of the ladies' footsteps. As may be imagined, they felt on thorns whilst walking to their places, and hurried on as fast as they possibly could, whilst Von Bülow accelerated his *tempo* in sympathy with their increasing pace. It was only when they had seated themselves that he took the proper speed of the *allegro*.

437

Sir Alexander Mackenzie* went one day with Bülow to hear a certain piece which its composer had expressed an ardent desire to play to the great pianist. Bülow listened, turned pale, then turned green – the music was revoltingly commonplace – and at last rushed out into the street and vomited on the pavement.

438

It was Bülow who invented the 'three B's' of music by means of a German witticism: *Mein musikalisches Glaubenbekenntniss steht in Es dur, mit drei B-en in der Vorzeichnung: Bach, Beethoven, und Brahms!* [My musical credo is in the key of E flat major whose key signature has three flats (♭ signs): Bach, Beethoven and Brahms!]

439

[Leschetizky] told of a young lady who asked Moszkowski† to write something in her birthday-book. He turned over the leaves and found a page upon which Hans von Bülow had written: '*Bach, Beethoven, Brahms, et tous les autres sont des crétins* [and all the others are cretins].' Moszkowski wrote underneath: '*Mendelssohn, Meyerbeer, Moszkowski, et tous les autres sont des Chrétiens* [and all the others are Christians].'

440

A lady asked her host to introduce her to the great man, and began her conversation with the question, '*Oh! Monsieur von Bülow, vous connaissez Monsieur Wagner, n'est ce pas* [you know Mr Wagner don't you?]?'

Bülow made a low bow and answered without a sign of surprise, '*Mais oui, Madame, c'est le mari de ma femme* [But of course, Madam, he's my wife's husband].'

❧

---

* (1847–1935); Scottish composer.
† Moritz Moszkowski (1854–1925); Polish-German pianist.

Theodor LESCHETIZKY (1830–1915)

Celebrated piano teacher in Vienna, numbering among his many pupils Paderewski, Schnabel, Ossip Gabrilowitsch and Mark Hambourg.

441

Upon entering the music room one morning, he found two ladies sitting there, dressed in deep black, as solemn as crows. When he came in, neither rose nor spoke. Leschetizky waited. At no word or sign from them, he waved his hand and exclaimed, '*Auf!*' [Up!] They rose to their feet, but still failed to express themselves in any way. Leschetizky then pointed to the piano. '*Spiel!*'[Play!] he commanded. One of them played, whereupon Leschetizky pointed to the door. '*Weg!*' [Out!] he said. With three words the visitors were received, heard, and dismissed. Needless to say, they were never seen again.

442

He said to me repeatedly throughout the years [recalled Artur Schnabel], 'You will never be a pianist. You are a musician.'

443

He never charged me anything for the lessons – never [wrote Paderewski]. But from the very first moment he said I could have become a great pianist if only I had begun to study earlier. This was heartbreaking.

444

The Professor had occasion to play to me* the Sonnambula Fantasia of Thalberg by heart which he said he had not played for fifty years. When he had finished he turned to me and said:

'What do you think of it?'

'Splendid!' said I, but boy-like I could not refrain from remarking, 'but you made a few mistakes.' To my horror he turned on me furiously and shouted:

'Impudent boy, did you say mistakes! You will please remember that as long as you remain my pupil, for you I must always be right, I cannot make any mistakes!'

〜✦〜

---

* Mark Hambourg (1879–1960); British pianist.

197

Joseph JOACHIM (1831–1907)

Influential Hungarian-Jewish violinist; protégé of Mendelssohn and friend of Liszt and the Schumanns, to whom he introduced his young discovery, Brahms.

445

Joachim had very amiably volunteered to play, and there happened to be no violin music handy except one set of the Beethoven Pianoforte and Violin Sonatas (that dedicated to Salieri), which was brought by our* hostess to the great virtuoso with the request that he would ask Brahms – she had not the courage to do so – to take the pianoforte part. Turning towards Brahms, Joachim smilingly asked, 'Dear master, will you vouchsafe to play this with me for the amusement of our friends here?' 'I am not an accompanist,' growled Brahms, and abruptly turning his back upon Joachim, strode angrily off into another room. The Hungarian violinist merely shrugged his shoulders, and looked around for a volunteer pianist. . . . To a look of inquiry I was unable to suppress, Joachim replied, 'It is his way when he is vexed; he means nothing by it.'

446

It was no doubt the great length of his public career which accounted for the absurd mistake of a Dutchman, who said to him, 'Allow me, sir, to congratulate you on your performance, which I thought very fine, but also to remind you that I had the privilege many years ago of hearing your father, the *great* Joachim.' Joachim replied that that must have been himself, for his father was a wool merchant and had never had a violin in his hand. This information, however, proved unavailing, and the admirer of the elder Joachim left the room muttering, 'It's all wrong; it *was* his father I heard!'

⌘

---

* The narrator here is W. Beatty Kingston, a British journalist.

Alexander BORODIN (1833–1887)

Russian nationalist composer, physician and professor of chemistry

447

He was . . . not at all suited to medical practice.

Once, . . . the coachman of some high-ranking official was brought into the hospital, and Borodin had to remove a bone that was choking him. While he was operating, the rusty instrument he was using broke in the patient's throat. But the young surgeon kept his presence of mind, and after a few unsuccessful attempts, removed the broken fragment of metal and the bone at the same time. Borodin tells how 'the coachman went down on his knees before me, and it was as much as I could do to restrain myself from doing likewise. Just think what might have happened if the broken piece of forceps had stuck in his throat! You can bet that I would have been court-martialled and ended up in Siberia.'

448

In his first year as house-surgeon at the hospital [writes D. S. Alexandrov], my brother happened to be on duty one day when they brought in six serfs belonging to Colonel V . . . who had flogged them for locking him in the stables because of the cruel way he treated them. Borodin had the job of pulling out the splinters from their backs. He fainted three times at the sight of the skin hanging in tatters from their backs. In the case of two of them, their bones were visible.

449

Turgenev was invited in May 1874 to hear Borodin, Cui, Mussorgsky and Rimsky-Korsakov play their music. First, Rubinstein played pieces by Beethoven, Chopin and Schumann, departing well before the Russian music was to start. Just as they were about to begin, Turgenev suffered a severe attack of arthritis. Borodin, the only doctor in the house, examined him and was obliged to order that he be taken straight home. Thus the great writer never got to hear the new music of Russian nationalism.

450

Borodin, letter to his wife
As I told Liszt I was only a Sunday musician, he answered me with ready wit, 'But Sunday is always a feast day, and you have every right to officiate.'

Borodin reports

After tea our hostess led the way to the piano in the drawing-room and gave Liszt one of his own rhapsodies, asking him to show us how such and such passages should be played.

It was a feminine ruse, but an innocent deception; Liszt began to laugh.

'You want me to play it,' he said; 'very well, but first I want to play Monsieur Borodin's symphony with the composer. Do you play treble or bass?' he asked me.

I refused absolutely.

At last I persuaded the Baroness [Olga von Meyendorff] to sit down to the piano. She consented to play the andante only. Liszt played the bass. How interesting to me was this performance to which I was the sole listener!

But Liszt was not satisfied.

'The Baroness is very kind,' he said, 'but I want to play with you. It is impossible that you cannot play your own symphony. You have arranged it so perfectly that I cannot believe that. Sit down there.' And without another word he took me by the hand and made me sit down to the bass, he himself taking the treble. I wished to protest.

'Play,' said the Baroness, 'or Liszt will be annoyed with you. I know him.'

I wanted to recommence the andante that was open before me, but Liszt turned over the pages and we attacked the finale, then the scherzo and the first movement. Thus we played the whole symphony with all the repeats. Liszt would not let me rest; after every movement he turned the pages, saying:

'Let us go on.'

When I made mistakes, or omitted anything, Liszt would say:

'Why did you not do that; it is so fine?' When we had finished he repeated several passages, growing enthusiastic over their novelty and the freshness of the ideas. He subjected my symphony to a most discriminating criticism; according to him, the andante is a perfect masterpiece.

'As to form,' he said, 'there is nothing superfluous; all is fine.'

The day before Borodin died, his son-in-law and colleague, A. P. Dianin, was sitting in the laboratory and heard him in the apartment playing music in a totally new style. There were tears in the composer's eyes when he came into the lab. 'Well Sashenka,' he declared, 'I know that some things I have written are not bad. But this finale!. . . What a finale!. . .' Unhappily, he did not manage to write down a single note of it.

453

Borodin's death was almost tragic. It was the last day of the carnival of 1887, and he had invited a number of friends to an evening party at his house. He was busy entertaining them with his usual sunny hospitality, and being in high spirits he did not wait to be asked to take part in the dancing. He also sang and played over to his guests fragments of the third symphony on the pianoforte. Then, just as he had entered on an animated conversation, he was suddenly seen to turn pale, stagger, and fall backwards before anybody had time to prevent him. They hurriedly gathered round him, picked him up . . . and he was dead.

◦◦◦

Johannes BRAHMS (1833–1897)

German symphonist who, like Beethoven, migrated to Vienna. His earliest musical activity was playing piano in squalid Hamburg taverns, until Joachim and Schumann recognized his ability.

454

On one evening early in June 1853, Liszt sent us* word to come up to the Altenburg next morning, as he expected a visit from a young man who was said to have great talent as a pianist and composer, and whose name was Johannes Brahms. . . .

We found Brahms and [Eduard] Reményi† already in the reception-room . . . I strolled over to a table on which were lying some manuscripts of music. They were several of Brahms' yet unpublished compositions, and I began turning over the leaves of the uppermost in the pile. It was the piano solo Op. 4, Scherzo, E Flat Minor, and, as I remember, the writing was so illegible that I thought to myself that if I had occasion to study it I should be obliged first to

---

* The narrator is William Mason (1829–1908); American pianist.
† (1830–98); widely travelled Hungarian violinist who toured in 1852 with Brahms as his accompanist.

make a copy of it. Finally Liszt came down, and after some general conversation he turned to Brahms and said: 'We are interested to hear some of your compositions whenever you are ready and feel inclined to play them.' Brahms, who was evidently very nervous, protested that it was quite impossible for him to play while in such a disconcerted state. . . .

Liszt, seeing that no progress was being made, went over to the table, and taking up the first piece at hand, the illegible scherzo, and saying, 'Well, I shall have to play,' placed the manuscript on the piano-desk. . . .

He read it off in such a marvellous way – at the same time carrying on a running accompaniment of audible criticism of the music – that Brahms was amazed and delighted. . . . A little later some one asked Liszt to play his own sonata, a work which was quite recent at that time, and of which he was very fond. Without hesitation, he sat down and began playing. As he progressed he came to a very expressive part of the sonata, which he always imbued with extreme pathos, and in which he looked for the especial interest and sympathy of his listeners. Casting a glance at Brahms, he found that the latter was dozing in his chair.

455

The door [to the tavern] opened again, admitting a rush of snow and three more patrons. In contrast to the other newcomers, these last were eminently more suited to the environment, the feminine member of the trio being a well-known street-walker and inhabitant of this old and dark section of the city. Her escorts were gigolos and all were very drunk. They seated themselves at a table next to Brahms and his friends and ordered drinks – as if they had not already drunk enough – all of them. Suddenly above the talking, the 'lady' called over to Brahms: 'Professor, play us some dance music. We want to dance.' I* had the impression that she knew him, which is not unlikely, for Brahms, like Beethoven, was somewhat divided in his patronage of idealist companionship and the more downright variety found in dark and unfrequented streets. At any rate, he rose from the table and with slow and deliberate steps went toward the old untuned piano which leaned against the dirty wall and began to play – waltzes, quadrilles – tunes which were for the most part *passés* and dated back a good many years. The lady who had succeeded so remarkably in getting Brahms to play, danced with her friends and

---

* Max Graf (1873–1958), Austrian critic.

others joined in. Brahms played uninterruptedly for an hour and then returned to his table, paid his bill and left. I have often thought the proprietor of this establishment should have put up a tablet in memory of this evening: 'Brahms played dance music in this pub.'

The following day I went to my coffee house and met an elderly gentleman who had been in Brahms' party the night before. This was Mr Bela Haas, a well-to-do socialite famous for his wit. I said to him, 'Please tell me what ever induced Brahms to play dance music for such a gathering,' and he answered, 'Well, I too was surprised and asked Brahms the same question. He told me, "When I was a boy in Hamburg I used to play in just such a place the whole night. I played dance music for drunken sailors and their girls. The place reminded me of that time and the pieces I played were those I used to play every night in Hamburg."'

456

Early one morning we* were walking along the road which leads by the lake from Beatenbucht to Merligen, and had somehow come to speak of women and family life. Brahms said, 'I have missed my chance. At the time I wished for it, I could not offer a wife what I should have felt was right.' Upon my asking him, if by that he meant that he had lacked confidence in his power to keep wife and children by his art, he replied, 'No, I did not mean that. But at the time when I should have liked to marry, my music was either hissed in the concert-rooms, or at least received with icy coldness. Now for myself, I could bear that quite well, because I knew its worth, and that some day the tables would be turned. And when, after such failures, I entered my lonely room I was not unhappy. On the contrary! But if, in such moments, I had had to meet the anxious, questioning eyes of a wife with the words "another failure" – I could not have borne that! For a woman may love an artist, whose wife she is, ever so much, and even do what is called believe in her husband – still she cannot have the perfect certainty of victory which is in his heart. And if she had wanted to comfort me . . . a wife to pity her husband for his non-success . . . ugh! I cannot bear to think what a hell that would have been, at least to me.'

Brahms uttered these words vehemently, in short, broken sentences, looking so defiant and indignant that I could think of no reply. . . .

---

* The narrator is Joseph Viktor Widmann (1842–1911); Swiss journalist, friend of Brahms.

'It has been for the best,' added Brahms, suddenly, and the next minute showed his usual expression of quiet content.

457

On the day before the concert there was, as usual, the final full rehearsal, to which in most places in Germany the public are admitted. Brahms had played Schumann's Concerto in A Minor and missed a good many notes. So in the morning of the day of the concert he went to the Concert Hall to practise. He had asked me* to follow him thither a little later and to rehearse with him the songs – his, of course – he was to accompany for me in the evening. When I arrived at the hall I found him quite alone, seated at the piano and working away for all he was worth, on Beethoven's Choral Fantasia and Schumann's Concerto. He was quite red in the face, and, interrupting himself for a moment on seeing me stand beside him, said with that childlike, confiding expression in his eyes, 'Really, this is too bad. Those people to-night expect to hear something especially good, and here I am likely to give them a hoggish mess. I assure you, I could play to-day, with the greatest ease, far more difficult things, with wider stretches for the fingers, my own concerto for example, but those simple diatonic runs are exasperating. I keep saying to myself: "But, Johannes, pull yourself together, do play decently," but no use; it's really horrid.'

458

At a Philharmonic rehearsal . . . at which one of his Serenades was played, the orchestra grew visibly restless, indicating disapproval of this composition. Brahms stepped to the director's stand and said, 'Gentlemen, I am aware that I am not Beethoven – but I am Johannes Brahms.'

459

Joachim, in a few well-chosen words, was asking us not to lose the opportunity of drinking the health of the greatest composer, when, before he could finish the sentence, Brahms bounded to his feet, glass in hand, and called out, 'Quite right! Here's Mozart's health!' and walked round, clinking glasses with us all.

460

'Yes, gentlemen,' observed [his Coblenz host] solemnly as the guests sat in almost reverential silence, inhaling the bouquet of some rare

---

* Sir George Henschel (1850–1934); conductor and baritone.

old Rauenthaler that had been reserved for the end of the repast, 'what Brahms is among the composers, so is this Rauenthaler among the wines.' 'Ah, then let's have a bottle of Bach now,' cried Brahms.

461

He was a great walker, and had a passionate love of nature. It was his habit during the spring and summer to rise at four or five o'clock, and, after making himself a cup of coffee, to go into the woods to enjoy the delicious freshness of early morning and to listen to the singing of the birds. In adverse weather he could still find something to admire and enjoy.

'I never feel it dull,' he said one day, in answer to some remark about the depressing effect of the long-continued rain, 'my view is so fine. Even when it rains, I have only another kind of beauty.'. . .

'How can I most quickly improve?' I* asked him one day. 'You must walk constantly in the forest,' he answered; and he meant what he said to be taken literally.

462

After many hours of wandering [in the Vienna Woods] he and his friends had come to an inn and asked for black coffee. The coffee was made with chicory – an economy exercised by many cooks – and Brahms did not like chicory in his coffee. He called the proprietress to his table and said, 'My dear old lady, have you some chicory?' When she said she had, he continued in an even more gracious tone, 'It's not possible! May I see it?' The old woman retreated to the kitchen and returned with two packages of chicory which she handed to Brahms. He looked them over solemnly and inquired, 'Is that all you have?' When she said yes, he pocketed both boxes and said, 'Well, now you can go back and make us some black coffee.'

463

We† retired to room No. 11, and it was my instant and most ardent endeavour to go to sleep before Brahms did, as I knew from past experience that otherwise his impertinently healthy habit of snoring would mean death to any hope of sleep on my part.

My delight at seeing him take up a book and read in bed was equalled only by my horror when, after a few minutes, I saw him blow out the light of his candle. A few seconds later the room was

---

* Florence May (1845–1923); English pianist.
† The narrator is Sir George Henschel.

fairly ringing with the most unearthly noises issuing from his nasal and vocal organs. What should I do? I was in despair, for I wanted sleep, and moreover, had to leave for Berlin early next morning. A sudden inspiration made me remember room No. 42. I got up, and went downstairs to the lodge of the porter, whom, not without some difficulty, I succeeded in rousing from a sound sleep. Explaining cause and object, I made him open room No. 42 for me. After a good night's rest, I returned, early in the morning, to the room in which I had left Brahms.

He was awake and, affectionately looking at me, with the familiar little twinkle in his eye and mock seriousness in his voice, said to me, well knowing what had driven me away, 'Oh, Henschel, when I awoke and found your bed empty, I said to myself, "There! he's gone and hanged himself!' But really, why didn't you throw a boot at me?'

The idea of my throwing a boot at Brahms!

464

Karl Goldmark (1830–1915), composer and friend of Brahms
Brahms was built on big lines and was absolutely truthful. He could not tell even the ordinary conventional fib. His friends were as wax in his hands. He was as great a man as he was an artist. There was not a blot on his superb character. But he was never accustomed to restraining himself nor to holding his tongue. If he disliked anything he would say so frankly. This bluntness combined with his rough manner frequently made him appear very harsh.

The following remark of some wit was current in Vienna. One evening, Brahms, on taking leave of his hostess at a party, said, 'Kindly excuse me if I by chance have forgotten to offend one of your guests.'

465

On one occasion Brahms, Goldmark and myself* had dined with Ignaz Brüll's father, Siegmund Brüll, and after dinner we retired for a smoke. A few recently published compositions by Ignaz were lying on the piano. Brahms turned over the leaves and suddenly exclaimed, 'How beautiful, how very beautiful!' (Modest Ignaz was doubtless silently enchanted.) But Brahms continued, 'It is the most beautiful title-page I have seen for a long time!'

---

* Sir Felix Semon, British laryngologist; Ignaz Brüll (1846–1907); Austrian composer.

After Dvořák had sent him a work which was not flawless in its workmanship, he answered, 'We cannot any longer write as beautiful music as Mozart did; so let us try to write as clean.'

At Leipzig he was always a little 'out of tune'. He never quite forgave the first reception of his D minor Concerto at the Gewandhaus, and he used to vent his bottled-up wrath by satirical remarks to the Directors. One of them, a tall and rather pompous gentleman who wore a white waistcoat, . . . asked Brahms before the concert with a patronizing smile, 'Whither are you going to lead us to-night, Mr Brahms? To Heaven?'

Brahms: 'It's all the same to me which direction you take.'

Brahms knew, and was well known to, all the children of the neighbourhood, and when starting on his country walks would fill his pockets with sweetmeats and little pictures, and amuse himself with the eagerness of the small bare-footed folk, who knew his ways and would run after him as he passed, on the look out for booty. 'Whoever can jump gets a gulden,' he would say; and, displaying beyond reach of the little ones a handful of sweatmeats made in imitation of the Austrian coin, he would increase his speed, and raise his hand higher and higher, drawing after him the flock of running, leaping children, until he allowed one and another to gain a prize.

I* can remember Bülow reproaching Brahms for sending the manuscript of the Fourth Symphony, of which no copy existed, as an ordinary postal packet, not even registered. 'What would we have done had the packet gone astray?' The composer answered: 'In that case I would have had to write the Symphony anew.'

Brahms, received the telegram [announcing Clara Schumann's death] in Vienna stating that the funeral was to take place in Endenich, near Bonn, and that she was to be buried beside her husband. He travelled to Frankfort-on-the-Maine to catch the con-

---

* Frederic Lamond (1868–1948); British pianist.

nection. In Frankfort a railway official foolishly told him to take the train running on the right side of the Rhine, instead of the left side, with the result that Brahms arrived too late in Endenich to be present at the funeral. The chagrin, the vexation, made him feel ill and sick: he, who had never known a day's illness, did not recognize himself in the looking-glass the next morning. An attack of jaundice had set in overnight.

471

Brahms made to attend the funeral of his old adversary Bruckner, in October 1896, but turned back at the cathedral door. 'Never mind,' he was heard to say, 'Soon my coffin.'

❧

Camille SAINT-SAËNS (1835–1921)

French composer remembered mainly for the opera *Samson and Delilah*, and *Carnival of the Animals*.

472

Saint-Saëns recalls
[My parents] took me to a symphony concert, and my mother held me in her arms near the door. Until then I had only heard single violins and their tone had not pleased me. But the impression of the orchestra was entirely different and I listened with delight to a passage played by a quartet, when suddenly, came a blast from the brass instruments – the trumpets, trombones and cymbals. I broke into loud cries, 'Make them stop. They prevent my hearing the music.' They had to take me out.

473

In November 1875 Camille Saint-Saëns came to conduct and play some of his works in Moscow. The short lively man, with his Jewish type of features, attracted Tchaikovsky and fascinated him not only by his wit and original ideas but by his masterly knowledge of his art. One day the friends discovered they had a great many likes and dislikes in common. In their youth both had been enthusiastic admirers of the ballet, and had often tried to imitate the art of the dancers. This suggested the idea of dancing together, and they brought out a little ballet, *Pygmalion and Galatea*, on the stage of the Conservatoire. Saint-Saëns, aged forty, played Galatea most conscientiously, while Tchaikovsky, thirty-five, appeared as Pygmalion. Nikolay Rubinstein formed the orchestra. Unfortunately, beside the three performers, no spectator witnessed this singular entertainment.

❧

Theodore THOMAS (1835–1905)

German-born musician, conductor for twelve years of the New York Philharmonic and founder of the Chicago Symphony Orchestra.

474

He made no concessions to the American public when he wished to instruct it. He performed the Mephisto Waltz of Liszt, thus, for the first time in New York. The audience, accustomed only to Italian or classical music, whistled and hissed down the orchestra and compelled Thomas to stop. Several attempts to resume were made in vain. Then Thomas took his watch in his hand, enforced quiet, and turned to the audience with the following words: 'I give you five minutes to leave the hall; then we shall play the waltz from the beginning to the end. Who wishes to listen without making a demonstration may do so; I request all others to go, I will carry out my purpose if I have to remain standing here until two o'clock in the morning – I have plenty of time.' The audience remained.

475

While I was walking with him one day in Chicago, four hoodlums approached us abreast and taking up the whole width of the sidewalk. To get by them it was apparently necessary to go out into the muddy street, but Mr Thomas was not in the habit of making such concessions. Squaring his elbows in front of him he collided with the unsavoury quartet directly in the centre. Two of them were flung against the building on their right and the other two went sprawling into the gutter. . . . He went on as unconcerned as if he had only brushed four straws out of his path.

❧

Henry WIENIAWSKI (1835–1880)

Polish violinist, composer of virtuoso showpieces.

476

While [Wieniawski was] touring the USA with Anton Rubinstein in 1872, one virtuoso was offensively given larger billing than the other. As a consequence, they went on to play the Kreutzer Sonata more than seventy times together without ever exchanging a word.

477

Once in London he was invited by some person of high rank to play at his house. When he stepped out to the front, all eyes and lorgnettes were on him, and there was not even a murmur in the audience; everybody was still and attentive; but he scarcely struck the first notes of Raff's* Cavatina, when all the people in the room began to talk. It was very provoking, and he was determined to teach them a lesson: knowing that every English man and woman had to rise and be silent when the hymn 'God save the Queen' was played, he gave a wink to the accompanist, then passed cleverly from Raff to the tune of the hymn and played it fortissimo. To his great satisfaction, the people stopped talking, and those who were seated rose to their feet. But when he resumed the Cavatina, they also instantly resumed their talk. He again intoned the hymn and gained a few minutes of silence, but the noise was stronger than ever when he changed the tune. He repeated the hymn trick five or six times. When he finished no one understood the hint; they only wondered at the strange composition in which the national hymn was so often repeated.

❧

Léo DELIBES (1836–1891)

Composer of the popular ballets *Coppélia* and *Sylvia*.

478

The violinist Fritz Kreisler remembered his teacher Delibes as 'a gay blade, flighty and irresponsible'. Daily lessons were often interrupted by the entrance of a pretty girl, who would entice the professor out to *déjeuner*, or for a stroll, or with an irresistible invitation. '*Allons*

---

* Joseph Joachim Raff (1822–82); Swiss composer famed for Cavatina for violin and piano.

danser!' Delibes, Kreisler said 'would hand me the beginnings of some composition on which he happened to be at work, suggest that I try to catch the spirit of it, and then charge me with going on from there. Even today, the waltz from *Coppélia* . . . is often played. Well I can truthfully claim the motif is mine. Delibes returning from one of his adventures with the fair sex, liked it so well that he took it into his ballet unchanged and developed and embellished it.'

✎✺✺✺✎

Sir William Schwenk GILBERT (1836–1911)

British lawyer who collaborated with Sir Arthur Sullivan on fourteen operettas.

479

Soon after the death of a well-known composer, someone, who did not keep pace with the news of the day, asked Mr Gilbert what the maestro in question was doing.

'He is doing nothing,' was the answer.

'Surely, he is composing?' persisted the questioner.

'On the contrary,' said Mr Gilbert, 'he is decomposing.'

480

He once directed an actor to sit down 'in a pensive fashion'. The man took his seat slowly but heavily, knocking over as he descended a large part of the scenery. 'I said "pensively",' flashed Gilbert. 'Not ex-pensively.'

✎✺✺✺✎

Mily BALAKIREV (1837–1910)

A disciple of Glinka's, Balakirev composed and encouraged others to create a distinctively Russian style of music.

481

Borodin writes

'I have already said in my letters that he'd been sulking at me for some time, and that he was off-hand, angry, and at times captious. I turn up at Liudma's* – and there was Mili; you'd hardly recognize

---

* Lyudmila Ivanovna Shestakinova (1816–1906); Glinka's sister.

him. He softened, melted, and gazed at me with loving eyes. In the end, at a loss as to how he could express his affection, he gently took me by the nose between two fingers and gave me a resounding kiss. I couldn't help but laugh! You must have guessed the reason for this change, of course. Korsinka [Rimsky-Korsakov] has told him that I'm trying my hand at another symphony and played him a bit of it.'

482

Balakirev, to Rimsky-Korsakov
From you, I expect a great deal. I place my faith in you, as an aged aunt does in a young jurist nephew.

483

He had the smallest regard for Mussorgsky, the most gifted of his protégés. 'Mussorgsky has no head,' he wrote to Stassov. 'His brains are weak.'

484

Rimsky-Korsakov recalls
While taking a walk, the concern about the conduct of his dog and its morals, and endeavours to keep him from courting the canine fair sex, went so far that occasionally he carried his hulk in his arms. As for the *dvorniks* who would chase the dog, which stuck his snout everywhere, they usually received suitable reprimands. The love and compassion for animals reached such heights with him that whenever some kind of filthy insect – a bedbug, for instance – turned up in the room, he would catch it carefully and throw it out of the casement window, accompanying the act with the words: 'Go thee, deary, in the Lord go!'

485

In general, his intolerance toward people who disagreed with him in anything or acted and reasoned in any way independently, on lines different from his, was as deep-rooted as before, and the epithet 'blackguard', dealt out right and left, did not leave his tongue. To this gracious epithet of his was now added a new one, '*Zhid*' ('sheeny'). Everybody for whom he felt a dislike he suspected to be of Jewish origin, and 'the sheenies' he hated, because they had crucified Christ. Very frequently his religious conversations with persons whom he liked would be closed with the entreaty: 'Please, just for my sake, put the sign of the cross over yourself; just once cross yourself. Now, do try!'

Georges BIZET (1838–1875)

Composer of *Carmen*, he died young, shortly after the opera's cool reception.

486

Bizet to his mother

Rome, 25 June 1858

A woman's virtue here is not worth more than one franc, and most of the men will do anything asked of them for a few sous. The same goes for the upper classes, only it is more expensive. There is not a woman here in a hundred who does not have a Cardinal, a Bishop or a priest according to her rank. . . . I had hoped, in leaving Paris, to escape light-hearted women, but I have been unlucky. I am sure you will be very angry, but what can I do? You, the rare virtuous women who live by duty, devotion and love of your families, are 1,000 times more deserving than the holy martyrs. You may not believe it, but we do.

487

Saint-Saëns
Bizet and I were great friends and we told each other all our troubles. 'You're less unfortunate than I am,' he used to tell me. 'You can do something besides things for the stage. I can't. That's my only resource.'

488

After *The Pearl Fishers'* débâcle, a friend told Bizet that he had purchased the score of the opera. 'What on earth for?' demanded the composer. 'I would have given you mine. Anyway, you will have no use for it.'

489

At the end of the first act of *Carmen*, a number of young musicians (among them Vincent D'Indy) gathered around Bizet and loudly praised the opera. 'You are the first to say [such things],' he lamented, 'and I fancy you will be the last.'

490

Madame Bizet married a rich lawyer in 1886 and founded a brilliant Parisian salon. One day she was asked by a titled lady whether she liked music. 'They played a great deal of it in my first family,' replied Halévy's daughter, Bizet's widow, cryptically.

Max BRUCH (1838–1920)

German composer whose best known work is Kol Nidrei, a composition based on the Jewish Yom Kippur prayer; he was not Jewish.

491

A rather celebrated composer* had asked Brahms to be allowed to play to him from the MS his latest composition, a violin concerto. Brahms consented to hear it and seated himself near the piano. Mr — played his work with great enthusiasm and force, the perspiration – it was a very warm day – streaming down his face.

When he had finished, Brahms got up, approached the piano, took a sheet of the manuscript between his thumb and middle finger and, rubbing it between them, exclaimed 'I say, where do you buy your music paper? First rate!'

❦

Modest MUSSORGSKY (1839–1881)

His operatic masterpiece, *Boris Godunov*, fell foul of Tsarist censors and fellow composers; Pieces at an Exhibition, a piano suite, achieved renown in an orchestration by Ravel.

492

When they began to omit the last act from performances of *Boris*, Mussorgsky not only approved this cut, but was especially pleased with it. Agreeing with him that this last act was obviously superfluous in the development of the drama and that it had the appearance of something hastily pasted on at the end (as it actually was) I† nevertheless regretted its complete omission because I found much that was good musically in it . . .

'In this act,' Mussorgsky answered me, 'and for the only time in my life, I lied about the Russian people. The mocking of the boyar by the Russian people – this is untrue, this is un-Russian. Infuriated people kill and execute, but they don't mock their victims.'

---

* Identified as Max Bruch in Semon's and Speyer's autobiographies.
† Count Arseni Arkadyevich Golenischev-Katuzov (1848–1913); poet.

Of my father's patients, Lev Tolstoy*, once dismissed the whole Mussorgsky question in a conversation with the doctor, 'I like neither talented drunks nor drunken talents.'

Borodin recalls

I soon learned that he was a composer himself, which increased the interest his personality had awakened in me. He then played a scherzo of his own.

I was quite astonished at these musical forms which were quite novel to me. I cannot say they pleased me at first. I was bewildered, but by dint of listening I soon began to appreciate them and find in them a certain charm. I must confess that when Mussorgsky had told me of his intention to devote himself seriously to music I took this declaration at first for a bit of braggadocia and laughed in my sleeve. But after hearing his scherzo, I asked myself, 'Can I believe it or not?'

Many often tried to talk Mussorgsky into marrying; but his unwillingness to marry was almost laughable: more than once he assured me† seriously that if I should ever read in the papers that he had shot or hanged himself, this would mean that on the day before he had got married.

One winter I‡ had to organize a concert for the benefit of medical students. . . .

Besides artists of the Russian Opera I was fortunate in obtaining, as a special favour, the splendid tenor of the Italian Opera, Ravelli, who was then singing at the Bolshoi Theatre. . . .

On the day before the concert Ravelli told me that he wished to meet his piano accompanist and asked me to bring him around next day for an early rehearsal.

Having [obtained] Mussorgsky's consent the day before, happily finding him in a lucid period, I went to him once more to carry out Ravelli's commission.

---

* The narrator is Sergei Bertensson.
† Lyudmila Ivanovna Shestakinova (1816–1906), Glinka's sister.
‡ Vasili Bertensson (1853–1933); Mussorgsky's physician.

But, to my horror, I found Mussorgsky drunker than wine! In a mumbling voice he tried to assure me, speaking in French, for some reason, that it was no use going to the Italian, that he would manage everything, etc.

No persuasions or pleas of mine had any effect, and with the stubbornness of the drunken he went on saying, '*Non, monsieur, non; maintenant c'est impossible. Ce soir je serai exacte.*' [No, sir, no; at the moment it is not possible. This evening I shall be alright.]

At that time Mussorgsky lived in a small, slovenly room. On the dirty table stood some vodka and some scraps of miserable food.

In saying goodbye to me he got up with difficulty, but saw me to the door and bowed me out in a manner which, though not quite worthy of Louis XIV, was quite amazing for anyone so completely 'tight', saying, '*Donc à ce soir!*' [Well then, till tonight!]

So I went back to my tenor and told him that I hadn't found Mussorgsky at home. . . .

In the meantime I located one of my colleagues who agreed to stand guard over Mussorgsky and bring him to the concert in plenty of time.

Sure enough, Modeste Petrovich showed up promptly at 7 at Kononov's hall where the concert was to take place.

Mussorgsky, unfortunately, remained long enough in the green-room to sample all the drinks on the table there, growing drunker and drunker. Suddenly my Italian tenor, after trying some runs, decided that his voice was a little strained and would therefore be compelled to sing his entire programme a half or even a whole tone lower than usual.

This was all we needed.

I rushed to Mussorgsky to ask him whether he could do this for Ravelli. Rising from his chair with a certain gallantry, Mussorgsky calmed me with the words, '*Pourquoi pas?*' [Why not?] (apparently Mussorgsky spoke only French with cultured people, even when he was drunk).

To prove his assuring words he suggested that the tenor at once run through his whole program *mezza-voce*.

Mussorgsky, who was probably hearing all Ravelli's Italian stuff for the first time, so charmed the Italian with his refined performance and his ability to transpose to any key that the tenor embraced him, saying repeatedly, '*Che artista!*' [What an artist!]

Pyotr (Ilyich) TCHAIKOVSKY (1840–1893)

The first Russian composer to attain worldwide popularity, Tchaikovsky taught harmony at the Moscow Conservatory until an unsought benefactress, Nadezhda von Meck, freed him to compose full-time. Fear and confusion over his homosexuality precipitated an appalling marriage, a nervous breakdown, suicide attempt and, ultimately, self-destruction.

497

'Tchaikovsky worked in an astonishing way,' said Nikolay Rubinstein, speaking of his pupil in later years. 'Once, at the composition class, I set him to write out contrapuntal variations on a given theme, and I mentioned that in this class of work not only quality but quantity was of importance. I thought perhaps he would write about a dozen variations. But not at all. At the next class I received over two hundred. To examine all these,' Rubinstein concluded, with a bland smile, 'would have taken me more time than it took him to write them.'

498

Tchaikovsky, letter to Nadezhda von Meck, 21 January 1878
In December 1874 I had written a piano concerto. As I am not a pianist, it was necessary to consult some virtuoso as to what might be ineffective, impracticable and ungrateful in my technique. Some inward voice warned me against the choice of Nikolay Rubinstein, however, as he was not only the best pianist in Moscow but also a first-rate all-round musician, and knowing that he would be deeply offended if he heard I had taken my concerto to anyone else, I decided to ask him to hear the work. It was on Christmas Eve 1874. We were invited to Albrecht's house and before we went Nikolay Rubinstein proposed I should meet him in one of the classrooms at the Conservatoire to go through the concerto.

I played the first movement. Never a word, never a single remark. Do you know the awkward and ridiculous sensation of putting before a friend a meal which you have cooked yourself, which he eats – and [then] holds his tongue? Oh, for a single word, for friendly abuse, for *anything* to break the silence! For God's sake say *something*! But Rubinstein never opened his lips. He was preparing his thunderbolt, and Hubert* (an onlooker) was waiting to see which way the wind would blow. Rubinstein's silence was eloquent. 'My dear friend,' he

---

* Nikolai Albertovich Hubert (1840–88), musician.

seemed to be saying to himself, 'how can I speak of the details when the work itself goes entirely against the grain?' I gathered patience and played the concerto straight through to the end. Still silence.

'Well?' I asked, and rose from the piano. Then a torrent broke from Rubinstein's lips. Gentle at first, gathering volume as it proceeded, and finally bursting into the fury of a Jupiter. My concerto was worthless, absolutely unplayable; the passages so broken, so disconnected, so unskilfully written, that they could not even be improved; the work itself was bad, trivial, common; here and there I had stolen from other people; only one or two pages were worth anything; all the rest had better be destroyed. I left the room without a word. Presently Rubinstein came to me and, seeing how upset I was, repeated that my concerto was impossible (but) said if I would suit it to his requirements he would bring it out at his concert. 'I shall not alter a single note.' I replied.

499

Speaking of criticism in general he said, 'Oblivion and neglect are the worst fate that can befall a composition, especially a new one. It does not so much signify *what* the critic writes; that he should write something is the important matter.'

500

A telephone wire had just been laid between Berlin and Leipzig. Tchaikovsky and Brodsky* arranged to speak through the telephone, the former from Berlin and the latter from Leipzig. At the appointed time Brodsky went to the telephone office hoping to have a chat with his friend, but he had only uttered a few words when he heard Tchaikovsky say in a trembling voice, 'Dear friend! Please let me go. I feel so nervous.'

'I have not got you by the buttonhole,' said A. B., 'You can go when you please.'

Later on Tchaikovsky explained to us that as soon as he heard his friend's voice and realized the distance between them his heart began to beat so violently that he could not endure it.

501

Sometimes Tchaikovsky would send us† a telegram from Berlin, or any other town where he happened to be, to this effect: 'I am coming

---

* Adolf Brodsky (1851–1929), Russian-born violinist who gave première of Tchaikovsky's concerto; the narrator is Brodsky's wife, Anna.
† The Brodskys.

to see you. Please keep it secret.' We knew well what this meant: that he was tired and homesick and in need of friends. Once after such a telegram Tchaikovsky just arrived in time for dinner; at first we had him quite to ourselves, but after dinner, as he was sitting in the music room with his head leaning on his hand as was his custom, the members of the Brodsky Quartet quietly entered the room bringing their instruments with them as had been previously arranged. They sat down in silence and played Tchaikovsky's own String Quartet No. 3, which they had just carefully prepared for a concert. Great was Tchaikovsky's delight! I saw the tears roll down his cheek as he listened, and then, passing from one performer to the other, he expressed again and again his gratitude for the happy hour they had given him. Then turning to Brodsky he said in his naïve way, 'I did not know I had composed such a fine quartet. I never liked the finale, but now I see it is really good.'

502

In the country he spoilt all the peasant children by giving them coins. Taneiev and Kashkin* reproached him for this bad habit, saying that it demoralized the children, and using other virtuous arguments. The next time they went for a walk, Tchaikovsky resolved to make an heroic effort to escape from the youthful beggars whose morals were corrupted by his kopecks. They started for the bridge which crosses the river on the road to Klin. Tchaikovsky's hour for walking was known to every child in the neighbourhood, and feeling sure that he would be waylaid on leaving the park, he tried to deceive his persecutors. Leaving Taneiev and Kashkin on the path, he descended to the river-bank and crept under the thick sallow-bushes, while Taneiev, from the upper road, watched his furtive movements, and recited with mock pathos, 'Behold the worthy fruits of evil-doing,' etc. Tchaikovsky's innocent ruse availed him nothing. The children, who had studied the character of their victim to some purpose, had posted sentries in ambush, and by the time Tchaikovsky reached the bridge a party of boys were awaiting him. His friends came up just in time to hear the joyful laughter of the victorious enemy as they moved off laden with booty. Tchaikovsky, blushing with confusion, hastened to explain that he really could not help it, that he had given the children the merest trifle, etc. M. Kashkin did not quite believe in this extenuating circumstance. On one occasion Tchaikovsky had given away at

---

* Nikolai Kashkin (1839–1920), Russian music critic; Sergei Taneiev (1856–1915), composer and pianist.

least fourteen shillings in an afternoon's walk, and, in addition, had borrowed all that his friend had with him at the moment.

503

Tchaikovsky reports the events of his wedding night, 18 July 1877
When the [rail] carriage started I was ready to cry out with choking sobs. Nevertheless, I still had to occupy my wife with conversation as far as Klin in order that I might earn the right to lie down in my own armchair when it was dark, and remain alone by myself. At the second station after Khinok, Meschchersky [one of Tchaikovsky's old friends from the School of Jurisprudence] burst into the carriage. When I saw him I felt that he simply had to take me away somewhere forthwith. This he did. Before beginning any sort of conversation with him I had to give vent to a flood of tears. Meshchersky showed much tender sympathy, and did a lot to prop up my fallen spirit. When, after Klin, I returned to my wife, I was much calmer. Meshchersky arranged that we should be accommodated in a sleeping compartment, and after this I slept the sleep of the dead. . . .

What I found most comforting of all was that my wife didn't comprehend or even perceive my ill-concealed anguish. Now and always she appears to be completely happy and contented. *Elle n'est pas difficile*. She is in agreement with everything and contented with everything. . . .

We had conversations which have still further clarified our relationship with each other. She is positively agreeable to everything, and will never want more. All she needs is to cherish and care for me. I have retained for myself complete freedom of action.*

504

Once, he told M. Kashkin, he was spending the evening quite alone at his country house. As his eye fell upon the volumes of his diary he was assailed by a sudden terror lest he might die with no friends at hand, and that some one should pry into these life-secrets. Under the influence of this feeling, he immediately ordered his fire to be lit, and burnt every volume before he went to bed. There was much in it

---

*Family letters revealing the agony of Tchaikovsky's marriage and his homosexuality were published in Moscow in 1940, but then promptly suppressed. The only copy to reach the West was smuggled out by the musicologist Alexandra Orlova, who has also published the authoritative account of the events leading to the composer's death (see anecdote 506).

which he regretted, but on the whole he believed that he had acted wisely.

505

Rimsky-Korsakov
I recall having asked him, during the intermission, after the performance of the Pathétique Symphony, whether he had a programme for this composition. He replied that there was one, of course, but that he did not wish to announce it. During that last visit of his to St Petersburg I saw him only at the concert. A few days later the news of his grave illness was in everybody's mouth. The whole world filed to his apartment several times a day to inquire about his health. How strange that, although death had resulted from cholera, admission to the Mass for the dead was free to all! I remember how Vyerzhbilovich, totally drunk . . . kept kissing the deceased man's head and face.*

506

In the autumn of 1893 Tchaikovsky was threatened with a terrible misfortune. Duke Stenbok-Fermor, disturbed by the attention which the composer was paying to his young nephew, wrote a letter of accusation to the Tsar and handed the letter to Jacobi, one of Tchaikovsky's fellow pupils at the School of Jurisprudence, to pass on to Alexander III. If exposed [as a homosexual] Tchaikovsky would be threatened with the loss of all his rights and exile to Siberia, and he would bring disgrace upon the School of Jurisprudence and all its old boys. To avoid publicity Jacobi invited all Tchaikovsky's former school friends in St Petersburg and set up a court of honour which included himself. This went on for a long time, almost five hours. Then Tchaikovsky came running headlong out of Jacobi's study without saying a word. He was very white and agitated. The others stayed for a long time inside the study, talking quietly. When they had gone, Jacobi told his wife that they had reached a decision by which Tchaikovsky had promised to abide. They required him to kill himself. A day or two later, news of the composer's mortal illness was circulating in St Petersburg.

---

* Cholera victims were quarantined and the corpse isolated for fear of infection. Rimsky-Korsakov's suspicions over the cause of Tchaikovsky's death were widely shared, but the truth did not come to light for almost eighty years (see following anecdote).

'I have just received very distressing news,' [Tolstoy] said ...
'Tchaikovsky died last night in St Petersburg.' I [Marie
Scheikevitch] looked up at my father. His head was bowed and tears
glistened on his cheeks. I had never seen him cry. His hand clenched
mine so that it nearly hurt. His tears formed a stream that dripped
from his white beard that was swaying above my head. . . . Then
Tolstoy's huge fist, clutching the telegram that he was showing my
father, obscured my view, like a small yellow screen shutting out the
darkening sky.

508

At nine in the morning there was a Requiem Mass for the soul of Peter
Ilitsch Tchaikovsky. I* drove in a sleigh to one of the chief churches
of Moscow and found all the professors of the Conservatoire gathered
in a small side-chapel. I stood between Scriabin and Taneiev. When
the officiating priest began to read the Mass for the dead I was aware
of an unnatural paleness on the part of Scriabin. Taneiev wept and
sobbed: knelt down and kissed the icy flags of the chapel: something
tense, even gloomy lay on the whole gathering. As the priest of the
Orthodox Greek Church, his deep, impressive bass half intoning, half
speaking, raised his voice to a threatening, booming cry, it was as if
the wings of the angels of Death were rushing over the gathering in
the semi-darkness of the ice-cold chapel.

509

'Poor Piotr Ilytch Tchaikovsky was always on the verge of suicide, so
afraid was he that people might discover that he was a pederast'
[said Diaghilev]; 'today, if you're a composer and *not* a pederast you
had better put a bullet through your head.' When I† protested and
cited the names of three especially successful living composers of
old-fashioned habits (that is, heterosexual), Diaghilev retorted, 'Nonsense. Two of them are *des tantes ratées* (would-be pederasts who
failed to make the grade) and the third is impotent.'

∾

---

* Frederic Lamond (1868–1948); British pianist.
† Vladimir Dukelsky (1903–69); Russian-born composer known by his American
pseudonym 'Vernon Duke'.

Antonín DVOŘÁK (1841–1904)

Czech composer whose immeasurably popular New World Symphony originated from three years (1892–5) spent in New York and among the Czech community of Spillville, Iowa.

510

Old Borax, as Dvořák was affectionately called, was handed over to me* by Madame Thurber when he arrived [in New York]. He was a fervent Roman Catholic, and I hunted a Bohemian church for him as he began his day with an early Mass. Rather too jauntily I invited him to taste the American drink called a whisky cocktail. He nodded his head, that of an angry-looking bulldog with a beard. He scared one at first with his fierce Slavonic eyes, but was as mild a mannered man as ever scuttled a pupil's counterpoint. I always spoke of him as a boned pirate. But I made a mistake in believing that American strong waters would upset his Czech nerves. We began at Goerwitz, then described a huge circle, through the great thirst belt of central New York. At each place Doc Borax took a cocktail. Now, alcohol I abhor, so I stuck to my guns, the usual three-voiced invention, hops, malt, and spring water. We spoke in German, and I was happy to meet a man whose accent and grammar were worse than my own. Yet we got along swimmingly – an appropriate enough image, for the weather was wet, though not squally. . . .

I left him swallowing his nineteenth cocktail. 'Master,' I said, rather thickly, 'don't you think it's time we ate something?' He gazed at me through those awful whiskers which met his tumbled hair half-way, 'Eat. No. I no eat. We go to a Houston Street restaurant. You go, hein? We drink the Slivovitch. It warms you after so much beer.' I didn't go that evening to the East Houston Street Bohemian café with Dr Antonín Dvořák. I never went with him. Such a man is as dangerous to a moderate drinker as a false beacon is to a ship-wrecked sailor. And he could drink as much spirits as I could the amber brew. No, I assured Mrs Thurber that I was through with piloting him. When I met Old Borax again at Sokel Hall, the Bohemian resort on the East Side, I deliberately dodged him.

---

* James Huneker (1860–1921), prominent New York critic; Jeanette M. Thurber, wealthy grocer's wife who founded National Conservatory of Music and engaged Dvořák as its director.

What the Master missed in America were his pigeons and loco-motives. He felt the want of these two 'hobbies' very much, but here, too, he at length found a modest substitute. One day we went with the Master to the Central Park where there is a small Zoological Garden and buildings with different kinds of birds. And then we came to a huge aviary with about two hundred pigeons. It was a real surprise for the Master and his pleasure at seeing the pigeons was great and even though none of these pigeons could compare with his 'pouters' and 'fantails', we made the trip to Central Park at least once and often twice a week.

With locomotives it was a more difficult matter. In New York at that time, there was only one station – the others were across the river (the city of New York is situated on the island of Manhattan). At the main station they did not allow anybody on to the platform except the passengers and it was in vain that we begged the porter to let us look at the 'American locomotive'. We travelled by overhead tram to 155th Street, a good hour from the Master's house, and there, on a bank, waited for the Chicago or Boston express to go by. Only it took up a lot of time, nearly the whole afternoon, as we always waited for a number of trains so that it would be worth the journey. . . .

And then the Master found a new hobby in steamships. For one thing the harbour was much nearer and then, on the day of departure, the public was allowed on board, an opportunity which the Master made full use of.

There was soon not a boat that we had not inspected from stem to stern. The Master always started a conversation with the ship's captain or with his assistants, and so, in a short time, we knew all the captains and mates by name. And when a ship was due to sail we went there and watched it from the shore till it was out of sight.

512

Brahms tried to persuade Dvořák to move to Vienna and, because he knew that he had a big family, he said, 'Look here, Dvořák, you have a lot of children and I haven't almost anybody. If you need anything, my fortune is at your disposal.' The tears came into Mrs Dvořák's eyes and Dvořák, deeply touched, seized the Master's hand. Then the conversation turned to faith and religion. Dvořák, as is well known, was possessed of a sincere and almost child-like faith, whereas Brahms' views were quite the opposite. 'I have read a lot of Schopen-hauer and look on things differently,' he remarked. . . . On the way

way to the hotel, Dvořák was more than usually silent. At last after some considerable time he exclaimed, 'Such a man, such a soul – and he doesn't believe in anything, he doesn't believe in anything!'

513

Fritz Kreisler called on Dvořák in 1903 in his impoverished home in Prague
'It was like a scene from *La Bohème*,' Kreisler remembered. 'Dvořák was lying in bed, sick and in visibly bad shape. He had sold all his compositions for a mere pittance and now had nothing to live on. Even the emoluments for his brilliant American tour had for some reason or other been used up.

'I had been playing some of Dvořák's Slavonic Dances and visited the old man to pay him my respects. I asked him whether he had nothing further for me to play. "Look through that pile," the sick composer said, pointing to a mass of unorganized papers. "Maybe you can find something." I did. It was the Humoresque.'*

છબાર

Arrigo BOITO (1842–1918)

Italian poet and composer, librettist of Verdi's *Otello* and *Falstaff*. His first opera, *Mefistofele*, appeared in 1868; his second, *Nerone*, was begun in 1862 but remained unfinished at his death fifty-six years later.

514

Chaliapin recalls
The performance [of *Mefistofele*] over, I was informed that he wished to see me as soon as possible at his home. I went off as soon as I was free. There was incense burning on the table in his study. He was a bachelor, and judging from the contents of his home, a great lover of beautiful things. He turned out to be a gay, jolly sort of person. I knew he was working on the opera, *Nerone*, and I asked him about it. His reaction was odd. He made a terrifying face, took an enormous pistol out of his desk drawer, laid it on my knee, and in a tone half-comic,

---

* In G-flat from Op. 101, which Kreisler arranged and transformed into an outstanding violinistic showpiece.

half-dismal, said, 'Shoot me. Yes, do. Please, for indulging in such nonsense.'

I realized he was a man who felt deeply about his work.

෴

Jules MASSENET (1842–1912)

French composer of twenty-seven operas including *Manon* and *Werther*.

515

When *Esclarmonde* was produced, the critical wits referred to him as 'Mlle. Wagner,' and the newspapers related with much zest an anecdote regarding the composer Reyer,* who, when he heard that Massenet had exclaimed: 'Wagner, a prodigious genius! I shall consider myself fortunate to reach his ankles!' retorted promptly and seriously: 'But he is reaching them!'

516

One evening at a dinner party, hearing Massenet praise Reyer, the hostess remarked how generous he was, for she said, 'Reyer always speaks disparagingly of you.'

'Dear Madame,' he replied, 'you know what inveterate liars we both are.'

517

A few weeks before the production of *Werther* in Paris, Massenet became a member of the Union Vélocipédique de France. A grand banquet was given in his honour, one of the features of which was an exhibition of proficiency on the part of the new member, who rode round the table on his bicycle. A spiteful critic wrote subsequently that he did this to advertise himself. But in 1893 Massenet was already a very famous man.

518

After a performance of *Manon* during which the tenor had sung flat all evening, Massenet, going behind the scene, was met by this singer, who came forward to receive congratulations. . . .

'I hope you were pleased, *cher Maître*?' inquired the culpable tenor.

---

* Ernest Reyer (1823–1909).

'Delighted, delighted,' replied the composer, 'but how could you sing with that dreadful orchestra; they accompanied you half a tone sharp all the evening?'

❦

Sir Arthur SULLIVAN (1842–1900)

Celebrated for his light operas with Gilbert; he also wrote the hymn, 'Onward Christian Soldiers'.

519

'It was on a very cold morning,' Sir Arthur said, 'with the snow falling heavily, that Gilbert came round to my place, clad in a heavy fur coat. He had called to read over to me the MS of *Trial by Jury* [their first important collaboration]. He read it through, as it seemed to me, in a perturbed sort of way, with a gradual crescendo of indignation, in the manner of a man considerably disappointed with what he had written. As soon as he had come to the last word he closed up the manuscript violently, apparently unconscious of the fact that he had achieved his purpose so far as I was concerned, inasmuch as I was screaming with laughter the whole time.'

520

Sullivan told this story against himself
Standing one night at the back of the dress-circle, he commenced in a contemplative fashion to hum the melody of a song that was being rendered on the stage. 'Look here,' declared a sensitive old gentleman, turning around sharply to the composer, 'I've paid my money to hear Sullivan's music – not yours.'

❦

Edvard GRIEG (1843–1907)

Norwegian composer whose youthful triumphs so boosted national morale that the government awarded him a state pension in 1874 – when he was twenty-nine.

521

Ethel Smyth praised one of Grieg's works but suggested that the coda of one movement was not of the same quality as the rest. 'Ah yes,' said Grieg, shrugging his shoulders, 'at that point inspiration gave out, and I had to finish without.'

In the midst of [Brahms'] rehearsal I* heard a ring at the bell, and expecting it would be Tchaikovsky, rushed to open the door. He was quite perplexed by the sound of music, asked who was there, and what they were playing. I took him into the room adjoining and tried to break, gently, the news of Brahms' presence. As we spoke there was a pause in the music; I begged him to enter, but he felt too nervous, so I opened the door softly and called my husband. He took Tchaikovsky with him and I followed.

Tchaikovsky and Brahms had never met before. It would be difficult to find two men more unlike. Tchaikovsky, a nobleman by birth, had something elegant and refined in his whole bearing and the greatest courtesy of manner. Brahms with his short, rather square figure and powerful head, was an image of strength and energy; he was an avowed foe to all so-called 'good manners'. His expression was often slightly sarcastic. When A. B.[rodsky] introduced them, Tchaikovsky said, in his soft melodious voice, 'Do I not disturb you?'

'Not in the least,' was Brahms' reply, with his peculiar hoarseness. 'But why are you going to hear this? It is not at all interesting.'

Tchaikovsky sat down and listened attentively. The personality of Brahms, as he told us later, impressed him very favourably, but he was not pleased with the music. When the trio was over I noticed that Tchaikovsky seemed uneasy. It would have been natural that he should say something, but he was not at all the man to pay unmeaning compliments. The situation might have become difficult, but at that moment the door was flung open, and in came our dear friends – Grieg and his wife, bringing, as they always did, a kind of sunshine with them. They knew Brahms, but had never met Tchaikovsky before. The latter loved Grieg's music, and was instantly attracted by these two charming people, full as they were of liveliness, enthusiasm and unconventionality, and yet with a simplicity about them that made everyone feel at home. Tchaikovsky with his sensitive nervous nature understood them at once. After the introductions and greetings were over we passed to the dining-room. Nina Grieg was seated between Brahms and Tchaikovsky, but we had only been a few moments at the table when she started from her seat exclaiming, 'I cannot sit between these two. It makes me feel so nervous.'

Grieg sprang up, saying, 'But I have the courage;' and exchanged places with her. So the three composers sat together, all in good

---

* Anna Brodsky, wife of the Russian violinist Adolf Brodsky.

spirits. I can see Brahms now taking hold of a dish of strawberry jam, and saying he would have it all for himself and no one else should get any. It was more like a children's party than a gathering of great composers. My husband had this feeling so strongly that, when dinner was over and our guests still remained around the table smoking cigars and drinking coffee, he brought a conjurer's chest – a Christmas present to my litle nephew – and began to perform tricks. All our guests were amused, and Brahms especially, who demanded from A. B. the explanation of each trick as soon as it was performed.

523

One day at Bergen, Grieg went fishing with his friend Frants Beyer. After a while a musical theme came into his head. Taking paper from his pocket, he quietly jotted it down and put the slip beside him on the bench. A moment later, a gust of wind blew it overboard. Unseen by Grieg, however, Beyer retrieved it. Some moments later he began whistling the tune.

'What was that?' demanded Grieg.

'Just an idea I had,' said Beyer nonchalantly.

'What the devil! I just had the same idea myself.'

Adelina PATTI (1843–1919)

The highest paid soprano of her time. Born in Madrid, she made her début as a child in New York and sang at Covent Garden for twenty-five seasons.

524

J. H. Haverly, the famous ministrel manager, at one time was ambitious to become an impresario. He was encouraged in this by Mrs Haverly, who one day said to him:

'John, why don't you go after Patti?'

'I will,' said the ministrel king, and he at once sought an interview with the diva, and, incidentally, he asked her what terms she would accept.

'For opera or for concert?' queried Adelina.

'For concert,' said Haverly.

'Four thousand dollars a night; $200,000 for fifty concerts,' answered Patti.

For once, the indefatigable Haverly was nonplussed. 'Why,

Madame, that is four times as much as we pay the President of the United States for a full year!' he remarked.

'Well, then,' said Patti, 'why don't you get the President to sing for you?'

525

Great was the curiosity of the public to see Mme Patti and Mme Scalchi together in the same opera. About five o'clock the crowd outside the Academy was already immense, and it was not until seven that we opened the doors. The rush was great, and a sad incident now took place. A lady in the crowd who had purchased her ticket beforehand was taken up from the bottom of the staircase to the top, though she died before reaching the first landing from disease of the heart, rendered fatal by the excitement. Borne upwards by the dense crowd she did not fall till she reached the gallery. Fearing the alarm this occurrence might cause, the servants, in order that I should not hear of it, had placed the lady on the floor of a little top private box, where she remained during the whole of the performance; her body not being removed by her friends until the next morning.

526

[In] her closing scene in *Aïda*, she and the tenor are supposed to be immured in a tomb of stone. At the close of the duet Patti, who had instructed the stage manager to make her comfortable, would carefully adjust a sofa cushion which had been placed conveniently at hand, would kick with one high-heeled Parisian slipper a train around behind her and assisted by the tenor would compose herself in graceful position – and die.

527

I* asked why she had never sung any of Wagner's rôles. She looked at me with her beautiful eyes, and simply asked me, 'Have I ever done you any harm?'

528

Patti was possibly the last great singer to resist the blandishments of the gramophone. Finally, in 1903, she relented and admitted the cumbersome recording equipment to her castle, Craig-y-Nos.

After a few days, she consented to sing Mozart's 'Voi che sapete',

---

* Sir Felix Semon (1849–1921); British laryngologist.

then demanded to hear it at once, rendering the record unusable for manufacture. 'I shall never forget the scene', wrote Landon Ronald, the producer. 'She had never heard her own voice, and when the little trumpet gave forth the beautiful tones she went into ecstasies! She threw kisses into the trumpet and kept on saying, "*Ah, mon Dieu! Maintenant je comprends pourquoi je suis Patti! Oh oui! Quelle voix! Quelle artiste! Je comprends tout!*" [Good heavens, now I understand why I am Patti! What a voice! What an artist! I understand all!] Her enthusiasm was so naïve and genuine that the fact that she was praising her own voice seemed to us all to be right and proper.'

⌂⌂⌂

Hans RICHTER (1843–1916)

Hungarian-born musician, assistant to Wagner, who chose him to conduct the first complete *Ring*.

529

During their residence in England Mrs Richter became ill and was afflicted with attacks of fainting, what the Germans call *schwindeln*, and had to lie down. When some one solicitiously inquired of the great conductor after the health of his wife, Doctor Richter replied, 'My vife, she is very bad; venn she does not lie she schwindles.'

530

He once pulled up the 'cellos in the passionate cantilena in the Introduction to *Tristan* with the words: 'Gentlemen of the violoncellos, you play that like married men!'

⌂⌂⌂

Nikolay RIMSKY-KORSAKOV (1844–1908)

Composer of Schéhérezade, teacher of Glazunov and Stravinsky.

531

Rimsky-Korsakov
In 1871 Mussorgsky and I agreed to live together, and we rented an apartment, or rather a furnished room. It was a unique example of two composers living together. How could we avoid disturbing each other? Like this. Mornings, till about noon, Mussorgsky used the piano and I copied or orchestrated something I had fully thought

out. At about noon he left for his duties at the Ministry, and I used the piano. The evenings were arranged by mutual agreement.

532

The critic M. D. Calvocoressi met Rimsky-Korsakov in Paris in 1907 and had the nerve to tell him that he preferred *Boris Godunov* in Mussorgsky's original version. The reviser of the opera was not offended. He merely smiled, shook his head and said, 'You young people in France go picking out in Mussorgsky's music just the specks of dirt; and then you put them all on an altar and worship them.'

533

Alexander Gretchaninov* approached him with a youthful work with which, he said, he was not entirely satisfied. 'Why not?' asked Rimsky-Korsakov.
'Because it resembles Borodin a little too much.'
'Don't be afraid if your music looks like something,' declared Rimsky-Korsakov, 'just beware if it doesn't look like anything!'

❧

Pablo de SARASATE (1844–1908)
[b. Sarasate y Navascuez]

Virtuoso Spanish violinist.

534

Apart from the beauty of his playing . . . I† shall always be grateful to him for his grand snub to the lady who invited him to dine *'avec votre violon'*.
'Chère Madame,' he replied, *'je viendrai avec plaisir, mais mon violon ne dîne pas.'* [I'll come with pleasure but my violin doesn't dine]‡

❧

---

* (1864–1956); Russian composer.
† Helen Henschel, daughter of Sir George Henschel, conductor and baritone.
‡ *However, this story has a life of its own*: When Johann Fischer [1733–1800], the celebrated oboe player, who was remarkable for the oddity of his manner, played concertos at the grand concerts given fifty years ago at the Rotunda in Dublin, a noble lord who had been enraptured with the rare talent he displayed, came up to him, and after having complimented him, gave him a pressing invitation to sup with him the following evening, adding, 'You'll bring your oboe with you!' Fischer, who was a little nettled at that sort of invitation, hastily replied, 'My Lord, my oboe never sups!'

Gabriel FAURE (1845–1924)

French composer, reforming director of the Paris Conservatoire, numbering Ravel, Enesco and Nadia Boulanger among his pupils.

535

Fauré was made head of the Conservatoire after the musical establishment provoked uproar by disqualifying Ravel from the Prix de Rome competition. The outgoing director, Théodore Dubois, solemnly warned his successor of his responsibilities, *'Monsieur, le Conservatoire, comme son nom l'indique, est fait pour conserver la Tradition'* (Sir, the Conservatoire, as its name implies, exists to conserve Tradition). The very act of Fauré's appointment caused so many resignations that the unassuming musician was nicknamed 'Robespierre' and Parisians talked of his 'daily cartload of victims'.

536

He was very conscious of the dignity of his position. He would arrive at the Conservatoire each day by cab, having travelled by Metro to the previous station.

537

Ravel once brought some songs to show him, but Fauré pushed them aside. At the next class he asked to see them again. 'I didn't bring them,' said Ravel, 'you rejected them.' 'I might have been wrong,' replied Fauré. Asked some time later what he had done with the songs, Ravel said, 'I burned them. Fauré was right.'

꠸꠸꠸

Thomas Alva EDISON (1847–1931)

The inventor of the phonograph listed 'reproduction of music' as only one of its ten possible uses.

538

[Twenty years ago, recalled Edison] when the talking machine was still a dubious proposition, a list of new records was often handed to me for approval. After hearing them I would mark 'good', 'fair' or 'rotten' to classify them for the trade. The 'rotten' records always made a hit with the public. Now all I have to do is condemn a bit of music and the factory works overtime to meet the demand.

Jean de RESZKE (1850–1925)
[b. Jan Mieczyslaw]

Polish singer, the outstanding tenor of the 'golden age of opera'.

539

Nellie Melba remembers

Chicago was in those days an even greater contrast to Boston and New York. In fact, all my early memories of Chicago were rather turbulent. I shall never forget an evening when I was singing with Jean de Reszke in *Romeo and Juliet*. It seemed to me as the performance progressed that we were not holding the audience as we usually did, and that somewhere in the back of the hall there was a disturbance brewing. And then there was a commotion, a general rising, a few startled screams, a confusion in the orchestra, and before I knew what had happened I saw clambering up over the footlights a man with staring eyes and the face of a lunatic, coming towards me.

It *was* a lunatic, a man who had in some way or other escaped from his asylum and had obtained entry to the house. For a moment everybody was paralysed. And then Jean came to the rescue. He ran forward, drawing his stage sword from its sheath and waving it fiercely in the man's face. The man looked as though he might give fight – and if he had done so I don't know what would have happened, for he was a powerful fellow and a theatrical sword is not a very good weapon against the strength of a maniac.

540

Jean de Reszke wished to sing the part of Werther in Massenet's opera of that name. Harris* thought the English public would not care for the work; Jean de Reszke swore that they would, and the manager consented to give it a chance.

To the shame of our opera-goers, Massenet's charming music was not appreciated. Neither was the touching, ultra-sentimental subject to which it is set. At the end of the performance Sir Augustus said to de Reszke:

'Well, you have had your way. *Werther* has been played, and for the present season this one representation will be enough.'

De Reszke, however, insisted on its being played again, and once more Sir Augustus gave in. On the afternoon of the day fixed for the second performance the manager was grieved to find that the seats

---

* Sir Augustus Harris (1852–96); English impresario.

were not letting at all. There would only be thirty pounds in a house which holds twelve hundred.

Suddenly there arrived from M. de Reszke a messenger bearing a letter. It was a request for a couple of stalls, 'if there were any left.'

'Come in here,' said Sir Augustus to the servant who had brought the letter, and he took him to the box office. 'Mr Hall,' continued Sir Augustus, addressing now the principal box-keeper, 'Mr Hall, give me eighty stalls, twenty boxes, and a hundred amphitheatre stalls. Make up into a parcel, please.'

Then, handing the packet to de Reszke's messenger, Sir Augustus told him to say that if M. de Reszke wanted twice as many tickets he could have them. Half an hour afterwards Sir Augustus received a telegram informing him that the distinguished tenor was ill, and would be unable to sing that night.

It was no longer necessary for Werther to commit suicide. *Werther* was already dead.

❦

Engelbert HUMPERDINCK (1854–1921)

Composer of *Hansel and Gretel*, the foremost children's opera.

541

When Augustus Harris himself went to America, it was to produce Humperdinck's *Hansel and Gretel* with the great Anton Seidl as conductor; but the opera was a 'frost', and the last touch of humour which nailed its coffin on the first night was a speech from Harris wherein he suggested 'a hope that there was enough artistic spirit in America to appreciate the wonderful work of this great composer, Pumpernickel.'

❦

Leŏs JANÁČEK (1854–1928)

Czech composer who waited until the age of fifty for his first success –
Jenufa – and followed it with a string of operatic masterpieces.

542

He was the first composer to reproduce the musical patterns of
everyday speech and constantly listened for the music that runs
through conversation. He met Smetana's daughter while out shop-
ping and immediately recorded her commonplace remarks on
staves that he drew in a notebook.

543

He kept altering the score of *The Makropoulos Affair* even during the
dress rehearsal until the conductor lost his temper and shouted, 'No
more changes!' Janáček acquiesced, and quietly departed. On the
opening night, in the middle of the opera, the leader of the 'cello
section and the conductor exchanged a look of astonishment as they
found themselves playing music they had never seen before.
Apparently, Janáček had gone into the library after the last rehearsal
was over and discreetly inserted a new solo for 'cello.

❦

John Philip SOUSA (1854–1932)

Composer of 'The Stars and Stripes Forever', 'The Washington Post',
and one hundred other rousing marches. A native of Washington DC,
he conducted the US Marine Corps band before touring the world with
his own band.

544

John Philip Sousa recalls
At the end of my concert in Hanover, the US consul approached,
radiant with joy. He and I went to his apartment, flushed with
triumph, and enjoyed a glass of Rhenish wine. He discussed every
piece on the programme, claiming each was better than the preced-
ing one and all of them excellent. Placing his hand on my shoulder,
he exulted:

'This is the happiest night of my life. Sousa, we are Americans! Let
us celebrate this great American victory. I have a bottle of Kentucky

whiskey. We will take it to the café, select a private room, and drink to your success!'

[Next day,] at the hotel, a bedraggled and woe-begone consul awaited my return from the matinée. His first words were, 'What did you do to-day?'

'Just what I intended to,' I replied.

'But did you go to the matinée?' he asked.

'I'm not here for my health,' I smiled, 'of course I went to the matinée, but why do you ask?'

'Man, don't you realize what we did last night?'

'Of course. We sat downstairs and had a few drinks, celebrating the success of the concert; that's all.'

'All!' he echoed, holding his head. 'All! Why, we drank an entire bottle of Kentucky whiskey. I've been in bed all day with a towel around my head. I've been so thoroughly knocked out that I couldn't even sign important official papers.'

'My dear consul,' said I impressively, 'you have been here twelve years. You have grown soft. Go back to America, my dear sir, and be a man again!'

⚮

Artur NIKISCH (1855–1922)

Hungarian conductor of the Berlin Philharmonic and Leipzig Gewandhaus orchestras. Known to his players as 'Der Magier', he was credited with supernatural powers.

545

Before going on holiday I* had worked out our programme in every detail, leaving a plan as to all rehearsals, etc., with my partner. According to this arrangement Artur Nikisch, then twenty-three, was to conduct the performance of *Tannhäuser*.

Presently there comes a telegram: 'Orchestra refuses to play under Nikisch. Too young!'

Just as I was about to leave for Leipzig an idea struck me and I telegraphed 'Don't postpone *Tannhäuser* on any account. Keep to programme, Nikisch conducting rehearsal to-morrow. Call meeting of orchestra.

'After having explained their rights and their limitations tell them, if they are still of the same mind, they may hand in their resignations

---

* Angelo Neumann (1838–1910); Austrian impresario.

at the *Tannhäuser* rehearsal tomorrow; and at the end of the overture may say whether they will hold to their decision or not. In case the orchestra should then resign I shall come directly back to Leipzig.'

The success of this young leader in that overture was so unqualified that the musicians themselves begged him with a storm of cheers and congratulations to continue the rehearsal at once; and with this performance of *Tannhäuser* Artur Nikisch entered the ranks of the foremost conductors of Germany.

546

Nikisch was reputed to be less conscientious with new works than with old, and Max Reger determined to test his preparedness. During the last orchestral rehearsal before a première, the composer called for a run-through of the final fugue. Nikisch, on the podium, paged through his score back and forth and eventually confessed to his embarrassment that he could not find the fugue. 'There is none,' growled Reger.

೮〜⌇

Sir Edward ELGAR (1857–1934)

Worcester-born composer, he won international recognition for English music with the Enigma Variations, a set of personality sketches concealing several unsolved puzzles. 'Land of Hope and Glory', one of the Pomp and Circumstance marches, became the anthem of late Imperial Britain.

547

I* loved the Enigma and had the cheek of a young pup. One evening, after hearing Elgar and my father reminisce about the Variations, I asked him straight out, 'What is the Enigma?' Elgar said, 'You shouldn't be asking me that. You should ask Troyte Griffith.' I knew Griffith, who was the subject of the seventh variation; he was an architect and no musician at all. So I said, 'How could Troyte tell me?' Elgar laughed, and told this story:

One day when I knew Troyte was coming, I marked with sticky paper certain keys on the piano, and on each paper I put a number, showing the sequence in which they were to be played. I

---

* E. Wulstan Atkins (b. 1904); son of Sir Ivor Atkins (1869–1953), organist at Worcester Cathedral 1897–1950.

asked Troyte to play them in the order they were marked. When he had finished, I removed the sticky paper and told him, 'Troyte, you now know the Enigma!' I knew I was safe, because he wouldn't remember which notes he had played.

Now was Elgar just pulling my leg, as he frequently did? Frankly, I don't believe a word of it.

548

It is strange to think that about forty-five years ago I was expecting to solve the secret of the Enigma any day [writes 'Dorabella', subject of the tenth variation]. Recounting to me a conversation in 1923, Troyte Griffith wrote, in a letter dated 21 September 1937:

'When I was visiting Elgar at Kempsey I asked him, "Can I have one guess? Is it 'God save the King'?"

"No, of course not; but it is so well known that it is extraordinary that no one has spotted it."

"It." Yes; we always spoke of the hidden matter as "it", never as tune or theme.

In November 1899, E. E. chaffed me:

"Haven't you guessed it yet? Try again."

"Are you quite sure I know it?" "Quite." And on another occasion:

"Well, I'm surprised. I thought that you of all people would guess it."

"Why me of all people?"

"That's asking questions!"'

549

One evening . . . Elgar had been working nearly all day, and we were sitting discussing the details of the construction and the possible lay-out of the orchestration which would follow, when he suddenly said, 'You know, Billy'* – I was Billy by this time – 'my wife is a wonderful woman. I play phrases and tunes to her because she always likes to see what progress I have been making. Well, she nods her head and says nothing, or just, "Oh, Edward!" – but I know whether she approves or not, and I always feel that there is something wrong with it if she doesn't. She never expresses her disapproval, as she feels she is not sufficiently competent to judge of the workings of the musical mind; but, a few nights before you came, we were at Plas Gwyn, Hereford. I played some of the music I had written that day,

---

* William Henry Reed (1876–1942); violinist, leader of the London Symphony Orchestra.

and she nodded her head appreciatively, except over one passage, at which she sat up, rather grimly, I thought. However, I went to bed leaving it as it was; but I got up as soon as it was light and went down to look over what I had written. I found it as I had left it, except that there was a little piece of paper, pinned over the offending bars, on which was written, "All of it is beautiful and just right, except this ending. Don't you think, dear Edward, that this end is just a little . . . ?" Well, Billy, I scrapped that end. Not a word was ever said about it; but I rewrote it; and as I heard no more I knew that it was approved.'

550

Sir Edward told a good one about his father who was demonstrating a piano to a client in his [music] shop at Worcester. 'Where do you get such fine children?' said the dear old lady. 'I pick them out myself in London,' replied Elgar senior, thinking only about his instruments.

551

As a young man, Elgar was conductor of the attendants' orchestra at Powick Lunatic Asylum. One of his favourite stories told of the visit by an Inspector of Asylums to the institution in Edinburgh while it was being redecorated. The decorators had been instructed that under no circumstances should they talk to the inmates.

'How many coats of paint are you putting on that door?' demanded the Inspector. The painter dutifully ignored him.

'Do you hear me, fellow?' demanded the Inspector. Still no reply.

'Are you deaf, or stupid?' he finally shouted. 'Are you aware that I am the Inspector and I am addressing you?'

The painter, terrified, turned round. 'Gang awa', ye deleerious deil!' he screamed, and took to his heels.

The word 'deleerious' became a favourite of Elgar's, inserted in his scores wherever the music rose to a tremendous climax.

552

We* walked slowly to the hall, first round Langham Place to kill time. As we were nearing the Artists' Entrance we passed an itinerant fiddler giving a fairly good rendition of Salut d'Amour. The delighted composer paused and from his pocket produced half a crown. Handing it to the bewildered musician, he said, 'Do you

---

* The narrator is Fred Gaisberg, record producer.

know what you're playing?' 'Yes,' he replied. 'It's Salut d'Amour by Elgar.' 'Take this, it's more than Elgar ever made out of it,' responded the donor.

553

On his deathbed, in February 1934, Elgar asked to see his friend, the critic Ernest Newman. 'He made a single short remark about himself' recalled Newman, which I have never disclosed to anyone and have no intention of ever disclosing, for it would lend itself too easily to the crudest of misinterpretations. . . . It has a particular bearing, I am convinced, on . . . his two "enigmas" – that of the Variations and that of the "Soul" enshrined in the violin concerto.'

Newman took the secret to his own grave four years later. 'Elgar's distressing remark consisted of only five words,' he explained to Gerald Abraham, 'but . . . they are too tragic for the ear of the mob.'

୧ᢀᣇᢀ୭

Ruggero LEONCAVALLO (1857–1919)

Composer of *Pagliacci*, which shares opera's most popular double-billing with Mascagni's *Cavalleria Rusticana* ('Cav & Pag', as they are known).

554

Leoncavallo was a fat, good-natured fellow, very fond of eating, and somewhat ponderous for an Italian. I* knew him in the nineties when he made a furore with his opera *Pagliacci*. I met him once many years after, and it was then that he recounted to me an incident which occurred in a little town in Italy called Forli, known for its silk factories, but, of course, boasting its own opera house, notwithstanding its population was not more than 40,000. He was there by chance and saw that a performance of *Pagliacci* was in the evening bill. Nobody knew he was there, and he decided to go and listen to it *incognito*. At the opera he sat beside an enthusiastic young lady, who noticed that he never applauded, but on the contrary showed signs of boredom. 'Why don't you applaud! Don't you like' it!' she asked. The composer, much amused, answered disagreeably, 'No; on the contrary, I find it great rubbish and unoriginal. It is the work of a *dilettante*.' 'Then you must be very ignorant of music,' she replied indignantly. 'On the contrary,' said Leoncavallo, 'it is because I

---

* Sir Landon Ronald (1873–1938); British conductor.

241

know what I am talking about that makes me so certain my opinion is correct'. He then tried to persuade her that this particular aria was stolen from Bizet, that another motive was from Wagner, and that such-and-such a bit was taken from Verdi, and so on and so on. She looked at him with pity in her eyes and remained quiet till the end of the performance. 'And all that you have told me is your honest opinion of *Pagliacci*?' she asked, rising to leave. 'Every word of it,' said the composer. 'All right,' she said, 'one day you'll be sorry for it.' He bowed low to her, and they separated. Next morning, reading the chief local paper, his eye fell upon an article, headed in big letters, 'Leoncavallo on his own Opera *Pagliacci*.'

. . . He swore to me that never since had he said an unkind word about his own music.

❧

Lillian NORDICA (1857–1914)
[b. Norton]

The first American to sing at Bayreuth.

555

Madame Nordica was married to a Hungarian singer, who considered himself engaged to the *prima donna* before she had left for America the previous year. It is said he was kept aware of her movements in America by her maid, who before long informed him that attentions were being paid to her by another. He thereupon set sail for New York, and on his arrival made his way to Nordica's hotel. Upon being announced and received by the beautiful artist, he, so the story goes, drew a pistol from his pocket and threatened to shoot her then and there unless she married him immediately. Influenced both by awe and admiration of so doughty a lover, the fair Lillian went with him to a clergyman near by who married them, the clergyman's wife being the witness. She later averred that the soprano was in such a torrent of tears that she could not answer the questions put by the clergyman during the wedding ceremony; while the bridegroom, with flashing eyes and moustache on end, commanded the minister, 'Go on! *Prima donnas* always behave this way when they are getting married.'

❧

Dame Ethel SMYTH (1858–1944)

English composer of ephemerally successful opera (*The Wreckers*); militant feminist.

556

Sir Thomas Beecham's broadcast reflections
She threw herself [into the Suffragette movement] with the same excitement, vigour and industry as she did into all things artistic. She led processions, she made speeches, she thumped many tubs here and there, and finally distinguished herself by throwing bricks – through the dining-room or drawing-room windows of Cabinet ministers. After a while (this was tolerated for a little while) it became too much of a habit to be encouraged and so Ethel was arrested, tried and convicted, and sent to Holloway Prison to reflect and, if possible, repent. Accompanying her were about a dozen other Suffragettes, for whom Ethel wrote a stirring march song of freedom. On one occasion (when) I went to see her the warden of the prison, a very amiable fellow, was bubbling with laughter. He said, 'Come into the quad!' There were the ladies marching up and down, singing hard. He pointed up to a window, where Ethel appeared, was leaning out, conducting – with a toothbrush – with immense vigour and joining in the chorus of her own song.

∾

Giacomo PUCCINI (1858–1924)

Composer of operas to realistic plots that touched occasionally upon the sordid.

557

While he was [in Vienna] he stayed at one of the best hotels, where he was besieged by admirers, ladies, and reporters, though he displayed a cunning worthy of a Red Indian in eluding these exhausting encounters, and was only too happy when, comfortably clad in pyjamas, he could abandon himself to the undisturbed enjoyment of his beloved cigarettes in the quiet ease of his handsome room. On this occasion there was a ring at the telephone, and he was informed that a lady urgently desired to speak to him. 'What is she like?' he replied. The porter assured him that she was young and charming, and received the order, 'Show her up!' a shy knock was heard, and a brother and sister appeared at the door, a really beautiful girl and her little brother – but, horrible to relate, the boy had a roll of music in his hand. The girl allayed the Master's consternation by saying that the boy had to go to his music lesson, but that, if the Master would allow her, she would stay with him in the meantime and let her brother call for her on his way back. Puccini good-humouredly raised no objection, being far from averse from a pleasant conversation with this attractive creature. He merely requested that, while the brother was taking his departure, he might change from his sleeping-suit into some more formal costume, during which time he asked the young girl to wait for him in the hall. She promptly consented; but when, a few minutes later, he came out of his dressing-room in an elegant visiting costume, he was transfixed with amazement for he found the young lady standing before him stark naked. '*Una povera pazza!*' (a poor madwoman) was the idea that flashed through his mind, and for a moment he hesitated whether to ring the bell or not, and commit the poor creature to the servants' care. But next he reflected that, after all, it was not without danger to oppose the will of a lunatic – and he decided that it would be better not to do so.

558

It was a stage accident in a Vienna rehearsal of *Tosca* that gave Puccini one of his most dramatic moments. While Maria Jeritza was walking towards the sofa where she was to sing 'Vissi d'arte' to the relentless police chief, she slipped, fell, and sang the aria from a prone position. 'At last!' exclaimed Puccini. 'That's how it is to be sung. Tosca struggles with Scarpia, falls to the ground and from there addresses her aria not to the tyrant but to Heaven.'

559

While Puccini was working at his opera at Torre del Lago with greater fervour than ever, the band of friends who were bidden every evening to the Maestro's villa formed itself into a club bearing the name of the new opera. . . .

One evening at the La Bohème Club started like all the previous ones, but ended very differently. . . .

The date was November 1895, and the time at night. The friends were playing at cards, while the Maestro sat at his Förster upright piano striking one chord after another. None of the club members were troubling about him, nor he about them. From time to time there would be a subdued cry of, 'Diamonds!' 'I trump it!' Next a murmur from the piano of 'F-e-f-g-, no, that will not do; B flat minor – that will be all right.' Then, from the table: 'Be careful, Cecco!' 'Pagno, you might take the game seriously!' 'Of course not' – from the piano – 'Of course it must be C sharp minor.' From the table: 'I trump it!' *Che ha detto il medico? – Verrà* (What said the doctor? – He'll come), hummed the Maestro, absorbed in Mimi's death-scene. Suddenly he turned to his friends. 'Be quiet, you fellows! It is finished!' All of them threw down their cards and crowded round him; and he sang them the last scene of the opera, that of Mimi's peaceful death, with its gently expiring the music full of stifled tears and the grief of young hearts. All of them wept, and Puccini, too, shed tears. They embraced him in silence; and one of them said, 'These pages will make you immortal.'

560

Caruso was dragging out his arias. *'Chi son? Chi son?'* [Who am I?] he sang slowly. *'Sei un imbecile!'* [You're a fool] retorted Puccini, to general delight.

561

Turandot received its first performance seventeen months after Puccini's death. Although a final scene had been added by Franco Alfano, Toscanini chose to end the opera with Liu's death, on the last notes Puccini had inscribed. He laid down his baton and, pre-empting applause, turned round to make the only speech of his life to an audience. 'Here Death triumphed over art,' he said, and left the pit. The lights went up, and the audience dispersed in silence.

❧

Eugène YSAYE (1858–1931)

Belgian violinist, conductor and composer; introduced many new works, including the Franck sonata.

562

There was nobody to meet us* at the little station; our telegram had somehow gone astray. So we trudged along the dusty road with our little overnight bags. At the Ysaÿe home we learned that Eugène had gone fishing; we were told where we would be likely to find him.

Sure enough, there he sat in the broiling sun, with a large sombrero

---

* The violinist Fritz Kreisler and his wife Harriet, the narrator here.

on his head, seemingly half asleep. We watched him for quite a while. He did not catch a single fish during that time. Now and then, nevertheless, he pulled in one of his lines. It wasn't a fish that he was hauling in – he had fastened beer bottles to this line which he kept on the bottom of the river for cooling purposes.

563

Arrived at his rooms, we* found him not only awake but sitting on a chair in his vast nightgown, pipe in mouth, and playing away for dear life. He told us to disregard him, for he had to do some work as he was playing in Glasgow (which he pronounced Glozgov) the following evening and had to play a concerto he had not played in quite some time. To my inexpressible joy, it was the rarely-heard Concerto in F by Lalo, which I knew, though I had never heard it played.

I leaned against a piece of furniture while he, with closed eyes and the huge pipe dangling from the right side of his mouth, was pouring forth his wealth of marvellous tone, staggering me with his mastery of the bow and ease of the left hand. However, there was another thing which dumbfounded me and it was that in the pages of passage-work there were scarcely two consecutive measures which contained the notes exactly as they had been written! Perhaps the composer, who doubtlessly had been an intimate friend of Ysaÿe, had made a revision of that work, for the passages, were different from the printed notes. Reaching a spot where the orchestra interrupts with loud chords, Ysaÿe relaxed for a moment, lowered his violin and, opening his eyes, winked at me. Then, in a high-pitched, thin voice imitated the 'meow' of a cat, re-lighting his pipe, he turned to me and said, 'Meow . . . *eh bien cochon, ça va, hein?* [not bad, pig, eh?]' He saw that I was transfixed with joy and as I made no response he guffawed: 'Well say something! It went well, didn't it? What do you think?' I was too confused to be able to find the right words and dreading to contradict him. I blurted the words which accomplished precisely that! I answered, 'Oh, it is marvellous, only it isn't quite right. It isn't that . . . it isn't accurate!'

'What!' he roared like a bull which had just been stabbed, and putting fiddle and pipe down, took his long hair in each fist and bellowed, 'René, René, did you hear that? René, this *cochon* has the effrontery to tell me that it wasn't right!' While he stood there, a fistful of hair in each hand, I begged his friend Ortmans to try explain to him that it was all, of course, marvellous, genial, overwhelming

---

* Two young violinists, Arthur Hartmann (1881–1956), and René Ortmans.

and staggering because he was not playing the actual notes in the pages of figurations, as published by Lalo. It was in vain I tried to tell him that I knew I had been very much out of order to make the comments that I had, that I did not know the French language sufficiently to pick quickly the right forms and words with which, with due apologies, to express my astonishment that a page of artistically woven figurations, so characteristic of Lalo, could have been so similar and yet dissimilar sufficiently to confound me, and so on. But he was too stunned and infuriated to pay any attention to Ortmans and my explanations and, still tearing at his hair, he stood over me menacingly while he kept on repeating, 'So you *know* the work – *you* know it? Do you hear that, René? This *cochon* here knows the Lalo, when I have played it before he was born.' . . .

But suddenly his mood changed and with thorough glee at my red-faced humiliation and wretchedness, he roared, 'René! Now you are going to see something! This *cochon* is going to play the Concerto in F of Lalo for me!' He winked his eyes, slapped his thighs and seizing his fiddle and bow thrust them at me with terrific imprecations and ordered me to play the pages containing the passage-work in question!

This was an encounter I had not expected, and paralysed with terror as this infuriated Goliath towered over me, I begged, actually begged tremblingly, to be forgiven and to be allowed to run from that room. But it was useless, for he kept thrusting fiddle and bow toward me and with terrific oaths ordered me to begin. He straddled a chair, turning it around so that his arms rested on its back, his enormous bare legs and thighs exposed to view, and smoking his pipe. I started the concerto, unprepared as I was, to play it. He watched me steadily and when I reached the passages in question, he closed his eyes, squeezing them together very hard, as if to impress something on his brain. Presently he stopped me by holding up his hand, and opening his eyes, he said to me in a normal, quiet voice, 'Play that place over again – a little more slowly.' Once more the eyes closed, were tightly squeezed, the head nodding. 'And now continue,' he said, and again all this had to be repeated. When I terminated the first movement, he turned to Ortmans and said in a matter-of-fact voice: '*Eh bien*, he is right. I must look through the score a little after lunch,' and approaching me, he gave me a slap on the back and said, 'Hm . . . *c'est un brave!* He has talent. We will have lunch together, won't we, *Cochon* . . .?'

Pulling his night-gown over his head, he told me to continue with the two remaining movements while he dressed. His clothes were strewn all over the place and I can now visualize him sitting there, pausing in the midst of pulling on a sock, or his trousers, while with closed eyes he was again making a mental record of something in the music at that particular point. This experience is not recounted to show that although unprepared and under such demoralizing conditions I did manage to play the concerto with such a colossal violinist and artist watching every finger-move and bow-stroke, but that Ysaÿe only one day before rehearsing and playing it publicly with orchestra, conceived the work as an entity and thus had woven things (scarcely less genial than those of Lalo himself) around the music, harmonies which he knew were in the background of the score, just as he, through habit, always filled in harmonies in the single-voiced or melodic phrases.

⌣∕∧∧∖⌣

Gustav MAHLER (1860–1911)

Son of Jewish distiller, Mahler's ancestry, his self-revealing symphonies and his reforms as director of the Vienna Opera aroused violent animosity; his last four conducting seasons were spent in New York.

564

I* wanted to know nothing less than how music is composed. 'God, how can you ask such a thing, Natalie? [he exclaimed]. Do you know how a trumpet is made? One takes a hole and wraps tin around it; that's more or less what composing is.'

565

It is said that when as a small boy he was asked what he wanted to be when he grew up, he replied, 'A martyr.'

566

Gustav Mahler to Natalie Bauer-Lechner, 9 July 1896
'My father . . . married my mother . . . who did not love him, hardly knew him before the wedding, and would rather have married another man. But her parents and my father made her submit to his will. They suited each other like fire and water. He was all obstinacy, she gentleness itself. Yet but for that union, neither I nor my Third Symphony would exist – I find that quite remarkable.'

---

* Natalie Bauer-Lechner (1858–1921); chamber musician who was Mahler's devoted friend until his marriage in 1902.

Mahler, in conversation with Freud

In the course of the talk [in 1910] Mahler suddenly said that he now understood why his music had always been prevented from achieving the highest rank, through the noblest passages, those inspired by the most profound emotions, being spoiled by the intrusion of some commonplace melody. His father, apparently a brutal person, treated his wife very badly, and when Mahler was a young boy there was a specially painful scene between them. It became quite unbearable to the boy, who rushed away from the house. At that moment, however, a hurdy-gurdy in the street was grinding out the popular Viennese air, [*Ach*] *Du Liebe Augustin*. In Mahler's opinion the conjunction of high tragedy and light amusement was from then on inextricably fixed in his mind, and the one mood inevitably brought on the other.

At the age of eleven, he was boarded at the Prague home of a wealthy leather merchant, Moritz Grünfeld, two of whose sons were to become celebrated pianists. Mahler told his wife that he was kept short of food and clothing at Grünfeld's, but 'his worst experience was being the involuntary witness, when he was sitting in a dark room, of a brutal love scene between the servant and the son of the house, and he never forgot the shock of disgust it caused him. He jumped up to go to the girl's help, but she did not thank him for his pains. He was soundly abused by both of them and sworn to secrecy . . . Gustav never forgave the young pianist* who had given him this shock.'

Ludwig Karpath† found Mahler looking sad and self-absorbed in a Vienna coffee house. When he asked him what was the matter, Mahler confessed that he had just learned that his father was ill. Next morning, while walking to the theatre, Karpath saw a man running sobbing through the streets. With some difficulty, he recognized Mahler and asked if something had happened to his father. 'Worse, worse, much worse,' wailed Mahler. 'The very worst has happened. The Master has died.' The date was 13 February 1883, and news had arrived from Venice of Wagner's death.

---

* Alfred Grünfeld (1852–1924).
† (1866–1936); Viennese music critic, formerly a singer.

Mahler and [his sister] Justi recalled an adventure at the two-storey Café in Budapest City Park, a favourite spot on fine days for elegant society to meet. They were sitting on the upper terrace, their backs to the balcony, having tea. When eating out, Mahler always wiped every piece of cutlery and crockery before using it. Even here, he rinsed a glass with water before drinking from it, and unthinkingly emptied it out over his shoulder – onto the lower terrace and some extremely well-dressed ladies, who cried out in alarm. 'So sorry,' gasped Mahler, realizing immediately what he had done. . . . Being Director of the Opera and a well-known personality whose absent-mindedness was legendary, he was forgiven and calm was restored. Five minutes later, when Justi asked for a glass of water, he rinsed out her glass as well and gave the lower terrace its second shower. This time there was general uproar, everyone laughing and shouting; a waiter just managed to put down a laden tray in time before he collapsed with laughter. It was quite a while before Mahler and Justi were seen again in the City Park.

Brahms was reluctantly taken to the Budapest Opera in 1890 to hear Mahler conduct *Don Giovanni*. He would have preferred to visit a beer-hall, but came along on the promise of a good sofa in the box to sleep on. During the overture, his friends heard grunts of approval from the sofa; gradually they rose to shouts of admiration. At the end of the first act Brahms rushed backstage to embrace the man who had given the finest *Don Giovanni* he had ever heard. 'He immediately became my fiercest partisan and benefactor,' said Mahler.

'The conductor here,' wrote Tchaikovsky from Hamburg to his nephew, 'is not merely passable but actually has genius and ardently desires to conduct the first performance [of *Eugene Onegin*]. . . . The singers, the orchestra, Pollini the manager and the conductor – his name is Mahler – are all in love with *Onegin*; but I am very doubtful whether the Hamburg public will share their enthusiasm.'

Encouraged by praise from the senior conductor, Mahler persuaded Hans von Bülow to listen to the 'Totenfeier' movement of his second symphony. Mahler began playing an excerpt on the piano but, when he looked up, saw Bülow standing beside the window, his hands over his ears. Mahler got up, but Bülow motioned him to continue. When he had finished the piece, there was a long silence. Then Bülow said, 'If that's music, I don't understand anything about music.'

574

Frustrated at 'remaining undiscovered like the South Pole' Mahler engaged the Berlin Philharmonic Orchestra and chorus of the Singakademie at his own expense to give the first full performance of the Second Symphony, on 13 December 1895. His ascent as a composer, wrote Bruno Walter, can justly be dated from that day. 'Yet how badly things might have turned out! Mahler used to suffer at times from a sick headache the violence of which was in proportion to his vehement nature. His strength would be quite paralysed. There was nothing for him to do on such occasions but to lie still, as in a swoon. . . . Here in Berlin he had staked his future fate as a composer upon a single card and, in the afternoon before the concert, he lay with one of the worst sick headaches of his life, unable to move or partake of anything. . . . I can still see him before me on the conductor's platform . . . deathly pale, mastering his affliction, the musicians and singers, and the audience, with a superhuman exertion of his will.'

'The triumph,' reported Justi Mahler to Natalie Bauer-Lechner, 'increased with every movement. Such rapture is witnessed only once in a lifetime. I saw grown men weeping and young men falling on each other's necks. And when the Bird of Death utters his last prolonged call over the graves – Mahler said he feared for a moment that the long silence in which the whole audience must hold its breath might not work – there was such a deathly silence that it seemed no one in the hall so much as batted an eyelid. And when the chorus entered, a shuddering sigh of relief broke from every breast. It was indescribable!'

575

The critic Max Graf asked him why he only composed symphonies. 'The only time I have to compose is in summer,' said Mahler. 'During this short holiday I have to write large works if I want to go down into posterity.'

576

In 1893 he rented rooms in the remote and often rainswept village of Steinbach on the Attersee, in Upper Austria. Peaceful though it was, the silence he required was absolute. His companions bribed children and farmers to keep their distance and hung their voluminous bathing costumes in the fields to scare off the birds. Even these measures, however, were insufficient, and in the following year Mahler had a small composing house built beside the lake. 'He would often say that the lake had its own language,' recalled the builder, Franz Lösch, 'that the lake spoke to him. He could not hear the lake from the inn, and needed to be beside it to compose more easily.'

577

It was a splendid day in July 1896 when the lake steamer landed me* at Steinbach. Mahler met me at the landing and, in spite of my protest, lugged my suitcase down the gangway with his own hands. When, on our way to his house, my glance fell on the Höllengebirge, whose forbidding rocky walls formed the background of an otherwise charming landscape, Mahler said, 'No need to look there any more – that's all been used up and set to music by me,' and immediately began to speak of the construction of the first movement of the Third Symphony, the introduction of which bore the tentative title: *Was mir das Felsgebirg erzählt* (What the rocks and mountains tell me).

578

The soprano, Lilli Lehmann
In Mahler's symphonic compositions, I was struck at once by the fact that the effect was caused by the simplicity of the melodies, which he knew how to present, of course, with an immense apparatus. The idea flashed into my mind, at the same time, that perhaps he might be the very one who would be willing, especially with regard to the machinery, to strike again into simple paths, and I put the question to him. He replied with scornful laughter, 'What are you thinking of? In a century my symphonies will be performed in immense halls that will hold from twenty to thirty thousand people, and will be great popular festivals.' I was silent, but I thought, involuntarily, that the more music is deprived of intimacy, the more it will be lacking in true genius.

579

'I am three times homeless,' he would say. 'As a native of Bohemia in Austria, as an Austrian among Germans, and as a Jew throughout the world.'

---

* The conductor, Bruno Walter (1876–1962).

At the beginning of his first *Ring* cycle in Vienna in August 1897 Mahler 'could hardly wait for seven o'clock: he was as excited as a child before Christmas.' In the last scene of *Das Rheingold* he gave the sign for a crucial tympani roll – and nothing happened. He looked up and saw that the tympanist was missing. After the performance he discovered that the man lived in a distant suburb and had left to catch the last train. At midnight, Mahler sent a telegram to the man, ordering him to report to his office first thing in the morning. There, he tore furiously into the wretched musician. The tympanist explained that on his salary of sixty-three guilders a month (less than £7) he could not afford to live in central Vienna and support a wife and child. Mahler decided on the spot to raise the orchestra's salaries, even if that meant cutting down on scenery and costumes.

He would let his baton shoot forward suddenly, like the tongue of a poisonous serpent. With his right hand he seemed to pull the music out of the orchestra as out of the bottom of a chest of drawers. Mahler was conscious of the extreme tension that emanated from him into the theatre. He once told me* . . . 'Believe me, people only realize what I am when I am gone.'

General Picquart recalled that during his unjust imprisonment over the Dreyfus scandal he had pledged to fulfil two missions if ever he was set free: to visit Beethoven's residences, and to hear Mahler conduct *Tristan*. He duly travelled to Vienna and on the evening the opera was to be performed, he took his seat an hour before the curtain rose. Just as the orchestra was tuning up, his hostess entered his box with a telegram from Georges Clémenceau, the French Prime Minister. It read, 'Please inform General Picquart that I have made him Minister of War. Return immediately.' Picquart blanched with rage at this news. 'It was your duty to keep it from me,' he shouted. 'Tomorrow morning would have been soon enough.'

When he crossed the street, hat in hand and gnawing his lip or the inside of his cheek, even the drivers of the cabs would turn their

---

* Max Graf (1873–1958); critic.

heads after him and whisper to each other tensely and in awe: 'Der Mahler!'

584

Arriving from Berlin on the overnight train for a performance of Beethoven's E flat major concerto with the Vienna Philharmonic, the pianist Ferruccio Busoni found a message ordering him to report to Mahler as soon as he had checked in at the hotel. Without pausing to wash or have breakfast, he raced over to the opera house. Mahler kept him waiting for an hour, then burst out of his office, shook his hand, declared, 'Not too fast in the last movement, Herr Busoni – all right?' and disappeared, whistling the main theme of the concerto.

585

Natalie coquettishly urged him to grow again the beard he had sported as a young man. 'What are you thinking of?' exclaimed Mahler. 'Do you think I go clean-shaven as a matter of personal vanity? There is a very good reason for it. When I conduct, I communicate with singers and orchestra not only with my hands and eyes but with facial expressions, through the mouth and lips. I could not do that if my face were hidden by a beard. I must be quite free.'

586

During the last summer which Mahler was permitted to witness, a strangely terrifying occurrence depressed his thoughts. He told me* that, while at work in his composer's cottage in Toblach, he was suddenly frightened by an indefinable noise. All at once 'something terribly dark' came rushing in by the window and, when he jumped up in horror, he saw that he was in the presence of an eagle which filled the little room with its violence. The fearsome meeting was quickly over and the eagle disappeared as stormily as it had come. When Mahler sat down, exhausted by his fright, a crow came fluttering from under the sofa and flew out. The peaceful abode of musical absorption had become a battle-ground upon which one of the innumerable fights of 'all against all' had taken place.

587

In 1910 Mahler took the Philharmonic on a concert tour of New York State. When they reached Niagara Falls he exclaimed, 'At last, a real fortissimo!'

---

* Bruno Walter.

Thomas Mann was in Brioni in the early summer of 1911, reading daily newspaper reports of Mahler's declining condition. He had met Mahler in Munich after the Eighth Symphony première; his 'intense personality left the strongest impression on me.' He borrowed Mahler's Christian name and bestowed his physical appearance on Aschenbach, tormented hero of *Death in Venice*, which he was just beginning to write.

589

Arnold Schoenberg's diary, February 1912
[A publisher] asked me about Mahler, and, when I expressed enthusiasm, asked whether he should, perhaps, not have the plates [of his Fifth Symphony] melted down. I replied, 'For God's sake, not that of all things. Today's young people worship Mahler like a God. His time will come in, at most, five or ten years!'

‿᪗᪘᪗‿

Ignacy Jan PADEREWSKI (1860–1941)

First prime minister of independent Poland, pianist, composer and international celebrity.

590

Arriving in Paris in January 1919, just before the Versailles Conference, Paderewski was told that the Allies were reconsidering the promised inclusion of Danzig and parts of Silesia and East Prussia in the new Polish state. He hastened to the Quai d'Orsay and demanded an immediate meeting with President Clémenceau. The French Foreign Minister, Stephen Pichon, asked him to wait. Fifteen minutes later, the door opened and Clémenceau entered.

'You wanted to see me,' he addressed Paderewski, 'here I am. Are you a cousin of the famous pianist?'

'I *am* the famous pianist,' replied Paderewski.

Clémenceau, with an expression of mock surprise, shook his head pityingly. 'And you, the celebrated artist, have become Prime Minister? What a comedown!'

591

When he first came to America, his English was very incomplete but even then he demonstrated his grasp of it in unmistakable fashion.

One evening he, my wife, and I* dined at the house of very dear mutual friends, Mr and Mrs John E. Cowdin, in Gramercy Park. Cowdin had all his life been an enthusiastic polo player, and after dinner Paderewski and I admìred some handsome silver trophies that he had won and that were placed in the dining-room. I said, 'You see the difference between you and Johnny is that he wins his prizes in playing polo while you win yours in playing solo.'

'Zat is not all ze difference!' Paderewski immediately exclaimed in his gentle Polish accents. 'I am a poor Pole playing solo, but Johnny is a dear soul playing polo.'

592

Not long before [Anton] Rubinstein's departure for Europe he wrote a large number of variations on 'Yankee Doodle', and meeting me† shortly afterward, he informed me of the fact, and added, 'I have inscribed your name at the head of the title-page, and they are now in the hands of the publisher.'. . .

The second season Paderewski was here I sat next to him at a dinner given just after his arrival. During conversation he said somewhat suddenly, 'Mr Mason, I have just composed a fantasy on "Yankee Doodle", and have dedicated it to you.' He looked at me, and thought he saw a curious expression in my face, – although I was quite unaware of such a thing, – and continued, 'You don't like it!' 'Oh, I do,' I protested, 'and esteem the dedication as a great honour.' 'I see you don't,' he said. 'Well,' I replied, 'I already have one "Yankee Doodle" from Rubinstein, and was thinking that the coincidence of your dedicating me another was very curious, that is all. Let me explain to you that "Yankee Doodle" does not stand in the same relation to the United States as "God Save the Queen" to England, "Gott erhalte Franz den Kaiser" to Austria, or the "Marseillaise" to France. "Yankee Doodle" was written by an Englishman in derision of us.' I am afraid that my remarks discouraged him, for he never finished the composition. He played it to me as far as he had progressed with it, and it is certainly the best treatment of the theme I have ever heard.

593

One day, about 1937, I‡ was walking down the long corridor at

---

* Walter Damrosch (1862–1950); conductor.
† William Mason (1829–1908); American pianist and composer.
‡ Miklós Rózsa (b. 1902); film composer.

Denham film studios when I saw a little old fellow with long white hair coming towards me. I recognized him as Paderewski, the famous pianist and former Polish Prime Minister, who was recording the soundtrack for the film *Moonlight Sonata*. Suddenly a stocky man came round the corner into the corridor. 'Churchill!' exclaimed Paderewski excitedly, and they pumped each other's hands and laughed. Winston Churchill was in Denham writing a film script on the life of his ancestor, the Duke of Marlborough. Both men were political outcasts; it must have been the first time they had met since Versailles.

❧

Hugo WOLF (1860–1903)

Austrian composer of song cycles.

594

In December 1875 the fifteen year-old Wolf, newly arrived in Vienna, wrote to his parents

I have been with – guess who? – *Meister* Richard Wagner. On Saturday 11 December at half past ten I saw Richard Wagner for the second time at the Hotel Imperial, where I stood on the staircase for half an hour waiting for him to arrive. At last the Master came down from the second floor and I greeted him very respectfully from a distance. He thanked me in a very friendly manner. As he reached the door, I leaped forward and opened it for him; at which, he stared hard at me for a few moments, then left for the rehearsal [of *Lohengrin*] at the Opera. I ran as fast as I could and arrived there just ahead of Richard Wagner's cab. I bowed to him again and tried to open the door for him, but couldn't manage and the driver had to jump down and open it. Wagner said something to the cabbie – I think it was about me. I tried to follow him to the stage, but was not allowed in.

As I had often waited for him at the Imperial, the hotel manager, whose acquaintance I had made, promised to bring me to Wagner's notice. Who could have been happier than I when he told me to come back the next day so that he could introduce me to Frau Cosima's chambermaid and Richard Wagner's valet? The next day I went with the maid to the Master's rooms. At last Wagner appeared, together with Cosima and [Karl] Goldmark. He was going into his room without noticing me when the maid said beseechingly, 'Ach,

257

Herr Wagner, a young artist who has waited upon you for a long time, wishes to speak to you.' He came out, glanced at me, and said, 'I have already seen you once, I believe, you are . . .' (he was probably going to say 'you are a fool'). Then he went in and opened the door of the reception room for me; it was furnished in truly regal style. When I was inside the room he asked me what I wanted.

To be continued in my next letter. . . .

I said to him, 'Honoured Master, I have long desired to hear an opinion of my compositions and it would be' – He broke in and said, 'My child, I cannot judge your compositions. I have no time and cannot even get my letters written. *I understand* nothing at all about music.' I asked the Master whether I should achieve anything in music, and he said, 'When I was your age and composing music, no one could tell if I would do anything great. . . .' When I told him that I took the classics as models, he said, 'Good, good, one can't be original all at once.' He laughed and said, 'I wish you, dear friend, much happiness in your career. Go on working hard and, if I come back to Vienna, show me your compositions.'

With that, I left the Master profoundly moved and impressed.

595

The Café Grünsteidl, nicknamed Café Grössenwahn [Megalomania], attracted a regular clientèle of famous musicians and writers, including Brahms, Hanslick, Hugo von Hofmannsthal, Arthur Schnitzler, Frank Wedekind and Hermann Bahr. Fritz Kreisler recalled that when Hugo Wolf dropped in, dressed in a brown velvet jacket and artist's black tie, he would make sure that Brahms was absent before taking a seat. Wolf and his songs were the target for considerable derision among the café's patrons until one day someone said, 'If they are so good, why don't you play them to us?' Wolf sat down at the piano and immediately captivated his audience. 'Why haven't you shown these songs to Meister Brahms?' he was asked. 'I sent him a song five years ago and asked him to mark a cross in the score wherever he thought it was faulty,' replied Wolf. 'Brahms sent it back unread, saying, "I don't want to make a cemetery of your composition."'

596

His classmate, Mahler, took a summer job in 1880 conducting opera at the Upper Austrian resort of [Bad] Hall. Wolf replied that he would not take just any job. 'I shall wait,' he said, 'until they make me God of the Southern Hemisphere.'

He began to have delusions that he, not Mahler, was Director of the Opera and would march beneath the external arches of the building shouting that he was now in charge. He even rang the bell at Mahler's flat, at Auenbruggergasse 2, and demanded that the servant let him enter as master of the house. After violent scenes at the homes of various friends, he was persuaded to ride in a carriage that would take him to Prince Liechtenstein, who could confirm his appointment at the Opera. Instead, the journey led to Dr Svetlin's private mental asylum, where attendants awaited him.

598

One day, in an advanced stage of his illness, he sighed, 'If only I were Hugo Wolf.'

∽∾∽

Dame Nellie MELBA (1861–1931)
[b. Helen Porter Mitchell]

Australian soprano whose stage name, taken from her native city (Melbourne), was later attached to sundry products, including an ice-cream and a toasted snack.

599

She habitually chewed chewing-gum, or for preference a piece of Australian wattle gum, on opera or concert nights to keep her mouth and throat moist. Making an entrance at Covent Garden, she took her gum from her mouth and put it on a little glass shelf, provided for the purpose in the wings. When she came off the stage, she went to the shelf, picked up her piece of gum, as she thought, and put it in her mouth. She spat it out, and two or three strong words with it. A stagehand had substituted a quid of tobacco for the gum. Melba demanded that all the stagehands should be sacked, but she was probably less furious with them than with Caruso, who thought the incident was the best joke of the Covent Garden season.

600

The chef of the Savoy Hotel in London, the renowned Escoffier, was desolate at being unable to get tickets for her sold-out gala performance. Melba somehow obtained him two seats. Next day at lunch, an extraordinary dessert made its début at her table accompanied by a note from the chef, saying he had named it after her: *Pêche Melba*.

601

Though I have no objection to *Pêche Melba*, I have the strongest objection to my name being calmly taken for any object which the proprietor considers suitable – from scent to hairpins. America is particularly prone to this sort of piracy. I was wandering down a street in New York one day when I suddenly stopped short before an immense drug store, across the windows of which were splashed glaring advertisements of Melba perfume. 'Ah!' I said to myself, 'I think I deserve a bottle of this.' And so I went inside.

I said: 'May I smell the perfume Melba?'

'Certainly,' said the assistant, and sprayed some on my wrist.

One sniff was enough. I hated the stuff.

Then I humbly asked who had given them permission to call this 'creation' Melba.

'Oh, that's all right,' drawled the assistant. 'We've found out that her name is Mrs Armstrong, and we've just as much right to call this stuff Melba as she has.'

❧

(Achille-) Claude DEBUSSY (1862–1918)

French composer whose style was called 'Impressionist' because of its pictorial images and delicate colourations. He became a somewhat notorious figure in Paris, when his abandoned mistress and wife both attempted suicide.

602

At the Press rehearsal of Debussy's *Pelléas et Mélisande*, I* heard a well-known professor at the Conservatoire say in an angry voice to a group of his pupils assembled around him during an interval: '*Le premier qui apporte cette cochonnerie de partition dans ma classe, le premier qui s'en autorise pour faire des fautes d'harmonie, je le f— à la porte de ma classe, et je le fais f— à la porte du conservatoire.*' [The first one to bring this filthy score into my class, the first to make these errors of harmony, I will — him to the door of my class and — him to the gate of the Conservatoire]' He was, no doubt, merely letting off steam: later, I think, he developed a genuine liking for *Pelléas*. But his

---

* Michel Dimitri Calvocoressi (1877–1944); critic and scholar.

attitude that day represented exactly the official stand taken by the Conservatoire. A little later one pupil, by name Emile Vuillermoz (who has since made a great reputation as a critic) was actually expelled, at another teacher's request, for having been found in possession of the forbidden score while attending a class.

603

The disruption of *Pelléas* reached its peak at the dress rehearsal. A subversive programme was circulated in the hall, Mary Garden's* Scots accent was greeted by howls of derision, and an elderly gentleman demanded plaintively to know when the orchestra would finish tuning up. Debussy organized a group of supporters to protect the first performance; their number was swiftly swelled by self-appointed *Pelléastres*, members of a new cult: 'Beautiful young men with long hair carefully brushed over their foreheads, with dull, smug faces and deep-set eyes. They wear velvet collars and puffed sleeves . . . loosely floating ties . . . precious rings of Egypt or Byzantium on their little fingers (for they all have pretty hands).' . . . Beneath the spell, they whisper in each other's ears, and their whispers descend deep into the soul.'

Before long Debussy was complaining that 'the so-called Debussyites will end up disgusting me with my music.'

604

The Orchestre Colonne refused to take La Mer seriously and its conductor, Camille Chevillard, had to plead with the players not to argue over every bar. Pierre Monteux, first viola, says the musicians were so irritated by the sounds they were making that they fabricated diversions. 'One jocular fellow concocted a small boat of music paper. With a slight push of the foot, it sailed on a wooden sea, from basses through the 'celli and violas, the length of the platform. This childish idea met with such success that there was soon a whole fleet of small ships made from all kinds of paper as Neptune, conceived by Claude Debussy, thundered his way to the end.'

605

Fauré, who had listened to the orchestra rehearsing the movement called 'De l'aube à midi sur la mer' [from dawn to moon on the sea], was asked if he liked the music. 'Indeed,' he replied, 'especially the little bit at thirteen minutes to twelve.'

---

* (1874–1967); Scottish soprano, the first Mélisande.

I* had rehearsed the [Queen's Hall] orchestra until there was practically nothing left for Debussy to do. The rehearsal went off smoothly enough but at the concert there was a peculiar accident. I do not remember ever witnessing anything quite like it. In the second of the Nocturnes (a movement called 'Fêtes') the time changes a good deal. To the surprise of all of us, Debussy (who, quite candidly, was not a good conductor even of his own works) suddenly lost his head, and his beat! Realizing what he had done, he evidently felt the best thing was to stop and begin the movement over again. He tapped the desk, and tapped again.

Then the most extraordinary thing happened. *The orchestra refused to stop*. It really was an amazing situation. Here was a famous composer directing a work of his own and, having got into difficulties was asking the orchestra to stop and was being met with refusal. They obviously did not intend to stop: they knew that the audience would think the fault was theirs. Moreover, the work (which they liked immensely) was going beautifully and they meant to give a first-rate performance of it; which they proceeded to do and succeeded in doing. I never knew them more unanimous.

The audience by no means missed the fact that something had gone wrong because it was evident that he had tried to stop the orchestra. At the end, in truly English fashion, they recorded their appreciation to such an extent that he was compelled to repeat the movement. This time nothing went wrong and the ovation was even greater than before. Debussy was non-plussed and certainly did not understand the English mind; but I was proud of my orchestra that afternoon.

Our meeting was quite formal. I† played the pieces, and he expressed himself satisfied. One little thing alone broke the stiffness of the occasion. After I played the last piece, 'Golliwog's Cake-Walk', he remarked:

'You don't seem to object today to the manner in which I treat Wagner.'

I had not the slightest idea what he meant and asked him to explain. He then pointed out the pitiless caricature of the first measures of *Tristan and Isolde* that he had introduced in the middle

---

* Sir Henry Wood (1869–1944); British conductor.
† Harold Bauer (1873–1951); Anglo-American pianist.

of the 'Cake-Walk'. It had completely escaped me. I laughed heartily and congratulated him on his wit.

The concert came off. The hall was full. To my chagrin, Debussy was not there. I played the suite and went out into the courtyard of the old house whose ballroom had been converted into an auditorium. I found the composer walking up and down with a very sour face. He came up to me and said, '*Eh bien!* How did they take it?'

I was immediately filled with an immense pity for him. I realized that this great man, who had struggled so long to obtain recognition of the new idiom he was bringing to our art, was *nervous*, scared to death at the thought that his reputation might be compromised because he had written something humorous.

I looked him straight in the eye.

'They laughed,' I said briefly.

I saw relief pour through him. He burst into a stentorian roar of glee and shook me warmly by the hand.

'*Vous savez? Je vous remercie bien!*' [You think so? I'm very grateful to you!] he said.

608

A pianist, playing some of his pieces, insisted that the tempo in a certain passage should be 'free'.

Debussy said afterwards, 'There are some who write music, some who edit it, and that gentleman who does as he pleases.' Asked what he had said to the pianist, Debussy replied, 'Nothing. I looked at the carpet – and he will never tread on it again.'

Ravel made Marguerite Long repeat this story to him time and again.

609

Satie's sardonic characterization of Debussy and his admirers

Les Commandements du catéchisme du Conservatoire	The Commandments of the Conservatoire Catechism
I Dieubussy seul adoreras Et copieras parfaitement.	One *God* Debussy alone shalt thou adore and copy him perfectly.
II Mélodieux point ne seras De fait ni de consentement.	Melodious thou shalt never by act or by condonement be.
III De plan toujours tu t'abstiendras Pour composer plus aisément.	Thou shalt abstain from planning altogether, in order to compose more easily.

IV	Avec grand soin tu violeras Des règles du vieux rudiment.	Thou shalt violate the old primer and all its rules deliberately.
V	Quintes de suite tu feras Et octaves pareillement.	Forbidden fifths shalt thou utter and consecutive octaves, similarly.
VI	Au grand jamais ne résoudras De dissonance aucunement.	Thou shalt never – but never – resolve a dissonance entirely.
VII	Aucun morceau ne finiras Jamais par accord consonnant.	No piece must finish ever upon a chord consonantly.
VIII	Des neuvièmes accumuleras Et sans aucun discernement.	Ninth chords upon ninths shalt thou gather undiscerningly.
IX	L'accord parfait ne désireras Qu'en marriage seulement.	Perfect harmony thou shalt abhor – except in holy matrimony.

Ad Gloriam Tuam
Erit Satis ('This will be enough')

❧

Frederick DELIUS (1862–1934)

Born in Yorkshire, Delius spent most of his life abroad in Florida, Norway and France. Blind and paralysed from 1922, he last works were 'dictated' to a young volunteer, Eric Fenby.

610

Delius recalls

[Strindberg's] interest in spiritualism caused Leclerq* and me to play a trick on him. I asked them both to my rooms one evening, and after dinner we had a séance of table-rapping. The lights were turned down and we joined hands round a small table. After ten minutes'

---

* Julien Leclerq (1865–1901); French poet.

ominous silence, the table began to rap and Leclerq asked it what message the spirits had for us. The first letter rapped out was M, and with each letter Strindberg's interest and excitement seemed to increase, until the momentous word MERDE had been spelled in its entirety. I do not think he ever quite forgave us for this.

611

Delius returned to England from France in 1918 with a new orchestral work for Sir Henry Wood's Prom. concerts. Wood, on meeting Delius was 'deeply distressed with his tired and tragic appearance' and as soon as they reached Wood's house, Mrs Delius insisted that her husband take a rest. Delius, recalled Wood, 'proceeded to unbutton his waistcoat, shirt and top trouser buttons, and, to my astonishment, pulled out sheet after sheet of manuscript which proved to be his new work, Once Upon a Time (Eventyr). 'What a relief to get it safely to London,' he murmured, and subsided into a chair. 'I, too, am relieved,' whispered Madame Delius. 'I was so afraid they might search him and commandeer it.' They had feared arrest throughout the journey, alarmed by rumours that a conductor in America had been transmitting coded war secrets to Germany in the guise of musical compositions.

സ്ക്ക

Pietro MASCAGNI (1863–1945)

Composer of the perennially popular *Cavalleria Rusticana* – and little else of note.

612

Mascagni at this time was flushed with the success of *Cavalleria*, and annoyed at the failure of *L'Amico Fritz* and one or two other later works to attain the same merit of success. Mascagni's anger was further accentuated by the prevalent remark that it was 'a fervent hope he would soon write another *Cavalleria*'. I* quote this sentence as *ipsissima verba* of general criticism and newspaper comment. He heard the cry everywhere – in the theatre, club, Press, society, 'A long way off *Cavalleria*,' 'Nothing like *Cavalleria*,' 'Never so popular,' etc., etc. Mascagni got very much hurt at this, so much so, that at a reception given him at Sir Augustus Harris' house when the impresario asked him to conduct a selection of the popular work,

---

* James [Jimmy] Glover (1861–1931); Irish conductor.

which was just about to be played by the Coldstreams, he point-blank refused, but ultimately succumbed to the gentle persuasion of Lady Harris. . . .

As a sop, Sir Augustus took the composer down to Windsor a few nights later to conduct his opera *L'Amico* there, but even then he was not safe from the old *Cavalleria* taunts. . . .

To the Royal presence he was ushered – the usual Royal formalities – congratulations, etc., and then one parting Royal word; the Queen addressing the composer, 'Signor Mascagni, I hope you will soon write another *Cavalleria*.'

613

He set the story of Lady Godiva to music in *Isabeau*, and was surprised to find that sopranos demurred at the prospect of a naked horseback ride 'because they might catch cold'. Nonetheless the opera aroused great anticipation at Buenos Aires, where it was premièred in 1911. Fifty thousand Argentines greeted Mascagni upon the pier and seventy-five banquets were thrown in his honour. 'If my *Isabeau* is a success,' he wailed, 'I am a dead man: dead of indigestion.'

Eugen d'ALBERT (1864–1932)

Scottish-born composer and pianist, who became renowned as much for his multiple marriages as for his virtuosity.

614

The most celebrated of his six wives was the Venezuelan pianist, Teresa Carreño. Some time after they were married, one of her concerts was advertised numerically: 'Eugen d'Albert's *first* concerto will be played on the *second* of March by his *third* wife.'

615

'My music is still alive,' he told the cellist Gregor Piatigorsky, 'but it will die young.' 'Pay no attention,' said a colleague. 'He may be about to divorce or marry again. It always makes him gloomy.'

Richard STRAUSS (1864–1949)

Bavarian composer of tone poems and fifteen operas, setting provacative themes from Nietzsche (Zarathustra), and Oscar Wilde (Salome) and making his fortune with *Der Rosenkavalier*.

616

The father of Richard Strauss was the celebrated horn player in the Royal Orchestra in Munich, when *Tristan* and the *Meistersinger* were produced for the first time under Bülow. Bülow's Meiningen Orchestra had finished a tour of nineteen concerts at Munich (where Richard had conducted his Serenade for thirteen wind instruments), meeting everywhere with great success. Strauss *père* went to the artists' room in the Odeon in Munich to thank Bülow for what he had done for his son. Bülow listened to his words, and replied: '. . . Strauss, you were my bitterest enemy in the Munich Orchestra: did everything in your power to injure me when *Tristan* and the *Meistersinger* were produced in 1865 and '68. But,' pointing to young Richard, 'such is the revenge of Hans von Bülow.' The two Strausses, father and son, slunk out of the room, without another word.

617

Conducting the Berlin Philharmonic Orchestra in his early tone poem *Macbeth*, at Bülow's invitation, Strauss found he had forgotten most of the piece and had to refer constantly to the score. For which Bülow famously rebuked him: 'The score should be in your head, not your head in the score – even if you composed it yourself.'

618

Strauss, terribly annoyed [with the singer Pauline de Ahna, after she had thrown a tantrum], laid down his baton, interrupted the rehearsal which had been so violently disturbed, and without knocking entered Pauline's artist's room. Those waiting outside heard through the closed door wild shrieks of rage and fragmentary insults – then all was quiet. Turning pale each looked at the other; who had killed whom? Strauss opened the door and stood in the doorway beaming radiantly. The representative of the orchestra stammered his speech: 'The orchestra is so horrified by the incredibly shocking behaviour of Fräulein Pauline de Ahna that they feel they owe it to their honoured conductor to refuse in the future to play in any opera in which she might have a part . . .' Strauss regarded the musicians smilingly. Then he said, 'That hurts me very much, for I have just become engaged to Fräulein de Ahna.'

At the dinner given for Strauss by the Lotos Club at its old home in Fifth Avenue near Forty-sixth Street, I* sat next him while he wrote some bars of one of his own most difficult compositions for me in spite of the hum of talk and the blare of quasi-popular music about us. During a discussion about making musical sounds mean anything he said, 'I can translate anything into sound. I can make you understand by music that I pick up my fork and spoon from this side of my plate and lay them down on the other side.'

My† performances of Strauss's *Don Quixote* are founded on the memories of an evening with him at 46 Grosvenor Street. Knowing that I was soon to direct his epic in character-study, he volunteered after dinner to play the work through to me on the piano from my full score. Never shall I forget how he played and acted and sang every mood portrayed in the variations. When Sancho Panza talked via the viola solo) Strauss put words to the phrases: 'Give me more money, money, more money!' This fitted exactly the particular musical phrase.

He shouted to the string players before the rising phrase at the opening of his poem, Don Juan, 'Gentlemen, I would ask those of you who are married to play this phrase as though you were engaged.'

His passion was the German card game of *skat*, which he played at every possible opportunity. 'Everybody,' grumbled his son, 'writes about my father as though all his life he had done nothing but play *skat*.' In *Intermezzo*, his hero calls *skat*, 'the only relaxation after music'. Strauss once admitted that playing cards, at least one doesn't think of silly music. His first remark when working with a new orchestra was, 'I need some players for *skat*. Who will join me?' Klaus Tennstedt's father was one of the volunteers from the Breslau orchestra, and lost a lot of money over the years, while gaining invaluable insights into Strauss's music. Artur Schnabel lost so much on a single occasion that he forfeited the pleasure of Strauss's company for some time afterwards.

---

* David Bispham (1827–1921); American baritone.
† The narrator is Sir Henry Wood, the conductor.

At the Bayreuth Festival, to keep him and the cast content, Winifred Wagner discreetly reimbursed the singers and musicians who nightly surrendered their earnings to the card-sharp conductor.

But his favourite partners were Viennese bankers who would cheerfully lose to him and then invest his winnings; this fortune he lost in the collapse of 1929.

623

Asked why he did not leave Germany during the Nazi era, Strauss said Germany had fifty-six opera houses, the United States had two. 'It would have reduced my income.'

624

In a bitter moment near the end of his life, he said, 'With Wagner, music reached its summit. I am only a straggler.'

625

As he lay dying he told his daughter-in-law, 'Death is just as I composed it [sixty years ago] in *Tod und Verklärung*.' [*Death and Transfiguration*]

ᑯᗅᗅᗅᑊ

Alexander GLAZUNOV (1865–1936)

Russian composer, director of St Petersburg Conservatory, teacher of Shostakovich.

626

An anniversary concert in Glazunov's honour was held in Moscow in 1922. He went, and after the gala Lunacharsky, the People's Commissar of Education, gave a speech. He announced that the government had decided to give Glazunov living conditions that would facilitate his creativity and be commensurate with his achievements. What would any other man have done in the guest of honour's place? He would have thanked him. The times were hard and lean. Glazunov, who had once been a substantial and handsome man, had lost a catastrophic amount of weight. His old clothes sagged on him as though he were a clothes hanger. His face was haggard and drawn. We knew that he didn't even have music paper on which to write down his ideas. But Glazunov manifested an absolutely amazing sense of his own dignity. And honour. He said that he needed absolutely nothing and asked not to be put in circumstances that differed from those of other citizens. But if the government had turned its attention to musical life, Glazunov said, well then, let it rest on the Conservatoire, which was freezing. There was no firewood, nothing with which to heat the place. It caused a minor scandal, but at least the Conservatoire received firewood.

∾

Carl NIELSEN (1865–1931)

Danish composer. Born of peasant stock, his symphonies remained uncelebrated outside Denmark until recent years.

627

Nielsen, in his memoirs
There is a memory which must derive from my earliest childhood. It is of my mother's bared breast. We children were suckled till we were nearly two, and I clearly remember the feel of her skin and a certain displeasure when my snub nose got in the way. But now comes a time I must treat with some reserve, because it is interwoven with the affairs of my younger brothers and sisters, which I observed so often and shared in so much that they seem like my own. My mother's nipple was pale pink against a white skin, and when we sucked we had a vague impression of small cracks and wrinkles. When we were being weaned, some yeast, or perhaps tansy juice, would be smeared on the breast, and I still seem to remember the shudder that went through me; but it may have been from watching my younger brothers and sisters that I felt this shudder, for they would cry dreadfully. When my mother sat with the youngest at her breast she was invariably happy and almost gay. It would then strike her fancy to take the baby away, play with her breast a little, and then pop it into the mouth of one of the bigger children, saying, 'Would *you* like a drop, my pet?' I have stood up in my clogs in front of my mother and shared in this feast.

∾

Jean SIBELIUS (1865–1957)

Finnish symphonist, Sibelius attained national standing in the 1890s with a succession of patriotic orchestral works of which Finlandia (1899) became a quasi-anthem.

628

In November 1907, while on a conducting visit to Finland, a definitive dialogue on the nature of the symphony took place between Mahler and Sibelius. 'Mahler's grave heart trouble forced him to lead an ascetic life, and he was not fond of dinners and banquets. Contact was established between us in some walks,' recalled Sibelius. 'When our conversation touched on the essence of the symphony, I said that I admired its severity and style and the profound logic that created an inner connection between all the motifs. . . .

'Mahler's opinion was just the reverse, *"Nein, die Symphonie muss sein wie die Welt. Sie muss alles umfassen."* [No, the symphony must be like the world. It must embrace everything]

629

'Never pay attention to what critics say,' he warned a pupil. 'Remember,' he said, 'a statue has never been set up in honour of a critic!'

630

On his first visit to Vienna in 1890 he presented himself to Brahms with a letter of introduction from Busoni. Brahms, however, refused to see him. Sibelius was later told that he had responded to the request for an interview with Schubert's catch-all criterion: '*Kann er was?*' [Is he capable?] and no one could provide a satisfactory answer.

631

The conductor Kajanus,* one of Sibelius's most intimate friends, sought to excuse himself [after dinner] and take his departure, as he was due to conduct a concert at Petrograd next day. The others present protested that the occasion was not one to be sacrificed to such sordid material considerations, and pressed Kajanus to telephone through to Petrograd and cancel the engagement. Seeming to comply with the suggestion, Kajanus left the table, but went to

---

* Robert Kajanus (1856–1933); Sibelius' favoured interpretor.

the station, took train to Petrograd, conducted the concert, and returned to Helsinki, where, on re-entering the restaurant, he found the company still seated at the same table, engaged in the same animated discussion. On seeing him, Sibelius mildly expostulated with him, saying, 'That was surely a very long telephone call of yours, Kajanus!'

Sir Thomas Beecham
All my life when I have made gramophone records and listened to the tests, I have annoyed those around me by turning up the knob so the music is played *fortissimo*. Obviously, in my case, it is a necessity. I want to hear every note played. Although the effect may be distressing to the average ear, it is illuminating and edifying to *mine*, who am a workman in this. I don't make records for my own amusement, I make them to sell in the open market and it is my duty to see that all I have striven to do, with the orchestra, singers or choruses, comes off – with the utmost clarity if possible.

I was delighted, therefore, when seeing Sibelius last year, and taking some records of mine of his music, that he eagerly grasped them, put them on the gramophone and turned the knob up *twice* as high as I had ever done. There were about twelve or fifteen people in his large sitting room. After about three minutes I had a sense of vacuum and, looking round, I found the whole lot had vanished into the garden, and even there were holding their hands over their ears. But Sibelius was hanging over the machine itself and trying to get more and more tone out of it. I said, 'You have the same feeling about this sort of thing that I do.' He said, 'Oh yes, I want to hear everything. I want to hear every little note, every semi-quaver.'

Once, while Kajanus was rehearsing the second symphony with only two trumpets – the third having succumbed to influenza – Sibelius interrupted him and departed abruptly. 'I can only hear the trumpet which isn't there,' he explained, 'and I can't stand it any longer.'

He was thought by his closest associates to be psychic – 'not dependent only on five senses,' as his secretary put it. His wife believed he was aware when one of his works was being broadcast anywhere in the world. 'He is sitting quietly reading a book or newspaper. Suddenly he becomes restless, goes to the radio, turns the knobs, and then one of his symphonies or tone-poems comes out of the air.'

635

He rarely invited musicians to his home. 'They talk of nothing but money and jobs. Give me businessmen every time,' he said. 'They really *are* interested in music and art.'

⤙⤚

Ferruccio BUSONI (1866–1924)

Italian-born composer, pianist and theorist.

636

Mahler and Busoni [had] worked with enthusiasm and exceptional application to give a rendering [of Beethoven's Piano Concerto in E flat major] that should owe nothing to stale traditions. After arduous preparation, in a state of prolonged tension, these two servants of the loftiest discipline hoped to resuscitate the very spirit of Beethoven.

The introduction was only just over, when an obese lady, with tortoiseshell-rimmed glasses on her millionairish pug-nose, stood up in the first row of stalls, bellowed, 'This will *never* do,' and removed her expensive body.

637

There was a Polish singer at Bologna who pestered him relentlessly; one day when she had attached herself to him at luncheon . . . [a friend] suddenly came in. Busoni seized his opportunity and sprang up to shake hands with him.

'Oh my dear doctor! Here's a fine bottle of wine for you! Here's a fine cigar for you! Here's a fine figure of a woman for you! Amuse yourself well! Goodbye!'

638

Ferruccio Busoni, letter to his wife
I must tell you about my dream last night! I was in an old town and, from the top of a gothic tower, I was obliged to go down an *outside* winding staircase. I stepped through a window into the inside and came straight into a chapel where a service was being held (I think it was 'Catholic'). Then – at a sign from the priest – a piano was brought in like lightning, half through the air, by three men and three demons. And that was '*le piano du diable*' (I know I thought in

273

French). Then I had to play at the church ceremony all the most godless stuff that I could remember. I know that, amongst other things, I played the 'Kaspar-Lied' from *Freischütz* and the 'Mephistofeles-Serenade' by Berlioz. If the passages were difficult, then the thing played by itself. Like lightning it was carried away again. I cried out, 'Stop, I must still play something *religious*,' but it was too late. This is all the fault of Liszt's Mephisto Waltz at which I am working industriously and which will be masterly.

❧

Erik SATIE (1866–1925)

French composer, satirist and eccentric.

639

Satie seemed to be a man whose chief concern in life was to think out and perpetrate jokes obviously intended for his own amusement rather than for that of others.

'One day,' Satie said, [for example] 'I had a saucepan full of water on the gas ring. Just as it was about to boil, I was suddenly called away. When I came back, twenty minutes later, the saucepan was quite empty. Now, I had locked the door; the window was closed, and the room was empty except for the cat. So obviously it was the cat who drank the water.'

640

He thought it might be amusing to compose music *not* to be listened to, '*musique d'ameublement*', or wallpaper music. Milhaud had some of it played in the interval of a concert of works by 'Les Six' and Stravinsky. No sooner had Satie's music started, than people began returning to their seats. Satie pleaded with them, 'Carry on talking! Walk about! Don't listen!' But no one paid him any attention.

❧

Enrique GRANADOS (1867–1916)

Spanish composer and pianist who earned fame with his Goya-inspired *Goyescas*.

641

Ignacio Tabuyo, a former operatic star and now leading professor of singing at the Madrid Conservatoire, friend of most of the older Spanish musicians such as Arbos, Albéniz, Granados and Sarasate, would talk for hours of the times when they were youths together, and Granados was evidently the instigator of most of their pranks. He, Tabuyo, would show me a yellow photograph cracking with age in which Albéniz and Granados, comically clad in exaggerated mountaineering-cum-tourist outfits complete with feather in hat and knickerbockers, are surrounded by a pile of miscellaneous instruments, flutes, trumpets, guitars, violins, drums, etc: This photograph was taken during one summer season at San Sebastian when a select group of famous men met now and then at a music shop to gossip and make informal concerts. To Granados occurred the brilliant idea that they should form an orchestra in which each member should play an instrument of which he knew nothing. Tabuyo, for instance, would scrape wildly on a famous violinist's fiddle, Albéniz would splutter and splurge with dolorous heavings on some wind instrument, while Granados would play on comb and paper or conduct as he felt inclined. Rehearsals took place in the open patio behind the shop, and, though caution was observed, the fame of this strange orchestra quickly spread, even reaching to the King's ear in his palace, so that Royal inquiry was made as to their progress.

But the cooks and domestic servants domiciled round the patio had other fish to fry, and one day when Granados was putting his men through the paces of a classical symphony, there was a sudden deluge, and the sky, innocent of all clouds, rained rotten fruit, eggs, vegetable peelings and other misplaced matter. Valiantly the orchestra pursued its laborious way in an increasing din of yells and cat-calls, banging of trays and kitchen utensils, but not until Granados gave a final flourish did the players desist, and then he turned and bowed most gravely and ceremoniously to right and left, and all quite imperturbably though his clothes were besmirched and completely ruined.

642

Poor Granados. He was delighted to come to New York to see his opera *Goyescas*, at the Metropolitan, but it was done so badly that it gave him more pain than pleasure.

For his children's sake he was glad of the money he got. On account of the war he was afraid to accept checks or banknotes and took all his gains in the form of gold which he wore in a belt under his clothes. When his ship went down in the English Channel some of the passengers were saved, but Granados was pulled to the bottom of the sea by the weight of the gold.

❧

Arturo TOSCANINI (1867–1957)

Italian conductor, he presided over distinguished periods at La Scala, the New York Metropolitan Opera and New York Philharmonic Orchestra. In 1937 the National Broadcasting Company of America created an orchestra specifically for Toscanini to conduct, broadcast and record with over the next seventeen years.

643

Yehudi Menuhin, recalls

In his apartment at the Hotel Astor on Times Square – which had an Italian proprietor and no doubt reliable pasta – we had reached the middle of the slow movement [of the Beethoven Concerto] where, after the second *tutti*, the sound marked *perdendosi* hangs by a thread, when the telephone rang. Naturally I ignored it; so did my father in his unobtrusive corner; so, fumbling at the piano (for he was not a great pianist), did Toscanini. There was a second ring. We went on playing, I at least tensely aware that the pressure in the room was boiling up to a reaction. At the third ring, Toscanini stopped, rose from the piano stool, and with light determined steps walked not to the telephone, but to the installation in the wall and jerked the whole thing bodily out, wooden fitting, plaster, dust, severed dangling wires; then, without a word uttered, he came back to take up where we had stopped, in total serenity. When the third movement ended there was a timid knock at the door. Relaxed, unembarrassed, amiable, Toscanini gently called, '*Avanti!*' – his first word since the incident – and the door opened on an abject trio, his wife, the hotel proprietor and an electrician.

644

Just before a concert, he paced up and down in [Gregor] Piatigorsky's dressing room, grunting, swearing to himself and muttering to the 'cellist, who was warming up, 'You are no good; I am no good.' Piatigorsky stopped practising and begged him to desist. 'Please Maestro, I will be a complete wreck.' Toscanini departed to begin the concert. After a short overture, while waiting in the wings with the soloist before the concerto, he repeated, 'We are no good – but the others are worse. Come on, *caro*, let's go.'

The soprano Geraldine Farrar, with whom he had a passionate affair, deviated from the score in the rehearsal of a Puccini aria, and objected when Toscanini interrupted and rebuked her. 'Maestro,' she retorted, 'please remember I am a star.'

'The place for stars is in heaven,' shouted Toscanini.

⚬⚬⚬

Leopold GODOWSKY (1870–1938)

Polish-American pianist whose virtuosity was the envy of his contemporaries, and his piano arrangements their despair.

646

'What's the difference between Godowsky and a pianola?' Busoni would ask.

'Godowsky can play ten times as fast, but the pianola has ten times as much feeling.'

⚬⚬⚬

Franz LEHAR (1870–1948)

Austro-Hungarian composer of The Merry Widow and many other operettas.

647

Mahler and his young wife went to see The Merry Widow in Vienna, loved it, danced to its tunes as soon as they got home, played the waltz from memory on the piano but could not remember the exact run of one passage. Next day they went to Döblinger's music shop, but could not bring themselves to admit to the assistant that they were interested in a low-brow operetta. So while Mahler questioned the staff about sales of his own compositions, Alma browsed feverishly through a piano score of The Merry Widow. As soon as they were out on the street, she sang the waltz to him complete and imprinted it on their memories.

⚬⚬⚬

Alexander SCRIABIN (1872–1915)

Russian composer, Scriabin's mystical views were applied to his music, in which he created a 'mystic' piano chord and works such as the 'Divine Poem', the 'Poem of Ecstasy' and the 'Prometheus' Symphony.

648

Sergei Rachmaninov writes

I remember one discussion which took place between Rimsky-Korsakov, Scriabin, and myself, while we were sitting at one of the little tables in the Café de la Paix. One of Scriabin's new discoveries was concerned with the relation existing between musical sound, that is, certain harmonies and keys, and the spectrum of the sun. If I am not mistaken he was just working out the plan of a great symphonic composition in which he was going to use this relation, and in which, together with the musical incidents, there was to be a play of light and colour. He had never reflected upon the practical possibilities of this idea, but that side of the question did not interest him very much. He said that he would limit himself to marking his score ['Prometheus'] with a special system of light and colour values.

To my astonishment Rimsky-Korsakov agreed on principle with Scriabin about this connection between musical keys and colour. I, who do not feel the similarity, contradicted them heatedly. The fact that Rimsky-Korsakov and Scriabin differed over the points of contact between the sound – and colour – scale seemed to prove that I was right. Thus, for instance, Rimsky-Korsakov saw F flat major as blue, while to Scriabin it was red-purple. In other keys, it is true, they agreed, as, for example, in D major (golden-brown).

'Look here!' suddenly exclaimed Rimsky-Korsakov turning to me, 'I will prove to you that we are right by quoting your own work. Take, for instance, the passage in *The Miserly Knight* where the old Baron opens his box and chests and gold and jewellery flash and glitter in the light of the torch . . . well?'

I had to admit that the passage was written in D major 'You see,' said Scriabin, 'your intuition has unconsciously followed the laws whose very existence you have tried in vain to deny.'

I had a much simpler explanation of this fact. While composing this particular passage I must unconsciously have borne in mind the scene in Rimsky-Korsakov's opera *Sadko*, where the people, at Sadko's command, draw the great catch of goldfish out of the Lake

Ilmen and break into the jubilant shout, 'Gold! Gold!' This shout is written in D major. But I could not prevent my two colleagues from leaving the café with the air of conquerors.

649

Arthur Rubinstein, recalls
'Who is your favourite composer?' he asked with the condescending smile of the great master who knows the answer. When I answered without hesitation, 'Brahms,' he banged his fist on the table. 'What, what?' he screamed. 'How can you like this terrible composer and me at the same time? When I was your age I was a Chopinist, later I became a Wagnerite, but now I can only be a Scriabinist!' And, quite enraged, he took his hat and ran out of the café, leaving me stunned by this scene and with the bill to pay.

650

Over dinner in New York, the conductor Vassily Safonov, gossiped about Wagner, who had been invited by a beautiful lady of great wealth to spend a weekend at her country home. In the evening, Wagner whispered loudly enough for her husband to overhear that he would come to her room that night. The husband duly ordered a houseboy to polish the floor of the corridor all night long. Every time Wagner emerged from his room in his red silk pyjamas, he saw the servant and retreated. Early in the morning, the husband ordered him to leave.

Safonov laughed loudly when he finished the story. Scriabin grew very pale. 'Your lady is a fool,' he cried. 'She should have considered it an honour that Wagner even noticed her.' Infuriated, he swept the tablecloth with the remains of the meal onto the floor and stormed out of the room.

Ralph VAUGHAN WILLIAMS (1872–1958)

English composer and folksong collector who achieved worldwide renown with his orchestration of Greensleeves.

651

He was taught to read by his grandmother from the same book with which she had instructed her younger brother, Charles Darwin. There was a great kerfuffle among the family – like everywhere else – when *The Origin of the Species* was published, and Ralph, when he was about seven, asked his mother about it. His mother was extremely sensible. She said, 'The Bible tells us that God made the world in six days. Great-uncle Charles thinks it took rather longer. But we needn't worry – it is equally wonderful either way.'

652

On his first expedition collecting English folksongs in December 1903, Vaughan Williams asked a retired farm worker, Mr Pottipher, where the tunes he was singing came from. 'If you can get the words,' replied the Essex villager, 'the Almighty sends you a tune.'

653

After conducting one of his own works Vaughan Williams, as he left the podium, was heard to mutter, 'If that's modern music – I don't like it!'

654

From his home in Surrey, Vaughan Williams was active in the 1930s on behalf of refugees from Hitler's Europe. His committee bought a house in Dorking to shelter the homeless, and the composer often put up individuals at his own home. Once, during a committee meeting, a representative of the refugees complained that the house they had been allocated was cold and damp. Things had been so much better in Germany, he grumbled, where most people had central heating. As soon as he had left, other members of the committee began muttering 'ungrateful wretch', and similar epithets. Vaughan Williams simply said, 'Isn't it wonderful that he can remember the *good* things in Germany . . .?'

∽✺∾

Enrico CARUSO (1873–1921)

Italian tenor, the first singer to make creditable gramophone records.

655

Dame Nellie Melba

Never shall I forget one night at Monte Carlo, before an immense audience 'thick' with Grand Dukes and Princesses and Marchesas, how I was suddenly startled in the middle of the death scene by a strange squeaking noise which seemed to come from Caruso as he bent over me. I went on singing, but I could not help wondering at the time if Caruso was ill, for his face was drawn and solemn, and every time he bent down there was this same extraordinary noise of squeaking. And then with a gulp which almost made me forget my part, I realized that he had a little rubber toy in his hand, which at the most pathetic phrases he was pressing in my ear. You know how difficult it is to stop laughing when you are supposed to be solemn; but when you are supposed to be dying the temptation is almost too much to be borne.

656

The record producer Fred Gaisberg heard Caruso for the first time in March 1902 in Milan, in the première of Franchetti's opera, *Germania*. He immediately went backstage and reached agreement that Caruso would record ten songs on the following afternoon for a fee of £100. Gaisberg cabled London for approval but was instructed: 'Fee exorbitant, forbid you to record.' He decided to proceed regardless. The ten records netted a profit of £15,000. Over the next twenty years Caruso earned almost £1 million pounds from records.

657

Caruso's powers of eating were prodigious. During the opera season he frequently lunched at Pagani's with Scotti and Sammarco. This became known and many of his admirers flocked there to lunch also, just to gaze upon the great tenor *intime* as it were. It was not an attractive sight.

Quite unconscious of his audience, Caruso would twist spaghetti round and round a fork until the plate was empty; then the whole would go down the throat that made him a fortune, at one gulp. The plate would be refilled from the dish, and the same operation repeated. . . .

One day, however, Caruso did shock his watching admirers. Whilst he was in deep talk with Sammarco, the favourite spaghetti having been despatched, the manager recommended a dish of particularly fine peaches. Apparently, Caruso took no notice, going on talking, but carefully felt each peach in turn. To the utter amazement of the onlookers a huge peach suddenly disappeared in the tenor's mouth. There was an equally sudden silence, only broken by the sound of the stone falling upon his plate.

658

Caruso was proud of his skill as a cartoonist and . . . greatly disappointed when Mark Twain failed to invite him to a dinner he once gave in New York to eminent cartoonists. 'Perhaps,' he said plaintively, 'he knows me only as a tenor.'

Feodor CHALIAPIN (1873–1938)

Russian bass, outstanding as Boris, Ivan the Terrible, Mefistofele and similar superhuman roles.

659

P. G. Wodehouse ('Plum') and Guy Bolton meet the mighty bass

'*Feodor!* Feodor, my *pet!*'

This time it was something spectacular, the great Chaliapin in person, looking, as he always did, like a benevolent all-in wrestler. Both Guy and Plum had often admired him, but never more so than now, for his first act was to thrust them back into their seats with a ham-like hand and insist jovially that they get on with the serious business of the evening.

'Zoop is zoop,' he said, speaking in English with an accent in which a spoon which would have stood upright, and they felt he could not have phrased it more neatly.

'These are two playwrights that I am dining with,' said Marguerite, performing a belated introduction.

'We do musical comedies,' said Guy, pegging away at his soup.

'A low form of art, of course,' said Plum, pegging away at his.

Chaliapin would have none of this self-deprecation.

'*Not* a low form of art,' he insisted vehemently. 'When I am a student at the gymnasium, I too write a musical comedy. In it there is a scene which I will give to you, Mr Bolton, as a present. It is a bum scene and very phoney.'

It seemed to Plum that the great man was too modest.

'Oh, I'm sure it isn't,' he said politely.

Marguerite interpreted.

'Bomb scene. Very funny.'

'Yes, so phoney you will laugh off your heads,' said Chaliapin. 'You are to imagine that I am a cruel Governor and you two are revolutionists who have come to blow me up with a bum. But I catch you, and my men they tie you to a bench and I put the bum beneath the bench. It is a time-bum and it goes tick-tock, tick-tock. I laugh. It tickles me like a horsehair undervest. Because it is a fine torture for 'you to hear that tick-tock, tick-tock, tick-tock.'

'Like someone reading the minutes at a meeting,' said Guy brightly. 'What happens then?'

'I tell you. The bum is going tick-tock, tick-tock, when a noise outside distracts my attention, and I turn my back for a moment. You have one hand free, and you take the bum and slip it into the pocket of my *palto*, my big overcoat. There are more noises outside and I go out to ask, "What the hell?", and the bum she goes with me.'

He illustrated this bit of action by turning away and squeezing past a party of two elderly ladies and a deaf old gentleman who were taking their places at the next table.

'But wait,' bellowed Chaliapin from a distance of several yards, his organ-tones ringing through the restaurant. 'You have not seen the last of me. I come back now to gloot over you.'

He began to creep back, his face wearing a hideous and menacing scowl. The two ladies at the next table stirred uneasily.

'Remember I have the bum in my pocket.' He patted his pocket. 'I am coming back to laugh, to gloot over you. The bum is ticking – any minute now she is going off – and I am glooting. Pigs! Children of pigs! In a little moment you will be sausage meat. You will be buttered all over the walls. It makes me laugh to think of it. Ha, ha, ha, ha.'

It was a good laugh, and it sent the two elderly ladies scurrying to the door, leaving their deaf escort to his fate. People were standing up, trying to see what the commotion was about. There was a sense of relief, mingled perhaps with a certain disappointment, when Chaliapin, reaching the table, sat down and helped himself to wine from the teapot, his face wreathed in smiles.

'Phoney?' he said.

'Very phoney,' agreed Guy faintly.

Chaliapin looked about him, inspecting the table closely. He seemed puzzled.

'Where is the other gentleman? There were two gentlemen two musical comedy writers, drinking zoop. Now there is one gentleman.'

'Mr Wodehouse had to leave hurriedly,' Guy explained. 'A sudden seizure. He gets them sometimes. I understand he hears buzzing sounds – '

'Like a bum going tick-tock, tick-tock, tick-tock?'

'Exactly. Accompanied by an occasional cow-bell.'

※

Sergei RACHMANINOV (1873–1943)

Rachmaninov, feeling unable to compose after initial successes, resorted to hynotherapy; the result was the famed Second Piano Concerto. The Russian composer finally settled in Switzerland and the United States and achieved a reputation as much for his piano playing as his music.

660

Rachmaninov writes

Amongst the Professors at the green table sat Tchaikovsky. The highest mark given was a five, which could, in exceptional cases, be supplemented by a plus sign. I knew already that I had been given this mark. When it was my turn to play and I had finished, Arensky drew Tchaikovsky's attention to the fact that I had been the only pupil who, during the last lesson, had written two-part 'songs without words', and asked whether he would like to hear them. Tchaikovsky nodded his assent, and as I knew my songs by heart I sat down and played them. When I finished Tchaikovsky rose and busied himself with the examination journal. It was only after a fortnight that I heard what he had been doing with it: he had added three more plus signs to my mark, one on top, one below, and one behind. This five with four plus marks – a unique occurrence in the annals of the Conservatoire – was naturally much discussed, and the story made the round of all Moscow.

661

Feodor Chaliapin

My first visit to Leo Tolstoy . . . took place in Moscow on 9 January 1900. Tolstoy was then living with his family at Khamovniki, a district of Moscow. Rachmaninov and I received an invitation to visit him. We climbed an unpretentious wood staircase to the second floor of a charming house, modest and intimate in character, built partially of wood. . . .

Tea was offered to us, but I was in such a state of excitement that I was in no fit state to drink it. Just think – for the first time in my life I was going to see in the flesh the man whose words had stirred the world. Up till then I had only seen portraits of Tolstoy, and now he himself appeared. . . .

My wretched acuteness of hearing informed me at this moment, significant as it was, that he spoke in a slightly bleating voice, and that a certain letter – no doubt because several of his teeth were missing – issued with a lisping, whistling sound. I noticed this, moved as I was by his nearness, and when he unostentatiously shook hands with me, my emotion increased. He asked me, as far as I can remember, how long I had been acting, as I looked so young, and I answered in [a] tremulous voice. . . .

Sergei Rachmaninov was not so shy as I was, but he was deeply moved, and his hands were cold. 'If I'm asked to play,' he whispered to me, 'I don't know what I shall do – my fingers are numb.' The next moment Tolstoy begged him to play. I can't remember what he played. I was too agitated by the thought that it would be my turn next. My agitation was doubled when Tolstoy said point-blank to Rachmaninov, 'Tell me, has that type of music any interest whatever?'

I was asked to sing. I remember that I sang 'Le Destin', a song that Rachmaninov had just composed round the leit-motif of Beethoven's Fifth Symphony with words by Apoukhtine. Rachmaninov accompanied me. We both did our utmost to give the song its full value, but we could not tell if it had pleased Tolstoy. He said nothing. Then as before, he asked, 'What kind of music is most necessary to men – classical or popular music?'

662

Rachmaninov recalls the same visit

To describe how Fedya sang is impossible. He sang – the way Tolstoy wrote. We were both twenty-six years old. We performed my song 'Fate'. When we finished, we felt that all were delighted. Suddenly the enthusiastic applause was hushed and everyone was silent. Tolstoy sat in an armchair a little apart from the others, looking gloomy and cross. For the next hour I evaded him, but suddenly he came up to me and declared excitedly, 'I must speak to you. I must tell you how I dislike it all!' And he went on and on, 'Beethoven is nonsense, Pushkin and Lermontov also.' It was awful. Sophia Andreyevna stood behind me; she touched my shoulder and whispered, 'Never mind, never mind. Please don't contradict him. Lyovochka must not get excited. It's very bad for him.' After a while Tolstoy came up to me again, 'Please excuse me. I am an old man. I did not mean to hurt you.' I replied, 'How could I be hurt on my own account, if I was not hurt on Beethoven's?' But I never went back. Sophia Andreyevna invited me to Yasnaya Polyana every year, but I always declined. And just think, the first time I went to him, I went to him as to a god.

663

Tolstoy's deprecations caught Rachmaninov at the lowest ebb of his nervous collapse; he sought solace with his friend Chekhov. 'Tolstoy's just like a stomach-ache,' said the dramatist. 'Nothing to do but ignore it.'

664

During a violin and piano recital in New York, Fritz Kreisler suffered a sudden lapse of memory. He sidled towards the piano and hissed urgently at Rachmaninov, 'Where are we?' The pianist, not missing a note, replied, 'in Carnegie Hall.'

665

In Hollywood, where he settled in 1940, Rachmaninov met Charlie Chaplin at the home of Vladimir Horowitz. The others present were Wanda Horowitz and Sir John Barbirolli. Someone began talking about religion and Chaplin declared himself to be an unbeliever. 'But how can you have art without religion?' asked Rachmaninov uncomprehendingly.

'I don't think we are talking about the same thing,' said Chaplin. 'Art is a feeling more than a belief.'

'So is religion,' replied the composer with finality.

666

Rachmaninov and Stravinsky had always spoken disparagingly of each other, so Arthur Rubinstein was astonished when one composer invited him to dinner with the other. Their wives, explained Rachmaninov, had met and become friendly. Conversation proceeded with difficulty at first, Rachmaninov quelling Stravinsky's social overtures. Then, after a few drinks, Rachmaninov began mocking Stravinsky's financial problems. 'Your *Petrushka*, your *Firebird*, ha-ha, never earned you a cent of royalties.' Stravinsky flushed, then paled. 'And what about the concertos and the C sharp minor Prelude you published in Russia?' he responded. 'You had to play the piano for a living.' Just as a violent confrontation seemed unavoidable, the two composers sat down amicably and began calculating the fortunes each might have earned if the history of the twentieth century had taken a different course.

Max REGER (1873–1916)

German composer admired chiefly in his own country; expert polyphonist and skilled organist.

667

Reger's appetites were enormous and certainly contributed to his early death. He would order a waiter to bring him 'two hours' worth of beefsteak' and his liquid consumption was of a similar dimension. Before inviting Reger to lunch in London, Sir Henry Wood, a considerate host, called the German Club to ascertain his guest's preferences. He was told to provide at least two dozen bottles of beer.

'Although the good Reger had lived up to his reputation and had consumed most of the beer without the slightest inconvenience to himself,' recalled Wood, 'I thought the poor fellow might be thirsty, so I offered him a whisky and soda. He was so pleased with the first that he had three more. He did not, however, remain to tea. . . .'

668

After an inspired performance of the piano part in Schubert's *Trout* quintet, a lady admirer sent Reger a freshly-caught trout. In his note of thanks, Reger enclosed the date of his next concert and the programme: Haydn's *Ox* minuet.

669

After receiving a particularly vicious review in a Munich newspaper, Reger replied to the critic:

I am sitting in the smallest room in my house.
I have your review before me. In a moment it will be *behind* me.

Charles IVES (1874–1954)

American composer and insurance magnate, Ives composed atonally, bitonally, quartertonally and polyrhythmically. Son of a town band-master, he studied music at Yale but took up life insurance as a vocation, founding one of the most successful US agencies (Ives & Myrick, part of Mutual Life).

670

Ives kept his business and his music strictly separate. His contribution to the expansion of life insurance was considerable – he founded the first training course for agents and invented the concept of 'estate planning' – but few of his associates knew that he was a musician. He enjoyed telling of his impassive demeanour in a conversation in the office elevator with a colleague who said, 'Ives, you know, yesterday I heard *Parsifal* at the opera. It's a fine thing. You should go to the opera sometimes.'

671

He was profoundly disillusioned by the political aftermath of the First War and by the materialism that replaced idealism in American society. He stopped taking New York newspapers and subscribed only to *The Times* of London, which reached him well after the events it reported. When his brother came to visit carrying a copy of *The New York Times*, Ives would exclaim in horror, 'Oh my gosh, here comes a newspaper.'

672

Despite the efforts of the conductor, Nicolas Slonimsky, the Chamber Orchestra of Boston failed to maintain perfect ensemble throughout Three Places in New England. Ives, however, was pleased with the performance. 'Just like a town meeting,' he congratulated Slonimsky, 'every man for himself. Wonderful how it came out!'

673

Ives recalls
Father had 'absolute pitch', as men say. But it seemed to disturb him; he seemed half ashamed of it. 'Everything is relative,' he said. 'Nothing but fools and taxes are absolute.'

A friend who was a 'thorough musician' – he had graduated from the New England Conservatory at Boston – asked him why with his sensitive ear he liked to sit down and beat out dissonances on the piano. 'Well,' he answered, 'I may have absolute pitch, but, thank

God, that piano hasn't.' One afternoon, in a pouring thunderstorm, we saw him standing without hat or coat in the back garden; the church bell next door was ringing. He would rush into the house to the piano, and then back again. 'I've heard a chord I've never heard before – it comes over and over but I can't seem to catch it.' He stayed up most of the night trying to find it in the piano. It was soon after this that he started his quarter-tone machine.

674

Upon hearing Haydn's 'Surprise' Symphony, he sang along satirically, '*Pret*-ty *lit*-tle *sug*-ar *plum sounds* . . .' and called it 'easy music for the sissies'.

675

When his Third Symphony was awarded the Pulitzer Prize in 1947, – forty-two years after it was composed, he told the award committee, 'Prizes are for boys – I'm grown up!' and gave the $500 away.

676

After Schoenberg's death in 1951, his widow sent Mr and Mrs Ives a note she had found among his papers. It read:

> There is a great Man living in this Country – a composer.
> He has solved the problem how to preserve one's self and to learn.
> He responds to negligence by contempt.
> He is not forced to accept praise or blame.
> His name is Ives.

677

He worked for some years on a 'Universe' Symphony, which he never intended to finish. Anybody else could add to it if they felt like it, he told one of his copyists. But he dreamed that one day it would be performed by several orchestras stationed on the tops of several hills, with huge choirs singing in the valleys.

❦

Arnold SCHOENBERG (1874–1951)
(b. Schönberg)

Viennese composer and visionary who abandoned tonality, originating the twelve-tone method of composition used in much of twentieth-century music.

678

[The première of Schoenberg's Chamber Symphony in 1907] has become a landmark in modern music history. It brought a terrible turmoil. In the audience people were booing. Just next to Mahler's box – Mahler himself applauded demonstratively – was standing a young man who booed at full voice. Mahler was reproaching him. 'Young man aren't you ashamed?' 'No, not at all, and I assure you for *your* next symphony I will do just the same.' After the performance I* asked Mahler what he thought of the work. He answered that he himself was unable to follow the younger (at that time thirty-[two] year-old) composer on his way; but that anyway it was a new way and this was the reason for supporting the man who followed it. From this man – and I had heard Mahler say this before – and from the direction he had taken, extraordinary things could be expected.

679

Schoenberg took up painting as a pastime and soon expressed himself so strikingly on canvas that he considered it as an alternative occupation to music. But his attempts to stage an exhibition were repeatedly thwarted. In 1910, when Schoenberg's canvases finally went on public view, a critic declared, 'Schoenberg's music and Schoenberg's pictures – they'll knock your ears and eyes out at the same time.'

680

Schoenberg to an unknown correspondent

Berlin, 22 April 1914

Dear Sir,

I regret that I am unable to accept your invitation to write something for Richard Strauss's fiftieth birthday.

In a letter to Frau Mahler . . . Herr Strauss wrote about me as follows:

---

* Klaus Pringsheim (1883–1972); composer, pupil of Mahler, brother-in-law of Thomas Mann.

'The only person who can help poor Schönberg now is a psychiatrist. . . .'

'I think he'd do better to shovel snow instead of scribbling on music-paper. . . .'

It seems to me that the opinion I myself and indeed everyone else who knows these remarks is bound to have of Herr Strauss as a man (for here is envy of a 'competitor') and as an artist (for the expressions he uses are as banal as a cheap song) is not suitable for general publication in honour of his fiftieth birthday.

I have no intention of damaging Herr Strauss 'morally'; . . . He is no longer of the slightest artistic interest to me, and whatever I may once have learnt from him, I am thankful to say I misunderstood.

681

In the latter stages of the First World War he was conscripted into the Austro-Hungarian Army in the week of his forty-third birthday. While in uniform, Schoenberg took care to conceal his civilian notoriety, but fellow-soldiers persisting in demanding, 'Aren't you that controversial modernist composer?' Eventually he replied, 'I must admit that I am: somebody had to be, and since no one else wanted to, I took it upon myself.'

682

'One could tell just by looking at him that he had been through the upheavals in Austria after the War,' recalled the Dutch composer, Herman Mulder, on seeing Schoenberg conducting in Amsterdam in 1912. 'I still see the gesture with which he cut the cigarette offered to him with a pocket knife in order to have part of it left for the afternoon. The Toonkunst choir wanted to offer him something in appreciation. He asked for a pair of trousers; he was very badly off for clothing.'

683

Schoenberg went to Venice in September 1925 to conduct his Serenade Op. 24, the first concerted piece to apply an organized method of composition with twelve notes, at the International Society for Contemporary Music festival. He overran his rehearsal time and was interrupted by Edward J. Dent, the Society's President, asking him to make way for the next performer. Schoenberg ignored him.

'Herr Schoenberg,' insisted Dent, 'You're not the only composer here.'

'*I* think so,' said Schoenberg.

684

A graphologist, shown a sample of his handwriting, concluded, 'This man thinks he is at least the emperor of China.' Schoenberg, told of the man's comment said, 'But did he believe I was justified?'

685

I* was friendly with Schnabel's son in Berlin and would often visit their flat. One day Schnabel announced, 'Mr Schoenberg is here. He has brought the manuscript of a new orchestral work and has dared me to sight-read it at the piano.' Schnabel tackled the work valiantly but suddenly stopped in puzzlement. 'I can't make it out: is this an A or B flat?' Schoenberg came over to the piano and peered at his own handwriting, raised his spectacles, replaced them again on his nose, and finally admitted, 'I don't know.' Then he said 'Wait a minute.' He rushed outside and fetched a battered briefcase from the hallway. From it he extracted a small notebook, of the kind used for keeping household expenses. He flipped through it until he came to a certain page. It was the famous 'row' of twelve notes. He studied it briefly and concluded, 'It must be B flat.'

686

After his one-act opera, *Von Heute auf Morgen*, was performed for the first time in Frankfurt, Schoenberg said to the orchestra, 'Gentlemen, the difference between what you played tonight and what I wrote in my score would make a new opera.'

687

Nuria Schoenberg-Nono, Schoenberg's daughter
In Berlin he and my mother were offered a vast amount for *Von Heute auf Morgen* (for which Mother wrote the text). They had very little money at the time and were not set up yet in an apartment. The publisher offered them something like 100,000 Reichsmarks, an incredible sum, more than they had ever been offered. But he said, 'I'm leaving tomorrow, you'll have to decide within ten minutes.' So Mother and Daddy went into the next room and started discussing it.

Mother said, 'I don't like the way this man wants to pressure us into

---

* Peter Diamand (b. 1913); musical administrator.

making a decision. Let's say, "No". Anyone can say "Yes" to 100,000 Reichsmarks, but how many can say, "No"?' So they refused the offer.

That decision, Mother would say, saved their lives. 'If we had taken the money, we would have bought a beautiful home, filled it with lovely furniture and, like so many others, would not have been able to leave immediately when Hitler came to power.'

688

When Schoenberg arrived in California it was the desire of his friends to see him employed in the movies and well paid for it. He was invited to an important première, following which the producer intercepted him and asked what he thought of the score. Schoenberg replied that he hadn't noticed it, thus bearing out the average producer's theory of what constitutes a good score, only in reverse.

Nevertheless, his friends continued the propaganda. . . .

It chanced then that the Columbia Broadcasting System was presenting a broadcast in Schoenberg's honor, of which a principal work was his early Verklärte Nacht. Its romantic flavor and poetic character deeply impressed [Irving] Thalberg, who thereafter sent an emissary to see Schoenberg, even though the music he might write now would have no possible resemblance to Verklärte Nacht. The emissary found the composer indifferent to the idea and thereupon launched into a long recitation of the possibilities for music in the film, *The Good Earth*, leading up to a dramatic exposition of its 'big scene'.

'Think of it!' he enthused. 'There's terrific storm going on, the wheat field is swaying in the wind, and suddenly the earth begins to tremble. In the midst of the earthquake Oo-Lan gives birth to a baby. What an opportunity for music!'

'With so much going on,' said Schoenberg mildly, 'what do you need music for?'

689

Thalberg, undeterred, summoned Schoenberg to a meeting to talk terms. The composer demanded $50,000 and an absolute veto on any changes in his music; he was politely dismissed. He reported the collapse of the venture to his wife with noticeable relief. The reason he had asked Thalberg for so much money was, he said, 'because if I am going to commit suicide, then I'd like to be able to live well afterwards.'

To make a living in California he had to teach courses at all levels, including a beginners' course in harmony. Confronted once with a class of kindergarten music teachers he asked, in wonderment, 'You are teachers? You mean there are people who know less than you do about music?'

On learning of Berg's death, Schoenberg wrote to Webern from Hollywood 'It is too terrible. One of us – who were anyway only three – is gone, and now we two alone have to bear this artistic isolation. The saddest thing is that it had to be the one of us who had success and might at least have enjoyed it.'

An acrimonious and public row in 1948 over Thomas Mann's *Doctor Faustus* (in which an ambiguous hero, Adrian Leverkühn, is portrayed as a composer who invented a method of composition with twelve notes) distressed Schoenberg deeply. Although the two eminent exiles saw each other socially, Mann never mentioned the novel to Schoenberg.

When the book was published, Schoenberg wrote a furious letter to the Press, accusing Mann of intellectual theft. Mann, in a reasoned reply, said the book was a tribute to Schoenberg's tremendous influence on music. For two years relations between the composer and author remained embittered.

Schoenberg's fear, he told his family, was that Leverkühn's unprincipled character would cast a shadow over his own music and ideas. 'If Mann had only told me he was writing this book,' he complained, 'I would have invented *another* method of composition for him – in an hour!'

He was awarded the freedom of the city of Vienna in 1949, but did not attend the ceremony. In a written response, he quoted a remark he had made in 1912, 'The second half of this century will spoil by overestimation what the first half's underestimation left unspoilt.'

Katia Mann writes
Schoenberg had a heart condition, and he was very superstitious. He was afraid of the number 13 and firmly believed that he would someday die on the thirteenth of the month. After all, he was already

seventy-six. When the thirteenth arrived, he was always restless; in the evening Gertrud Schoenberg would have to sit with him and hold his hand. On the other side of the room was a clock, and he would watch it until the thirteenth was past. On 13 July 1951, exactly the same thing happened. They were sitting there, and the clock was ticking; finally midnight came. Schoenberg went upstairs to go to bed. Gertrud Schoenberg went as always to the kitchen to fix his bedtime drink – he always drank a cup of Bovril at night. When she took the cup up to him, he was lying dead in his room. Gertrud was terrified and looked at the clock. She had become just as obsessed with the clock as he. She saw that it wasn't yet midnight; the clock in the room downstairs had been several minutes fast.*

〜〜〜

Maurice RAVEL (1875–1937)

The repetitive Bolero brought him widespread fame, but Ravel never became rich from his music.

695

To hear a whole programme of Ravel's works [wrote *The Times* in 1924] is like watching some midget pygmy doing clever but very small things within a limited scope. Moreover, the almost reptilian cold-bloodedness, which one suspects of having been consciously cultivated, of most of M. Ravel's music is almost repulsive when heard in bulk; even its beauties are like the markings on snakes and lizards.

---

* Nuria Schoenberg-Nono: On 13 July 1951, the situation was very different from Katia Mann's tale. My father did not go 'upstairs to go to bed'; unfortunately he had been 'upstairs' for months and had not gone to bed for at least *three years* since he slept sitting in a chair opposite the bed, because of his attacks of asthma during the night. On that night Mother was lying awake in bed, the big clock was behind my father's head. Mother later said that she was watching the clock, hoping that my father would outlive the 13th, that she had thought: only fifteen more minutes, when he had the attack which ended his life.

There was no bedtime drink, I don't even know what Bovril is; certainly my father never drank it. Katia Mann confuses the truth with some movie she must have seen. What Mother may have said to her was: how ironic it is, that in *Europe it was already the 14th*.

It is true that Schoenberg was superstitious about the number 13. When my father was about to have his 76th birthday he received a letter from an astrologer to the effect that due to the sum of the digits that made up his age that year (7+6=13), it would be a very dangerous year for him.

The Hollywood romantic idea of Gertrud sitting with Arnold holding his hand on every 13th of the month is ridiculous.

The 'Valses nobles et sentimentales' were first performed anonymously at a concert for cognoscenti in which works by unnamed living and long-dead composers were intermingled.

Half the audience identified Ravel as the composer; others said the piece was by Satie, Kodály, Blanche Selva, or Theodor Szánto.

A clique of Ravel enthusiasts who would normally swoon at the first sound of his music, believing the Valses to be by another composer, jeered them vigorously hoping to please Ravel by their fealty. Ravel betrayed no detectable emotion.

Stravinsky's body was small, taut and compact, but in common with small men, he was fashion crazy, not unlike Ravel, who spent a young fortune on a light-blue tailcoat once, 'launched' it at one of the Princesse de Polignac's bigger *soirées* and then, to his mortification, heard a marquis ask a count, 'Who is the little fellow who didn't bother to dress?'

In 1920 he caused a scandal by refusing Ministerial nomination as a Chévalier of the Légion d'Honneur. To decline such elevation was unheard-of, but Ravel had consistently proclaimed a Baudelairean disdain of the State's right to judge its citizens. 'Ravel refuses the Légion d'Honneur,' cackled Satie, 'but all his music accepts it.'

At the première of Bolero, a woman in the audience called out, 'He's mad!' Ravel replied, smiling, that she had understood the piece.

George Gershwin asked Ravel to give him lessons, but nothing came of it. Soon, the story circulated that Ravel had asked Gershwin, 'How much do you earn a year from your compositions? 'Around $100,000,' replied Gershwin. 'In that case,' said Ravel, 'you give *me* lessons.'

A similar tale was told about Gershwin and Stravinsky. 'A nice story,' said Stravinsky, 'but I heard it about myself from Ravel a year before I met Gershwin.'

He once told Georges Auric that he would like to write a treatise on orchestration, illustrated with examples of failure from his own works.

కావుదు

Albert SCHWEITZER (1875–1965)

Editor of Bach's organ works, Schweitzer was an eminent organist, as well as a theologian, physician, minister to the lepers of equatorial Africa and recipient of the Nobel Peace Prize (1952).

702

Schweitzer organized a series of Bach concerts in Strasbourg from 1896 and in Paris from 1906. In 1905 he published an important Bach biography, and rewrote it himself in German. Then one day, over lunch with his teacher, Widor,* he announced that he was going to Gabon to build a hospital. The old organist pleaded with him to give up the idea, to consider the disruptive effect it would have on his Bach researches but to no avail. 'What can you do,' sighed Widor afterwards, 'when a man says to you, "God calls me"?'

కావుదు

Pau (Pablo) CASALS (1876–1973)

Casals revolutionized 'cello technique, and restored the Bach solo suites to performance. A native of Spain, he went into lifelong exile in protest against the Franco régime.

703

The young Gregor Piatigorsky† played for him once in Berlin and, inhibited by shyness, made a mess of music by Beethoven, Schumann and Bach. Casals, nonetheless, applauded energetically and embraced the diffident 'cellist. Some years later, when playing duos together late into the night, Piatigorsky confessed that he had been hurt by the undeserved praise. 'Casals reacted with sudden anger. He rushed to the 'cello. "Listen!" He played a phrase from the Beethoven sonata. "Didn't you play this fingering? It was novel to me . . . it was

---

* Charles Marie Widor (1844–1937); organist and composer.
† (1903–76); 'cellist.

good . . . and here, didn't you attack that passage with up-bow, like this? And for the rest," he said passionately, "leave it to the ignorant and stupid who judge by counting only the faults. I can be grateful, and so must you be, for even one note, one wonderful phrase."'

❧

Carl RUGGLES (1876–1971)

American modernist.

704

During the performance of a Ruggles work in New York, Charles Ives leapt to his feet to confront a disrupter. 'Stop being such a god-damned sissy!' he thundered, 'Stand up . . . and use your ears like a man!'

705

At Paris rehearsals of *Men and Mountains*, one of the violists was so alienated by the sounds he made that he scrawled the word *Il* on his score before the title *viola* and *la musique* after it – implying that the composer violated music.

❧

Sir Thomas BEECHAM (1879–1961)

English conductor, impresario and wit, who squandered his inheritance from his father's firm, Beecham's Pills, on operatic ventures. He founded Beecham Opera Company (1915–20), ran Covent Garden (1932–9) and created the London Philharmonic (1932) and Royal Philharmonic (1947) orchestras.

706

Something went disastrously wrong during a performance of the Beethoven G major Concerto with the pianist Alfred Cortot*. As Beecham explained afterwards, 'M. Cortot started playing the Beethoven, so I conducted the Beethoven. He went on to the Schumann, so I conducted the Schumann. He went on to play all sorts of concerti. I conducted as long as I knew what he was playing. Then he started on a concerto with which I was completely unfamiliar, so I had to withdraw.'

---

* (1877–1962)

A soprano in Massenet's *Don Quixote* complained that she had missed her entry in an aria, 'because Mr Chaliapin always dies too soon'. 'Madam, you must be profoundly in error,' said Sir Thomas. 'No operatic star has yet died half soon enough for me.'

'My father,' Beecham confided, 'came to me one Christmas and said, "Look here, my lad, I've been spendin' a lot o'brass on your musical education, and now Ah wants you to help me." (Every year a *Christmas Carol Annual* was published by Beecham's Pills.) "Now, Tom," continued my father, "I want you go go through th' *Annual* and alter some of th' verses so as to advertise th' business, you know?" So,' Sir Thomas told me, 'I retired into my study and, after some meditation, I produced the following:

> Hark! the herald angels sing!
> Beecham's Pills are just the thing,
> Two for a woman one for a child . . .
> Peace on Earth and mercy mild!

'These sentiments,' continued Sir Thomas, 'especially the ellipsis, seemed to me admirably to express the rapture which is occasioned by a good effortless release. . . .'

During his tour of Australia, he one midnight howled and gurgled through Siegfried's Forging Songs until a rapping was heard on the other side of the wall of the room. Sir Thomas immediately stopped his noise sforzando. 'Did I hear a knock?' he asked, and rising from the piano stool, with his arms clasped behind his dressing-gown, he walked processionally to the door, his face eager with inquiry. The rapping was repeated.

'Come,' he said to me,* 'let us investigate.'

He opened the door of his sitting-room and peered outwards.

'Ah, ha,' he cried, 'sayst thou so? Art thou there, true-penny?'

Then he knocked at next door, and I overheard the following dialogue:

An Australian Voice: 'Shut that bloody row at this time of night. How do you expect anybody to go to sleep?'

Sir Thomas: 'I don't expect it. This is not the time for sleep. To be

---

* Neville Cardus (1889–1975); English critic.

up at midnight and to go to bed then is early, so that to go to bed after midnight is to go to bed betimes.'

The Australian Voice (not at all mollified): 'How do you expect a fellow to get any sleep in all that hell row? I've got to get up early and do a day's work.'

Sir Thomas: 'My dear fellow, *I* have to get up early and conduct the Brisbane'Orchestra at a rehearsal, which is worse. Come, come, rouse ye. Thou art a scholar; let us therefore eat and drink.'

And in a few minutes the tired business man was sitting in his pyjamas with us in Beecham's suite, filling himself with champagne, until Sir Thomas and I carried him back to his bed, and by now he was dead to all physical phenomena. Next day he departed from the hotel but left a note to Sir Thomas vowing he had never enjoyed himself so much in all his life, and regretting he had 'passed out' so soon; as Sir Thomas said to me, showing me the letter, 'The Australian is a heavy, but not a strong drinker.'

ᑲᗑᗑᑯ

Béla BARTÓK (1881–1945)

Fervent Hungarian patriot who based his musical language on extensive researches into folk music; he left Hungary in protest against rising Fascist influence and died in American exile.

710

Béla Bartók, collecting folk songs in Turkey

. . . On we went then to the next camp of nomadic tribes. Our cart drove across rivers (big and small), the road grew stonier and ceased altogether, and our cart just went on and on rattling over rocky hillsides. This manner of travelling was not very pleasant. It might have been all right without the care of our instruments. But we had to keep the phonographs and the records firmly on our laps. At last we had enough of that business; we walked on, on foot, carrying our fragile treasures on our backs and in our hands. At sunset we at last reached the winter camp of a tribe called Tecirli. They are also a nomadic tribe, but live in clay huts and not in tents for the winter. Our guide took us to the 'house' of a man who seemed rather influential among the families of the tribe, and whom he knew well. This man received us most amiably. A well-mannered and tactful man, he did not ask questions about the purpose of our visit or about the funny apparatus we carried with us. He at once ordered a sheep

300

to be killed for our meal, but we said a hen would be sufficient. He invited us to enter his house. . . .

Slowly the room got filled with people from the neighbourhood and we talked and talked very amicably. This went on till seven, and apparently our guide had not even mentioned yet what had brought us here. I was sitting on coals. At seven I heard our guide saying words like '*türkü*' '*türk halk müsiki*,' etc., etc. At last I could hear that folk songs were mentioned and hoped the ice would soon be broken. And indeed, without shyness and hesitation a 15-year-old boy sang the first song, and it was again a melody that sounded Hungarian to me. I quickly prepared my instruments on the mattresses spread out on the floor and took down the song in writing by the light of the wood fire. Well, I thought, now let us begin with the recording. But this did not prove as easy as all that. My good singer was frightened he might lose his voice by singing into a machine obviously driven by a devil; this instrument, he thought, might not only take down his voice, but take it away altogether. It took me long to dispel his fright. Then he worked incessantly, undisturbed till midnight. I thought the time had then come to ask a few delicate questions, especially regarding women. Whether women sing other songs than men. Oh no, by no means, was the short but decided answer. Well, I went on, but surely they knew the same songs and it would be so nice for us to hear these songs sung by women. After some embarrassment they informed us that women never sung in the presence of men. Not even a husband had the right to ask his wife for a song. I had to resign myself to this fact, since naturally I could not claim rights greater than those of a husband, and gave up all hope with a sad heart. What a pity! It is an impossible situation to have to record lullabys in croaking men's voices when it was obvious that men never lulled their babies to sleep either with or without songs!

711

I* remember only too well the occasion [in 1921] when I was first introduced to the recently completed music of the ballet, *The Miraculous Mandarin*. It was a day of scorching heat in August [in Budapest], in a street in the centre of the town where the din of the traffic was intolerable; and Bartók played to me the piano score on an inferior instrument which was also decidedly out of tune. Even in orchestral performance this work is a severe strain on the nervous system, to say nothing of one's aesthetic sensibilities; consequently

---

* Cecil Gray (1895–1951); British composer.

my sufferings under the aggravated circumstances of the performance can perhaps be estimated, without much exercise of imagination. I have seldom suffered so much from music. It was even too much for the composer himself. About three-quarters' way through the work he suddenly stopped playing, saying that he did not feel in the right mood. I searched my brain desperately for some complimentary and appreciative words which would not sound too insincere, but failed. I could find nothing to say. But later, when walking back with Kodály,* with whom I was staying, to his flat, I confessed my misgivings and disillusionment, and was comforted to learn that my feelings were to some extent shared, and at any rate completely understood. 'This harmonically exacerbated style,' said Kodály, 'is a phase through which Bartók has to pass. He will emerge from it, you will see.'

712

The Miraculous Mandarin received its first performance in Cologne in 1926 and created a terrible fracas. People were shouting, stink bombs were thrown and the music was drowned out. The Major of Cologne, Konrad Adenauer, demanded the resignation of Eugen Szenkár.† After the chaotic performance, Bartók came to the conductor's dressing room. 'Eugen,' he said mildly, 'on page thirty-four the second clarinet is marked *mezzo forte*. I couldn't hear it. Would you please make it *forte*?'

713

The conductor, Antal Doráti
One instance when Bartók made important revelations about one of his works was an hour at his small service-flat in New York shortly after he completed his Concerto for Orchestra. We were alone and he was in a mellow mood. Our conversation concentrated on this work and Bartók was unusually communicative. 'Do you know what music I quote in the "Intermezzo interotto" (the concerto's fourth movement)?' he asked.

I thought I knew, but I guessed wrong.

Thereupon Bartók, first exacting my solemn promise not to tell anyone during his lifetime – which I gave and kept – confided that it was a tune by Shostakovich which he caricatured as the interrupting element. That confession seemed to have broken a dam, for it was followed by a general unburdening from what evidently had been

---

* Zoltan Kodály (1882–1967); Hungarian composer.
† (1891–1977); Hungarian conductor.

stored in his soul for a long time. This was the only time he spoke of his feelings, his disappointment in the great and sudden acclaim that some musical works – among others some of Shostakovich's – enjoyed, which he thought not worthy of such success. He spoke with restraint and real dignity, but it was evident that he was hurt by the neglect of his own music. Turning back to his 'Intermezzo interrotto' he wistfully concluded, 'Well, that is how I gave vent to my anger.'

714

[When living in America] he longed for Hungary and its countryside. Walking in Manhattan one day he announced, 'I smell horses.'

'In the middle of 66th Street?' exclaimed his wife.

'Yes, horses,' said Bartók, looking around and proceeding to cross the road. His wife and a friend watched him enter an unmarked building. They followed him inside and found it to be a riding academy. 'What a peaceful natural smell,' said Bartók, inhaling deeply in the stables, 'Sleeping horses.'

715

At the first big Bartók festival in post-war Hungary, Zoltan Kodály was placed in the front row next to the bloodthirsty tyrant, Matyas Rakosi. Many tributes were paid, and one speaker proclaimed that 'if Bartók was alive today, he would be a prominent member of the Hungarian Communist Party.' Kodály immediately stood up and, oblivious of personal risk, declared, 'In memory of my dear friend, no party in the world can claim Béla Bartók.'

∽∾∾∾∾

Percy GRAINGER (1882–1961)

Australian-born pianist and composer, he staged his wedding at a Hollywood Bowl concert before an audience of 20,000 and bequeathed his skeleton to the University of Melbourne 'for preservation and possible display'.

716

He was an extraordinarily athletic man and would often run from one concert to the next. On his first concert tour of South Africa, he misjudged the distance to his next destination and the audience were already taking their seats when Grainger's friends, searching the horizon with binoculars, perceived a cloud of dust. It cleared, to reveal a band of Zulu warriors heading for the township, with Grainger jogging along beside them. Arriving just in time for the concert, he demanded seats for his companions. However, he was forced to leave them outside; their admission would have resulted in his immediate deportation.

❦

Artur SCHNABEL (1882–1951)

Austrian-born pianist and revered teacher.

717

Rehearsing a Beethoven concerto with Otto Klemperer in Los Angeles, he began to signal his own preferred *tempi* to the orchestra from the piano stool. As soon as the conductor noticed what he was doing, he stopped the rehearsal. 'Schnabel,' rasped Klemperer, *'here* is the conductor!' 'I know that,' Schnabel replied, 'and *here* is the soloist. Only, *where* is Beethoven?'

718

In 1933, to mark the centenary of Brahms' birth, Hindemith, together with Schnabel, Bronislaw Hubermann* and Piatigorsky, arranged to give a cycle of his music for piano and strings in Berlin and Hamburg but could not agree how to share the fees. 'Let's leave it to the managers,' said Hubermann, thinking he would get the best deal. Schnabel refused, and the argument became heated. Finally, Schnabel proposed: 'We will divide the fee into 35 parts.'

'Why 35?' demanded the others.

'Easy,' said Schnabel. 'We will play three trios, three quartets, three violin sonatas, two viola sonatas, and two cello sonatas – 35 parts in all. As pianist I will receive 13 thirty-fifths, the violin will take 9/35, the cello 8/35 and the viola 5/35.' Even Hindemith, who received least, acknowledged the Solomonian wisdom of the arrangement. 'It was lucky that Schnabel's ingenuity did not extend to counting the notes,' reflected Piatigorsky, 'for I would have come out much worse.'

❦

---

* (1882–1947); violinist who founded symphony orchestra in Palestine.

Leopold STOKOWSKI (1882–1977)

British-born conductor of the Philadelphia Orchestra (1912–38), he popularized music in many forms, most famously in Walt Disney's *Fantasia*.

719

There was a player in Stokowski's orchestra who was remarkable for the fact that never once in all the long years had he been five minutes late or missed a rehearsal. But now, at last, all the other members of the Philadelphia Orchestra thought he would be late because he was just about to become the father of his first child, the child to be born during the morning rehearsal.

Everyone knew that his wife would not stand for his not being present for that event.

However, that morning he was present as always; moreover, he did not miss a single cue.

The mystery (as I* heard the story) was explained later by the fact that the wife's hospital was near the Academy of Music and that the piece rehearsed that morning had a five-hundred-bar rest. The chap had simply laid down his instrument, kept counting bars all the way to the hospital, kissed his new baby (still counting bars) kissed his wife (still counting), and returned to the Academy just in time to take up his instrument and come in on the split second of the downbeat of the 501st bar.

I asked Stokowski if it was true, and he said, 'Yes.'

❦

Igor STRAVINSKY (1882–1971)

Born in St Petersburg, Stravinsky made his mark with three Paris ballets commissioned by Diaghilev; the third, *Rite of Spring*, announced a new era in music. But in mid-life Stravinsky adopted a neo-classical style and in his last years turned to Webernian serialism.

720

The young Stravinsky took a new composition to Rimsky-Korsakov. 'This is disgusting, Sir,' said his teacher, 'No, Sir, it is not permissible to write such nonsense until one is sixty.' Rimsky remained in a bad

---

* George Antheil (1900 59); American composer.

temper all day, and at dinner complained to his wife, 'What a bunch of nonentities my pupils are! Not one of them is capable of producing a piece of rubbish such as Igor brought me this morning.'

721

On 29 May 1913, at the Champs-Élysées Theatre, the *Sacre du Printemps* was performed for the first time, on the very anniversary of the première of *Faune*, for Diaghilev was superstitious. I* wondered what the reaction of the brilliant, excited audience would be. I knew the music of *Sacre*, and had seen bits of the dancing from back stage during the last rehearsals, I thought the public might fidget, but none of us in the company expected what followed. The first bars of the overture were listened to amid murmurs, and very soon the audience began to behave itself, not as the dignified audience of Paris, but as a bunch of naughty, ill-mannered children.

One of the witnesses, Carl van Vechten†, wrote about this memorable evening: 'A certain part of the audience was thrilled by what it considered to be a blasphemous attempt to destroy music as an art, and, swept away with wrath, began, very soon after the rise of the curtain, to make cat-calls and to offer audible suggestions as to how the performance should proceed. The orchestra played unheard except occasionally, when a slight lull occurred. The young man seated behind me in the box stood up during the course of the ballet to enable himself to see more clearly. The intense excitement under which he was labouring betrayed itself presently when he began to beat rhythmically on the top of my head with his fists. My emotion was so great that I did not feel the blows for some time.'

Yes, indeed, the excitement, the shouting, was extreme. People whistled, insulted the performers and the composer, shouted, laughed. Monteux threw desperate glances towards Diaghilev, who sat in Astruc's box and made signs to him to keep on playing. Astruc in this indescribable noise ordered the lights turned on, and the fights and controversy did not remain in the domain of sound, but actually culminated in bodily conflict. One beautifully dressed lady in an orchestra box stood up and slapped the face of a young man who was hissing in the next box. Her escort rose, and cards were exchanged between the men. A duel followed next day. Another society lady spat in the face of one of the demonstrators. La Princesse de P. left her box, saying 'I am sixty years old, but this is the

---

* Romola Nijinsky; wife of Vaslev Nijinsky (1889–1950), dancer and choreographer of *Rite of Spring*.
† (1880–1964); American music and dance critic.

first time anyone has dared to make a fool of me.' At this moment Diaghilev, who was standing livid in his box, shouted, *'Je vous en prie, laissez achever le spectacle'* [please let them finish the show].

722

The conductor, Pierre Monteux (1876–1964) remembers
'You may think this strange, but I have never seen the ballet. The night of the première, I kept my eyes on the score, playing the exact *tempo* Igor had given me and which, I must say, I have never forgotten. As you know, the public reacted in a scandalous manner. They filled the new Champs Elysées Theatre to overflowing, manifested their disapprobation of the ballet in a most violent manner. . . .

The gendarmes arrived at last. Well, on hearing this near riot behind me I decided to keep the orchestra together at any cost, in case of a lull in the hubbub. I did, and we played it to the end absolutely as we had rehearsed it in the peace of an empty theatre. After that performance, we played it five times, and five times the public reacted in the same way. . . .

We played *Le Sacre* a few times in London to very polite audiences, obviously bent on showing greater sophistication in regard to music and ballet than Paris. Then, as the saying goes, the work was 'shelved'.

A year later I suggested to Stravinsky that I programme *Le Sacre* alone in concert. I had not seen the ballet, but friends had described it to me and I was convinced half the manifestations were rebellion at a new form of choreographic art. Stravinsky agreed and, before a theatre completely sold out, with everyone who was anyone in Paris musical circles in attendance, the work was performed. My mother had a box and Camille Saint-Saëns sat with her. She told me afterwards that the great French composer did nothing but repeat over and over, *'Mais il est fou, il est fou!* He is crazy, he is crazy!' As the work progressed, Saint-Saëns became very angry, as much with me I believe as with Stravinsky, and left in high dudgeon. The reaction of those musicians who had played the première of the work was very different; many said to me, 'That music has already aged!'

723

When Stravinsky's mother visited him from the Soviet Union in 1922, she refused to acknowledge his fame in western Europe. They quarrelled violently in the presence of George Antheil, who saw Stravinsky come close to tears because his mother had reproached him for not composing like Scriabin. Stravinsky said he hated

Scriabin. 'Now, now, Igor,' said Mrs Stravinsky, 'you haven't changed a bit – you were always contemptuous of your *betters*.'

724

Proust approached Stravinsky at a party after the 1922 première of *Renard* and asked him, 'Do you like Beethoven?'

'I detest him,' said Stravinsky.

'But the late quartets?'

'Worst things he ever wrote.'

He explained later, 'I should have shared his enthusiasm for Beethoven were it not a commonplace among intellectuals of that time.'

725

It was a Saturday, the day when the Russian choir opposite had its longest and loudest rehearsal. And every time, at the height of a fortissimo, the choir would stop because the sopranos – perhaps due to a mistake in the parts – would make the same mistake. They would move half a tone upwards instead of a whole tone.

Stravinsky had been complaining about the *coda* of the last movement of the Symphony of Psalms. 'I simply can't find an end for the last movement. Every time I think I have found it, it goes wrong and then, *pas de pitié*, I erase it.'

Suddenly I* heard him come into my studio and put his hands on my shoulders. 'From where comes this singing?'

'Oh,' I said, 'listen to that Igor Fedorovich. They have been singing the same phrase over and over again for the last fifteen minutes and every time, on the third repeat of the phrase, the sopranos make the same mistake. . . .'

'Shh . . . Shhh,' Stravinsky interrupted and whispered in my ear, 'be quiet, let me listen'.

'You see, there it comes again, the mistake.'

But Stravinsky grinned from ear to ear and said, still whispering; 'But this is beautiful . . . this is exactly what I need.' And he ran back to his study.

At half-past-twelve Stravinsky opened my door and exclaimed in a jovial tone: 'Nika, come on, let's go and celebrate. We'll have vodka and caviar. I have found the coda.'

726

Relieved at having received his immigration papers and 'searching about for a vehicle through which I might best express my

---

* Nicolas Nabokov (1903–78); Russian-born composer.

gratitude,' Stravinsky composed a new orchestration for 'The Star-Spangled Banner' and dedicated it 'to the American people.' He knew Congress had made it a civil offence (maximum fine $100) to embellish or otherwise tamper with the national anthem, but found the existing harmonization (by Damrosch) to be 'characterless'. After the first performance of his revision on 13 January 1944 in Cambridge, Massachusets, members of the audience filed complaints with the Boston Police Commissioner, Thomas F. Sullivan. At a second concert two nights later, Police Captain Thomas F. Harvey and six members of the 'radical squad' attended the performance, preparing to charge Stravinsky with an offence under chapter 264, section 9, of Massachusetts law. 'Let him change it just once,' said the captain, 'and we'll grab him.' Warned of the danger, Stravinsky conducted a faultlessly conventional rendition of the anthem. The police did not remain for the rest of the concert.

727

In his first years in Hollywood, Stravinsky badly needed money.

The early works, registered in Tsarist Russia, were not protected by copyright and earned him no income; his inter-War compositions were not greatly performed. Eventually, Louis B. Mayer was persuaded to offer him employment.

'I hear you are the greatest composer in the world,' said Mayer. Stravinsky bowed.

'Well, this is the greatest movie studio in the world.' Stravinsky bowed again.

To prove his point, Mayer demonstrated the battery of technological wonders he had installed in his enormous desk.

'How much will you charge for a music score?' he finally asked.

'How long is it?' asked Stravinsky.

'Say 45 minutes.'

Stravinsky did a mental caculation of the amount of work that had gone into *Petrushka* and the *Rite of Spring*, compositions of the desired length, and said '$25,000.'

'That's a lot of money, Mr Stravinsky,' said Mayer, 'much more than we normally pay. But since you're the greatest composer in the world, you shall have it. Now, when can I have the score?'

'In about one year,' said Stravinsky.

Mayer stared at him in disbelief. 'Good day, Mr Stravinsky', he said.

728

Billy Rose commissioned a piece from Stravinsky for a New York revue, staged in 1945. On the opening night he cabled the composer:

'Your music great success stop could be sensational success if you would authorize robert russell bennett retouch orchestration stop bennett orchestrates even the works of cole porter'

Stravinsky replied:

'SATISFIED WITH GREAT SUCCESS'

729

[At the opening concert of the 1952 Holland Festival] Stravinsky was presented to Queen Juliana. He was for various reasons, in the foulest of all moods. The Queen, knowing very little about music but wanting to be as friendly as possible, said she was a great admirer of his. Stravinsky said, 'Which of my works do you specially like?' The Queen was nonplussed. There was an interminable moment of silence. Stravinsky began to make a few suggestions, naming works that even Stravinskologists would not remember that he had written. If she had said 'yes' to any of them he would have made a complete fool of her. I*, standing behind Stravinsky, shook my head frantically each time he named a piece. The Queen said, 'Ah, I don't think I know that work.' 'What about that one?' he persisted, naming another. I shook my head at her again and contemplated suicide. Then he relented and said, '*Petrushka*', and I could at last nod approval. 'That's the one,' said the Queen. The conversation came quickly to an end and Stravinsky trotted off with me, giggling uninhibitedly.

Edgard VARESE (1883–1965)

Franco-American composer and conductor, pioneer of taped and electronic music, and explorer of unconventional sounds. 'I refuse,' he once said, 'to submit myself only to sounds that have already been heard.'

730

On arrival in New York in 1915, he disdained an offer to conduct the orchestra at a new motion picture theatre. Then he was introduced to John Barrymore, who, scrutinizing him carefully, asked how he was going to make a living. 'If you want to make some money,' he suggested, 'I can put you in a picture I'm doing in Chicago.' After

---

* Peter Diamand [b. 1913], artistic director of the Holland Festival.

protesting that he was not an actor – 'you don't have to be,' said Barrymore – the handsome Varèse agreed. He was thus the first serious composer to appear in a movie, though the name of the picture is not known.

૮ઝ૦

Anton von WEBERN (1883–1945)

A disciple of Schoenberg's, Webern's aphoristic compositions inspired the post-war *avant garde* compositions of Boulez and Stockhausen.

731

Webern reports to Schoenberg on his venture into psychoanalysis
5 August 1913

There were only two physicians in Vienna who could come into question for me, Freud and a certain Adler.* The latter, was telephoned at once, and I was able to go to him yesterday at seven o'clock in the evening. After I had told him all, he began at once with questions about everything, just everything. He voiced the opinion that he could cure me, but I would have to come daily to him for a month. Some of what he said was indeed astounding, and it appears to me, too, as if one could find out through analogies the real connections that uncover the cause. To be sure, I still have reservations and a strong antipathy towards it all. For the time being, I want to go to the fellow a few times; I will then see what develops. I can always quit.

6 August

Well then, yesterday I was for the second time with the psychoanalyst. I just do not know at all what he is driving at. Yesterday, by means of a thousand questions, he tried to establish how much of the effeminate there is in me. Ah, what sense does all this make!. . .

I go every day to Dr Adler. I have to tell him everything, simply everything. There is not much left in my life that he does not know by now. From it all he concludes always the same thing: my spells of indisposition were a transference of the battleground from the real world into that of illness.

21 August

After everything that I told him of my illnesses and of my life from childhood on, he has arrived at the following conclusion: the cause

---

* Alfred Adler (1870–1937); Austrian psychiatrist who broke with Freud in 1911.

lay in too tendentious a desire to be 'on top', in a mania not to let myself be guided under any circumstances. I had set for myself a high goal in all respects, in my career, in married life, and so forth; on the other hand, however, I shrank from decisions because of a timidity – yes, indeed, a softness and exaggerated sensitivity – beginning in childhood. In order to delay such decisions, my body created these symptoms of illness so that it could offer, as it were, an excuse for my backing away. Now since I did not want to let myself be guided by anyone, so naturally I did not wish him [Adler] to lead me either. And the culmination of the cure, its goal, consisted in my overcoming this, too, in my convincing myself that he was right.

732

Schoenberg, letter to a Dutch patron of the Arts

Traunkirchen, 9 July 1923

Dear Mr Boissevain,

I myself have received many a proof of our friendship, yet I cannot help feeling somewhat diffident about now asking you for yet another. This time it is, into the bargain, a matter of financial support. It is for my former pupil, my friend, Dr Anton von Webern. He is in very dire need. He is the father of four children and every summer, when private lessons stop, he finds himself without any income, without any prospect of earning anything. In earlier days there was frequently help from abroad. But now, with the ever rising cost of living, the sums he receives scarcely cover a quarter of what he needs. Since I myself have very few rich acquaintances, I have myself repeatedly helped him out with fairly large sums (far beyond what I can afford). At the moment I could scarcely do more. And indeed I think my resources would not stretch to it.

You know Webern; you know that he is an extraordinarily gifted composer. I don't have to introduce him to you. You undoubtedly have a flair for remarkable people and must long ago have realized that he is one of them: Do help to keep him going!

733

Days before Vienna fell on 10 April 1945, Webern and his wife fled to the village of Mittersill, near Salzburg, to be with their daughters and grandchildren. They were also joined there by a son-in-law, formerly a member of the SS but now flourishing as a black market trader with soldiers of the US 42nd Division. On 15 September he invited his parents-in-law to a festive dinner, promising Webern an American cigar. 'Do you know what a historic day this is?' Webern joked as he left for the fateful meal.

After supper some soldiers called. Webern, his wife and daughter retired to the room where the children slept.

'At 9.45 pm exactly', wrote Wilhelmine von Webern, 'my husband said we had to leave soon for our home, because we had to be there by 10.30 pm [the curfew hour for civilians]. He wanted to smoke the cigar that he had received the same evening from our son-in-law. He stated that he wanted to smoke it only partly, and outside the room in order not to bother the children. This was the first time that he left the room. My husband was only outside for two to three minutes when we heard three shots. I was very frightened but did not think that my husband could be involved in any way. Then the door to our room was opened by my husband, who said "I was shot." Together with my daughter, I laid him on a mattress and started opening his clothes. My husband was just able to say the words, "It is over." [Webern was accidentally shot and killed by an American soldier.]

❧

Alban BERG (1885–1935)

Pupil of Schoenberg's, Viennese composer of two major operas, *Wozzeck* and *Lulu*.

734

Arnold Schoenberg

When Alban Berg came to me in 1904, he was a very tall youngster and extremely timid. But when I saw the composition he showed me – songs in a style between Hugo Wolf and Brahms – I recognized at once that he had real talent. Consequently I accepted him as pupil, though at this time he was unable to pay my fee. Later his mother inherited a great fortune and told Alban, as they now have money, he could enter the conservatory. I was told that Alban was so upset by this assumption that he started weeping and could not stop weeping before his mother had allowed him to continue with me.

735

When excerpts from *Lulu* were first performed in Vienna in 1935 the customary demonstrations were reinforced by Nazi troublemakers. Some members of the audience shouted, 'Long live Tchaikovsky!' Berg observed them pityingly and said, 'Poor boys! Their grandfathers behaved just the same when Tchaikovsky's Fifth was played in this hall forty years ago. Only *then* they shouted for some Schubert.'

736

'When I compose I feel I am like Beethoven,' he told his pupil, Adorno*. 'Only afterwards do I realize that I am at best only a Bizet.'

737

Adorno writes
Berg said about himself that in his life he had really never known the full bliss of sexuality as he imagined it – this, despite his extraordinary handsomeness and despite the fact that women were greatly attracted to Berg, notably since he became famous. He derived a certain pleasure in setting other people erotically on one another. For this purpose he once invited me together with a very charming singer who was considerably older than I and made us drunk. He himself had many love affairs which ended, however, always unhappily, in a sense the unhappy end was 'composed' into them, and one had the feeling that from their inception these affairs formed a part of his creative apparatus, that they were, as in the Austrian joke, desperate but not serious.

❦

Wilhelm FURTWÄNGLER (1886–1954)

Principal conductor of the Berlin Philharmonic Orchestra from 1922, in the Nazi era he remained in Germany, protecting his musicians to the extent that he was able.

738

After a Berlin Philharmonic concert in December 1944, Furt-wängler invited Albert Speer, Minister of Armaments, to his dressing room. According to Speer, the conductor asked with disarming unworldliness whether there was any prospect of winning the war. Speer said defeat was at hand and advised the conductor to remain in Switzerland after a forthcoming concert as he might be in danger from his Nazi enemies. 'But what is to become of my orchestra?' he protested. Speer promised to protect the Philharmonic and, greatly relieved, Furtwängler left Germany.

---

* Theodor Wiesengrund Adorno [1903–69]; German Marxist, social and musical philosopher.

On 12 April 1945, in Furtwängler's absence, the orchestra played the last aria and finale from *Götterdämmerung*, Beethoven's Violin Concerto and a performance which Speer had warned friends would signify the end of the war – Bruckner's Fourth Symphony.

739

During the Nazi years, Goebbels and Goering had fostered a fierce rivalry between Furtwängler and Herbert von Karajan for musical supremacy in Berlin. The feud persisted after the war until Furtwängler's death. Elisabeth Schwarzkopf remembers lunching with her husband, Walter Legge, and Furtwängler. The subject of the Salzburg Festival came up, and Legge happened to mention Karajan's name. 'Furtwängler's face grew darker and darker. Finally he said, "If that man K" – he would not take Karajan's name into his mouth – "if that man K is there, I will give them a programme that they will *hate*."'

⌒⌒⌒

Sergei PROKOFIEV (1891–1953)

The young Prokofiev scandalized St Petersburg with two piano concertos (1911–12) and was recruited by Diaghilev to write three ballets for Paris. He emigrated from Russia in 1918 but returned in the 1930s, only to have his music attacked during Stalin's purge in 1948.

740

Prokofiev announced one day that there had not been a first-rate French composer since Bizet. 'I know,' he brushed aside Nabokov's[*] protests, 'you like that old crank Satie. You think his followers are important. Well they're not: they're pure mush. The only one in France who knows what he's doing is Ravel.'

'But what about Debussy?' objected Nabokov.

'You know what Debussy is! Calf's-foot jelly. It's spineless music. Except perhaps,' – and he grinned – 'it's very "personal" jelly, and the jelly-maker knows what he's doing.' Prokofiev raised the index finger of his right hand, but did not elaborate.

---

[*] Nicolas Nabokov (1903–78); Russian born composer.

Nathan Milstein, recalls

We used to stay in the same hotel in Hollywood and would meet for breakfast. Ever since I was a child, I had always believed that inspired, creative people were not like ordinary human beings: they don't go to the WC, they don't eat. Then I saw Prokofiev eating bacon and eggs for breakfast, the fat spattering over his clothes, the foam gathering at the corners of his mouth. He had such full-blooded lips that you had the feeling that if you squeezed them blood would come spurting out. It was not a pleasant sight. I looked at him and thought, 'It's not possible.' Well, it was possible. Probably Beethoven was the same.

742

I* have seen Prokofiev for weeks on end in his little room furnished with an upright piano, a small table and a few chairs, composing for fourteen hours a day, not going to eat except occasionally and then in complete silence. At these times he only emerged from his office to give the manuscript pages covered with a fine calligraphy in pencil, to his secretary, or, moved by an unusual nerviness, to take the flat green ruler with which he ruled his scores and make for the room where the children were being over noisy. Justice done and calm restored by a few strokes on the seat of the pants, he would return to the piano or the table, for he could compose equally well either through his fingers or through his brain (in this latter case he would hear the music with complete precision, although in practice he could not sing two notes in succession). To be exact, he no longer composed at the piano, letting it suffice just to confirm certain harmonic combinations, for he had often been turned out of various lodgings for making too much noise. Even this confirmation was not, however, without danger to his domestic peace and that of his neighbours. One day when he was working, a process-server arrived – yet another one! – with an order to quit. 'You have just played two hundred and eighteen times in succession the same wildly barbaric chord,' affirmed the civil officer of justice. 'Don't deny it; I was in the flat below, I counted them. I summon you to vacate these premises.'

743

Gregor Piatigorsky pestered Prokofiev for a 'cello concerto.
   'But I don't know your crazy instrument,' the composer protested.

---

* Serge Moreaux, critic.

Piatigorsky insisted, showing him some of the greatest works for 'cello.

'You should not keep this stuff in the house. It smells,' said Prokofiev.

At Piatigorsky's continued urging, the composer eventually produced the first movement of a concerto, accompanying it with a warning.

'It will lead to nothing,' said Prokofiev. 'I cannot compose away from Russia. I will go home.'

Back in his native country, Prokofiev completed the work and it was premièred by Piatigorsky and Koussevitsky in Boston without further excuse or comment from the composer (who later revised it for Mstislav Rostropovich).

❧

Andrés SEGOVIA (b. 1893)

Spanish virtuoso who established the guitar as a concert instrument.

744

Towards the end of a recital in Berlin, just as he was concluding with a *pianissimo*, there was a loud cracking noise. Segovia rushed off. Gregor Piatigorsky, who visited him backstage, found him muttering 'my guitar, my guitar', as if it was the only word he knew.

Some time afterwards Segovia told Piatigorsky that his friend who had made the guitar had died in Madrid at the precise moment the instrument had split in Berlin.

❧

Paul HINDEMITH (1895–1963)

Blacklisted by the Nazis, Hindemith left first for Turkey, where he founded the Ankara Music School, and then for the United States, where he taught at Yale.

745

Carlo-Maria Giulini observed Hindemith rehearsing Bach with a famous German orchestra, whose strings played a consistent *staccato*, without *vibrato* or variations in dynamics. After some minutes, he stopped them and asked for a more beautiful sound. The leader of the orchestra apologized but insisted, 'We descend from the Bach tradition and this is the style, the right way.' Hindemith retorted

317

mildly, 'I don't know how, with no *vibrato*, Bach could have so many sons.'

746

Hindemith was persuaded by an American *avant-gardist* to listen to a new work. After an uncomfortable half-hour he asked, 'Is this your last composition?'

'No,' replied the aspirant.

'Pity.' muttered Hindemith.

❧

Erich Wolfgang KORNGOLD (1897–1957)

Viennese boy prodigy, hailed as a second Mozart, Korngold became the classiest composer in Hollywood (*The Sea Hawk, Robin Hood*, etc.)

747

During the Hollywood production of *Midsummer Night's Dream*, for which he adapted Mendelssohn's music, Korngold was introduced to James Cagney. No sooner had [he] been presented to Cagney than he stepped back and said, 'Hold still, Mr Cagney. Hold still a minute.' Then he rubbed his chin reflectively and began to hum a little. Walking around to the other side, he continued the inspection and the humming, while whistling contentedly under his breath.

Finally, when the image of Cagney had been securely captured in musical terms, he thanked his subject and departed. Cagney said he almost felt as if he should ask when to come in and try on the theme for which Korngold had fitted him.

❧

Georg SZELL (1897–1970)

Hungarian conductor who made the Cleveland Orchestra one of the world's finest.

748

Szell's manner, aloof and autocractic, made him few friends. After he had stalked out of the New York Met. in 1954, someone observed to Rudolf Bing, the manager, that Georg Szell was his own worst enemy. 'Not while I'm alive,' said Bing.

❧

George GERSHWIN (1898–1937)

Born of Jewish immigrants in New York and influenced by Negro jazz and blues, Gershwin composed both for Broadway and the concert hall.

749

He was forever seeking lessons from anyone he felt might improve his technical skills – from Ravel, Stravinsky, the violinist Joseph Achron and many others. In Hollywood he became a friend and tennis partner of Schoenberg's and duly asked the older composer to accept him as a pupil. Schoenberg refused. 'I would only make you a bad Schoenberg,' he said, 'and you're such a good Gershwin already.'

750

The Gullah Negro prides himself on what he calls 'shouting'. This is a complicated pattern beaten out by feet and hands as an accompaniment to the spirituals and is indubitably an African survival. I* shall never forget the night when, at a Negro meeting on a remote sea-island, George started 'shouting' with them. And eventually to their huge delight stole the show from their champion 'shouter'. I think he is the only white man in America who could have done it.'

ભ્જ્જ

Ernst KŘENEK (b. 1900)

Composer of the first jazz-based opera, *Jonny Spielt Auf*. Born in Vienna, he emigrated to the USA in 1938.

751

When Ernst Křenek, the composer came to town [Hollywood] Ben [Hecht] and I† decided that Sam Goldwyn would have to hire him to write the score of a picture which Sam was then planning, one with a Czech background. Because Křenek was Czech, had just arrived from Europe (where he had been persecuted by the Nazis), because

---

* DuBose Heyward, author of the novel from which *Porgy and Bess* was created.
† George Antheil (1900–59); American composer.

he was an old and very good friend of mine, and finally because he was out of a job, Ben and I immediately went to Sam and started screaming at him that the greatest composer in the world was in town.

'Is that so?' said Goldwyn, without falling off his chair. 'What's his name?'

'Křenek, Ernst Křenek!'

'Never heard of him! What has he written?'

'What's he written, what's he written!' screamed Ben. 'Listen to that!'

'Well, what *has* he written? I never heard tell of the guy before.'

'You tell him, Georgie,' said Ben. I took over.

'He wrote one of the world's most successful operas, *Jonny Spielt Auf*. It made over a million in Germany before Hitler came in.'

'Never heard of it.'

'Well.' I said, reaching, 'he wrote *Threepenny Opera*.' (Kurt Weill wrote it, and I knew it, but all of Křenck's operas, symphonies, and other pieces seemed so feeble now.)

'Never heard of it.'

'And *Rosenkavalier*,' interrupted Ben. 'He wrote *Rosenkavalier*. It grossed over two million dollars last year on the Continent.'

Goldwyn brightened up a bit. He thought he might have heard of *Rosenkavalier*.

'And *Faust*, too; Křenek wrote that.'

'No kiddin!' said Goldwyn speculatively. I could see Křenek was going to get the job.

'And *La Traviata*, too,' said Ben, to clinch it.

'So he wrote *La Traviata* did he!' Goldwyn's smiling face suddenly turned black. "Just bring that guy around here so's I can get my hands on him. Why, his publishers almost ruined me with a suit just because we used a few bars of that lousy opera. We had to retake half of the picture for a few lousy bars.'

As we quickly withdrew from his wrath, both Ben and I sadly realized that we over-sold our product.

752

The newly-exiled Křenek was applauded politely when he played the piano in the US première of his aggressive and atonal Second Piano Concerto in Boston in November 1938. Afterwards, his publisher heard one patrician lady comment on it to another, 'Conditions in Europe,' she observed, 'must be dreadful.'

❧

Aaron COPLAND (b.1900)
(b. Kaplan)

The first of several Americans to study in Paris with Nadia Boulanger, Copland drew on elements of jazz, New England hymns and folk songs to achieve an American musical style.

753

His First Symphony, including an organ part for Nadia Boulanger to play on her first US tour, received its first performance in New York on 11 January 1925. Hearing some hissing at its conclusion, the conductor, Walter Damrosch, swung round and declared loudly to the audience, 'If a young man at the age of twenty three can write a symphony like that, in five years he will be ready to commit murder.'

754

While Copland was in Hollywood in 1943 writing tuneful music for a Sam Goldwyn movie, he met Groucho Marx at a contemporary music concert at which his dissonant piano sonata was being played.

'I have a split personality,' explained Copland.

'Well it's OK,' said Groucho, 'as long as you split it with Mr Goldwyn.'

❧

Jascha HEIFETZ (b. 1901)

Russian-born violinist.

755

News of Heifetz's European triumphs ran ahead of him to the United States and his début there, at Carnegie Hall in October 1917, was attended by many of the outstanding soloists of the day. During a break between two pieces, the violinist Mischa Elman mopped his brow and, turning to his neighbour, the sharp-witted pianist Leopold Godowsky, exclaimed, 'Phew, it's hot in here!' 'Not for pianists,' said Godowsky.*

❧

---

* Alternative version of Godowsky's quip: 'Only for violinists'.

Vladimir HOROWITZ (b. 1903)

Virtuoso pianist.

756

Nathan Milstein recalls
On doctor's orders he would take a walk every day between four and
five in the afternoon. Usually he would go along Fifth Avenue and
Central Park and on his way home would stop at my apartment and
sit down at the piano, often breaking its string. One day as he played
my daughter asked me, 'Is that good?'

'Good?' I exclaimed, 'it's miraculous, he's the greatest pianist in
the world!' I will never forget her response. She said, 'Does he know?'

757

Vladimir Horowitz
'I asked Schnabel if he played Chopin and Liszt. "No, I don't," he
replied, "but after I have played all of Mozart, Schubert, Beethoven,
Schumann and Brahms, perhaps I will." You know what I said? I said,
"I am doing exactly vice versa."'

❧

Dmitri SHOSTAKOVICH (1906–1975)

Born in St Petersburg, Shostakovich achieved instant success with
his graduation work, the First Symphony. Soviet literature portrays
Shostakovich as a faithful servant of the State, but in 1936 *Pravda*
attacked his opera, *Lady Macbeth of Mtsensk*, as 'chaos instead of
music', and he fell again into disfavour during Stalin's 1948 purge.

758

Mstislav Rostropovich recalls
Shostakovich was much more introverted than Ben (Britten) but in
a very different way. Ben suffered for his personal, intimate life, but
Shostakovich suffered for his whole country, for his persecuted
colleagues, for thousands of people who were hungry. After I played
the 'cello concerto for him for the first time at his *dacha* in Leningrad (in 1958), he accompanied me to the railway station to catch
the overnight train to Moscow. In the big waiting hall we found many
people sleeping on the floor. I saw his face, and the great suffering in
it brought tears to my eyes. I cried, not from seeing the poor people
but from what I saw in the face of Shostakovich.

That is the difference between Britten and Shostakovich. It is like the music of Tchaikovsky and Mussorgsky: in one the substance is himself, in the other it is the experience of his people.

Shostakovich, memoirs
After my trip to Turkey, which got a lot of coverage in the Soviet papers, I was offered guest performances at very flattering terms. I went on one of these trips, to Arkhangelsk, with the cellist Viktor Kubatsky. He played my 'cello sonata. On 28 January 1936, we went to the railway station to buy a new *Pravda*. I opened it up, leafed through it – and found the article 'Muddle Instead of Music'. I'll never forget that day, it's probably the most memorable in my life.

That article on the third page of *Pravda* changed my entire existence. It was printed without a signature, like an editorial – that is, it expressed the opinion of the Party. But it actually expressed the opinion of Stalin, and that was much more important. . . .

The title, 'Muddle Instead of Music', belongs to Stalin. The day before, *Pravda* had printed the leader and teacher's brilliant comments on the outlines of new history textbooks, and he talked about muddles there, too. . . .

So, my opera was taken off the stage. Meetings were organized to drum 'the muddle' into everyone's head. Everyone turned away from me. There was a phrase in the article saying that all this 'could end very badly'. They were all waiting for the bad end to come. . . .

From that moment on I was stuck with the label 'enemy of the people', and I don't need to explain what the label meant in those days. Everyone still remembers that.

I was called an enemy of the people quietly and out loud and from podiums. One paper made the following announcement of my concert: 'Today there is a concert by enemy of the people Shostakovich.'

Maxim Shostakovich
I began to understand the problem of life in the Soviet Union in 1948. My father had suffered under Stalin once before in 1936, before I was born. But in '48 I can clearly remember that people threw stones through our windows. The newspapers had said that Shostakovich was an enemy of the people. Yet my father could not have left Russia. Like the great writers Akhmatova and Pasternak, he needed to be with his people in their time of torment.

Soon after the Decree of 10 February 1948, in which the Central Committee of the Party attacked leading composers and their music I* remember meeting Khrennikov at a Molotov reception, and he started talking about Shostakovich's *Lady Macbeth of Mtsensk*. He was positively grundyish. 'Ugh,' he said, 'why, he gives you there a musical rendering of – ugh! – the Sexual Act!' I remarked that, after all, Wagner had done much the same in *Tristan* and the *Walküre*. 'Ugh, yes, horrible,' said Khrennikov, 'but Shostakovich is *even more naturalistic, even more horrible!*'

762

I† visited him in February 1948, the day after the central committee [of the Communist Party of the USSR] passed its resolution against the composers. Shostakovich was very tense; almost ill with tension. He thanked me many times for coming. I was with him for several hours. He drank a bottle of red wine and smoked many cigarettes. He did not talk about the resolution. He said, 'We must be quiet. And patient.'

763

Mstislav Rostropovich
Sometimes Shostakovich was unable to talk at all. He just wanted to have the presence of a person he liked, sitting without a word in the same room. Before we lived in the same apartment building (the Composers' House in Moscow) he lived quite a long way away. He would telephone me and say, 'Come quickly, hurry.'

So I'd arrive at his flat, and he'd say, 'Sit down, and now we can be silent.' I would sit for half an hour, without a word. It was most relaxing, just sitting. Then Shostakovich would get up and say, 'Thank you. Goodbye, Slava.'

It was very special, sitting like that with him. When I left I felt as though I'd been through some kind of catharsis; the relaxation was purifying. And afterwards, when somebody would start to talk, I'd get irritated; and if they asked a question I'd say, 'It's obvious, don't be silly!'

---

* The narrator is Alexander Werth, a British foreign correspondent; Tikhon Khrennikov (b. 1913) secretary-general of the Union of Soviet Composers since 1948, assiduous implementer of Party resolutions against composers; Vyacheslav M. Molotov (b. 1890), Soviet Foreign Minister 1939–56, a cousin of Scriabin.
† The conductor Rudolf Barshai (b. 1924)

Shostakovich, memoirs

Naturally, Stalin didn't give a damn about the West, and the Western intelligentsia in particular. He used to say, 'Don't worry, they'll swallow it.' But the West did exist and he had to do something with it. They had started a peace movement, and they needed people for it. And Stalin thought of me. That was his style completely. Stalin liked to put a man face to face with death and then make him dance to his own tune.

I was given the order to get ready for a trip to America. I had to go to the Cultural and Scientific Congress for World Peace in New York. A worthy cause. It's obvious that peace is better than war and therefore struggling for peace is a noble effort. But I refused; it was humiliating for me to take part in a spectacle like that. I was formalist, a representative of an anti-national direction in music. My music was banned, and now I was supposed to go and say that everything was fine.

No, I said, I won't go. I'm ill, I can't fly, I get airsick. Molotov talked to me, but I still refused.

Then Stalin called. And in his nagging way, the leader and teacher asked me why I didn't want to go to America. I answered that I couldn't. My comrades' music wasn't played, and neither was mine. They would ask about it in America. What could I say?

Stalin pretended to be surprised. 'What do you mean, it isn't played? Why aren't they playing it?'

I told him that there was a decree by the censors, that there was a blacklist. Stalin said, 'Who gave the orders?' Naturally I replied, 'It must have been one of the leading comrades.'

Now came the interesting part. Stalin announced, 'No, we didn't give that order.' He always referred to himself in the royal plural. . . .

He began rehearsing the thought that the censors had overreacted, had taken an incorrect initiative. . . .

This was another matter, this was a real concession. And I thought that maybe it would make sense to go to America, if as a result they would play the music of Prokofiev, Shebalin, Miaskovsky, Khachaturian, Popov and Shostakovich again.

And just then, Stalin stopped going on about the question of the order and said, 'We'll take care of that problem, Comrade Shostakovich. What about your health?'

And I told Stalin the pure truth. 'I feel sick.'

Stalin was taken aback and then started mulling over this unexpected bulletin. 'Why do you feel sick? From what? We'll send you a physician, he'll see why you feel sick.' And so on.

So finally I agreed, and I made the trip to America. It cost me a great deal, that trip. I had to answer stupid questions and avoid saying too much. They made a sensation out of that too. And all I thought about was: How much longer do I have to live?

Thirty thousand people were jammed into Madison Square Garden when I played the scherzo from my Fifth Symphony on the piano, and I thought, this is it, this is the last time I'll ever play before an audience this size.

765

Mstislav Rostropovich
He gave me the manuscript of the First 'Cello Concerto on 2 August 1958. On the sixth I played it to him from memory, three times. After the first time he was *so* excited, and of course we drank a little bit of vodka. The second time I played not so perfect, and afterwards we drank even more vodka. The third time I *think* I played the Saint-Saëns concerto, but he still accompanied *his* concerto. We were enormously happy.

766

The music of Shostakovich was the first to be performed extra-terrestially. On 12 April 1961, Yuri Gagarin, the first cosmonaut, sang for the benefit of an audience at Mission Control the Shostakovich song, 'My homeland hears, my homeland knows where in the skies her son soars on'.

❦

Herbert von KARAJAN (b. 1908)

The most recorded conductor in history, Karajan has directed the Berlin Philharmonic for more than thirty years. He was also director of the Vienna Opera and Salzburg Festivals.

767

He explained once to a German journalist why he preferred the Berlin to the Vienna Philharmonic. 'If I tell the Berliners to step forward, they do it. If I tell the Viennese to step forward, they do it. But then they ask why.'

❦

Olivier MESSIAEN (b. 1908)

French composer whose music reflects devout Catholicism and love of nature.

768

Messiaen

Bird-song is my refuge. In dark hours, when my uselessness is brutally revealed to me and all the musical languages of the world seem to be merely an effort of patient research, without there being anything behind the notes to justify so much work – I go into the forest, into fields, into mountains, by the sea, among birds . . . it is there that music dwells for me; free, anonymous music, improvized for pleasure.

I have been collecting bird-song for twenty years. I did this instinctively, for my own personal pleasure; then I was ashamed of working blindly. I made contact with ornithologists and accompanied them on expeditions. . . .

Birds alone are the great artists.

ᑲᗢᑐ

John CAGE (b. 1912)

American *avant-gardist*, inventor of the 'prepared piano' (1938), in which screws, coins and other objects are placed between the strings.

769

John Cage writes

So it was that about 1949 I gave my *Lecture on Nothing* at the Artists' Club on Eighth Street in New York City. This *Lecture on Nothing* was written in the same rhythmic structure I employed at the time in my musical compositions. One of the structural divisions was the repetition, some fourteen times, of a single page in which occurred the refrain, 'If anyone is sleepy let him go to sleep.' Jeanne Reynal, I remember, stood up part way through, screamed, and then said, while I continued speaking, 'John, I dearly love you but I can't bear another minute.' She then walked out. Later, during the question period, I gave one of six previously prepared answers regardless of the question asked. This was a reflection of my engagement in Zen.

ᑲᗢᑐ

Benjamin BRITTEN [1913–1976]
(Lord Britten of Aldeburgh)

Britten's opera *Peter Grimes* was the first major British opera since Purcell's day. Many of Britten's works were inspired by his lifelong companion, the tenor Sir Peter Pears, and by his native Suffolk seaboard.

770

On tour with *The Rape of Lucretia* his librettist, Ronald Duncan, found Britten [then thirty-three years old] in a hotel corridor in Edinburgh hobbling along as if permanently crippled. 'What I'm trying to do,' Britten explained, 'is walk down the corridor and back without touching any of the red lines in the carpet.' Duncan asked what he hoped to achieve by that. 'If I can get up and down the corridor without touching the lines' said Britten, 'it will mean that I am a composer.'

771

The composer, Sir Michael Tippett, recalls
Ben and I first met in the War when we were both conscientious objectors. Here is a small anecdote of those times. It is customary for artists to give concerts free to inmates of HM prisons. Britten and Pears had already offered to do so before I was sent to prison myself*. They managed to arrange it that they gave a recital at Wormwood Scrubs (West London gaol, 11 July 1943) when I was there. On my side, I am ashamed to mention the untruthful wrangling by which I convinced the authorities that the recital was impossible unless I turned the pages for the pianist. To the last moment it was touch and go. But finally I stepped out of the ranks and sat down on the platform beside him. A strange moment for us both.

772

When Britten visited Russia, he and Shostakovich became friends.
'What do you think of Puccini?' Shostakovich asked once.
'His operas are dreadful,' said Britten.
'No, Ben, you're wrong,' said Shostakovich. 'He wrote marvellous operas but dreadful music.'

773

His anger was terrifying: one look was the equivalent of a twenty-minute harangue by anyone else. After a rehearsal in Holland, the

---

* For infringement of his status as a conscientious objector.

musicians emerged to tell me* that Britten was in a frightful mood, a fearful temper. 'What did he say to you?' I asked. No one could remember exactly. 'He put down his baton and looked at us,' one man recalled. 'Then he said, "Now gentleman, *please!*"'

❧

Leonard BERNSTEIN (b. 1918)

Through his television broadcasts, recordings, concerts and books, Bernstein has become the first American conductor to achieve success in Europe. Music director of the New York Philharmonic Orchestra for eleven years, his best known composition is *West Side Story*.

774

Confronted at an opera rehearsal in Vienna with an uncomprehending singer, Bernstein finally blew up. 'I know it's the historical prerogative of the tenor to be stupid,' he yelled, 'but you, sir, have abused that privilege.'

775

On 16 November 1943, after the unknown Bernstein had taken over a coast-to-coast broadcast from the indisposed Bruno Walter, the New York Times editorialized
There are many variations of the six best stories in the world: the young corporal takes over the platoon when all the officers are down; the captain, with the dead admiral at his side, signals the fleet to go ahead; the young actress, fresh from Corinth or Ashtabula, steps into the star's role; the junior clerk, alone in the office, makes the instantaneous decision that saves the firm from ruin. The adventure of Leonard Bernstein, twenty-five-year-old assistant conductor of the Philharmonic, who blithely mounted the podium at Carnegie Hall Sunday afternoon when Conductor Bruno Walter became ill, belongs in the list. . . .

776

The composer Ned Rorem recalls
Lenny Bernstein once said . . . (c. 1946): 'The trouble with you and me, Ned, is that we want everyone in the world to personally love us, and of course that's impossible: you just don't *meet* everyone in the world.'

❧

---

* Peter Diamand (b. 1913), music administrator.

Maria CALLAS (1923–1977)
(b. Kalogeropoulos)

Supreme dramatic soprano, last of the legendary divas, her *Tosca* and *Norma* were legendary.

777

An American reporter asked her: 'Madame Callas, you were born in the United States, raised in Greece and live in Italy: which language do you think in?' Callas replied, 'I count in English.'

778

'What a lovely voice,' she exclaimed on hearing a recording of her more sedate rival, Renata Tebaldi, 'but who cares?'

779

She refused to re-emerge after the first act of *Norma* in Rome on 2 January 1958, offending the Italian President who was attending the gala opening and provoking ructions in the audience. 'Go back to Milan,' they shouted. Menenghini, her husband, told the Press that she was suffering from an 'inflammation of the vocal chords and bronchial complications'. These were complicated still further by eyewitness accounts of how she had celebrated the New Year at an exclusive night club in the small hours of the eve of her première. The newspapers shrieked, 'Disgrace', questions were asked in Parliament, and the Rome Opera 'in the interests of publc order' obtained a court injunction to bar her from singing the remaining performances of *Norma* and restrain her from entering the house. Callas sued the opera house and won restitution of her fees of 2.7 million lire.

❧

György LIGETI (b. 1923)

Hungarian-born composer of intricate orchestral and vocal scores; he describes his style as 'micropolyphony'.

780

Ligeti recalls

As a small child I once had a dream that I could not get to my cot, to my safe haven, because the whole room was filled with a dense confused tangle of fine filaments. It looked like the web I had seen silkworms fill their box with as they change into pupas. I was caught up in this immense web together with both living things and objects of various kinds . . . enormous dirty pillows were suspended in this substance, their rotten stuffing hanging out through the slits in the torn covers. There were blobs of fresh mucus, balls of dry mucus, remnants of food all gone cold and other such revolting rubbish. Every time a beetle or moth moved, the entire web started shaking. . . . An indescribable sadness hung over these shifting forms and structure, the hopelessness of passing time and the melancholy of unalterable past events.

781

Interviewer: I'm intrigued by one title from 1951, your 'Grand symphonie militaire' op. 69.
Ligeti: Oh that was a joke: the opus number refers of course to the sexual position.

ᓚᘏ

Pierre BOULEZ (b. 1925)

French composer, conductor, philosopher and founder of the Institut de recherche et co-ordination acoustique/musique (IRCAM), a unique government-funded musical research centre in Paris. He has sought to create a new musical language. In the 1970s he was chief conductor simultaneously of the BBC Symphony and New York Philharmonic orchestras.

782

On holiday at his sister's home in Provence in 1970, Boulez was summoned to the phone. 'It's the Elysée Palace,' his sister said excitedly, 'President Pompidou wants to speak to you.' Boulez was unimpressed. 'It's just Howard Hartog* pulling my leg: take his number and I'll call him back.'

He returned the call, and found himself invited to dine alone with the President and his wife. 'President Pompidou asked me outright: would you come back to France?' recalled Boulez, who had lived for most of the past decade in Germany. 'I said: I have no phobia against the French. But if I return it will not be to conduct an orchestra, when I have better opportunities in London and New York. For the idea of IRCAM, though, I would leave everything.'

He went on to outline his vision of an institute in which com-

---

* Friend and London agent of Boulez.

posers, scientists and engineers would work side by side to carry music into its next phase of evolution. Almost without qualification, Pompidou endorsed his dream at a cost of ninety million francs.

783

The title of *e.e. cummings ist der Dichter* (1973) is a product of Boulez' whimsy. The work was scheduled for performance in West Germany and he was being pressed by the concert organizers for a title they could print in the programmes.

'I haven't got one,' wrote Boulez in German, 'all I can tell you now is e. e. cummings is the poet I have chosen.'

Some days later he received a reply, 'As regards your work *e. e. cummings ist der Dichter* [is the poet]. . . .'

'I could not have a better title,' said Boulez, 'than that which had come about completely by accident.'

❦

Hans Werner HENZE (b. 1926)

German composer whose recent works, in particular the opera, *We Come to the River*, are meant to serve the aims of Marxism.

784

We Come to the River, commissioned by Covent Garden, was not the Royal Opera House's most successful première. Certain members of the cast disapproved of the music, others of the politics, others still of Henze's role as producer; neither critics nor public were over-enthusiastic. . . .

One evening, the tenor Robert Tear announced backstage that the audience were being allowed in free. Having paused to allow his colleagues to reflect on this gloomy news, Tear added, 'But they are having to pay to get out.'

❦

Mstislav ROSTROPOVICH (b. 1927)

Russian 'cellist and conductor. He was exiled from the USSR over his friendship with the dissident writer, Alexander Solzhenitsyn.

785

Olga Ivinskaya, lover of Boris Pasternak, found herself sharing a sleeping compartment with a stranger on the Leningrad to Moscow train I unpacked my things and took out a magazine where a work by a well-known Soviet author was appearing in instalments.

'How can you possibly read such rubbish?' My companion asked . . . 'the only modern authors I read are those who are not published.'

'For example?' I asked.

'Well, Solzhenitsyn, for example. I rate him higher than Tolstoy. But you don't read him, I suppose?'

We sat up the whole night, drinking champagne and talking about Solzhenitsyn and the people who supported him. We argued and even quarrelled. [He said,] 'he was not someone to disown himself like Pasternak.'

'Do you know that after Rostropovich had seen Solzhenitsyn only once at a recital in Ryazan, he invited him to come and stay at his home and shared everything he had with him? And now he's not only going to get him a residence permit to live in Moscow, but permission to have a *dacha* there as well. He'll go right up to the people at the top and won't stop at anything.'

For a long time he went on heatedly like this about the friendship between Rostropovich and Solzhenitsyn – little did I know at the time that I was hearing it from none other than Rostropovich himself.'

❧

Karlheinz STOCKHAUSEN (b. 1928)

German composer and leader of the *avant-garde*. After meeting Boulez and Messaien in Darmstadt in 1951 he studied for two years in Paris. Of his many works, *Stimmung* for six voices and electronics, and *Gesang der Jünglinge*, for unbroken boy's voice and echo, have commanded widespread attention.

786

'Have you heard any Stockhausen?' Sir Thomas Beecham was asked.

'No,' he replied, 'but I believe I have trodden in some.'

❧

NOTES

Place of publication of each documentary source is London, unless stated otherwise. Sources quoted several times are named in full on first appearance and abbreviated thereafter.

1. Quoted in Martin Gerbert: *Scriptores ecclesiastici de musica*. San Blasianis, 1784; transl. by Lawrence Rosenwald in *Music in the Western World: A History in Documents*. Selected and annotated by Piero Weiss and Richard Taruskin. (Reprinted by permission.)

2. Thirteenth-century chronicle quoted in Thomas Busby: *General History of Music* (Busby: *History*), 1819. Discredited in Jerome and Elizabeth Roche: *A Dictionary of Early Music*, 1981, as 'bizarre but largely untrue'.

3. From Guillaume de Machaut: *Le Livre du voir-dit*; summarized in Siegmund Levarie: *Guillaume de Machaut*. NY, 1954.

4. Introductory quotation from Paul Nettl: *Luther and his Music*. Philadelphia, 1948. Anecdote derived from Heinrich Glareanus: *Dodekachordon*; transl. by Clement A. Miller. Rome, 1965. (Reprinted by permission of Dr Armen Carapetyan, director of the American Institute of Musicology.)

5. Glareanus; quoted in Charles Burney: *A General History of Music* (Burney: *History*). 1776–89.

6. Ratzeberger: *Martin Luther*. Jena, 1850; transl. revised from Nettl: *op. cit.*

7. In James R. Sterndale-Bennett, 'Lassus' in Sir George Grove (ed.): *Dictionary of Music and Musicians (Grove I)*. 1879–89.

8. Busby: *History*.

9. Introductory quotation from Cecil Gray and Philip Heseltine: *Carlo Gesualdo*. 1926. Anecdote derived from Giovanni Battista Spaccini (1588–1636): *Cronaca Modenese*; quoted in Glenn E. Watkins: *Gesualdo, the Man and his Music*. Oxford, 1973.

10. Don Ferrante della Marra. 1632; quoted in Gray and Heseltine, *op. cit.*

11. Quoted in Hans F. Redlich's: *Claudio Monteverdi, Life and Works*; transl. Kathleen Dale. Oxford, 1952. (Reprinted by permission of OUP.)

12. From Erich Müller von Asow (ed.): *Heinrich Schütz, Gesammelte Briefe und Schriften*. Regensburg, 1931.

13. George Hogarth: *Memoirs of the Musical Drama* (Hogarth: *Memoirs*). 1838.

14. Lecerf de la Viéville: *Comparaison de la musique italienne et de la musique française*. Brussels, 1705.

15. Sir John Hawkins: *General History of the Science and Practice of Music* (Hawkins: *History*). 1776.

16. From Burney: *History*.

17. From Pierre Bennet-Bourdelot: *Histoire de la musique et de ses effets*. Paris, 1715.

18. Rev. John Mainwaring: *Memoirs of the Life of the Late George Frederic Handel*. 1760.

19. From Francesco Geminiani's account in Burney: *History*.

20. Edmond van der Straeten: *History of the Violoncello, the Viola da Gamba, their Precursors and Collateral Instruments*. 1914.

21. Manuscript notes by Hawkins printed in the introduction to the second edition of his *History*. 1853.

22. Hawkins: *History*. Hawkins doubts the 'tradition'.

23. From François Couperin: 'Aveu de l'auteur au public'. 1726. In M. Couchie (ed.): *Œuvres complètes de François Couperin*. Paris, 1932–3; transl. from W. S. Newman: *The Sonata in the Baroque Era* (4th edn). NY, 1983. (Reprinted by permission of W. W. Norton & Co. Inc.)

24. Hogarth: *Memoirs*.

25. Telemann's autobiography in Johann T. Mattheson's: *Grundlage einer Ehrenpforte*. Hamburg, 1740; quoted in C. Burney: *An Account of the Musical Performances in Westminster Abbey and The Pantheon, 1784, in Commemoration of Handel* (Burney: *Handel Comm*.). 1785.

26. From Richard Petzoldt: *Georg Philipp Telemann – Leben und Werk*. Leipzig, 1967.

27. Hugues Maret: *Eloge historique de M. Rameau*. Dijon, 1766; quoted in Cuthbert Girdlestone: *J.-P. Rameau*. 1957.

28. R. B. Douglas: *Sophie Arnould*. Paris, 1898.

29. Hugues Maret quoted in Girdlestone, *op. cit*.

30. Douglas, *op. cit*.

31. From Girdlestone, *op. cit*.

32. C. H. Bitter: *The Life of Johann Sebastian Bach* (abbr. transl.) 1873.

33. From H. T. David and A. Mendel: *The Bach Reader*. NY, 1945.

34. Johann Nicolaus Forkel: *Life of Johann Sebastian Bach*. 1820.

35. Bitter, *op. cit*.

36. Johann Friedrich Reichardt: *Musikalischer Almanach*. Berlin, 1796.

37. Burney: *History*.

38. Forkel, *op. cit.*

39. Philipp Spitta: *Johann Sebastian Bach*. 1884–5.

40. Reichardt, *op. cit.*

41. Forkel, *op. cit.*

42. *Ibid.*

43. *Ibid.*

44. Bitter, *op. cit.*

45. *Ibid.*

46. *Ibid.*

47. In Arthur Duke Coleridge (ed.): *Goethe-Zelter Correspondence*. 1892.

48. Eduard Devrient: *My Recollections of Felix Mendelssohn-Bartholdy and his Letters to Me*. 1869.

49. Pablo Casals, his own story as told to Albert E. Kahn: *Joys and Sorrows*. NY, 1970. (Reprinted by permission of Simon & Schuster, Inc.)

50. Hogarth: *Memoirs*.

51. Rev. John Mainwaring: *Memoirs of the Life of the Late George Frederic Handel*. 1760.

52. Mainwaring, *op. cit.*

53. Burney: *Handel Comm.*

54. Thomas Busby: *Concert Room and Orchestra Anecdotes of Music and Musicians* (Busby: *Anecdotes*). 1825.

55. Mainwaring, *op. cit.*

56. William S. Rockstro: *The Life of George Frederick Handel*. 1883.

57. Busby: *Anecdotes*.

58. Burney: *Handel Comm.*

59. Busby: *Anecdotes*.

60. Rockstro, *op. cit.*

61. In William C. Smith: *A Handelian's Notebook*. 1965.

62. *Biographica Dramatica*: 'On the authority of the Earl of Kinnoul'; quoted in G. Hogarth: *Musical History, Biography and Criticism* (2nd edn; Hogarth: *History*). 1838.

63. Rockstro, *op. cit.*

64. Burney: *Handel Comm.*

65. *Ibid.*

66. A. W. Schmidt: *C. W. Ritter von Gluck*. Leipzig, 1854.

67. Burney: *Handel Comm.*

68. Hawkins: *History*.

69. Busby: *Anecdotes*.

70. William Coxe: *Anecdotes of G. F. Handel and J. C. Smith*. 1799.

71. Henry E. Krehbiel: *Music and Manners in the Classical Period*. NY, 1898.

72. 'A Day with Beethoven', *The Harmonicon*. 1824.

73. Hogarth: *History*.

74. Michael Kelly: *Reminiscences*. 1826.

75. From Quantz's autobiography. Berlin, 1755; Eng. transl. in Paul Nettl: *Forgotten Musicians*. NY, 1951.

76. *The Lives of Haydn and Mozart with Observations on Metastasio and on the Present State of Music in France and Italy* (Stendhal: *Lives*); transl. from the French of L. A. C. Bombet (2nd edn). 1818.

77. Burney: *History*.

78. *Ibid.*

79. Roger Lonsdale: *Dr Charles Burney*. 1974. (By permission of OUP.)

80. George Dubourg: *The Violin*. 1852.

81. Busby: *Anecdotes*.

82. From Angus Heriot: *The Castrati in Opera*. 1956.

83. *Frederick the Great: Memoirs of his Reader, Henri de Catt*. 1916.

84. From Louis Engel: *From Mozart to Mario* (Engel: *Mozart*). 1886.

85. Jacques Henri Bernardin de Saint Pierre: *Œuvres*; ed. A. Martin; Paris, 1818–1820; quoted in Lord Morley: *Rousseau*. 1873.

86. Hogarth: *Memoirs*.

87. *The Confessions of J.-J. Rousseau*. 1856.

88. Louis Engel: *From Handel to Hallé* (Engel: *Handel*). 1890.

89. Hogarth: *History*.

90. Michael Kelly: *Reminiscences*. 1826.

91. R. B. Douglas: *Sophie Arnould*. Paris, 1898.

92. Engel: *Handel*.

93. Busby: *Anecdotes*.

94. André Philidor, quoted in G. Allen: *The Life of Philidor*. Philadelphia, 1863.

95. From André Grétry: *Mémoires*. Paris, 1789; quoted in G. Allen, *op. cit.*

96. Albert Christoph Dies: *Biographische Nachrichten von Joseph Haydn*. Vienna, 1810. There is a similar account in G. A. Von Griesinger: *Biographische Notizen über Joseph Haydn*. Leipzig, 1810. Both originate from Haydn himself.

97. Griesinger, *op. cit.*

98. *Ibid*.

99. Stendhal: *Lives*.

100. From Griesinger, *op. cit.*

101. *Ibid*.

102. Dies, *op. cit.*

103. William Gardiner: *Music and Friends*. 1838–1853.

104. Quoted in Henry E. Krehbiel: *Music and Manners in the Classical Period*. NY, 1898.

105. William Reeve: *Residence at Vienna and Berlin*. 1879.

106. William T. Parke: *Musical Memoirs* (Parke: *Memoirs*). 1830.

107. From Frederick S. Silverstolpe: *Reminiscences*. Stockholm, 1841.

108. Busby: *History*.

109. Griesinger, *op. cit.*

110. John Ella: *Musical Sketches*. 1878.

111. Johann Friedrich Reichardt: *Musikalischer Almanach*. Berlin, 1796.

112. From Otto Jahn: *Life of Mozart* (2nd edn). 1882.

113. From Parke: *Memoirs*.

114. From Henry Angelo: *Reminiscences of Harry Angelo*. 1828.

115. Gardiner, *op. cit.*

116. Quoted in Krehbiel, *op. cit.*

117. From Cecil Roberts: *And So to Bath*. 1940.

118. H. Sutherland Edwards: *History of the Opera*. 1862.

119. Michael Kelly: *Reminiscences*. 1826.

120. Ella, *op. cit.*

121. Reverend Hugh Reginald Haweis: *My Musical Life*. 1884.

122. Hogarth: *History*.

123. Busby: *Anecdotes*.

124. Edmond Michotte: *La visite de R. Wagner à Rossini*. Paris, 1906.

125. Charlotte Moscheles: *Life of Moscheles, with a Selection from his Correspondence*. 1873.

126. Parke: *Memoirs*.

127. G. Dubourg: *The Violin*. 1852.

128. Told by Ferdinand Langlé to Adolphe Adam; recounted in G. T. Ferris: *The Great Violinists and Pianists*. NY, 1881.

129. Introductory quotation from a letter written by Leopold Mozart to his daughter, Maria Anna, 16 February 1785. Anecdote quoted in Friedrich Schlichtegroll: 'Johannes Chrysostomus Wolfgang Gottlieb Mozart', *Nekrolog auf das Jahr 1791*. Gotha, 1793.

130. Johann Peter Eckermann: *Conversations with Goethe*. 1850.

131. Edward Holmes: *Life of Mozart*. 1845.

132. *Allegemeine Musikalische Zeitung*. Leipzig, 22 January 1800.

133. Schlichtegroll, *op. cit.*

134. In Georg Nikolaus Nissen: *Biographie W. A. Mozarts nach Originalbriefen*. Leipzig, 1828.

135. Otto Jahn: *Life of Mozart* (2nd edn). 1882.

136. *Ibid.*

137. *Ibid.*

138. *Ibid.*

139. Parke: *Memoirs*.

140. Adalbert Gyrowetz: *Selbstbiographie*. Vienna, 1850.

141. Jahn, *op. cit.*

142. Quoted by Otto Erich Deutsch in *Mozart: Documents from his Life* (2nd edn). 1966. (Reproduced by permission of Cassell & Co.)

143. Told by Theodor von Karajan (1810–73); philologist and music historian, whose informant was Loibl's daughter, 'Frau Klein of Vienna'; quoted in Jahn, *op. cit.*

144. Jahn, *op. cit.*

145. Recounted by Wenzel Swoboda in Wilhelm Kuhe: *Memoirs of a Musician*. 1913.

146. Georg Nikolaus Nissen; quoted in H. Sutherland Edwards: *Famous First Representations*. 1886.

147. Kuhe, *op. cit.*

148. From *The Memoirs of Lorenzo da Ponte*; ed. Arthur Livingstone; transl. Elisabeth Abbott. NY, 1929.

149. Jahn, *op. cit.*

150. Holmes, *op. cit.*

151. From Jahn, *op. cit.*; Alexander Wheelock Thayer: *Life of Ludwig van Beethoven* (Thayer: *Life*); transl. Henry E. Krehbiel. Berlin, 1866–79 (rev. Leipzig, 1910–17); NY, 1921.

152. Jahn, *op. cit.*

153. J. F. Rochlitz's account of a letter written by Constanze Mozart, cited in Jahn, *op. cit.*

154. Holmes, *op. cit.*

155. Stendhal: *Lives*.

156. Sophie Haibl, letter to Georg Nikolaus Nissen; transl. in Holmes, *op. cit.*

157. Franz Xaver Niemetschek: *Leben des k.k. Kapellmeisters Wolfgang Gottlieb Mozart nach Originalquellen beschrieben*. Prague, 1798; quoted in Jahn, *op. cit.*

158. Jahn, *op. cit.*

159. Letter to Johann Michael Puchberg; quoted in H. C. Robbins Landon: *Haydn: A Documentary Study*. 1981.

160. In Sir Charles Villiers Stanford: *Pages from an Unwritten Diary* (Stanford: *Diary*). 1914.

161. Told by Cramer's widow; quoted in Thayer: *Life*.

162. Edward Bellasis: Cherubini: *Memorials Illustrative of his Life*. 1874.

163. *Ibid.*

164. H. Berlioz: *Memoirs*; transl. Rachel and Eleanor Holmes. 1884.

165. Gottfried Fischer (1780–1857), boyhood memories of Beethoven; in Oscar Sonneck (ed.): *Beethoven, Impressions by his Contemporaries*. NY, 1926.

166. Gottfried Fischer, in Sonneck, *op. cit.*

167. MS in the archives of the Gesellschaft des Musikfreunde, Vienna; quoted in Ludwig Nohl: *Beethoven Depicted by his Contemporaries*. 1880.

168. Thayer: *Life*.

169. Wenzel Tomaschek's recollections. Prague, 1845; quoted in Nohl, *op. cit.*

170. In Thayer: *Life*.

171. *Ibid*.

172. Karl Czerny in Maynard Solomon: *Beethoven*. NY, 1978. (Reprinted by permission of Schirmer Books.)

173. Ferdinand Ries and Franz Gerhard Wegeler: *Biographische Notizen über Ludwig van Beethoven*. Koblenz, 1838; in Sonneck, *op. cit.*, Thayer: *Life*.

174. Thayer: *Life*.

175. Alexander Wheelock Thayer, notes for his Life of Beethoven; quoted in Henry E. Krehbiel: *Music and Manners in the Classical Period* (Thayer: *Notes*). NY, 1898.

176. *Leaves from the Journals of Sir George Smart*; eds H. B. and C. L. E. Coxe. (Coxe: *Smart*). 1907.

177. Louis Spohr: *Autobiography*. 1865.

178. In Nohl, *op. cit.*

179. Charlotte Moscheles: *Life of Moscheles*. 1873.

180. A. D. Coleridge (ed.): Goethe-Zelter correspondence. 1892.

181. From Anton Schindler (ed. Ignaz Moscheles): *The Life of Beethoven* (Schindler/Moscheles). 1841.

182. Thayer: *Life*.

183. *Ibid*.

184. Anton Schindler in Thayer: *Life*.

185. In Schindler/Moscheles.

186. In A. B. Marx: *Ludwig van Beethoven*. Berlin, 1911; transl. in Sonneck (ed.), *op. cit.*

187. In Schindler/Moscheles.

188. Told by Nanette Streicher, 'the lady friend', to Dr Müller; in Nohl, *op. cit.*

189. Schindler/Moscheles.

190. *Ibid*.

191. In Nohl, *op. cit.*

192. Schindler/Moscheles.

193. Thayer: *Notes*.

194. Thayer: *Life*.

195. Baron Max Maria von Weber: *Life of Weber*. 1865.

196. Thayer: *Life*.

197. *Ibid*.

198. Schindler/Moscheles.

199. Friedrich Starke in Nohl, *op. cit*.

200. *Ibid*.

201. Gerhard von Brenning in Sonneck, *op. cit*.

202. From Maynard Solomon: *Beethoven*. NY, 1978. (Reprinted by permission of Schirmer Books.)

203. Schindler/Moscheles.

204. Thayer: *Notes*.

205. Schindler/Moscheles.

206. Austrian Federal Press Service, 'Franz Schubert'. Vienna, 1977; Marion M. Scott: *Beethoven*. 1934.

207. Ernest Legouvé: *60 Years of Recollections*. 1893.

208. Heinz Unger: *Hammer, Sickle and Baton*. 1939. (Reproduced by permission of The Cresset Press.)

209. François Castil-Blaze: *L'Opéra italien 1548–1856*. Paris, 1856; quoted in G. T. Ferris: *The Great Italian and French Composers*. NY, 1882.

210. Richard Wagner: *My Life*. Munich, 1911.

211. Lillie de Hegermann-Lindencrone: *In the Courts of Memory*, NY, 1911.

212. Engel: *Mozart*.

213. From Ignaz Moscheles' diary in C. Moscheles: *Life of Moscheles*. 1873.

214. Alexander Dubuk: *Memories of John Field*. Moscow, 1898. (Cited in doctoral thesis by Heinrich Dessauer. Leipzig, 1912; and by Maria Kelly in a paper read before the Old Dublin Society, 7 February 1944, and in Patrick Piggott: *The Life and Music of John Field*. 1973.)

215. L. H. Houtchens and C. W. Houtchens (eds): *Leigh Hunt's Dramatic Criticism: 1808–31*. NY, 1949. (Reprinted by permission of Columbia University Press.)

216. Engel: *Mozart*.

217. Coxe: *Smart*.

218. In François-Joseph Fétis: *Biographical Notice of N. Paganini*. 1852.

219. Louis Vidal (1820–91), music historian, in Jeffrey Pulver: *Paganini, the Romantic Virtuoso* (2nd edn). 1969.

220. C. E. and M. Hallé (eds): *Life and Letters of Sir Charles Hallé*. 1896.

221. H. Berlioz: *Memoirs*; transl. Rachel and Eleanor Holmes. 1884.

222. Fétis, *op. cit.*, quoting an Italian writer.

223. From Paul David, 'Spohr' in *Grove I*.

224. Louis Spohr: *Autobiography*. 1865.

225. Baron Max Maria von Weber: *Life of Weber*. 1865.

226. Coxe: *Smart*.

227. Sir Julius Benedict: *Weber*. 1881.

228. Charlotte Moscheles: *Life of Moscheles*. 1873.

229. Engel: *Mozart, op. cit.*

230. Berlioz, *op. cit.*

231. Stanford: *Diary*.

232. Felix Moscheles: *Fragments of an Autobiography*. 1899.

233. Engel: *Mozart*.

234. From Herbert Weinstock: *Rossini: a Biography*. NY, 1968.

235. John Ella: *Musical Sketches*. 1878.

236. Henri Beyle [Stendhal]: *Memoirs of Rossini*. 1824.

237. From Edmond Michotte: *La visite de R. Wagner à Rossini*. Paris, 1906.

238. Engel: *Mozart*.

239. Lillie de Hegermann-Lindencrone: *In the Courts of Memory*. NY, 1911.

240. Leopold Auer: *My Long Life In Music*. 1924.

241. Henry F. Chorley: *Music and Manners in France and Germany*. 1841.

242. Engel: *Mozart*.

243. Max Maretzek: *Crochets and Quavers*. NY, 1855.

244. de Hegermann-Lindencrone, *op. cit.*

245. Emil Naumann: *Italienischer Tondichter von Palestrina bis auf die Gegenwart*. Munich, 1876.

246. Engel: *Mozart*.

247. William Gardiner: *Music and Friends*. 1838.

248. In Arthur Lawrence: *Sir Arthur Sullivan*. 1899.

249. Engel: *Mozart*.

250. Introductory quotation from *Grove* I, 'Schubert'. Anecdote in Heinrich Kreissle von Hellborn: *Life of Schubert*. 1869.

251. From *ibid*.

252. Eduard von Bauernfeld: *Einiges von F. Schubert*. Vienna, 1869; quoted in Austrian Federal Press Service (AFPS): *Franz Schubert*. Vienna, 1977.

253. Kreissle von Hellborn, *op. cit*.

254. H. von Chezy: *Unvergessenes: Denkwürdigkeiten aus dem Leben*. Leipzig, 1858; quoted in Kreissle von Hellborn, *op. cit*.

255. Bauernfeld, *op. cit*.

256. Attributed to Lachner, this story appeared in American, Austrian and German publications between 1905 and 1913, with variations in detail. It is unauthenticated. From Otto Erich Deutsch (ed.): *Schubert, Memoirs by his Friends*; transl. R. Ley and J. Nowell. 1958. (Reproduced by permission of A. and C. Black.); and AFPS.

257. Kreissle von Hellborn, *op. cit*.

258. From Ferdinand Hiller: *Künstlerleben*. Cologne, 1880.

259. Randhartinger, told to A. B. Bach in: *The Art Ballad, Loewe and Schubert*. Edinburgh, 1890.

260. AFPS: *Schubert*. Vienna, 1977.

261. Notes by Josef von Spaun, condensed from Deutsch, *op. cit*.

262. In *Grove I*, 'Schubert'.

263. Engel: *Mozart*.

264. C. E. and M. Hallé (eds.): *Life and Letters of Sir Charles Hallé*. 1896.

265. From Federico Alborghetti and Michelangelo Galli: *Gaetano Donizetti &c*. Bergamo, 1875.

266. Hallé, *op. cit*.

267. Mme. Emile de Girardin: *Lettres parisiennes*. Paris, nd; quoted in C. L. Kenny: *A Memoir of M. W. Balfe*. 1875.

268. Max Maretzek: *Sharps and Flats*. NY, 1870.

269. Heinrich Heine: *Florentine Nights*. 1891.

270. Heine, *op. cit*.

271. From Ernst von Decsey: *Johann Strauss*. Stuttgart, 1922.

272. Ernest Legouvé: *60 Years of Recollections*. 1893.

273. Berlioz, *op. cit*.

274. *Ibid*.

275. Mathilde Marchesi: *Marchesi and Music*. 1897.

276. Legouvé, *op. cit.*

277. Heinrich Heine: *Collected Works*. 1893.

278. Legouvé, *op. cit.*

279. Berlioz, *op. cit.*

280. Stanford: *Diary*.

281. Berlioz, *op. cit.*

282. In Robert Baldick (ed. and transl.): *Pages from the Goncourt Journal*. Oxford, 1962. (Reproduced by permission of OUP.)

283. Mikhail I. Glinka: *Memoirs*. Moscow, 1870; transl. Richard B. Mudge. Norman, Oklahoma, 1963. (Reprinted by permission of the University of Oklahoma Press.)

284. From Glinka, *op. cit.*

285. Karoline Bauer quoting 'the Hungarian Kertberg' in Karoline Bauer: *Memoirs*. 1885.

286. Bauer, *op. cit.*

287. Richard Hoffman: *Some Musical Recollections of 50 Years*. NY, 1910.

288. C. L. Kenney: *A Memoir of M. W. Balfe*. 1875.

289. Rev. J. E. Cox: *Musical Recollections of the last Half-Century*. 1872.

290. William Glover: *Memoirs of a Cambridge Chorister*. 1885.

291. Coxe: *Smart*.

292. Ludwig Rellstab: *Aus Meinem Leben*. Berlin, 1861.

293. In an undated article in *The Musical World*; cited in F. Crowest: *Musical Anecdotes*. 1878.

294. Hallé, *op. cit.*

295. Elise Polko: *Reminiscences of Felix Mendelssohn-Bartholdy*. 1869.

296. Quoted in Francis Hueffer: *Half a Century of Music in England 1837–87*. 1889.

297. Felix Moscheles: *Fragments of an Autobiography*. 1899.

298. Quoted in Bertha Geissmar: *The Baton and the Jackboot*. 1944. (Reprinted by permission of Hamish Hamilton.)

299. Sara C. Bull: *Ole Bull – a Memoir*. 1886.

300. Lillie de Hegermann-Lindencrone: *The Sunny Side of Diplomatic Life*. NY, 1913.

301. Bull, *op. cit.*

302. Count Stanislaw Tarnowski: *Chopin, as Revealed by Extracts from his Diary.* 1899.

303. William Mason: *Memories of a Musical Life.* NY, 1901; quoting Dreyschock.

304. Quoted in Moritz Karasowski: *Life and Letters of Chopin.* 1879.

305. Nowakowski, in Karasowski, *op. cit.*; similar account by Charles Rollinat, friend of Georges Sand, in *Le Temps*, 1 September 1874.

306. Niecks reports that Liszt had 'not the slightest recollection of ever having imitated Chopin's playing in a darkened room'. F. Niecks: *Frederick Chopin as Man and Musician.* 1888–90, quoting Rollinat, *op. cit.*

307. Ernest Legouvé: *60 Years of Recollections.* 1893.

308. Niecks, *op. cit.*

309. Ferdinand Hiller: *Mendelssohn, Letters and Recollections.* 1874.

310. Legouvé, *op. cit.*

311. Quoted in Niecks, *op. cit.*

312. Wilhelm von Lenz: *Die Grossen Pianoforte-Virtuosen.* Berlin, 1872.

313. Niecks, *op. cit.*

314. Tarnowski, *op. cit.*

315. Quoted in James Huneker: *Chopin, the Man and his Music.* NY, 1900.

316. Hallé, *op. cit.*

317. Josef Wilhelm von Wasiliewski: *Life of Robert Schumann.* Boston, 1871.

318. Wasiliewski, *op. cit.*

319. Mason, *op. cit.*

320. Edward Speyer: *My Life and Friends.* 1937.

321. Albert Dietrich: *Recollections of Johannes Brahms.* 1899.

322. Frederick Niecks: 'Schumanniana', in *Monthly Musical Record.* 1884.

323. Wasiliewski, *op. cit.*

324. Joseph Joachim, letter to Waldemar Bargiel, Clara's half brother, 6 March 1884; in *Letters from and to Joseph Joachim.* 1914.

325. From Ronald Taylor: *Robert Schumann: His Life and Work.* 1982. (Reprinted by permission.)

326. From Rev. Hugh Reginald Haweis: *My Musical Life.* 1884. Footnote: *see* Alan Walker: *Franz Liszt, Vol. I.* 1983.

327. Mason, *op. cit.*

328. Hallé, *op. cit.*

329. Speyer, *op. cit.*

330. *Memoirs of the Life and Correspondence of Henry Reeve*; ed. S. Laughton. 1898.

331. Charles Salaman, 'Pianists of the Past', *Blackwood's Magazine*, September, 1901.

332. Janka Wohl: *François Liszt: Recollections of a Compatriot.* 1887.

333. *Ibid.*

334. William Beatty Kingston: *Music and Manners.* 1887.

335. Wohl, *op. cit.*

336. From Walker, *op. cit.*

337. Stanford: *Diary.*

338. Lillie de Hegermann-Lindencrone: *The Sunny Side of Diplomatic Life.* NY, 1913.

339. Henry Theophilus Finck: *Grieg and his Music.* 1909.

340. Lillie de Hegermann-Lindencrone: *In the Courts of Memory.* NY, 1911.

341. *The Memoirs of Count Apponyi.* 1935.

342. Lilli Lehmann: *My Path through Life.* NY, 1914.

343. Judith Gauthier. *Wagner at Home.* 1910.

344. Wohl, *op. cit.*

345. Felix Weingartner: *Buffets and Rewards.* 1937 (Reprinted by permission of Hutchinson Ltd.)

346. Wohl, *op. cit.*

347. *Ibid.*

348. Jules Rivière: *My Musical Life and Recollections.* 1893.

349. Thomas Ryan: *Recollections of an Old Musician.* NY, 1899.

350. Willert Beale: *The Light of Other Days.* 1890.

351. William Maynard (pseudonym of Willert Beale): *The Enterprising Impresario.* 1867.

352. Beale, *op. cit.*

353. Arthur Pougin: *Verdi, an Anecdotic History of his Life and Works.* 1887.

354. Verdi, autobiographical narrative related to Giulio Ricordi on 19 October 1879, reproduced in Pougin, *op. cit.*

355. C. V. Stanford, article in *The Daily Graphic*, 14 January 1893; quoted in Frederick J. Crowest: *Verdi, Man and Musician, his Biography, with Especial Reference to his English Experiences*. 1897.

356. Pougin, *op. cit.*

357. Unidentified Italian account, in Pougin.

358. Pougin, *op. cit.*

359. Stanford: *Diary*.

360. Sir George Henschel: *Musings and Memories of a Musician*. 1918.

361. Engel: *Mozart*.

362. F. Crowest: *Verdi, man and musician*. 1897.

363. H. Sutherland Edwards: *Personal Recollections*. 1800.

364. Pougin, *op. cit.*

365. Mathilde Marchesi: *Marchesi and Music*. 1897.

366. Wilhelm Ganz: *Memories of a Musician*. 1913.

367. Pougin, *op. cit.*

368. From Giulio Gatti-Casazza: *Memories of the Opera* (2nd edn). NY, 1969; and Mosco Carner: *Puccini* (2nd edn). 1975.

369. From Gatti-Casazza, *op. cit.*

370. From Howard Taubman: *Toscanini*. NY, 1951.

371. 'Verdi at the Time of Otello', in *The Musical Times*, XXVIII. 1887.

372. William Mason: *Memories of a Musical Life*. NY, 1901

373. Richard Wagner: *Mein Leben*. Munich, 1911.

374. Eduard Dannreuther, 'Wagner' in *Grove I*.

375. Leopold Auer: *My Long Life in Music*. 1924.

376. Louise Héritte-Viardot: *Memories and Adventures*. 1913.

377. J. W. Davison in *The Musical World*. nd.

378. From Wagner, *op. cit.*

379. From Richard Count du Moulin Eckart (ed.): *Letters of Hans von Bülow*; transl. Hannah Walter. NY, 1931. (Reprinted by permission of Alfred A. Knopf Inc.)

380. Judith Gauthier: *Wagner at Home*. 1910.

381. Sir George Henschel: *Musings and Memories*. 1918.

382. Dame Ethel Smyth: *Impressions that Remained*. 1923. (Reprinted by permission of Longmans Green.)

383. Gauthier, *op. cit.*

384. William M. Quirke: *Recollections of a Violinist*. 1914.

385. From Ludwig Karpath: *Lachende Musiker*. Munich, 1929.

386. Stanford: *Diary*.

387. *The Memoirs of Count Apponyi*. 1935.

388. H. T. Finck: *Massenet and his Operas*. 1910.

389. Lilli Lehmann: *My Path Through Life*. NY, 1914.

390. Wohl, *op. cit.*

391. Francis Neilson: *My Life in Two Worlds*. Appleton, Wisconsin, 1952. (Reproduced by permission of C. C. Nelson Publishing Co.)

392. Sir Felix Semon: *Autobiography*. 1928.

393. Louis Charles Elson: *European Reminiscences*. Philadelphia, 1892.

394. Charles Kenney, 1879.

395. Engel: *Mozart*.

396. James Henry Mapleson: *The Mapleson Memoirs*. 1888.

397. Stanford: *Diary*.

398. In Edward Grierson: *Storm Bird, the Strange Life of Georgina Weldon*. 1959. (Reprinted by permission of Chatto & Windus.)

399. Stanford: *Diary*.

400. From Alexander Faris: *Jacques Offenbach*. 1980.

401. From K. F. Glasenapp: *Das Leben Richard Wagners*. Munich, 1894–1911.

402. Frederick Niecks, 'Schumanniana' in *Monthly Musical Record*. 1884.

403. Clara Louise Kellogg: *Memories of an American Prima Donna*. NY, 1913.

404. Arthur Duke Coleridge: *Musical Recollections*. 1921.

405. H. Sutherland Edwards: *History of Opera*. 1862.

406. Elise Polko: *Reminiscences of Mendelssohn*. 1869.

407. William Maynard (Willert Beale): *The Enterprising Impresario*. 1867.

408. Walter Macfarren: *Memories*. 1905.

409. Leopold Auer: *My Long Life in Music*. 1924.

410. From Leon Vallas: *César Franck*. 1951.

411. From Vallas, *op. cit.*

412. From George D. Painter: *Marcel Proust*. 1959–65.

413. Gustav Mahler, in Natalie Bauer-Lechner: *Erinnerungen an Gustav Mahler*. Leipzig, 1923.

414. Louis P. Lochner: *Fritz Kreisler*. 1951. (Reprinted by permission of Rockliff & Co.)

415. From Werner Wolff: *Anton Bruckner, Rustic Genius*. NY, 1942; and Walter Damrosch: *My Musical Life*. NY, 1916. (Reprinted by permission of Scribner & Sons.)

416. From Damrosch, *op. cit.*

417. Rafael Joseffy (1852–1915), in H. T. Finck: *Musical Laughs*. 1924. Corroborated by Artur Nikisch in Sir Adrian Boult: *My Own Trumpet*. 1973.

418. From Max Graf: *Legends of a Musical City*. NY, 1945. (Reprinted by permission of the Royal Philosophical Society.)

419. From Bauer-Lechner, *op. cit.*

420. Richard Wagner: *Mein Leben*. Munich, 1911.

421. Eduard Hanslick, *Neue Freie Presse*.

422. Auer, *op. cit.*

423. William Beatty-Kingston: *Music and Manners*. 1887. This anecdote is uncorroborated.

424. Ferdinand Scherchen, introduction to Karl Goldmark: *Notes from the Life of a Viennese Composer*. NY, 1927.

425. Morrison Foster: *Biography, Songs and Musical Compositions of Stephen C. Foster*. Pittsburgh, 1896.

426. Louis Moreau Gottschalk: *Notes of a Pianist*. Philadelphia, 1881.

427. George Titus Ferris: *Great Pianists and Violinists*. NY, 1881.

428. Gottschalk, *op. cit.*

429. Damrosch, *op. cit.*

430. From *Ferruccio Busoni: Letters to his Wife*; transl. R. Ley. 1938. (Reprinted by permission of E. J. Arnold.)

431. Sir George Henschel: *Musings and Memories of a Musician*. 1918.

432. Louise Héritte-Viardot: *Memories and Adventures*. 1913.

433. Lilli Lehmann: *My Path through Life*. 1913.

434. Stanford: *Diary*.

435. From Josef Bohuslav Förster: *Der Pilger*. Prague, 1955.

436. John Francis Barnett: *Musical Reminiscences and Impressions*. 1906.

437. H. Sutherland Edwards: *Personal Recollections*. 1900.

438. From Nicolas Slonimsky: *A Thing or Two about Music*. NY, 1948.

439. Wilhelm Ganz: *Memories of a Musician*. 1913.

440. Stanford: *Diary*.

441. Ethel C. Newcomb: *Leschetizky as I Knew Him*. NY, 1921.

442. Artur Schnabel: *My Life and Music*. 1971.

443. Ignaz J. Paderewski and Mary Lawton: *The Paderewski Memoirs*. 1939. (Reprinted by permission of William Collins Ltd.)

444. Mark Hambourg: *From Piano to Forte*. 1931.

445. W. Beatty-Kingston: *Music and Manners*, 1887.

446. Edward Speyer: *My Life and Friends*. 1937.

447. Serge Dianin: *Borodin*; transl. Robert Lord. Oxford, 1963. (Reprinted by permission of OUP.)

448. In Dianin, *op. cit.*

449. From Dianin, *op. cit.*

450. In Alfred Habets: *Borodin and Liszt*; transl. Rosa Newmarch. 1896. (Reprinted by permission of Digby, Long & Co.)

451. In Habets, *op. cit.*

452. From Dianin, *op. cit.*

453. Arthur Pougin: *A Short History of Russian Music*. 1915.

454. William Mason: *Memories of a Musical Life*. NY, 1901.

455. Max Graf: *Legends of a Musical City*. NY, 1945. (Reprinted by permission of The Philosophical Library.)

456. Joseph Viktor Widmann: *Recollections of Johannes Brahms*. 1899.

457. Sir George Henschel: *Musings and Memories*. 1918.

458. Karl Goldmark: *Notes from the Life of a Viennese Composer*. 1927.

459. Charles Villiers Stanford: *Studies and Memories*. 1908.

460. Florence May: *The Life of Johannes Brahms*. 1905.

461. May, *op. cit.*

462. Graf, *op. cit.*

463. Henschel, *op. cit.*

464. Goldmark, *op. cit.* According to Max Graf this tale is untrue; it was made up by a well-known Viennese wit, and friend of Brahms', Bela Haas.

465. Sir Felix Semon: *Autobiography*. 1926.

466. Stanford: *Diary, op. cit.*

467. *Ibid.*

468. May, *op. cit.*

469. Frederic Lamond: *Memoirs.* Edinburgh. 1949. (Reprinted by permission.)

470. Lamond, *op. cit.*

471. From Hans-Hubert Schönzeler: *Bruckner.* 1970.

472. Camille Saint-Saëns: *Musical Memories.* Boston, 1919.

473. From Modeste Tchaikovsky: *Life and Letters of P. I. Tchaikovsky*; ed. and transl. Rosa Newmarch. 1906. (Reprinted by permission of The Bodley Head.)

474. Lilli Lehmann, *op. cit.*

475. George P. Upton: *Reminiscence and Appreciation*; in Theodore Thomas: *A Musical Autobiography.* Chicago, 1905.

476. From Percy Scholes: *Oxford Companion to Music.* 1938.

477. Helena Modjeska: *Memories and Impressions.* NY, 1910.

478. From Louis P. Lochner: *Fritz Kreisler.* NY, 1951.

479. H. Sutherland Edwards: *Personal Recollections.* 1900.

480. From Henry A. Lytton: *The Secrets of a Savoyard.* 1921.

481. Quoted in Serge Dianin: *Borodin*; transl. Robert Lord. Oxford, 1963. (Reprinted by permission of OUP.)

482. From Dianin, *op. cit.*

483. Balakirev's letters; quoted in Nikolay A. Rimsky-Korsakov: *My Musical Life*; transl. from 5th revised Russian edition by Judith A. Joffe. NY, 1942. (Reprinted by permission of Alfred A. Knopf, Inc.)

484. Rimsky-Korsakov, *op. cit.*

485. *Ibid.*

486. *Lettres de Georges Bizet.* Paris, 1907.

487. Saint-Saëns, *op. cit.*

488. From Edmond Galabert: *Georges Bizet, souvenirs et correspondance.* Paris, 1877.

489. From D. C. Parker: *Georges Bizet, his Life and Works.* 1926.

490. From George D. Painter: *Marcel Proust.* 1959–65.

491. Sir George Henschel: *Musings and Memories.* 1918.

492. Arseni Golenischev-Katuzov: *Reminiscences of M. P. Mussorgsky*. Moscow, 1935; in Jay Leyda and Sergei Bertensson: *The Mussorgsky Reader*. NY, 1947. (Reprinted by permission of Alfred A. Knopf Inc.)

493. 'A Personal Note' in Leyda and Bertensson, *op. cit*.

494. In Alfred Habets: *Borodin and Liszt*; transl. Rosa Newmarch. 1896. (Reprinted by permission of Digby, Long & Co.)

495. In Leyda/Bertensson, *op. cit*.

496. *Ibid*.

497. Nikolay Kashkin: *Reminiscences of P. I. Tchaikovsky*. Moscow, 1897; quoted in Rosa Newmarch: *Tchaikovsky, his Life and Works: with extracts from his writings and the diary of his tour abroad in 1888*. 1908. (Reprinted by permission of the estate of Rosa Newmarch.)

498. In Modeste Tchaikovsky: *The Life and Letters of P. I. Tchaikovsky*; transl. Rosa Newmarch. 1906. (Reprinted by permission of the estate of Rosa Newmarch.)

499. Anna Brodsky: *Recollections of a Russian Home*. Manchester, 1904.

500. *Ibid*.

501. *Ibid*.

502. Kashkin/Newmarch, *op. cit*.

503. *Tchaikovsky: Letters to his Relatives*. Moscow, 1940; in D. Brown: *Tchaikovsky, the Crisis Years*. 1982. (Reprinted by permission of the author and Victor Gollancz Ltd.)

504. Kashkin/Newmarch, *op. cit*.

505. Nikolay Rimsky-Korsakov: *My Musical Life* (5th edn). NY, 1942 (Reprinted by permission of Alfred A. Knopf, Inc.)

506. From Alexander Voitov, graduate of the School of Jurisprudence, quoting Elizaveta Karlovna Jacobi, widow of Tchaikovsky's 'judge'; in Alexandra Orlova, 'Tchaikovsky: the last chapter', *Music & Letters*, April 1981.

507. Marie Scheikevitch: *Souvenirs d'un temps disparu*. Paris, nd; quoted in Gerald Norris: *Stanford, the Cambridge Jubilee and Tchaikovsky*. Newton Abbot, Devon. 1980. (Reprinted by permission of David and Charles Ltd.)

508. Frederic A. Lamond: *Memoirs*. Edinburgh, 1949. (Reprinted by permission.)

509. Vernon Duke: *Passport to Paris*. Boston, 1955. (Reprinted by permission of Little, Brown. Inc.)

510. James Huneker: *Steeplejack*. NY, 1921.

511. J. J. Kovařik's reminiscences in Otakar Sourek: *Antonín Dvořák, Letters and Reminiscences*. Prague, 1954. (Reprinted by permission of Artia.)

512. Josef Suk, 'Aus meiner Jugend', in Sourek, *op. cit.*

513. Louis P. Lochner: *Fritz Kreisler*. 1951. (Reprinted by permission of Rockliff & Co.)

514. Chaliapin: *An Autobiography as Told to Maxim Gorky* (translated, compiled and edited by Nina Froud and James Hanley). 1967. (Reprinted by permission of Macdonald & Co.)

515. Henry Theophilus Finck: *Massenet and his Operas*. NY, 1910.

516. Isidore de Lara: *Many Tales of Many Cities*. 1928.

517. Finck, *op. cit.*

518. de Lara, *op. cit.*

519. Arthur Lawrence: *Sir Arthur Sullivan; Life Story, Letters and Reminiscences*. 1899.

520. Henry A. Lytton: *The Secrets of a Savoyard*. 1921.

521. From Dame Ethel Smyth: *Impressions that Remained*. 1923. (Reprinted by permission of Longmans Green.)

522. Anna Brodsky: *Recollections of a Russian Home*. Manchester, 1904.

523. Christian Schott, in Henry Theophilus Finck: *Musical Laughs*. 1924.

524. Robert Grau: *40 Years Observation of Music and Drama*. NY, 1909.

525. James Henry Mapleson: *The Mapleson Memoirs*. 1888.

526. David Bispham: *A Quaker Singer's Recollections*. NY, 1920.

527. Sir Felix Semon: *Autobiography*. 1926.

528. From Sir Landon Ronald: *Variations on a Personal Theme*. 1922. (Reprinted by permission of Hodder & Stoughton Ltd.)

529. Bispham, *op. cit.*; also in F. Cowen: *My Art and Friends*. 1913.

530. Edward Speyer: *My Life and Friends*. 1937.

531. From Nikolay A. Rimsky-Korsakov: *My Musical Life* (5th edn). Moscow, 1935.

532. From Michel Dimitri Calvocoressi: *Musicians Gallery*. 1933.

533. From Alexandre Gretchaninov: *My Life*; transl. Nicolas Slonimsky. NY, 1952.

534. Helen Henschel: *When Soft Voices Die*. 1944. (Reprinted by permission of John Westhouse, Publishers Ltd.); Footnote: Parke: *Memoirs*.

535. From Philippe Fauré-Fremiet: *Gabriel Fauré*. Paris, 1929.

536. Henriette Canter (b. 1898), interviewed by Margaret Campbell, *The Strad*, May 1984.

537. From Marguerite Long: *Au piano avec Fauré*. Paris, 1963.

538. Article in *The Etude*; quoted in Finck, *op. cit.*

539. Dame Nellie Melba: *Melodies and Memories*. 1925.

540. H. Sutherland Edwards: *Personal Recollections*. 1900.

541. From J. M. Glover: *Jimmy Glover – His Book*. 1911.

542. From Vilem and Margaret Tausky (eds): *Jaňacék: Leaves from his Life*. 1982.

543. From Margaret Tausky: *Vilem Tausky tells his Story*. 1979.

544. John Philip Sousa: *Marching Along*. Boston, 1923.

545. From Angelo Neumann: *Personal Recollections of Wagner*. NY, 1906.

546. From Artur Schnabel, lecture at Chicago University. 1945.

547. E. Wulstan Atkins; author's interview.

548. Mrs Richard Powell: *Edward Elgar, Memories of a Variation* (3rd edn). 1979. (Reprinted by permission of OUP.)

549. William H. Reed: *Elgar as I Knew Him*. 1938. (Reprinted by permission of Victor Gollancz.)

550. Fred Gaisberg: *Music on Record*. 1946. (Reprinted by permission of Robert Hale.)

551. Reed, *op. cit.*

552. Gaisberg, *op. cit.*

553. From Newman's article in *The Sunday Times*, 6 November 1955, and Michael Kennedy: *Portrait of Elgar* (2nd edn). 1982.

554. Sir Landon Ronald: *Variations on a Personal Theme*. 1922. (Reprinted by permission of Hodder & Stoughton Ltd.)

555. David Bispham: *A Quaker Singer's Recollections*. NY, 1920.

556. Centenary reflections on Dame Ethel in *BBC Music Magazine*, broadcast on 20 April 1958. (Reprinted by permission of the BBC.)

557. Richard Specht: *Giacomo Puccini, the Man, his Life, his Work*. NY, 1933.

558. From Maria Jeritza: *Sunlight and Song*. NY, 1924.

559. Guido Narotti and Ferruccio Pagui: *Giacomo Puccini Intimo*. Florence, 1926; quoted in Specht, *op. cit.*

560. From Henry Russell: *The Passing Show*. 1926.

561. From Mosco Carner: *Puccini* (2nd edn). 1974, and Howard Taubman: *Toscanini*. NY, 1951.

562. Harriet Kreisler in Louis P. Lochner: *Fritz Kreisler*. (Reprinted by permission of Rockliff & Co.)

563. Arthur Hartmann: *Ysaÿe, Colossus of the Violin*. nd.

564. Natalie Bauer-Lechner: *Erinnerungen an Gustav Mahler*. Leipzig, 1923.

565. From Alma Maria Mahler, introduction to *Gustav Mahler Briefe, 1879–1911*. Vienna, 1924.

566. Bauer-Lechner, *op. cit.*

567. Ernest Jones: *The Life and Work of Sigmund Freud*. 1953–7. (Reprinted by permission of The Hogarth Press.)

568. From Alma Mahler: *Gustav Mahler, Memories and Letters* (A. Mahler: *Gustav Mahler*); ed. Donald Mitchell; transl. Basil Creighton. 1968; Henry Louis de la Grange: *Mahler*, Vol I. 1973.

569. From Kurt Blaukopf: *Mahler, a Documentary Study*. 1976.

570. From Bauer-Lechner, *op. cit.*

571. From de la Grange, *op. cit.*; Blaukopf, *op. cit.*

572. From Modeste Tchaikovsky: *Life and Letters of Peter Ilich Tchaikovsky*; transl. Rosa Newmarch. 1906.

573. From Josef Bohuslav Förster: *Der Pilger*. Prague, 1955.

574. From Bruno Walter: *Themes and Variations*; transl. James A. Galston. 1946; Bruno Walter: *Gustav Mahler*; transl. James A. Galston. 1937. (Reprinted by permission of Routledge & Kegan Paul.); Bauer-Lechner, *op. cit.*

575. From Max Graf: *Legends of a Musical City*. NY, 1945.

576. From documents discovered in Steinbach by the author; and Bauer-Lechner, *op. cit.*

577. Walter: *op. cit.*

578. Lilli Lehmann: *My Path through Life*. NY, 1914.

579. A. Mahler: *Gustav Mahler*.

580. From Bauer-Lechner, *op. cit.*

581. Max Graf: *Legends of a Musical City*. NY, 1945. (Reprinted by permission of The Philosophical Library.)

582. From Berta Szeps-Zukerkandl: *My Life and History*. 1938.

583. Walter, *op. cit.*

584. From *Ferruccio Busoni: Letters to his Wife*; transl. R. Ley. 1938.

585. From Bauer-Lechner, *op. cit.*

586. Walter, *op. cit.*

587. Buffalo Press report, located by Jack Diether, author's interview.

588. From *The Letters of Thomas Mann*; transl. Richard and Clara Winston. NY, 1970.

589. From Arnold Schoenberg: *Berliner Tagebuch*; ed. Josef Rufer. Berlin, 1974.

590. From Rom Landau: *Paderewski*. 1934.

591. Walter Damrosch: *My Musical Life*. NY, 1924. (Reprinted by permission of Scribners Inc.)

592. William Mason: *Memories of a Musical Life*. NY, 1901.

593. Miklós Rózsa (b. 1907), film composer; author's interview.

594. Ernst von Decsey: *Hugo Wolf*. Berlin, 1904–6.

595. From Louis P. Lochner: *Fritz Kreisler*. 1951.

596. From A. Mahler: *Gustav Mahler*; de la Grange, *op. cit.*

597. From Frank Walker: *Hugo Wolf, a Biography* (2nd edn). 1968; A. Mahler: *Gustav Mahler*.

598. From Walker, *op. cit.*

599. John Hetherington: *Melba*. 1967. (Reprinted by permission of Faber & Faber.)

600. From Josef Szigeti: *With Strings Attached*. NY, 1947.

601. Dame Nellie Melba: *Melodies and Memories*. 1925.

602. Michel Dimitri Calvocoressi: *Musicians Gallery*. 1933. (Reprinted by permission of Faber & Faber.)

603. From Norman Lebrecht: *Discord: Conflict and the Making of Music*. 1982; Jean Lorain in *Le Journal*, Paris, May 1902.

604. From Doris Monteux: *It's All in the Music: the Life and Works of Pierre Monteux*. 1965.

605. From Harriet Cohen: *A Bundle of Time*. 1969.

606. Sir Henry Wood: *My Life of Music*. 1938. (Reprinted by permission of Victor Gollancz Ltd.)

607. *Harold Bauer – His Book*. NY, 1948. (Reprinted by permission of W. W. Norton & Company Inc.)

608. From Marguerite Long: *Au piano avec Debussy*. Paris, 1960.

609. Published in *La Semaine musicale*, Paris, 11 November 1927.

610. In Philip Heseltine: *Frederick Delius*. 1923.

611. From Sir Henry Wood: *My Life of Music*. 1938.

612. J. M. Glover: *Jimmy Glover – His Book*. 1911.

613. From Nicolas Slonimsky: *Music Since 1900* [Slonimsky: *Music*] (4th edn). NY, 1971.

614. From Marta Milinowski: *Teresa Carreño 'By the Grace of God'*. NY, 1940.

615. From Gregor Piatigorsky: *Cellist* (Piatigorsky: *Cellist*). Garden City, New Jersey. 1965.

616. Frederic A. Lamond: *Memoirs*. Edinburgh, 1949.

617. From Richard Strauss: *Recollections and Reflections*; ed. Willi Schuh. 1953.

618. Lotte Lehmann: *My Many Lives*. 1948. (Reprinted by permission of Hamish Hamilton Ltd.)

619. David Bispham: *A Quaker Singer's Recollections*. NY, 1920.

620. Sir Henry Wood: *My Life of Music*. 1938. (Reprinted by permission of Victor Gollancz Ltd.)

621. Gustav Samazeuilh, 'Richard Strauss as I knew him', *Tempo*, Summer 1964.

622. From Lotte Lehmann: *Singing with Richard Strauss*. 1964. Max Graf: *Legends of a Musical City*. NY, 1945; Klaus Tennstedt, author's interview; Artur Schnabel: *My Life and Music*; Friedelind Wagner. *The Royal House of Bayreuth*. 1944.

623. From *Conversations with Klemperer*; ed. Peter Heyworth. 1983.

624. From Willi Schuh: *Richard Strauss, a Chronicle of the Early Years 1864–98*; transl. Mary Whittall. Cambridge, 1982.

625. From Michael Kennedy: *Strauss*. 1976.

626. *Testimony: The Memoirs of Shostakovich*; as related to and edited by Solomon Volkov. NY, 1979. (Reprinted by permission of Harper & Row.)

627. Carl Nielsen: *My Childhood*. 1953. (Reprinted by permission of Hutchinson Ltd.)

628. From Karl Ekman: *Jean Sibelius, the Life and Personality of an Artist*. Helsingfors, Finland, 1935.

629. From Bengt de Törne: *Sibelius, a Close-Up*. 1937.

630. From Ekman, *op. cit.*

631. Cecil Gray: *Musical Chairs*. 1948. (Reprinted by permission of the estate of Cecil Gray.)

632. Sir Thomas Beecham, broadcast reflections on Sibelius's 90th birthday, 24 November 1955. (Reprinted by permission of the BBC)

633. From Bengt de Törne, *op. cit.*

634. From Santeri Levas: *Sibelius, a Personal Portrait*; transl. by Percy M. Young. 1972.

635. From Harriet Cohen: *A Bundle of Time*. 1969.

636. Bernard van Dieren: *Down Among the Dead Men*. 1935. (Reprinted by permission of OUP.)

637. Edward J. Dent: *Ferruccio Busoni*. 1933. (Reprinted by permission of OUP.)

638. *Ferruccio Busoni: Letters to His Wife* transl. R. Ley. 1938. (Reprinted by permission of E. J. Arnold.)

639. Michel Dimitri Calvocoressi: *Musicians Gallery*. 1933. (Reprinted by permission of Faber & Faber.)

640. From Darius Milhaud: *Notes Without Music*. NY, 1953.

641. A. L. Mason, 'Granados', *Music and Letters*, July 1933. (Reprinted by permission of the editor.)

642. Henry Theophilus Finck: *My Adventures in the Golden Age of Music*. NY, 1926.

643. Yehudi Menuhin: *Unfinished Journey*. 1977. (Reprinted by permission of the author and Macdonald & Company.)

644. From Piatigorsky: *Cellist*.

645. From Henry Russell: *The Passing Show*. 1926.

646. From Carl Flesch: *Memoirs*. 1957.

647. From Alma Mahler: *Gustav Mahler, Memories and Letters*; ed. Donald Mitchell; transl. Basil Creighton. 1968.

648. *Rachmaninov's Recollections*; told to Oskar von Riesemann. 1934. (Reprinted by permission of Allen & Unwin.)

649. Arthur Rubinstein: *My Young Years*. NY, 1972. (Reprinted by permission of Alfred A. Knopf Inc.)

650. From Faubion Bowers: *Scriabin*. Tokyo, 1969. (Reprinted by permission of Kodansha International.)

651. Ursula Vaughan Williams, composers's wife; author's interview.

652. From Imogen Holst: *Gustav Holst*. 1974

653. From Bernard Shore: *The Orchestra Speaks*. 1938.

654. Ursula Vaughan Williams; author's intervew.

655. Nellie Melba: *Melodies and Memories*. 1925

656. From Fred Gaisberg: *Music on Record*. 1946. Roland Gelatt: *The Fabulous Phonograph* (2nd edn). 1977.

657. Dettmar Dressel: *Up and Down the Scale*. 1937. (Reprinted by permission of Selwyn & Blount.)

658. Henry Theophilus Finck: *Musical Laughs*. 1924.

659. P. G. Wodehouse and Guy Bolton: *Bring on the Girls*. 1954. (Reprinted by permission of Century Hutchinson.)

660. *Rachmaninov's Recollections, op. cit.*

661. Feodor Chaliapin: *Man and Mask*; transl. P. Megroz. 1932. (Reprinted by permission of Victor Gollancz Ltd.)

662. In Alfred and Katherine Swan: 'Rachmaninov, personal reminiscences', *Musical Quarterly*, 1944. (Reprinted by permission of *MQ*, Editor.)

663. From Faubion Bowers: *Scriabin*. Tokyo, 1969. (Reprinted by permission of Kodansha International.)

664. From Abram Chasins: *Speaking of Pianists*. NY, 1952.

665. From Charles Chaplin: *My Autobiography*. 1964.

666. From Arthur Rubinstein: *My Many Years*. 1980.

667. From Uwe Kramer: programme note to Reger's Variation and Fugue on a Theme of Mozart; Sir Henry Wood, *op. cit.*

668. From *Berliner Tagesblatt* report, quoted in Finck, *op. cit.*

669. From Nicolas Slominsky: *Lexicon of Musical Invective*. NY, 1955. (Reprinted by permission of the author.)

670. From Elliott Carter in Vivian Perlis: *Charles Ives Remembered*. New Haven, Connecticut, 1974.

671. From Brewster Ives, Chester Ives, Elliott Carter in Perlis, *op. cit.*

672. From Henry and Sidney Cowell: *Charles Ives and his Music*. NY, 1955. (Reprinted by permission of OUP.)

673. Charles Ives: *Some Quarter-tone Impressions*. NY, 1961. (Reprinted by permission of W. W. Norton & Co. Inc.)

674. From Cowell, *op. cit.*

675. From *Ibid*.

676. From Perlis, Cowell, *op. cit.*

677. From George F. Roberts; in Perlis, *op. cit.*

678. Taped recollections of Mahler by Klaus Pringsheim, reproduced by permission of Professor Pringsheim, McMaster University, Canada.

679. From Jelena Hahl Koch: *Arnold Shoenberg, Wassily Kandinsky, Letters, Pictures and Documents*. 1984.

680. *Arnold Schoenberg: Letters*; ed. Erwin Stein; transl. Eithne Williams and Ernst Kaiser. 1964. (By permission of Faber & Faber.)

681. From article by Hanns Eisler in Schoenberg issue of *Musikblätter des Anbruch*. Vienna, 1924.

682. From article in *NRC-Handelsblad*, 14 May 1971; quoted in *Journal of the Arnold Schoenberg Institute*.

683. From Alma-Mahler Werfel: *Mein Leben*. Frankfurt, 1960.

684. From Clara Steuermann, 'From the Archives', *Journal of the Arnold Schoenberg Institute*, June 1978.

685. Peter Diamand (b. 1913), musical administrator; author's interview.

686. Slonimsky: *Music*.

687. Nuria Schoenberg-Nono (b. 1932), daughter of the composer; author's interview.

688. Oscar Levant: *A Smattering of Ignorance*. NY, 1940. (Reprinted by permission of Doubleday & Company Inc.)

689. From Salka Viertel: *The Kindness of Strangers*, NY, 1969; Schoenberg-Nono; author's interview.

690. Schoenberg-Nono; author's interview.

691. From Arnold Schoenberg: *Gedenkausstellung*. Vienna, 1974.

692. Slonimsky: *Music*; Schoenberg-Nono; author's interview.

693. From Hans Heinz Stuckenschmidt: *Arnold Schoenberg*. 1977.

694. Katia Mann: *Unwritten Memories*. 1971. (Reprinted by permission of André Deutsch Ltd.); Footnote: Nuria Schoenberg-Nono, letter to the author.

695. *The Times*, 28 April 1924.

696. From *Maurice Ravel par quelques-uns de ses familiers*. Paris, 1939.

697. Vernon Duke: *Passport to Paris*. Boston, 1955. (Reprinted by permission of Little, Brown, Inc.)

698. From Roland-Manuel: *Maurice Ravel*. 1947; *The Writings of Erik Satie*; ed. Nigel Wilkins. 1980.

699. From Hans Heinz Stuckenschmidt: *Maurice Ravel*. 1969.

700. From Arthur Rubinstein: *My Many Years*. NY, 1979; Merle Armitage: *George Gershwin*. NY, 1958; Igor Stravinsky and Robert Craft: *Dialogues and Diary*. 1968.

701. From Aaron Copland: *Copland on Music*. 1961.

702. From Marcel Dupré. *My Recollections*. NY, 1975.

703. From Piatigorsky: *Cellist*.

704. From Henry and Sidney Cowell: *Charles Ives and His Music*. NY, 1955.

705. From Slonimsky: *Music*.

706. From Ivor Newton: *At the Piano*. 1966; Fred Gaisberg: *Music on Record*. 1946.

707. From Bertha Geissmar: *The Baton and the Jackboot*. 1944.

708. Neville Cardus: *Sir Thomas Beecham*. 1961. (Reprinted by permission of William Collins & Sons Ltd.)

709. Neville Cardus: *Autobiography*. 1947. (Reprinted by permission of William Collins & Sons Ltd.)

710. Béla Bartók: *On Collecting Folk Songs in Turkey*; transl. Eva Hajnal-Konyi. 1937. (Reprinted by permission of the Editor of *Tempo*.)

711. Cecil Gray: *Musical Chairs*. 1948. (Reprinted by permission of the estate of Cecil Gray.)

712. Eugen Szenkar to Miklós Rósza, author's interview.

713. *Classical Music*, 7 March 1981. (Reprinted by permission of the editor.)

714. From Agatha Fassett: *The Naked Face of Genius: Béla Bartók's American Years*. 1958.

715. George Mikes, Hungarian writer; author's interview.

716. From John Bird: *Percy Grainger* (2nd edn). 1982.

717. Peter Diamand; author's interview.

718. From Piatigorsky: *Cellist*.

719. George Antheil: *Bad Boy of Music*. Garden City, New Jersey, 1945. (Reprinted by permission of Doubleday & Company Inc.)

720. From Diaghilev's memoirs, MS in the possession of Boris Kochno; quoted in Richard Buckle: *Diaghilev*. 1969.

721. Romola Nijinsky: *Nijinsky*. 1933. (Reprinted by permission of Victor Gollancz Ltd.)

722. Doris Monteux: *It's All in the Music*. 1965. (By permission of William Kimber Ltd.)

723. From Antheil, *op. cit.*

724. From George D. Painter: *Marcel Proust*. 1959–65.

725. Nicolas Nabokov: *Bagazh*. NY, 1975. (Reprinted by permission of Atheneum.)

726. From Nicolas Slonimsky: *A Thing or Two About Music*. NY, 1947: Slonimsky: *Music*; Vera Stravinsky and Robert Craft: 'Stravinsky in pictures and documents', *Musical America*, January 1944.

727. Miklós Rósza (b. 1907), film composer; author's interview.

728. From Slonimsky: *Music*.

729. Peter Diamand; author's interview.

730. From Louise Varèse: *Varèse, a Looking-Glass Diary*. NY, 1972.

731. Hans Moldenhauer: *Anton von Webern*. 1978. (Reprinted by permission of Victor Gollancz Ltd.)

732. *Arnold Schoenberg: Letters*; ed. Erwin Stein, 1964; transl. Eithne Williams and Ernst Kaiser. (By permission of Faber & Faber.)

733. From Moldenhauer, *op. cit.*

734. Arnold Schoenberg, article (in his own English) on Berg; reproduced in Hans F. Redlich: *Alban Berg*. 1957. (Reprinted by permission of the Schoenberg heirs.)

735. From Josef Szigeti: *With Strings Attached*. NY, 1967.

736. From Theodor W. Adorno: *Alban Berg, der Meister des kleinsten Übergangs*. Vienna, 1968.

737. Theodor W. Adorno: *Aufzeichnungen über Berg*; transl. in Mosco Carner: *Alban Berg* (2nd edn). 1983. (Reprinted by permission of Duckworths.)

738. From Albert Speer: *Inside the Third Reich*. 1970.

739. From Elizabeth Schwarzkopf (b. 1915), German soprano; author's interview.

740. From Nicolas Nabokov: *Old Friends and New Music*. 1951. (Reprinted by permission of Hamish Hamilton.)

741. Nathan Milstein (b. 1904), violinist; author's interview.

742. Serge Moreaux: *Prokofiev, an Intimate Portrait*. (By permission of the Editor of *Tempo*.)

743. From Piatigorsky: *Cellist*.

744. From Piatigorsky: *Cellist*.

745. From Robert Jacobson: *Reverberations*. 1976.

746. Unsubstantiated account in E. Herzog and G. von Turnitz: *Musikeranekdoten*. Munich, 1981.

747. Oscar Levant: *A Smattering of Ignorance*. NY, 1940. (Reprinted by permission of Doubleday & Company Inc.)

748. From Martin Mayer: *The Met*. 1983; *The Memoirs of Sir Rudolf Bing: 5000 Nights at the Opera*. 1972.

749. Nuria Schoenberg-Nono; author's interview.

750. Du Bose Heyward; in David Ewen: *A Journey to Greatness*. 1956. (Reprinted by permission of W. H. Allen.)

751. George Antheil: *Bad Boy of Music*. Garden City, New Jersey. 1945. (Reprinted by permission of Doubleday & Company Inc.)

752. From Hans W. Heinsheimer: *Menagerie in F sharp*. Garden City, New Jersey. 1947.

753. From Juan Orrego Salas, 'Aaron Copland, New York composer', published by the University of Chile, nd, and reprinted in *Tempo*.

754. From sleeve notes to *The Best of Aaron Copland*, CBS 61431.

755. Godowsky, Slonimsky: *Music*.

756. Nathan Milstein; author's interview.

757. Horowitz in Piatigorsky: *Cellist*.

758. Mstislav Rostropovich: author's interview.

759. From *Testimony: The Memoirs of Shostakovich*; as related to and edited by Solomon Volkov; transl. Antonina W. Bouis. NY, 1979. (Reprinted by permission of Harper & Row.)

760. Maxim Shostakovich (b.1938), conductor and son of the composer; author's interview.

761. Alexander Werth: *Musical Uproar in Moscow*. 1949. (Reprinted by permission of Turnstile Press.)

762. Rudolf Barshai (b. 1924). Russian conductor; author's interview.

763. Rostropovich, interview with Gillian Widdicombe in *The Observer*, 7 November 1977. (Reprinted by permission of the editor.)

764. Volkov, *op. cit.*

765. Rostropovich; author's interview.

766. From Slonimsky: *Music*.

767. Brian Moynahan, 'Funeral in Berlin', *The Sunday Times*, 30 January 1983. (By permission of the Editor.)

768. Interview with Bernard Gavoty, music critic of *Figaro*, in *Journal musical français* (Reproduced by permission of the Editor of *Tempo*.)

769. John Cage: *Introduction to Silence*. Middletown, Connecticut, 1968. (By permission of the author.)

770. Ronald Duncan, English poet and translator; author's interview.

771. Sir Michael Tippett, interviewed in Alan Blyth: *Remembering Britten*. 1981. (Reprinted by permission of Century Hutchinson.)

772. From Lord Harewood: *The Tongs and the Bones*. 1979.

773. Peter Diamand (b. 1913); author's interview.

774. Widely circulated, though unverified, Viennese legend.

775. Editorial in the *New York Times*, 16 November 1943.

776. *The Paris Diary of Ned Rorem*. NY, 1966. (Reprinted by permission of the author.)

777. From *The Memoirs of Sir Rudolf Bing: 5000 nights at the Opera*. 1972.

778. From Lanfranco Rasponi: *The Last Prima Donnas*. 1984.

779. From *The Times*, 4 January 1958; Ariana Stassinopoulos: *Maria Callas*. 1980.

780. In *György Ligeti in Conversation*. 1983. (Reprinted by permission of Ernst Eulenberg Ltd.)

781. Paul Griffiths: *György Ligeti*. 1983. (Reprinted by permission of Robson Books.)

782. Howard Hartog; author's interview; Pierre Boulez; author's interview.

783. From *Par volonté et par hasard: entretiens avec Celestin Deliège*. Paris, 1975.

784. From Michael Langdon (with R. Fawkes): *Notes from a Low Singer*. 1982.

785. Olga Ivinskaya: *A Captive of Time*. Paris, 1978. (By permission of William Collins Ltd.)

786. Apocryphal; source unknown.

INDEX